Author
Jerzy Kluczewski
English translation
Agata Skutela

iTSt@rt

COMPUTER NETWORKS IN PACKET TRACER

FOR ADVANCED USERS

The book "**COMPUTER NETWORKS IN PACKET TRACER FOR ADVANCED USERS**" is a continuation of the book, published under the title **PACKET TRACER FOR YOUNG, INTERMEDIATE ADMINS** and contains a set of schedules and network simulations for the users with at least basic knowledge about networks and experience in working with administering basic devices and also managing the network architecture.

The subject matter of this book is expanded and varied. Multiuser mode, visualization, Bluetooth connections, cellular networks, WLAN network controllers, industrial routers, IPV6 protocol, are only a few issues that the Author provided schedules to and also ready-made simulation files, which can be downloaded from the publishing house's site.

Restricted companies' names, organizations and products have been used in the book only in order to identify them.

The cover's design: ***Marcin Król***

Editorial Staff and composition: ***Marek Smyczek and Marcin Kaim***

English translation: ***Agata Skutela***

IT publishing house: **ITSTART**

www: http://www.itstart.pl

email: itstart@itstart.pl

ISBN: 978-83-65645-88-3

The first edition – Piekary Śląskie 2023

TABLE OF CONTENTS

Introduction

CHAPTER 1

INTRODUCTION

Introduction

1 Introduction

1.1 Who is this book for ?

What were the reasons of writing this book ?

- *firstly* – in the previous books of our Publishing House the advanced exercises concerning exercises in Packet Tracer program were not included.
- *secondly* – in July 2021 the Cisco company released new options in the Packet Tracer program 8.0.1, e.g. NET CONTROLLER.
- *thirdly* – in July 2022 the Cisco company released the latest Packet Tracer version 8.2.

That is why in this book item we include more advanced options of exercises. The book contains descriptions and examples of solutions concerning:

- the use of Multiuser mode in Windows (chapter 2),
- the use of Multiuser mode in virtual Ubuntu and Windows (chapter 3),
- Bluetooth connection and Tethering technique (chapter 4),
- creating mobile networks (chapter 5),
- using Network controller (chapter 6),
- configuring wireless network controllers (chapter 7),
- configuring integrated industrial routers (chapter 8),
- installing and analyzing power derived from hot swapping devices (chapter 9),
- routers' clocks and switches synch (chapter 10),
- creating server services (chapter11),
- configuring the IPV6 protocol (chapter 12),
- the HSRP protocol uses (chapter 13),
- advanced physical topology (chapter 14),
- commands in Command Prompt (chapter 15).

1.2 The EULA license conditions for Packet Tracer

Cisco Packet Tracer can be freely distributed and used by any instructor, a student or a graduate of Cisco Network Academy. The license allows pupils and students to use Cisco Packet Tracer with any computer, even after classes, working at home, practicing and learning.

Source (Cisco, End User License Agreement, 2022) [1]

1.3 The main changes in Packet Tracer 8.2

On July 28th, 2022 the version 8.2 of the program Packet Tracer was released. The main changes compared to the previous version are:

- simplified way of logging in (**the option of logging in the visitor is not available any more**),
- the mistakes have been improved (e.g. in VTP the Transparent mode works correctly),
- the visualization of transferring devices and wiring in the patch cabinet.

1.4 Detailed comments applying to the program version.

- The files made in Cisco Packet Tracer in 7.2.2 version or older might work differently in Cisco Packet Tracer 8.2 version.
- Depending on the efficiency of your computer, running Packet Tracer Activity (**PKA**) files or Packet Tracer (**PKT**) might take a **few minutes!**
- Not all offered functionalities work correctly!

1.5 "Keep me logged in" option

„Keep me logged in" option was designed to ensure the access (for 3 months) to Cisco Packet Tracer without the necessity of logging in again each time .

[1] Cisco End User License Agreement

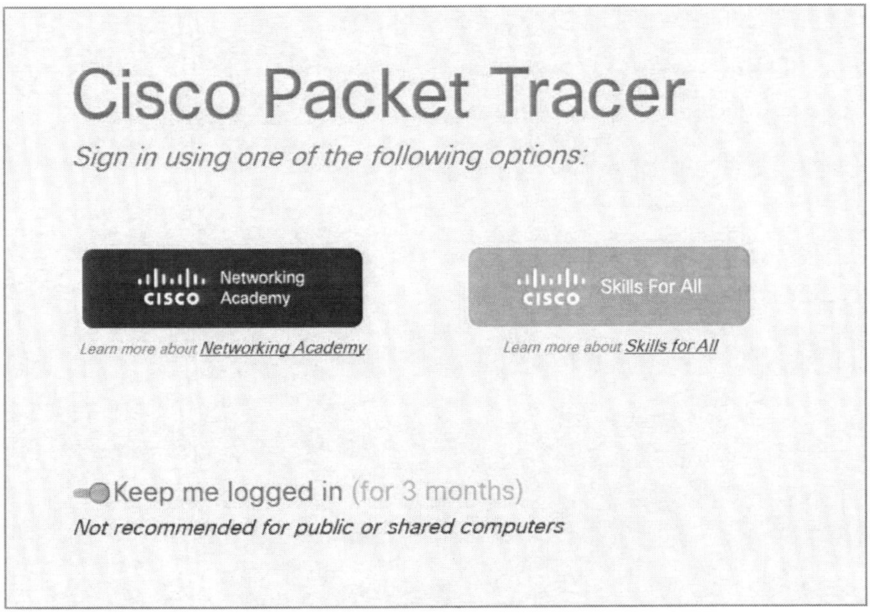

Figure 1.1 Keep me logged in option

Using „**Keep me logged in**" option is recommended for private computers.

If you use public or any shared computer, DO NOT use "Keep me logged in" option or log out before closing Cisco Packet Tracer to unable the other users of the computer the access to PT using Your credentials.

1.6 The minimum system requirements and installing.

Part 1. System requirements for Cisco Packet Tracer 8.2 (64 bit).

- operating systems: Microsoft Windows 8.1, 10, 11 (64bit), Ubuntu 20.04 LTS (64bit), macOS 10.14 or newer versions
- amd64(x86-64) CPU
- 4GB of free RAM
- 1.4 GB of free disk space

Part 2. System requirements for Cisco Packet Tracer 8.2 (32 bit).

- operating systems: Microsoft Windows 8.1, 10 (32bit)
- x86 compatible CPU
- 2GB of free RAM
- 1.4 GB of free disk space

Part 3. Downloading and installing a program in Windows.

Step 1. Downloading an installation file from Netacad.com. Use the website **netacad.com** and download the installation file:

CiscoPacketTracer_820_Windows_64bit_setup.exe

or

CiscoPacketTracer820_Windows_32bit_setup.exe.

Step 2. Run the installation file.

Step 3. Accept the **EULA license**.

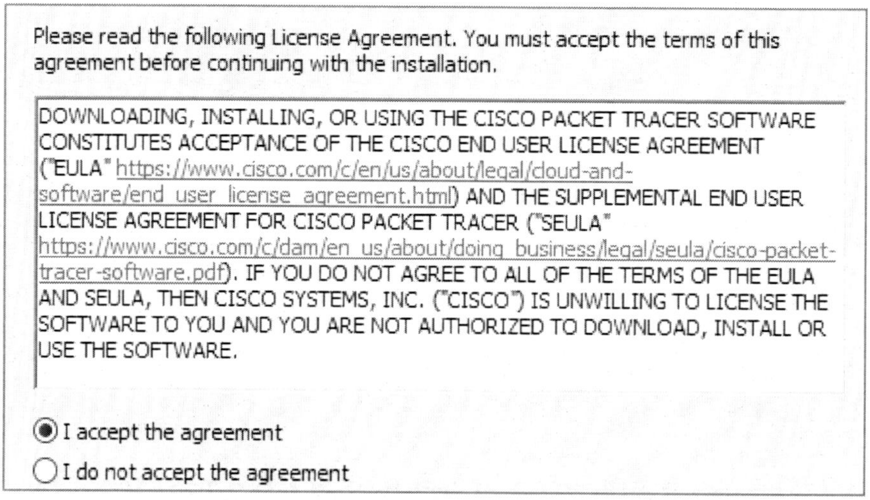

Figure 1.2 Accepting the EULA licence

Step 4. Specify the program localization.

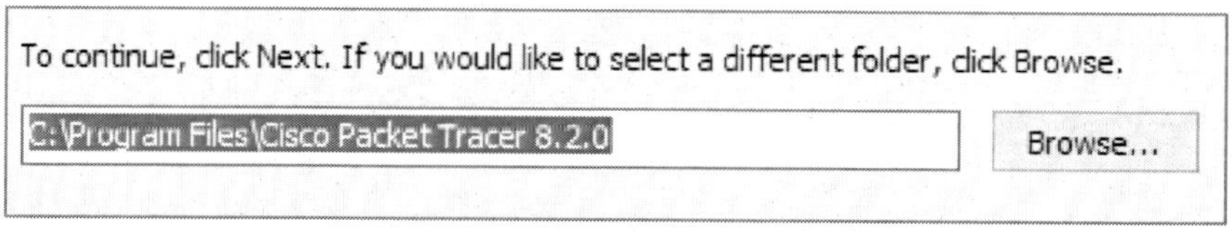

Figure 1.3 Specifying the program localization

Step 5. Specify the localization of the program shortcut

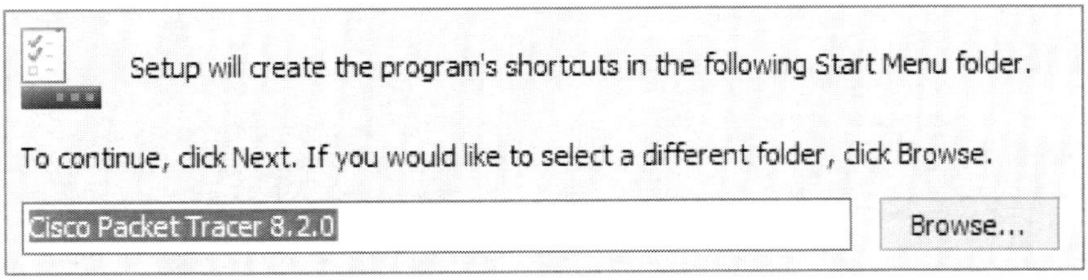

Figure 1.4 Specifying the localization of the program shortcut

Step 6. Create shortcuts to the program.

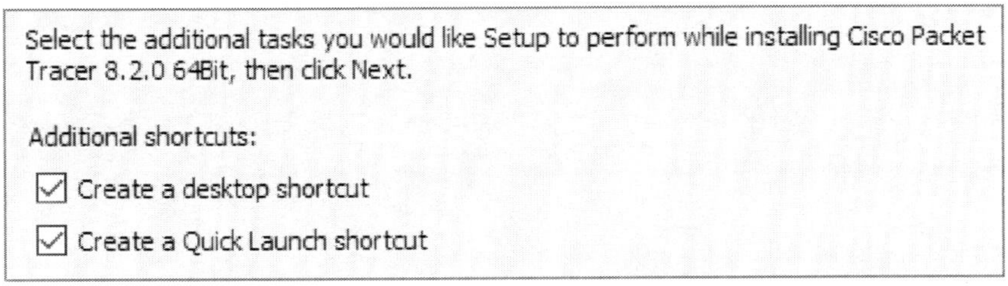

Figure 1.5 Creating shortcuts to the program

1.7 The first run of the Packet Tracer program

Step 1. The first run of the program – boot logo.

Figure 1.6 The first run of the program – boot logo.

Step 2. The first run of the program – should the Multi-user mode be activated during application start? (it doesn't matter what is chosen).

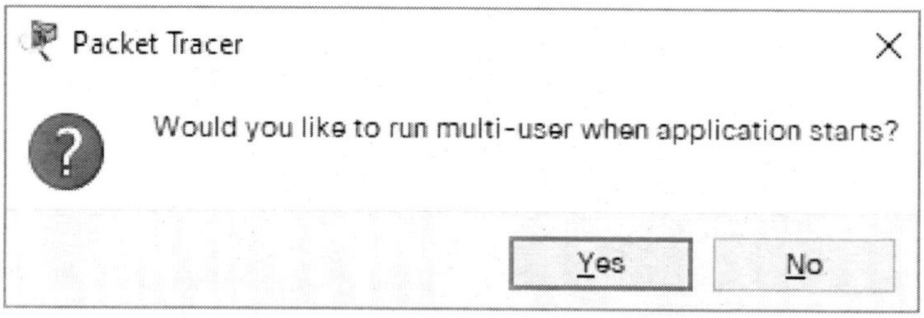

Figure 1.7 The first run of the program – activating a multi-user mode

Step 3. The first run of the program – it is necessary to enable the „**Keep me logged in**" option.

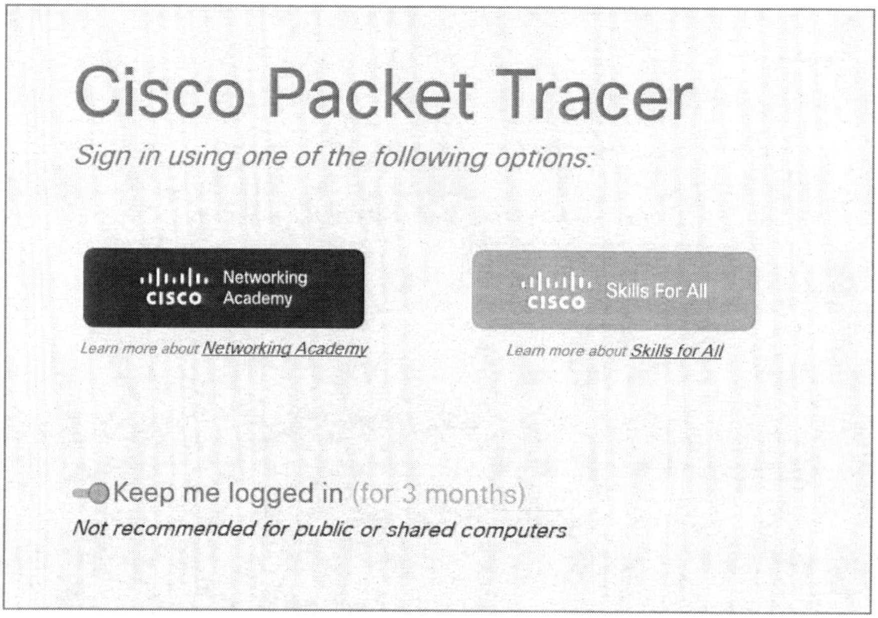

Figure 1.8 The first run of the program - Keep me logged In Option

Step 4. The first run of the program - choose „**Networking Academy**".

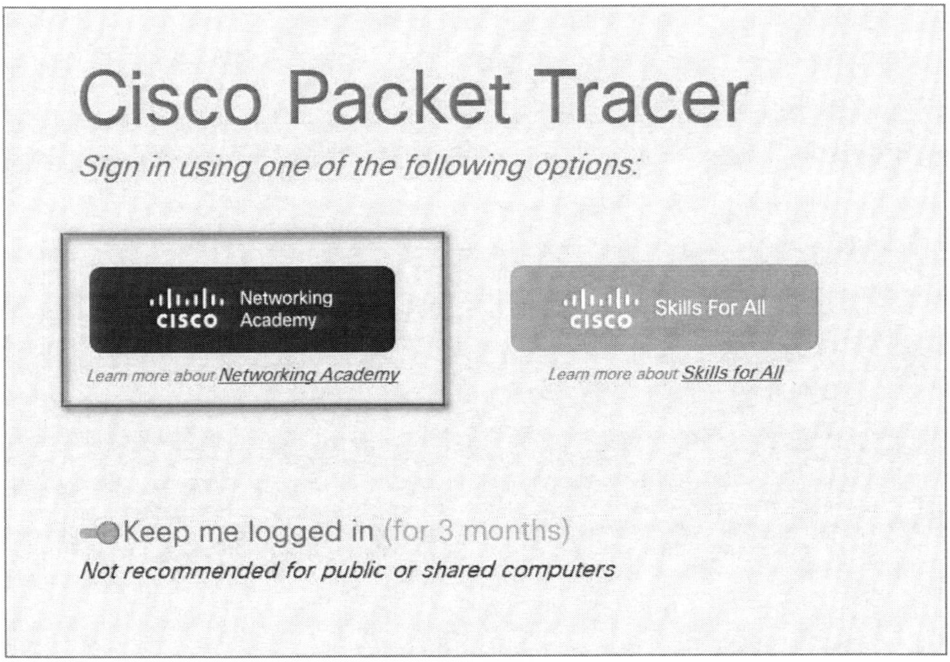

Figure 1.9 The first run of the program - choosing Networking Academy

Step 5. The first run of the program - you should check if the newest version of the Packet Tracer has been run. From the main menu choose **Help → About** and check the version.

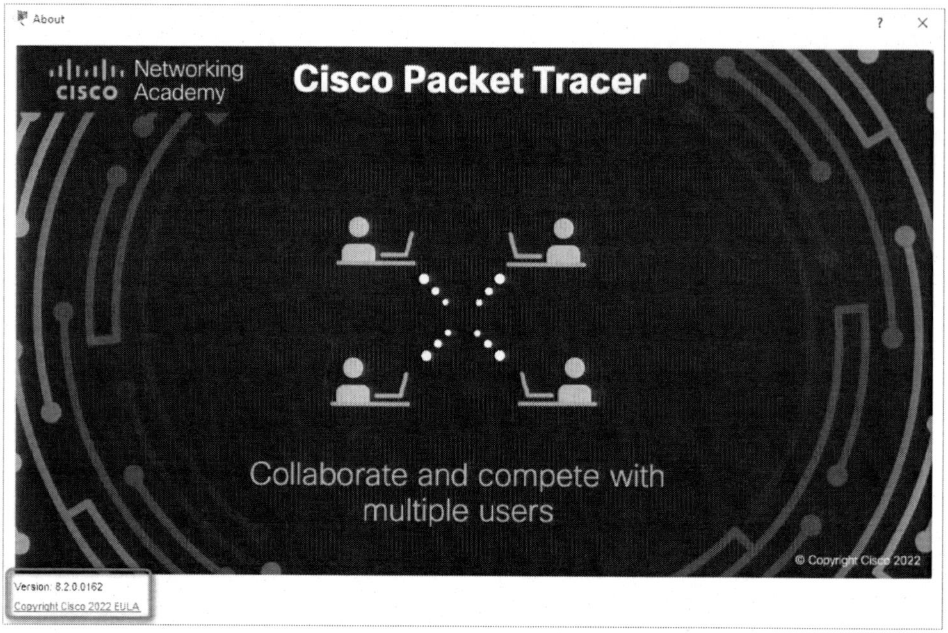

Figure 1.10 The first run of the program – check the version.

1.8 Files necessary to analyze the content

The author has prepared a lot of exercises just to make learning easier. Their aim is to help in the process of learning and they were put together on the special site of our publishing house. The address is: **http://ptfyaadv.itstart.pl**. If you want to obtain a full access to the files you should log in using: **ptfyaadv** login and a password: **ptfya#ADV**

CHAPTER 2

USING MULTIUSER MODE

COMPUTER NETWORKS IN PACKET TRACER

FOR ADVANCED USERS

2 Using Multiuser Mode

2.1 Multiuser mode description

Part 1. Goal.

The connection of virtual topologies PT in an actual network.

Part 2. Introduction.

Packet Tracer program can be used in the environment of a local network (the actual LAN network), allowing for organizing connections between many people (many Packet Tracer programs). The exercises shown may be done between many users in the same actual LAN network.

To make use of this method you should use the configuration of the mode known as ***multiuser mode***.

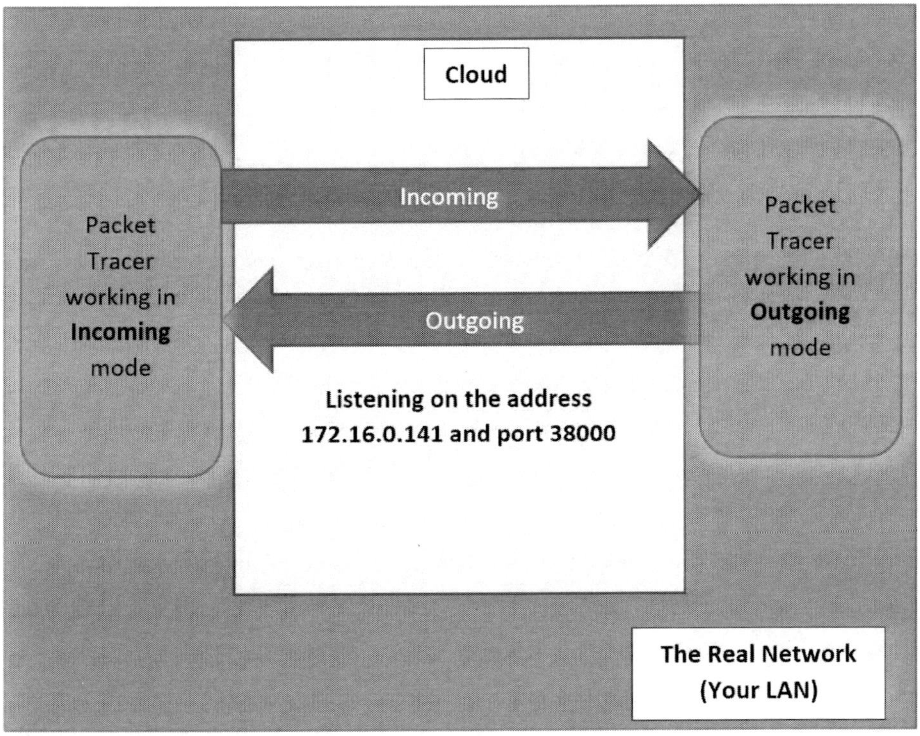

Figure 2.1 Working model in Multiuser mode.

Notice: In your case the IP address of your computer can be different. The address shown is only an example. During exercises pay attention to this notice!

Part 3. Technical comments.

In order to communicate between many Packet Tracer programs an internal protocol **PTMP** is used (**Point-To-Multipoint Protocol**), which makes use of TCP protocol.

In **Multiuser** mode a default, base TCP port with a number **38000** is used to communicate between given PT programs.

If there are many Packet Tracer programs running on one computer, then the port numbers are increased by 1 in relation to the base port (the port number **38000**). In case of more advanced configurations PT automatically generates the ports' numbers.

Default password for every connection in the cloud is: **cisco**.

Part 4. Restrictions.

- Wireless devices are not supported.
- Switching from the real mode to the simulation mode is not possible while working in **Multiuser mode**.

Part 5. Connection states in Multiuser mode.

While testing and doing exercises in multiuser mode there might occur lacks of communication between remote networks both on the server side and the customer. In such cases Packet Tracer program signals the condition of the connection by a specific form of a graphic cloud.

Part 6. Comments.

Patience and careful observation of the conditions in certain PT programs running is required, because depending on the level of the network and its capacity; changes of the cloud's condition can last from a few seconds to a couple of minutes.

In case of any problems in connecting, checking the condition of the connection by using **Extensions → Multiuser → Listen …** function is recommended.

Part 7. Description of connections' status.

In **Multiuser mode** there are five states of connections with the cloud, which are displayed by a specific cloud's form:

- **Error** – a mistake in connection between clouds; probably a lack of a cloud or the cloud is disabled on the other side of the connection or there is the wrong password or name of the cloud.
- **Disconnected** – the network is disconnected; probably there is no remote network given.
- **Initializing** – the process of initializing the cloud is in progress (depending on the level of the network and its capacity, changes of the cloud's condition can last from a few seconds to a couple of minutes),
- **Connecting** – the process of connecting with the remote network is in progress (depending on the level of the network and its capacity this process can last from a few seconds to a couple of minutes),
- **Connected** – the process of connecting the two remote networks has been completed successfully- the two remote networks were connected.

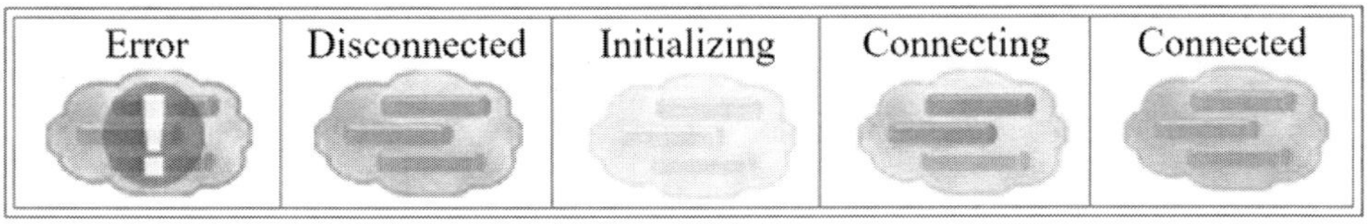

Figure 2.2 Connection statuses in Multiuser mode.

2.2 Setting up a Server Room (Exercise 1)

Part 1. Preparing a SERVER ROOM

Step 1. Prepare the following files for the SERVER ROOM

```
BODY, P, UL, TD, TH, DIR, .bodyText {
    font-family: Arial, Helvetica, Verdana, Geneva, Arial, sans-serif;
    font-size : 10pt;
    color: Black;
    background-color: Silver;
}

h1  {font-size: 14pt/14pt; font-weight: bold; color: Red;}

div {font-size: 24pt; font-weight: bold; color: Red; text-align: center;}

.head {font-size: 12pt; font-weight: bold; color: #990000;}

p.textbody {text-align: justify; line-height: 17pt;}
```

Figure 2.3 style.css file.

```
<html>

<head>
<link rel="stylesheet" href="style.css">
<script>
function info()
{
   alert("ADDRESS of HTTP SERVER 192.168.1.1\n
    ADDRESS of FTP SERVER 192.168.1.2\n
    ADDRESS of DNS SERVER 192.168.1.3\n
    ADDRESS of EMAIL SERVER EMAIL 192.168.1.4\n
    ADDRESS of RADIUS SERVER 192.168.1.5");
}
</script>
</head>

<body>
<div>SERVER ROOM</div>
<hr>
<div>www.server.com</div>
<div>ftp.server.com</div>
<div>dns.server.com</div>
<div>email.server.com</div>
<div>radius.server.com</div>
<p><center><button type="button" onclick="info()">INFO</button></center></p>

</body>
</html>
```

Figure 2.4 index.html file.

```
-----------------------------------
A Records
-----------------------------------
www.server.com        192.168.1.1
ftp.server.com        192.168.1.2
dns.server.com        192.168.1.3
email.server.com      192.168.1.4
radius.server.com     192.168.1.5
```

Figure 2.5 dns-config.txt file.

```
FTP SERVER ADDRESS  192.168.1.2
------------------------------------
Login: cisco Password: cisco
------------------------------------
```

Figure 2.6 ftp-config.txt file.

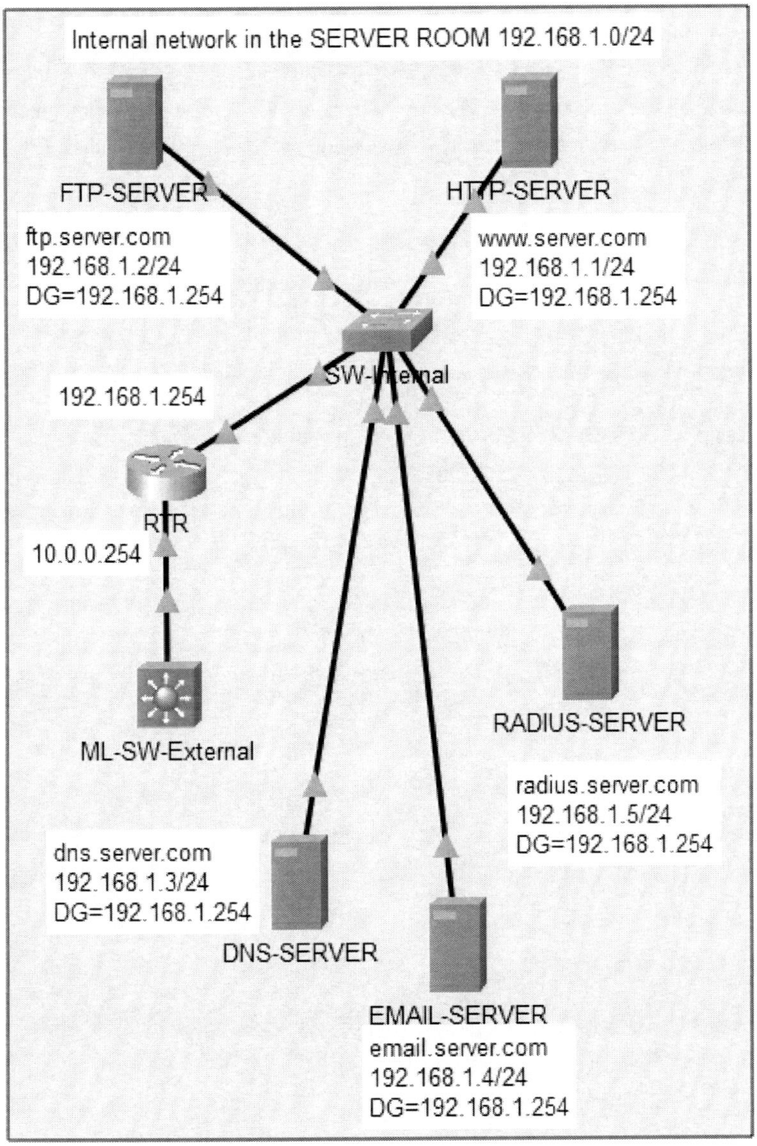

Figure 2.7 Internal network topology in the SERVER ROOM.

Step 2. Create a network topology in the SERVER ROOM according to the drawing.

The SERVER ROOM by the use of separate servers, will offer the following services:

- http,
- ftp,
- dns,
- email,
- radius.

Assumptions: servers are connected with the router 2811 (**RTR**) by the use of the switcher 2960 (**SW-Internal**). The switcher **SW-Internal** is connected with the multilayer edge switch 3650 (**ML-SW-External**). Using the **ML-SW-External** edge switch, devices from the external networks will be able to connect with the SERVER ROOM and benefit from it.

Additionally logging in to the **RTR** router is only possible by the SSH, using an authenticated account by the use of the **radius.server.com** server.

Part 2. Configuring the SERVER ROOM.

Step 1. Set up HTTP-SERVER server according to the given assumptions.

IP address / Subnet Mask	192.168.1.1/24
Default gateway	192.168.1.254
DNS server's address	192.168.1.3
Files for http service	index.html, style.css
Notice	import the files using **Import** button

Table 2.1 HTTP Service configuration data

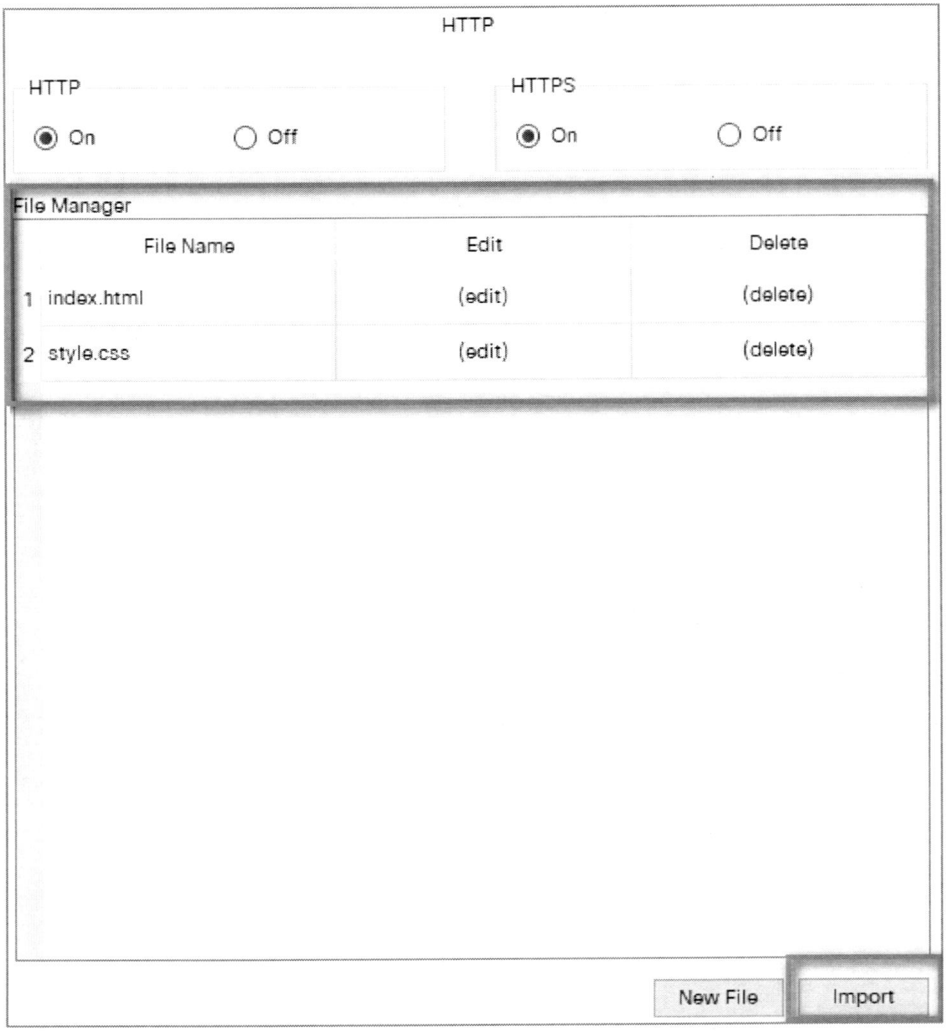

Figure 2.8 Files of HTTP service in HTTP-SERVER

Step 2. Set up the FTP-SERVER server according to the given assumptions.

IP address/Subnet Mask	192.168.1.2/24
Default gateway	192.168.1.254
DNS server's address	192.168.1.3
Account for ftp service	cisco, cisco
Rights for the ftp account	RWDNL
Files for ftp service	Delete all existing files
Files for http service	index.html, style.css
Notice	files should be imported by an **Import button**

Table 2.2 FTP service configuration data

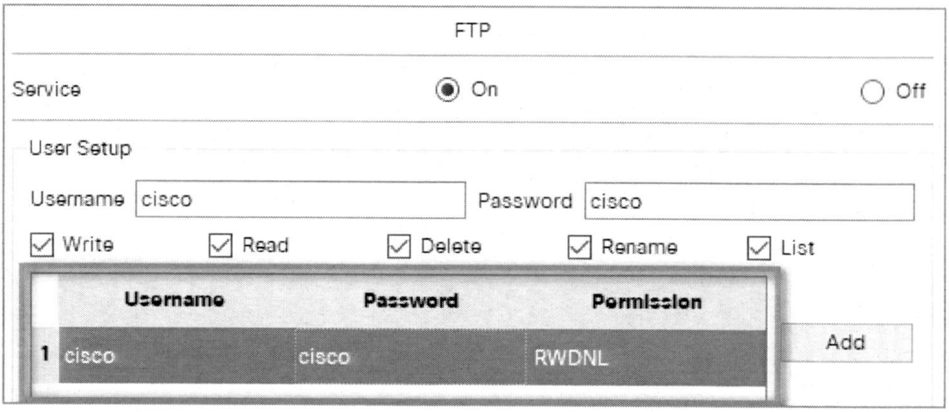

Figure 2.9 FTP account service in FTP-SERVER

Step 3. Delete existing files in **FTP-SERVER**. Use **delete** command. Next check the content of C:\ catalog using **dir** command.

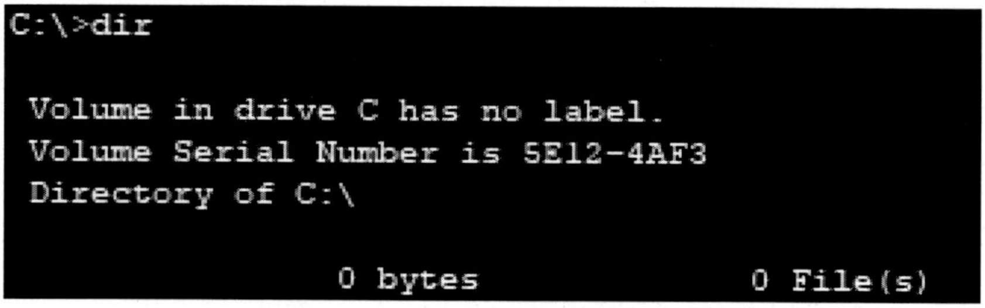

Figure 2.10 The dir command result.

Step 4. To the computer **FTP-SERVER** import files (using an application **Text Editor.** Menu **File→Import**):

- dns-config.txt
- ftp-config.txt

Figure 2.11 Text Editor application menu.

The imported files in the computer **FTP-SERVER** are:

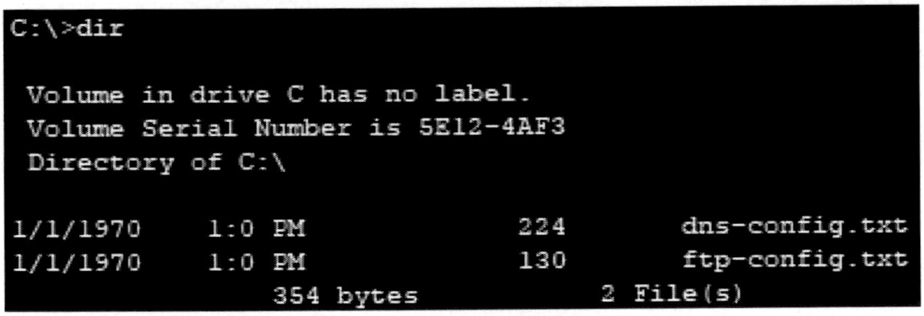

```
C:\>dir

 Volume in drive C has no label.
 Volume Serial Number is 5E12-4AF3
 Directory of C:\

1/1/1970     1:0 PM                 224        dns-config.txt
1/1/1970     1:0 PM                 130        ftp-config.txt
                354 bytes                2 File(s)
```

Figure 2.12 The dir command result.

Step 4. Set up the DNS-SERVER according to the given assumptions.

IP address / Subnet Mask	192.168.1.3/24
Default gateway	192.168.1.254
DNS server's address	192.168.1.3
A Records	
Name	**Address**
www.server.com	192.168.1.1
ftp.server.com	192.168.1.2
dns.server.com	192.168.1.3
email.server.com	192.168.1.4
radius.server.com	192.168.1.5

Table 2.3 DNS configuration serivice's data

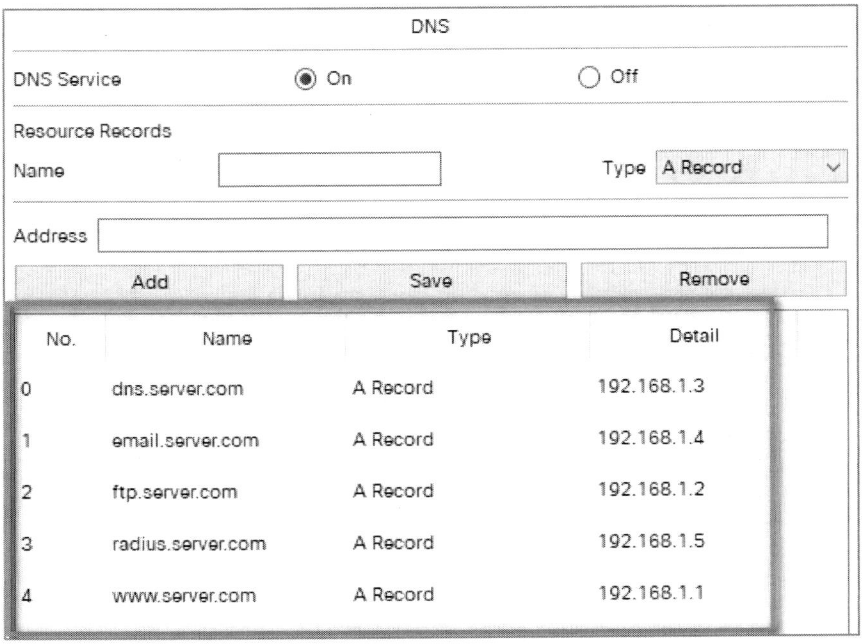

Figure 2.13 Configuring DNS service.

Step 5. Configurate the EMAIL-SERVER according to the given assumptions.

IP Address/ Subnet Mask	192.168.1.4/24
Default gateway	192.168.1.254
DNS server's address	192.168.1.3
Email domain	email.server.com
Email accounts	
User	**Password**
Tom	tom123
Eve	eve123

Table 2.4 EMAIL service configuration data

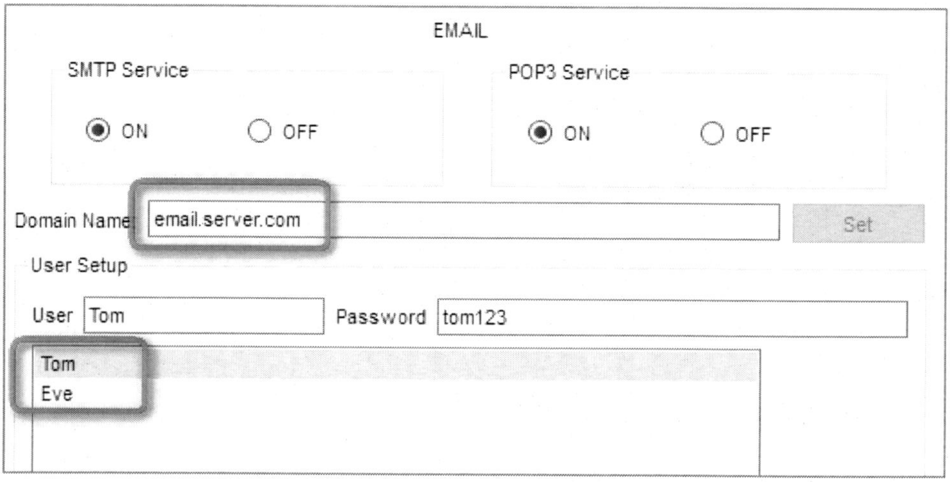

Figure 2.14 Configuring EMAIL service.

Step 6. Set up the RADIUS-SERVER according to the given assumptions.

IP Address/ Subnet Mask	192.168.1.5/24
Default gateway	192.168.1.254
DNS server's address	192.168.1.3
AAA service	enabled
AAA Configuration	
Client Name	RTR
Client IP	192.168.1.254
Secret	Krakers456
Server Type	RADIUS
Username	admin1
Password	admin456

Figure 2.5 The RADIUS service configuration data

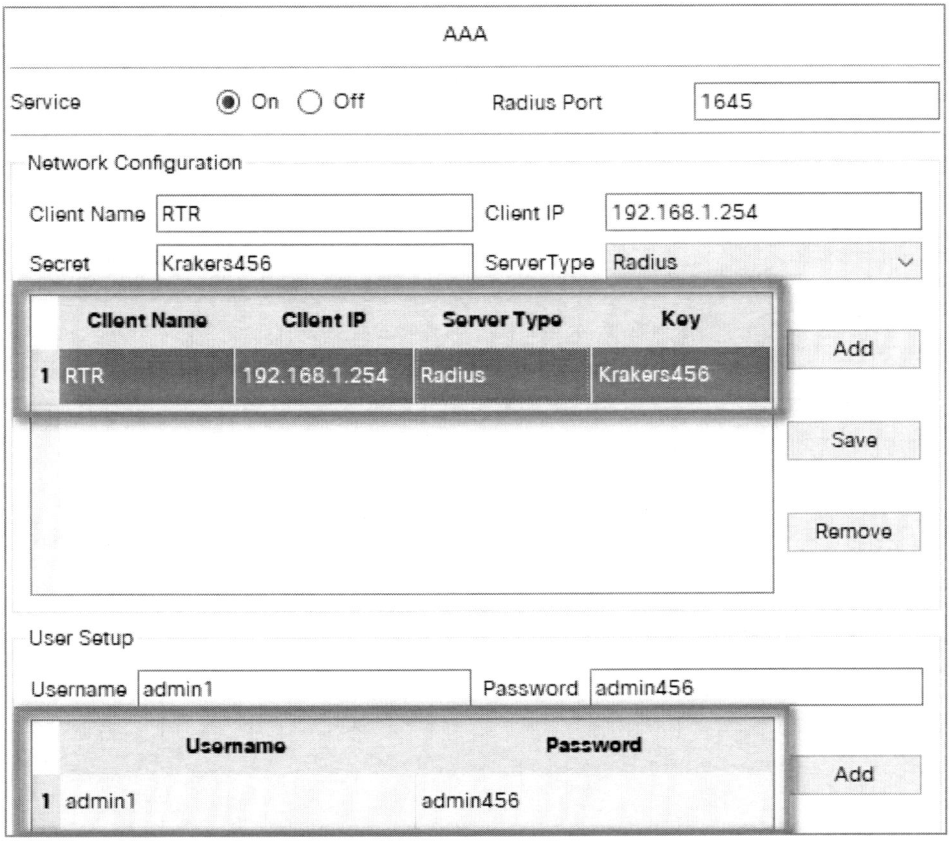

Figure 2.15 The RADIUS protocol configuration in AAA service.

Step 7. Set up the basic RTR router parameters according to the given assumptions. The IOS system commands are presented in the last column of the table.

Interface Fa0/0	192.168.1.254/24	**interface FastEthernet0/0** **ip address 192.168.1.254 255.255.255.0** **no shut**
Interface Fa0/1	10.0.0.254/8	**interface FastEthernet0/1** **ip address 10.0.0.254 255.0.0.0** **no shut**
Password for the privileged mode	ciscoen	**enable secret ciscoen**
Addresses excluded from the DHCP pool	10.0.0.254	**ip dhcp excluded-address 10.0.0.254**
The DHCP pool name	EXTERNAL-DHCP	**ip dhcp pool EXTERNAL-DHCP**
DHCP pool parameters	10.0.0.0 255.0.0.0 10.0.0.254	**network 10.0.0.0 255.0.0.0** **default-router 10.0.0.254**

	192.168.1.3 server.com	**dns-server 192.168.1.3** **domain-name server.com**
Routing protocol	OSPF	-
ID	1	**router ospf 1**
Area No.	10	-
Subnet/wildcard mask	192.168.1.0 / 0.0.0.255	**network 192.168.1.0 0.0.0.255 area 10**
Subnet/wildcard mask	10.0.0.0 / 0.255.255.255	**network 10.0.0.0 0.255.255.255 area 10**

Table 2.6 Router RTR parameters

Step 8. Set up SSH server in router RTR according to the given assumptions. The IOS system commands are presented in the last column of the table.

SSH Account	admin1 admin456	**username admin1 privilege 15 secret admin456**
SSH Domain	server.com	**ip domain-name server.com**
The RSA key length	1024	**crypto key generate rsa**

Table 2.7 SSH parameters

Step 9. Set up AAA (RADIUS) authentication for SSH in RTR router according to the given assumptions. The IOS system commands are presented in the last column of the table.

RADIUS server's address	192.168.1.5	**radius-server host 192.168.1.5**
RADIUS server's key	Krakers456	**radius-server key Krakers456**
The inclusion of the authentication for SSH	-	**aaa new-model** **aaa authentication login default group radius local** **line vty 0 4** **login authentication default transport input ssh**

Table 2.8 AAA (RADIUS) parameters

Step10. Ready-made topology should be recorded in the file **exercise1-internal-network-topology-in-the-server-room.pkt**

2.3 Creating external networks (Exercise 2)

Part 1. Preparing and configuring external topologies

Assumptions: this exercise is a continuation of the previous exercise. External networks will connect with the SERVER ROOM and make use of its services, through the edge switch **ML-SW-External**), which is located in the SERVER ROOM.

Step 1. Prepare topologies of external networks according to the drawing.

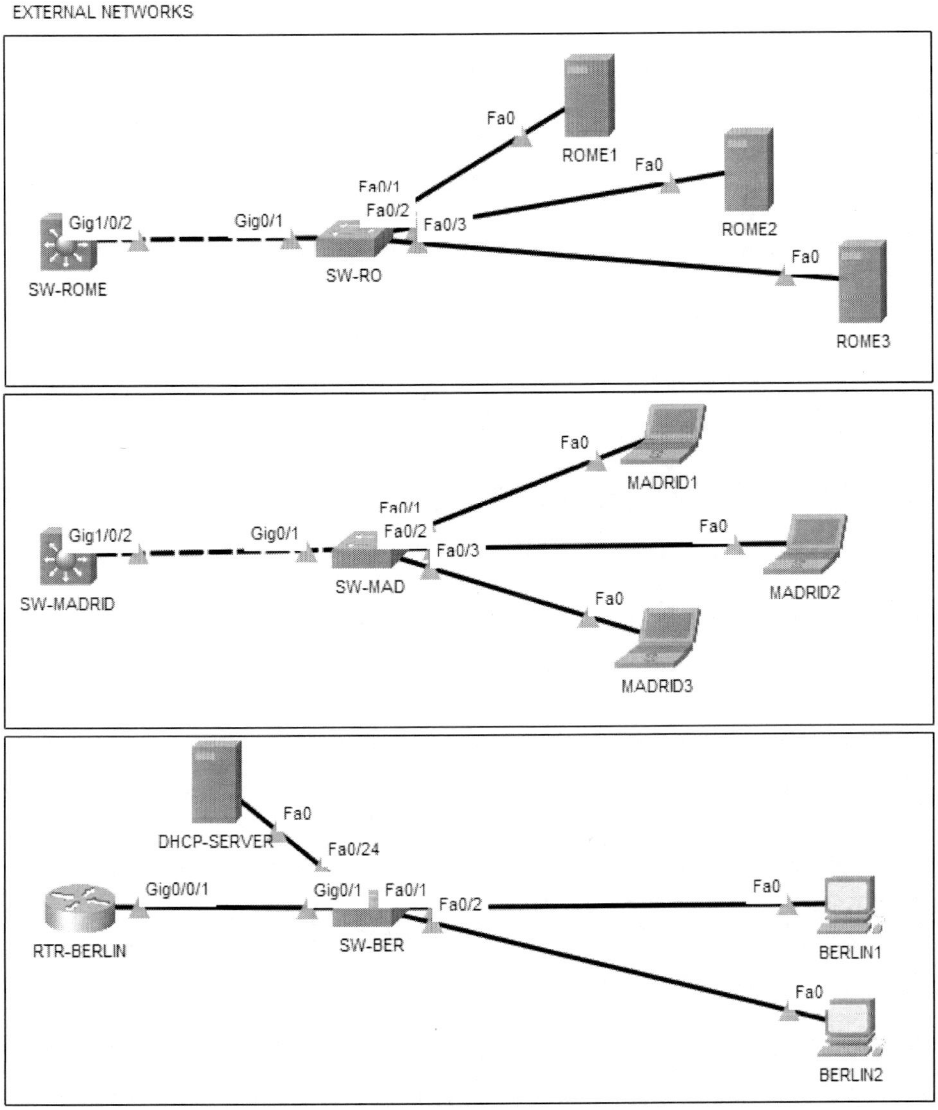

Figure 2.16 Topology of external networks

Step 2. Set up ROME network according to the assumptions.

Device	Interface	Action
SW-ROME	Gi1/0/2	Connect with Gi0/1 in SW-RO
ROME1, ROME2, ROME3	Fa0	Connect with Fa0/1-Fa0/3 in SW-RO
ROME1	Fa0	Enable DHCP
ROME2	Fa0	Enable DHCP
ROME3	Fa0	Enable DHCP

Table 2.9 ROME network parameters

Step 3. Set up MADRID network according to the assumptions.

Device	Interface	Action
SW-MADRID	Gi1/0/2	Connect with Gi0/1 in SW-MAD
MADRID1, MADRID2, MADRID3	Fa0	Connect with Fa0/1-Fa0/3 in SW- MAD
MADRID1	Fa0	Enable DHCP
MADRID2	Fa0	Enable DHCP
MADRID3	Fa0	Enable DHCP

Table 2.10 MADRID network parameters

Step 4. Set up BERLIN network according to the assumptions.

Device	Interface	Action
RTR- BERLIN	Gi0/0/1	Connect with Gi0/1 in SW- BER
DHCP-SERVER	Fa0	Connect with Fa0/24 in SW- BER
BERLIN1, BERLIN2	Fa0	Connect with Fa0/1- Fa0/2 in SW- BER
BERLIN1	Fa0	Enable DHCP
BERLIN2	Fa0	Enable DHCP
RTR- BERLIN	Gi0/0/0	**interface Gi0/0/0** **ip address dhcp** **no shudown**
RTR- BERLIN	Gi0/0/1	**interface Gi0/0/1** **ip address 172.16.1.1 255.255.0.0** **no shudown**
DHCP-SERVER	Fa0	**IP = 172.16.1.2** **Maska podsieci = 255.255.0.0** **Gate= 172.168.1.1** **DNS Server = 192.168.1.3**

Table 2.11 BERLIN network topology

Step 5. Set up DHCP in DHCP-SERVER according to the assumptions.

Pool	**serverPool**
Default Gateway	**172.16.1.1**
DNS Server	**192.168.1.3**
Start IP Address	**172.16.1.3**
Subnet Mask	**255.255.0.0**
Maximum Number of Users	**512**

Table 2.12 DHCP-SERVER parameters

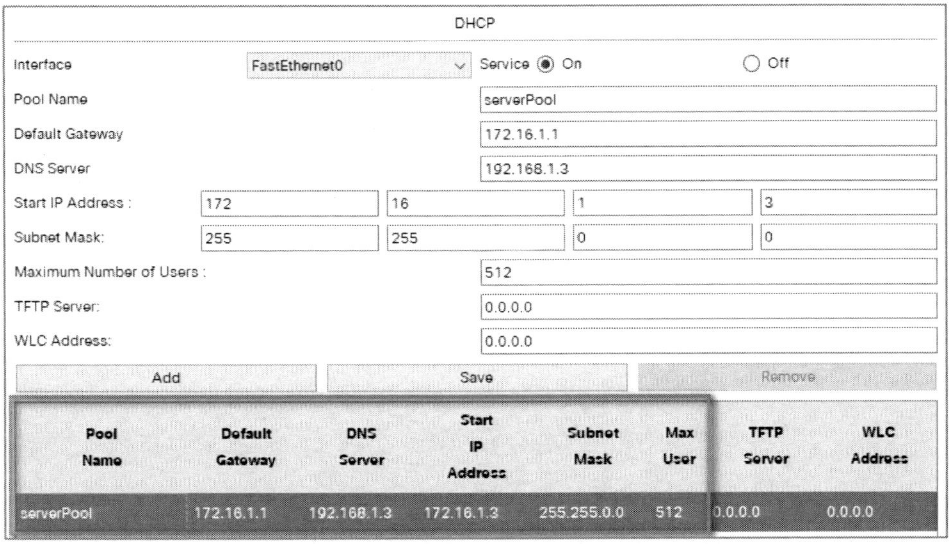

Figure 2.17 Configuring DHCP protocol.

Step 6. In router RTR-GSP configure OSPF protocol according to the assumptions.

Routing protocol	OSPF	-
ID	1	**router ospf 1**
Area No.	10	-
Subnetwork/ wildcard mask	10.0.0.0 / 0.255.255.255	**network 10.0.0.0 0.255.255.255 area 10**
Subnetwork/ wildcard mask	172.16.1.0 / 0.0.255.255	**network 172.16.1.0 0.0.255.255 area 10**

Table 2.13 OSPF parameters

Step 7. Record the ready-made topology in the file **exercise2-external-networks-topology.pkt**

2.4 Connecting the SERVER ROOM with external networks (Exercise 3)

Part 1. Introduction.

In the previous exercises you have prepared the file with the SERVER ROOM topology and the file with the topology of the external networks. This exercise is a continuation of the previous exercises.

You should prepare yourself now to connect both topologies through Your actual LAN network. In order to do so you have to obtain basic data about Your actual network.

Part 2. Obtain actual real IPs in the local area network.

For example, if you already have two actual running devices in Your network eg. a PC and a laptop (or another PC).

Let's assume that there is SERVER ROOM topology running on the first computer, and there is a topology of external networks running on the other computer. Let's name them as **PC1** and **PC2**.

Step 1. In order to obtain IP address of your first computer, type **ipconfig** command on the command line in **PC1**.

```
Ethernet adapter Ethernet:

   Connection-specific DNS Suffix  . :
   Link-local IPv6 Address . . . . . : fe80::54f8:d34c:6c84:c297%8
   IPv4 Address. . . . . . . . . . . : 172.16.0.141
   Subnet Mask . . . . . . . . . . . : 255.255.240.0
   Default Gateway . . . . . . . . . : 172.16.0.1
```

Figure 2.18 PC1 address.

Step 2. In order to obtain IP address of your second computer, type **ipconfig** command on the command line in **PC2**.

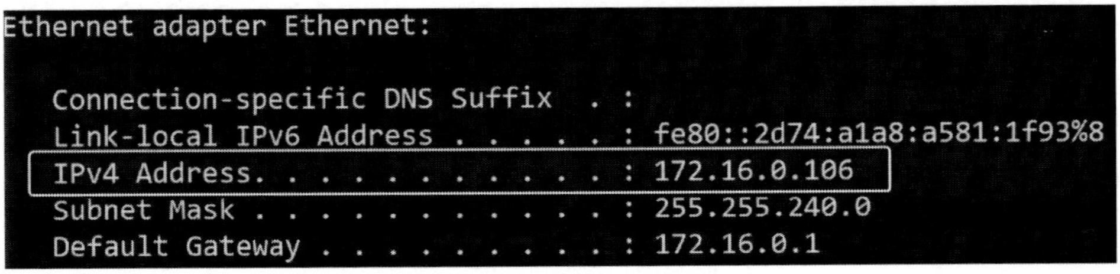

Figure 2.19 PC2 address.

Step 3. Type the results of the commands into the table.

Current Real IP *)	Real computer	Comments
172.16.0.141	**PC1**	The SERVER ROOM topology will work here.
172.16.0.106	**PC2**	The external networks topology will work here.

Table 2.14 The actual local area network's parameters.

Notice *): Current IP addresses will be visible and also used in the next subsections , but in your case they can vary.

Step 4. Now copy the file **exercise1-internal-network-topology-in-the-server room.pkt** to the real computer **PC1**.

Step 5. Change the name of the file **exercise1-internal-network-topology-in-the-server-room.pkt** into **exercise3-server-room-pc1.pkt**

Step 6. Next copy the file **exercise2-external-networks-topology.pkt** to the real computer **PC2**.

Step 7. Change the name of the file **exercise2-external-networks-topology.pkt** into **exercise3-external-networks-pc2.pkt**

Current real IP	Real computer	The name of the file
172.16.0.141	**PC1**	**exercise3-server-room-pc1.pkt**
172.16.0.106	**PC2**	**exercise3-external-networks-pc2.pkt**

Table 2.15 Names of PKT files in the real local area network

Part 3. Configuration of PT Multiuser into PC1

Step 1. Run the **exercise3-server-room-pc1.pkt** file which is located in your computer **PC1**.

Step 2. Check the following PT settings [**Options→Preferences→Administrative**]. See the figure.

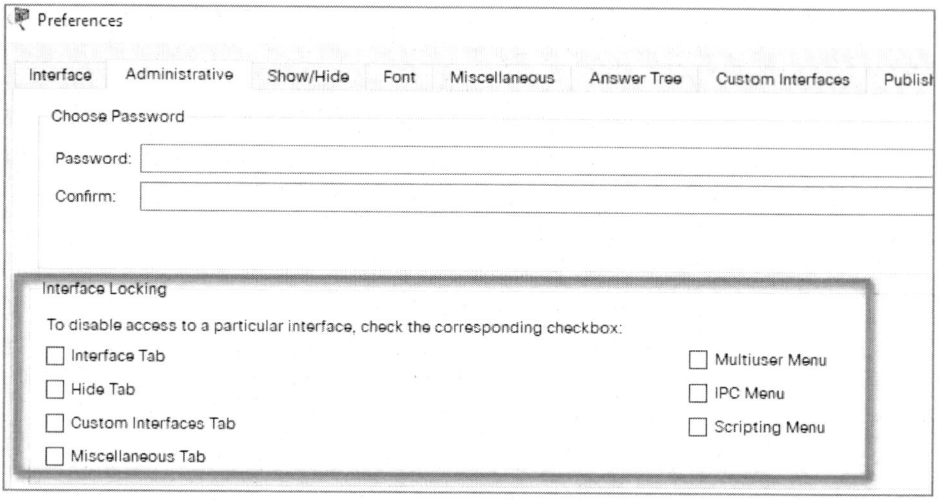

Figure 2.20 Interface Locking options in the Preferences menu.

The options shown in the figure should be disabled.

Step 3. Check the following PT settings [**Extensions→Multiuser→Options**]. See the following figure.

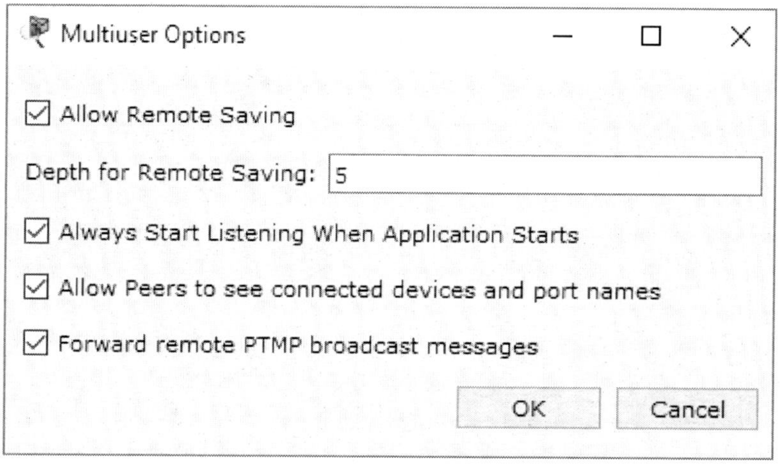

Figure 2.21 Extensions→Multiuser→Options.

The options shown in the figure should be enabled.

Step 4. Choose the ports that are supposed to be visible in PT in the **PC2** computer [**Extensions→Multiuser→Port Visibility**].

In our case those are going to be the following port ranges in the edge switch **ML-SW-External**: GigabitEthernet1/0/1 - GigabitEthernet1/0/23. See the figure.

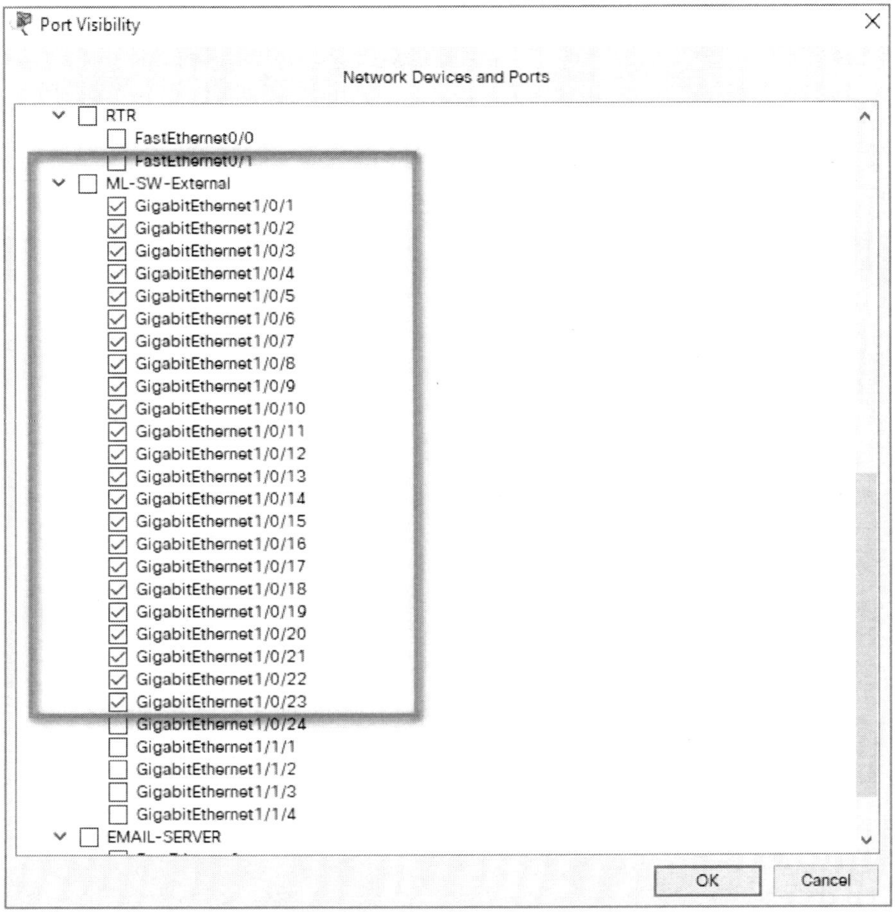

Figure 2.22 Extensions→Multiuser→Port Visibility.

Step 5. In PT in the **PC1** computer set the listening parameters on the port **38000**.

Local Listening Address	172.16.0.141
Port Number	38000
Password	**cisco** (default value)
Existing Remote Networks	Always Accept
New Remote Networks	Always Accept

Table 2.16 Listening parameters in PC1

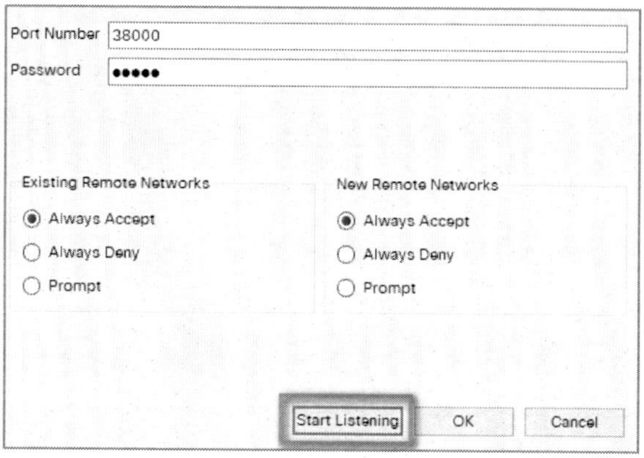

Figure 2.23 Extensions→Multiuser→Listen…

Step 6. Click [**Start Listening**] button.

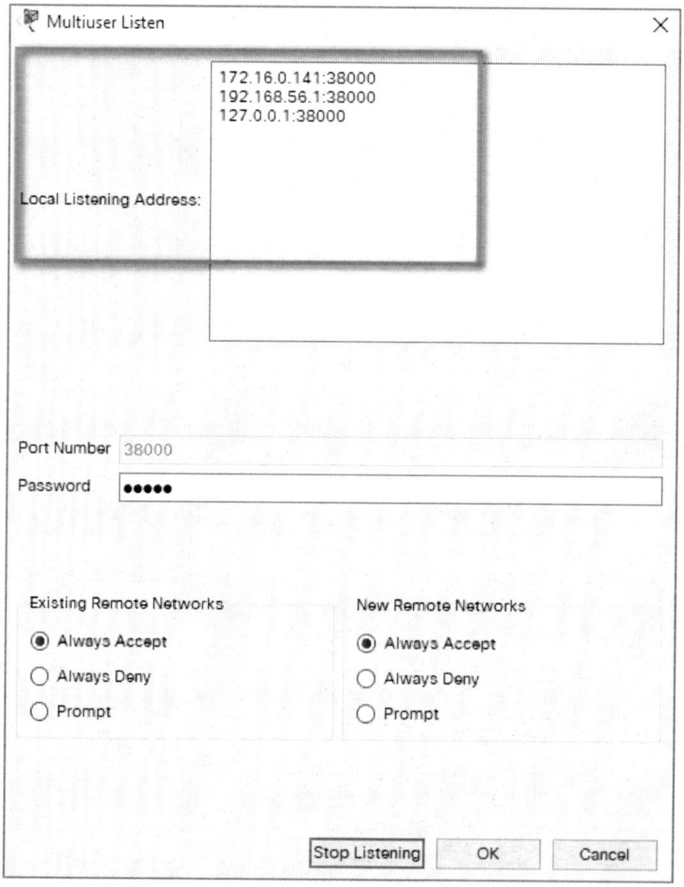

Figure 2.24 The program is listening at the address 172.16.0.141 and 38000 port.

Part 4. Insertion of a cloud of the Incoming type in PT in PC1.

Step 1. In PT in the computer **PC1** insert a cloud of **Incoming** type and configure it according to the given steps.

Step 2. Move to the group of program device icons, which are in the lower left corner of the program.

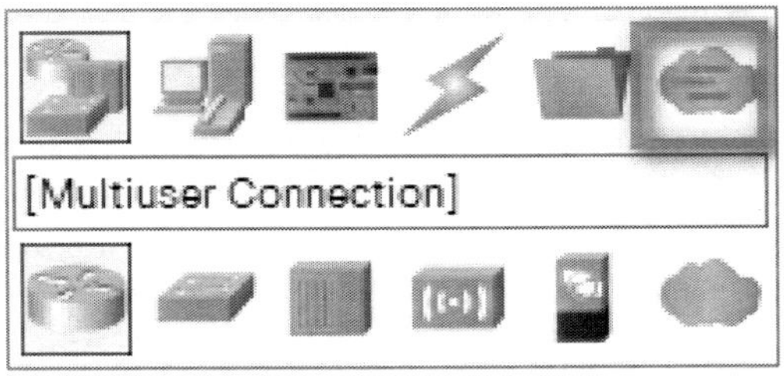

Figure 2.25 Group [Multiuser Connection].

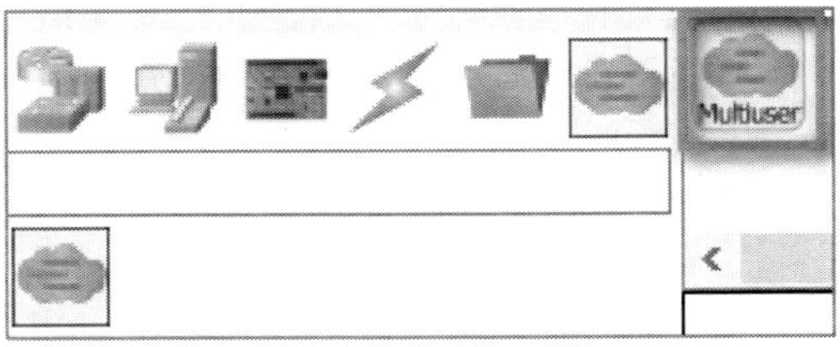

Figure 2.26 Cloud of „Multiuser" type.

Step 3. Choose a cloud **Multiuser** type and insert it to the topology. The cloud's name will be **Peer0**.

Figure 2.27 Peer0 cloud.

Step 4. Click **Peer0** cloud and set connection type [**Connection Type**] for '**Incoming**' and tick the [**Use Global Multiuser Password**] option. Notice: the second option means that a default password (**cisco**) is used.

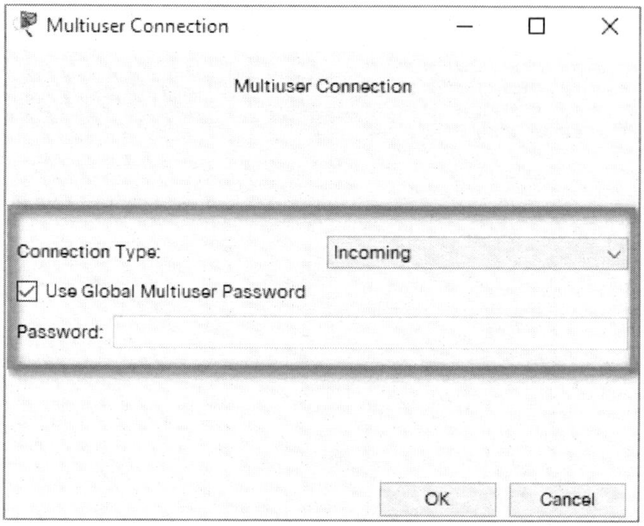

Figure 2.28 The [Incoming] mode of the cloud.

Step 5. Connect ports **ML-SW-External**: GigabitEthernet1/0/1 - GigabitEthernet1/0/2 with the **Peer0** cloud. Use Cooper Cross-Over cables.

Step 6. Connect port **ML-SW-External**: GigabitEthernet1/0/3 with **Peer0** cloud. Use Cooper Straight-Through cable.

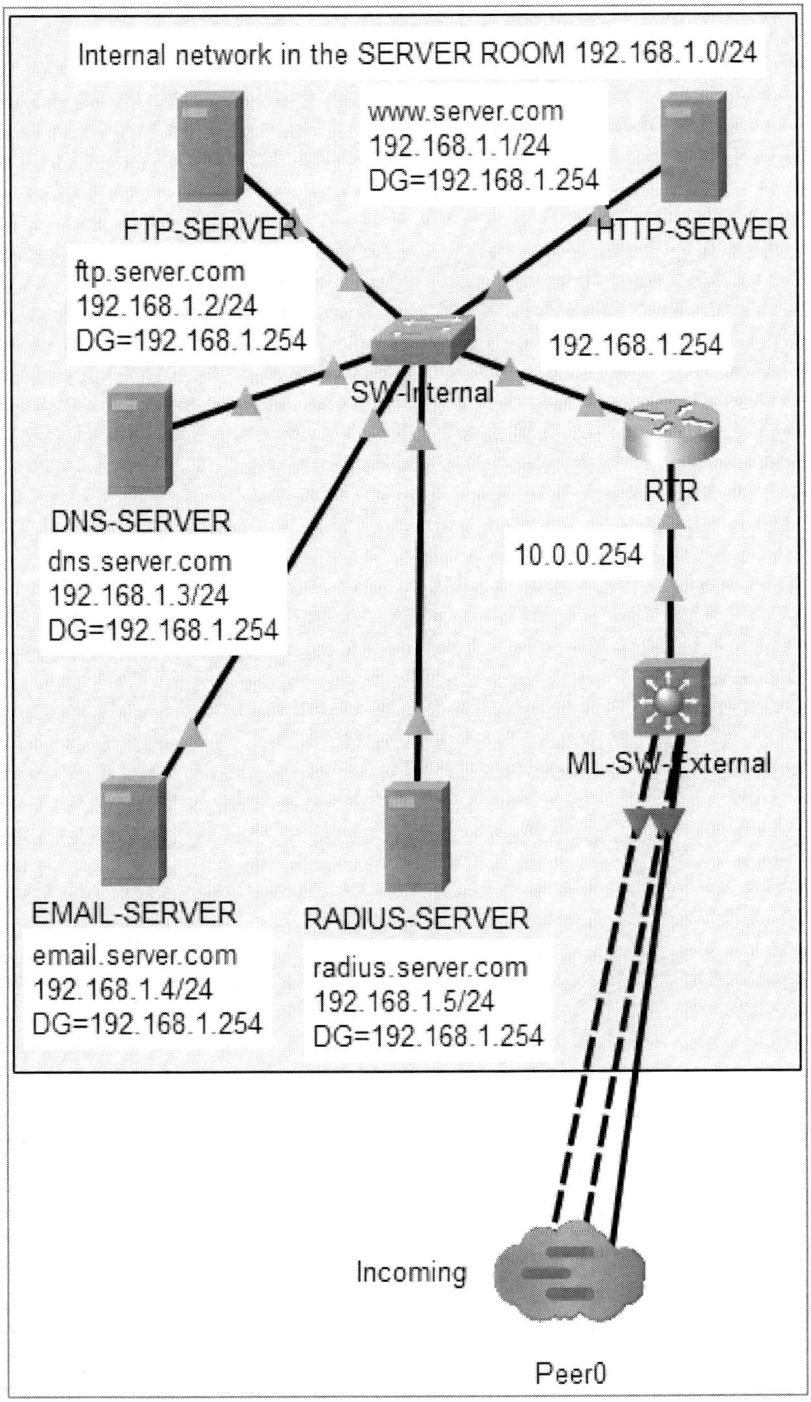

Figure 2.29 The server room topology connected to the cloud.

Part 5. PT Multiuser configuration in PC2.

Step 1. Run the **exercise3-external-networks-pc2.pkt** file which is in your computer **PC2**.

Step 2. Similarly as in case of PC1 perform a PT settings check.

[**Options→Preferences→Administrative**] and [**Extensions→Multiuser→Options**].

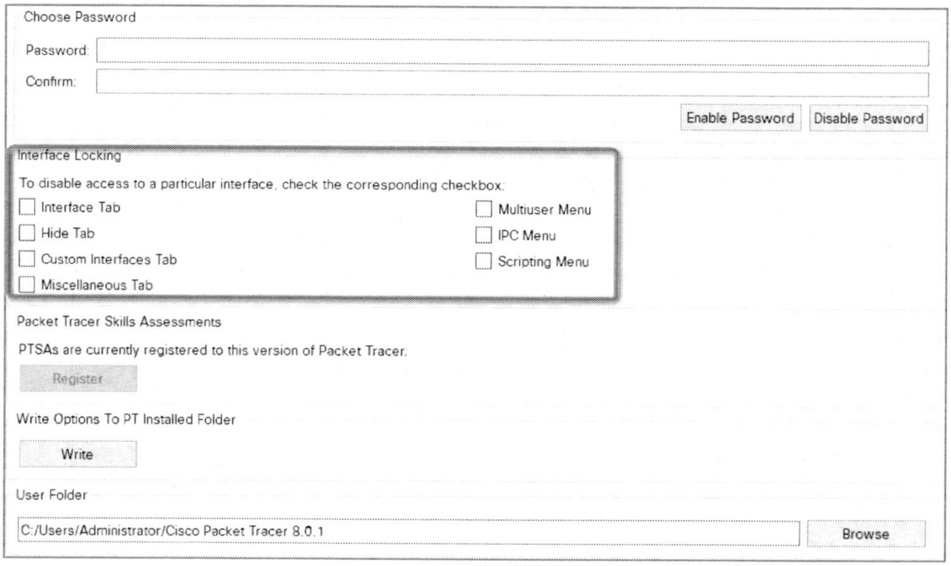

Figure 2.30 Interface Locking options in Preferences menu.

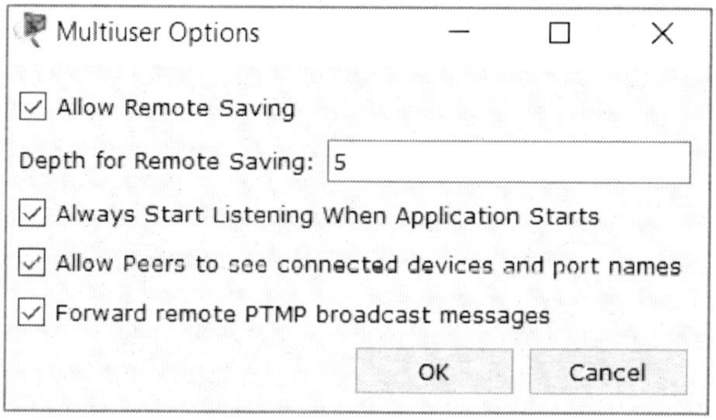

Figure 2.31 Options [Extentions→Multiuser→Options].

Step 3. Configure listening parameters in PT in the computer **PC2.** In PT, running on computer **PC2**, set the following listening parameters on the port **38000**. In PT execute the command [**Extensions→Multiuser→Listen…**]

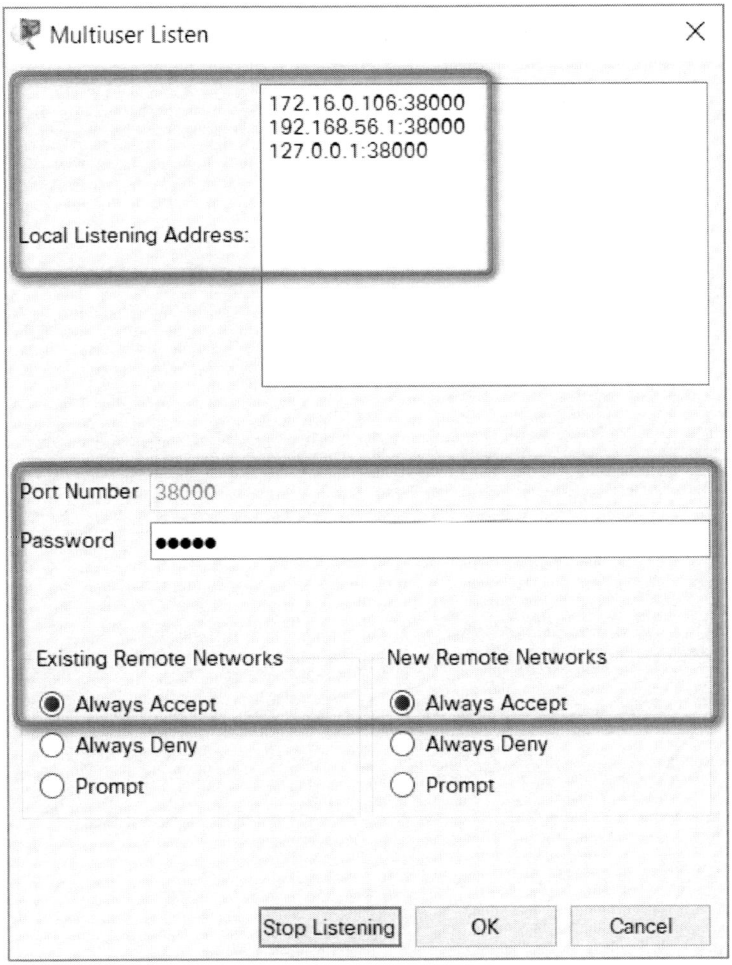

Figure 2.32 Extensions→Multiuser→Listen…

Part 6. Inserting Outgoing type cloud in PT in PC2.

Step 1. In PT in the computer **PC2** insert the cloud of **Outgoing** type and configurate it according to the given steps.

Step 2. Move to the group of program device icons, which are in the lower left corner of the program.

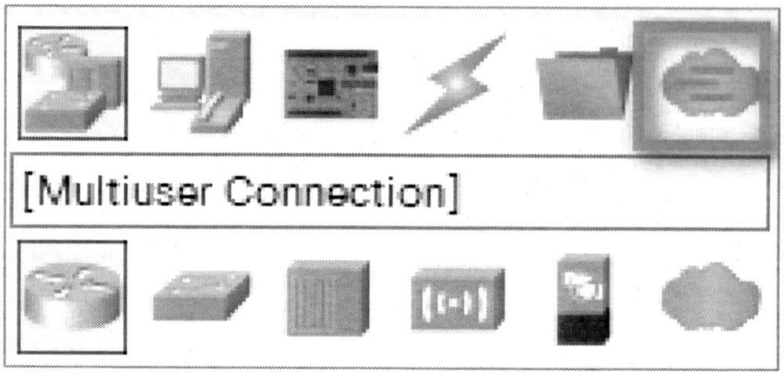

Figure 2.33 Group [Multiuser Connection].

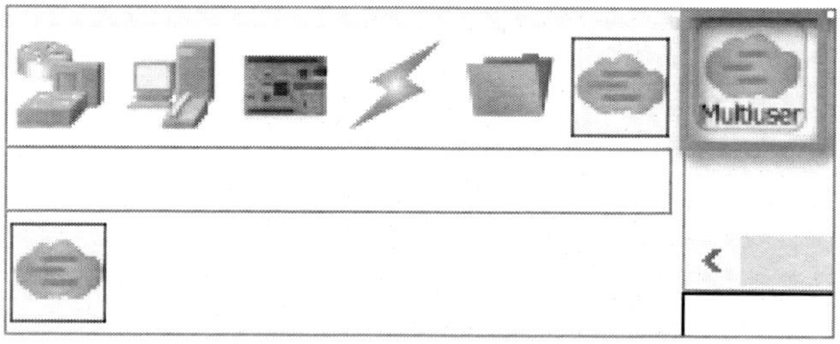

Figure 2.34 'Multiuser' type cloud.

Step 3. Choose a cloud of '**Multiuser**' type and insert it to the topology. The cloud's name will be **Peer0**.

Figure 2.35 Peer0 cloud.

Step 4. Click **Peer0** cloud

Step 5. Set the type of connection at **Outgoing**

Step 6. Set the Peer Address at **172.16.0.141**

Step 7. Set the Peer Port's Number at **38000**

Step 8. Set the Peer Network's Name at **Peer0**

Step 9. Set the Password at **cisco**

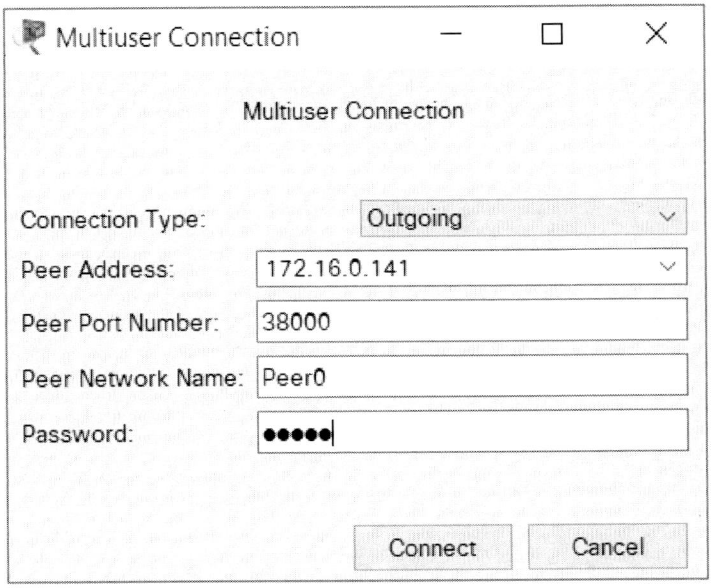

Figure 2.36 The program is listening at the address 172.16.0.141 and 38000 port.

Step 10. Click [**Connect**].

Step 11. Connect **Peer0** cloud with the devices' ports according to the table.

Device in PC2	Port	Device in PC1	Port	Cable's type
SW-ROME	Gi1/0/1	ML-SW-External	Gi1/0/1	Cooper Cross-Over
SW-MADRID	Gi1/0/1	ML-SW-External	Gi1/0/2	Cooper Cross-Over
RTR-BERLIN	Gi0/0/0	ML-SW-External	Gi1/0/3	Cooper Straight-Through

Table 2.17 The devices' connections in OUTGOING cloud.

Step 12. Wait till the clouds are connected.

Step 13. Check if the topology in PC2 matches the topology in the following figure.

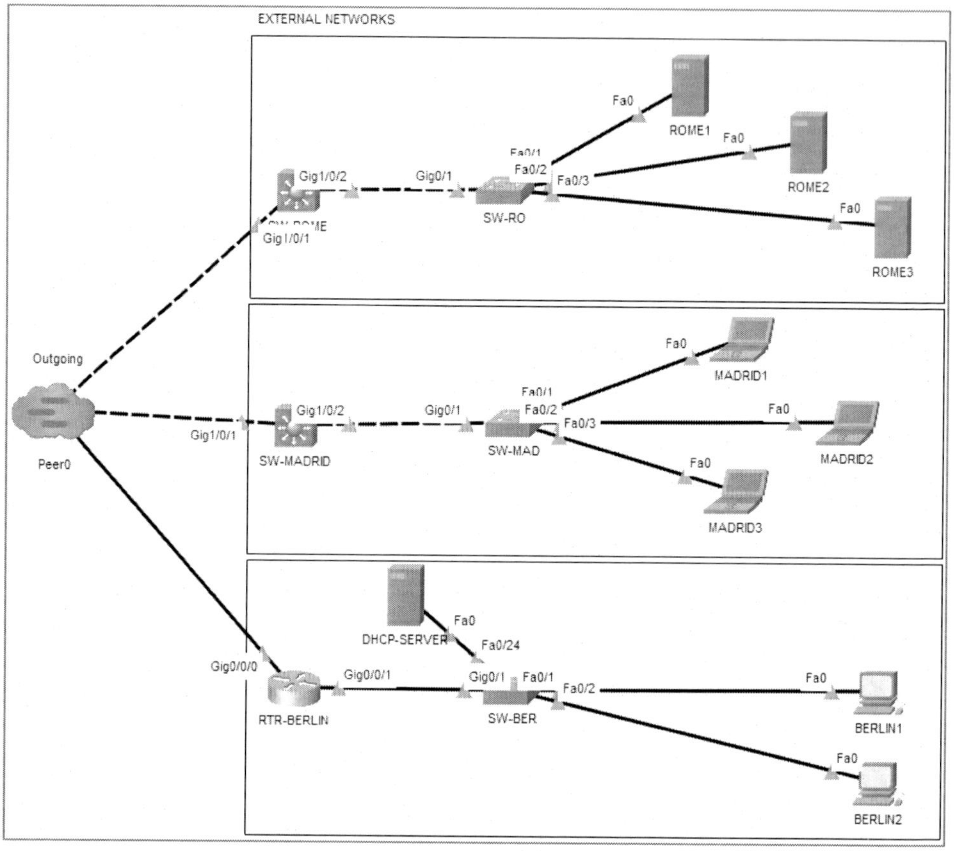

Figure 2.37 The external network topology connected to the cloud.

Step 14. To activate in Gi0/0/0 RTR-BERLIN automatic obtaining an IP address, follow the instructions in RTR-BERLIN:

```
enable
conf t
interface GigabitEthernet0/0/0
ip address dhcp
```

Part 7. Checking communication between networks.

Step 1. Check ping communication with BERLIN2 to the address 192.168.1.1 in the SERVER ROOM.

```
C:\>ping 192.168.1.1

Pinging 192.168.1.1 with 32 bytes of data:

Reply from 192.168.1.1: bytes=32 time=22ms TTL=126
Reply from 192.168.1.1: bytes=32 time=24ms TTL=126
Reply from 192.168.1.1: bytes=32 time=19ms TTL=126
Reply from 192.168.1.1: bytes=32 time=39ms TTL=126

Ping statistics for 192.168.1.1:
    Packets: Sent = 4, Received = 4, Lost = 0 (0% loss),
Approximate round trip times in milli-seconds:
    Minimum = 19ms, Maximum = 39ms, Average = 26ms
```

Figure 2.38 The result of ping command from BERLIN2 to 192.168.1.1

Step 2. Check ping communication from BERLIN2 to the address 192.168.1.2 in the SERVER ROOM.

```
C:\>ping 192.168.1.2

Pinging 192.168.1.2 with 32 bytes of data:

Reply from 192.168.1.2: bytes=32 time=28ms TTL=126
Reply from 192.168.1.2: bytes=32 time=48ms TTL=126
Reply from 192.168.1.2: bytes=32 time=22ms TTL=126
Reply from 192.168.1.2: bytes=32 time=23ms TTL=126

Ping statistics for 192.168.1.2:
    Packets: Sent = 4, Received = 4, Lost = 0 (0% loss),
Approximate round trip times in milli-seconds:
    Minimum = 22ms, Maximum = 48ms, Average = 30ms
```

Figure 2.39 the result of ping command from BERLIN2 to 192.168.1.2

Step 3. Check ping communication from BERLIN2 to the address 192.168.1.3 in the SERVER ROOM.

```
C:\>ping 192.168.1.3

Pinging 192.168.1.3 with 32 bytes of data:

Reply from 192.168.1.3: bytes=32 time=37ms TTL=126
Reply from 192.168.1.3: bytes=32 time=17ms TTL=126
Reply from 192.168.1.3: bytes=32 time=35ms TTL=126
Reply from 192.168.1.3: bytes=32 time=27ms TTL=126

Ping statistics for 192.168.1.3:
    Packets: Sent = 4, Received = 4, Lost = 0 (0% loss),
Approximate round trip times in milli-seconds:
    Minimum = 17ms, Maximum = 37ms, Average = 29ms
```

Figure 2.40 The result of ping command from BERLIN2 to 192.168.1.3

Step 4. Check ping communication from BERLIN2 to the address 192.168.1.4 in the SERVER ROOM.

```
C:\>ping 192.168.1.4

Pinging 192.168.1.4 with 32 bytes of data:

Reply from 192.168.1.4: bytes=32 time=38ms TTL=126
Reply from 192.168.1.4: bytes=32 time=48ms TTL=126
Reply from 192.168.1.4: bytes=32 time=50ms TTL=126
Reply from 192.168.1.4: bytes=32 time=21ms TTL=126

Ping statistics for 192.168.1.4:
    Packets: Sent = 4, Received = 4, Lost = 0 (0% loss),
Approximate round trip times in milli-seconds:
    Minimum = 21ms, Maximum = 50ms, Average = 39ms
```

Figure 2.41 The result of ping command from BERLIN2 to 192.168.1.4

Step 5. Check ping communication from BERLIN2 to the address 192.168.1.5 in the SERVER ROOM.

```
C:\>ping 192.168.1.5

Pinging 192.168.1.5 with 32 bytes of data:

Reply from 192.168.1.5: bytes=32 time=35ms TTL=126
Reply from 192.168.1.5: bytes=32 time=29ms TTL=126
Reply from 192.168.1.5: bytes=32 time=57ms TTL=126
Reply from 192.168.1.5: bytes=32 time=5ms TTL=126

Ping statistics for 192.168.1.5:
    Packets: Sent = 4, Received = 4, Lost = 0 (0% loss),
Approximate round trip times in milli-seconds:
    Minimum = 5ms, Maximum = 57ms, Average = 31ms
```

Figure 2.42 The result of ping command from BERLIN2 to 192.168.1.5

Part 8. Checking the operation of services between networks.

Step 1. Check if it is possible to log in to the router RTR in the SERVER ROOM, from BERLIN2 using SSH (account: **admin1**, password: **admin456**).

```
C:\>ssh -l admin1 10.0.0.254

Password:
RTR>en
Password:
RTR#
```

Figure2.43 Logging into RTR using SSH.

Step 2. Display routing table for OSPF.

```
C:\>
C:\>ssh -l admin1 10.0.0.254

Password:
RTR>en
Password:
RTR#
RTR#show ip route ospf
O    172.16.0.0 [110/2] via 10.0.0.4, 00:02:07, FastEthernet0/1

RTR#
```

Figure2.44 Routing table

Step 3. Display allocated IP addresses in the pool DHCP

```
RTR#show ip dhcp binding
IP address       Client-ID/              Lease expiration        Type
                 Hardware address
10.0.0.2         0050.0F89.BB8A           --                     Automatic
10.0.0.1         0060.47AA.49D3           --                     Automatic
10.0.0.3         00E0.A349.5DB7           --                     Automatic
10.0.0.4         000B.BE8D.9701           --                     Automatic
10.0.0.5         000D.BD50.3D6B           --                     Automatic
10.0.0.6         0006.2A39.9C83           --                     Automatic
10.0.0.7         0002.1794.C024           --                     Automatic
RTR#
```

Figure2.45 IP addresses allocation in DHCP

Step 4. Display pool DHCP parameters

```
RTR#show ip dhcp pool

Pool EXTERNAL-DHCP :
 Utilization mark (high/low)    : 100 / 0
 Subnet size (first/next)       : 0 / 0
 Total addresses                : 16777214
 Leased addresses               : 7
 Excluded addresses             : 1
 Pending event                  : none

 1 subnet is currently in the pool
 Current index        IP address range                    Leased/Excluded/Total
 10.0.0.1             10.0.0.1         - 10.255.255.254    7    / 1      / 16777214
RTR#
```

Figure2.46 Pool DHCP parameters

Step 5. Check if it is possible to open www.server.com webpage from BERLIN2

Figure 2.47 Opening www.server.com webpage

Step 6. Check if it is possible to connect with ftp.server.com from BERLIN2.

```
C:\>ftp ftp.server.com
Trying to connect...ftp.server.com
Connected to ftp.server.com
220- Welcome to PT Ftp server
Username:cisco
331- Username ok, need password
Password:
230- Logged in
(passive mode On)
ftp>
ftp>
ftp>dir

Listing /ftp directory from ftp.server.com:
ftp>
ftp>quit

221- Service closing control connection.
C:\>
```

Figure 2.48 The connection with ftp.server.com.

Step 7. Check if it is possible to open ftp.server.com webpage from ROME1.

Figure 2.49 Opening the ftp.server.com website.

Step 8. Check if after clicking the button [**INFO**] the JavaScript works

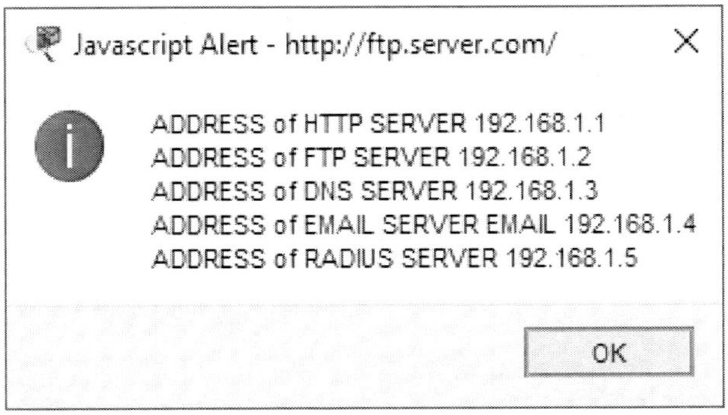

Figure 2.50 The result of clicking the [INFO] button.

Step 9. Check if you can open the website dns.server.com from ROME1.

Figure 2.51 Opening the dns.server.com website.

Step 10. Configure a mail account on MADRID1 computer for Tom. **[Desktop→Email]**

Your name	Email Address	User Name	Password
Tom	tom@email.server.com	Tom	tom123
Server Information			
Incoming Mail Server	email.server.com		
Outgoing Mail Server	email.server.com		

Table 2.18 Configuring Tom's mail account.

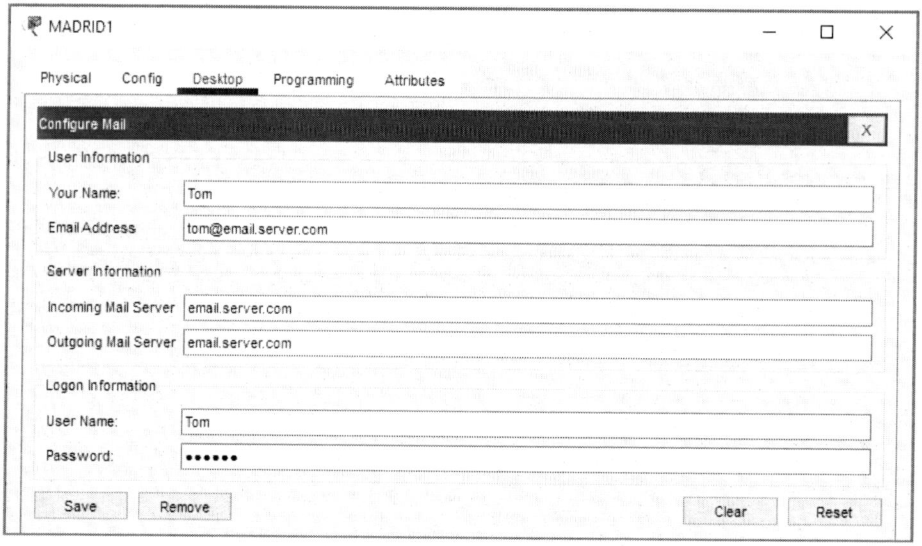

Figure 2.52 Configuring Tom's mail account.

Step 11. Configure a mail account on MADRID2 computer for Eve. **[Desktop→Email]**

Your name	**Email Address**	**User Name**	**Password**
Eve	eve@email.server.com	Eve	eve123
Server Information			
Incoming Mail Server	email.server.com		
Outgoing Mail Server	email.server.com		

Table 2.19 Configuring Eve's mail account.

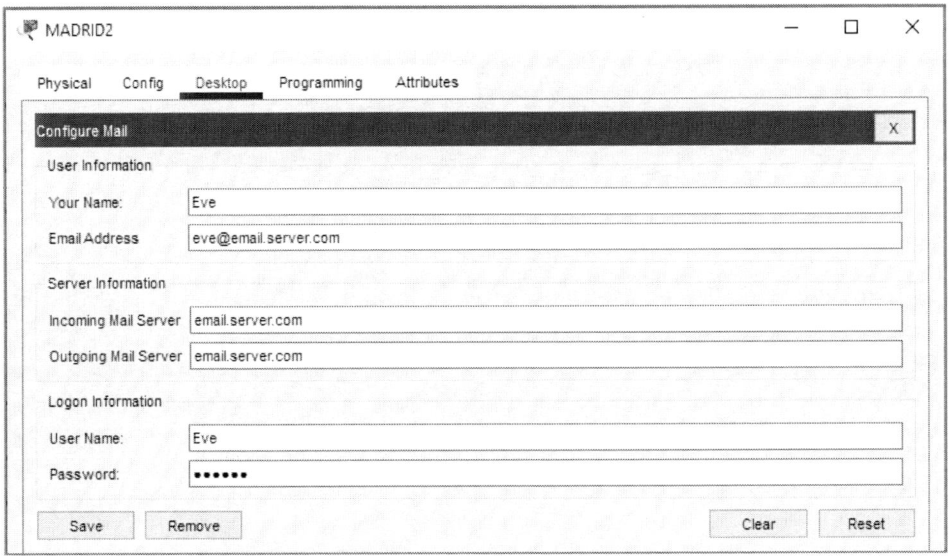

Figure 2.53 Configuring Eve's mail account.

Step 12. Using Tom's mail account from the MADRID1 computer send an email to Eve.

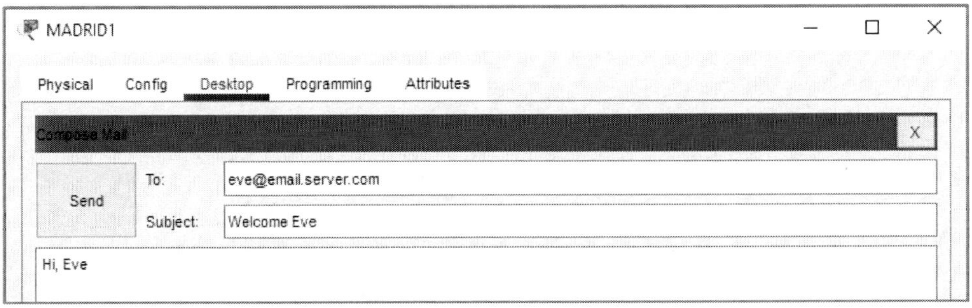

Figure 2.54 Sending email from Tom to Eve.

Step 13. Using Eve's mail account answer the email from the MADRID2 computer.

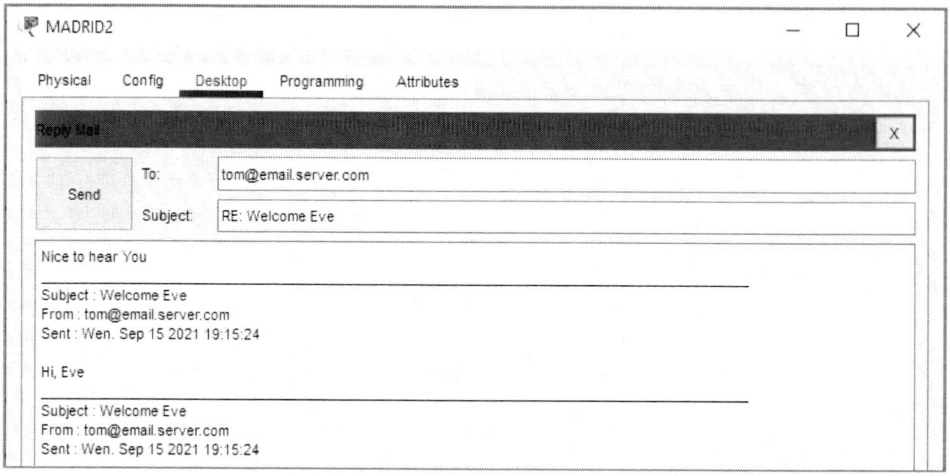

Figure 2.55 Answering to Tom's email.

Step 14. Closing the PT Multiuser file on the PC2.

After closing the **exercise3-external-networks-pc2.pkt** file, it will there an immediate LAN connection breakdown and the topology in the file **exercise3-server-room-pc1.pkt** looks as follows.

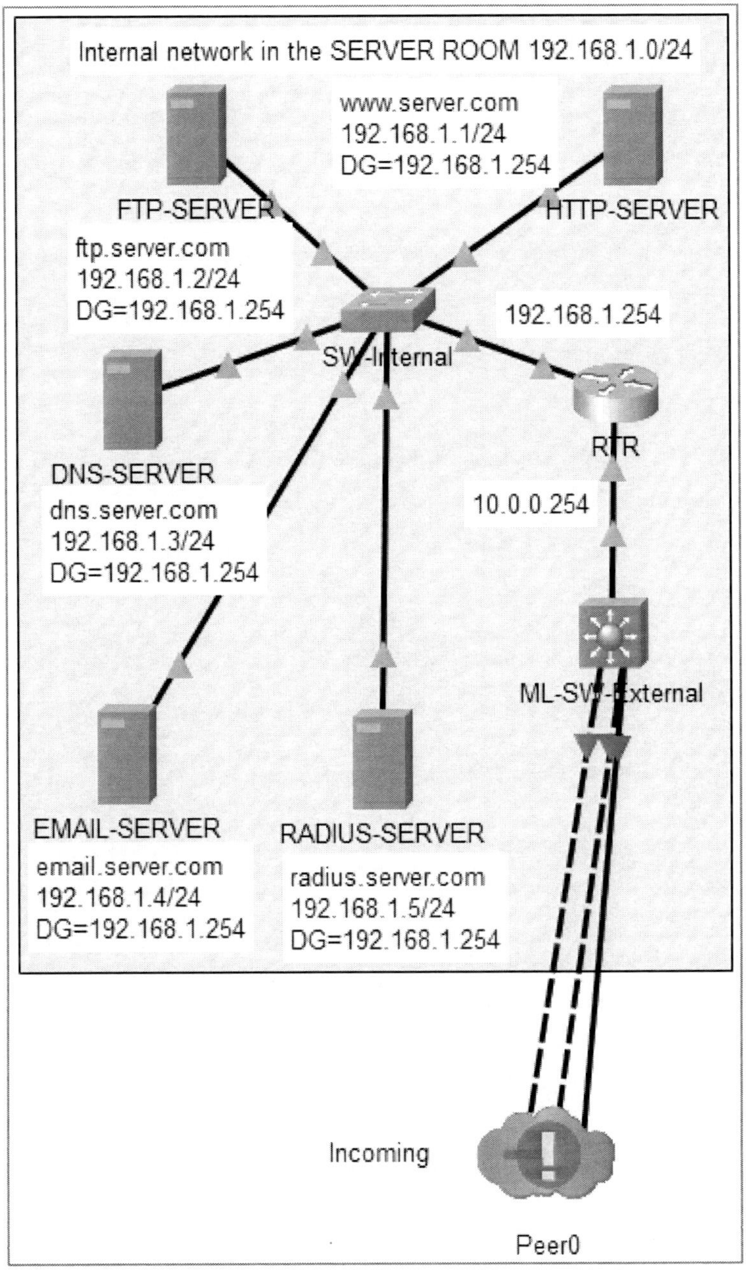

Figure 2.56 „Incoming"cloud connection status after „Outgoing" cloud connection breakdown.

2.5 List of auxiliary files

- dns-config.txt
- ftp-config.txt
- index.html
- style.css
- exercise1-internal-network-topology-in-the-server-room.pkt
- exercise2-external-networks-topology.pkt
- exercise3-server-room-pc1.pkt
- exercise3-external-networks-pc2.pkt

CHAPTER 3

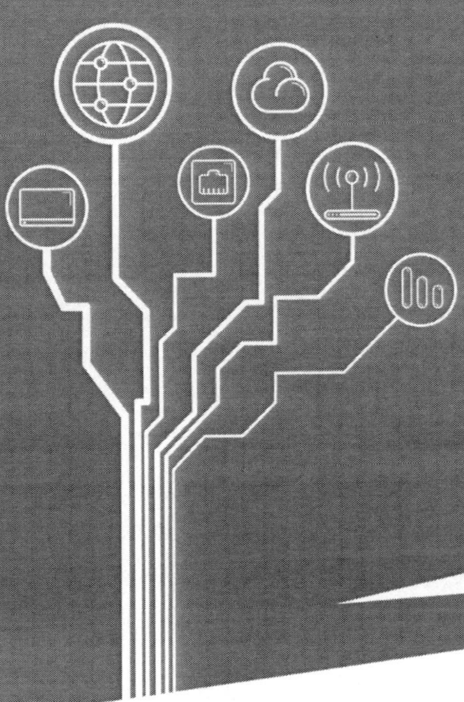

PACKET TRACER IN LINUX

COMPUTER NETWORKS IN PACKET TRACER

FOR ADVANCED USERS

3 Packet Tracer in Linux

In this chapter there is a description of creating a virtual Ubuntu Linux machine, installing the Packet Tracer program in Ubuntu Linux system and also connecting and communicating of **PT topologies** between Windows and Linux systems.

3.1 Creating the Virtual Ubuntu Linux machine

Step 1. Install the VirtualBox.

Download and install the program from the producer's website.

Source : https://www.virtualbox.org/

File: VirtualBox-7.0.0-153978-Win.exe

Figure 3.1 VirtualBox 7.0 program installation begin.

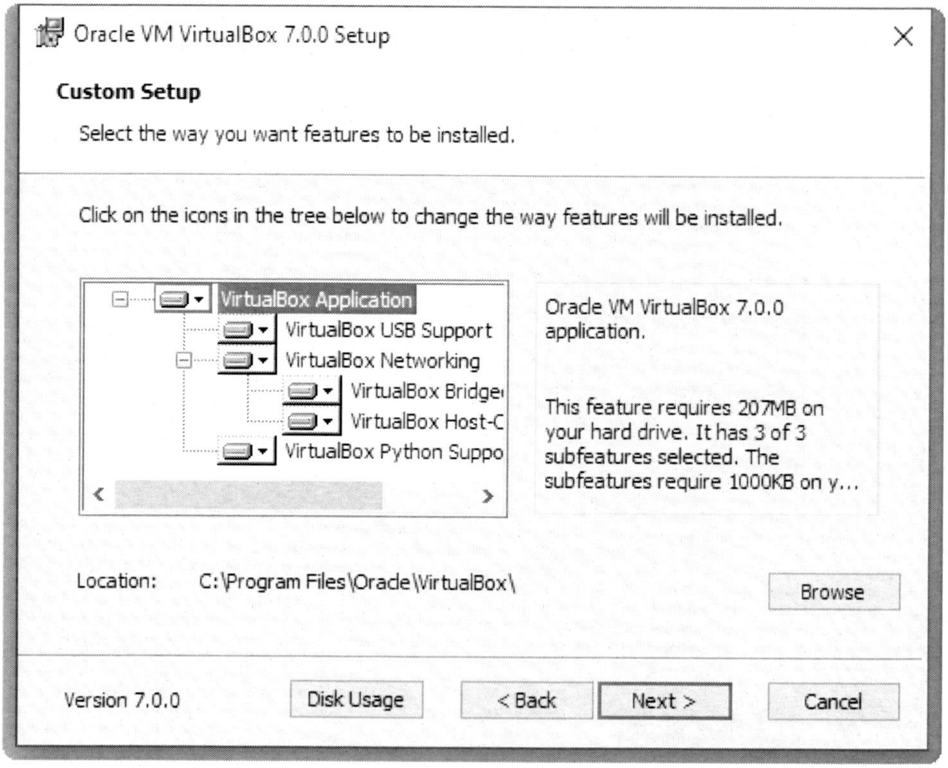

Figure 3.2 VirtualBox 7.0 program features installation.

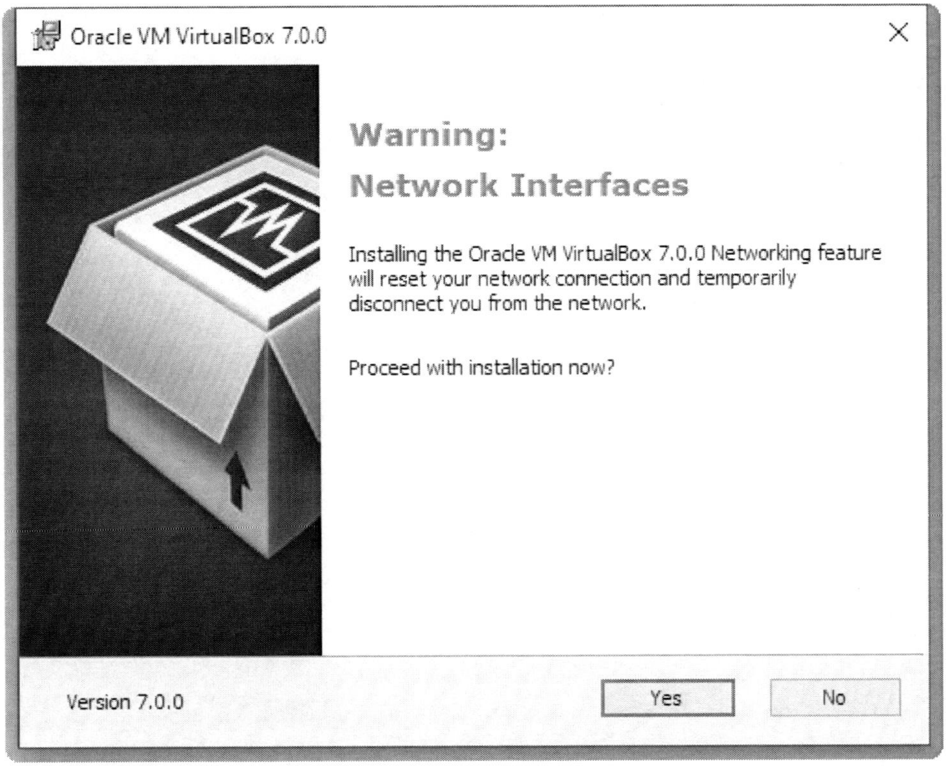

Figure 3.3 VirtualBox 7.0 program installation (warning about network).

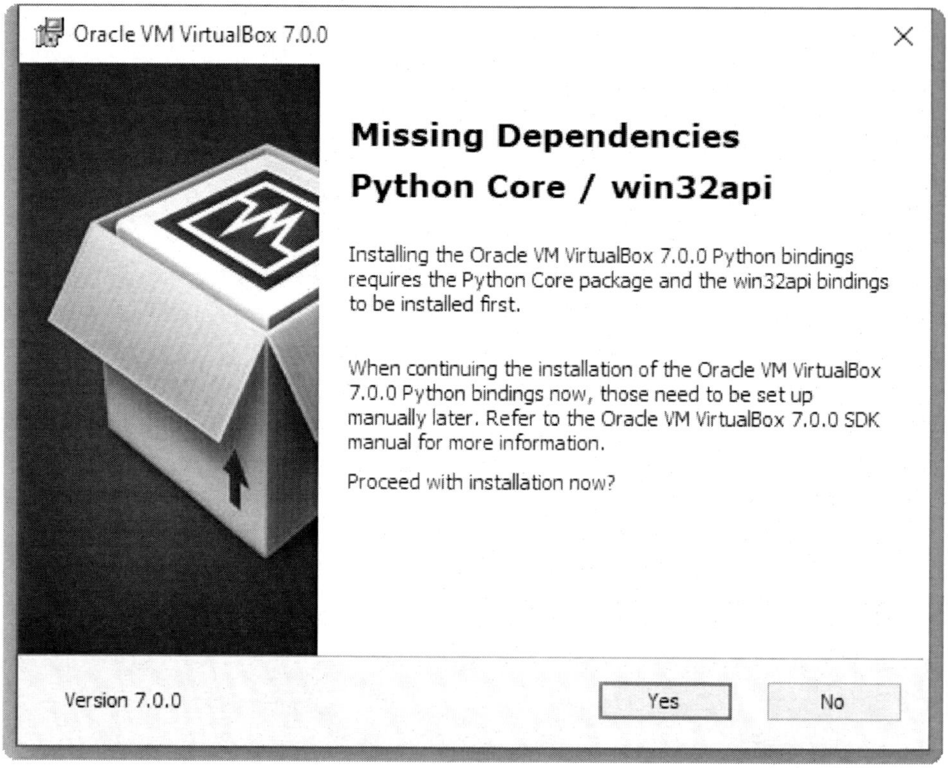

Figure 3.4 VirtualBox 7.0 program installation (bindings to Python Core).

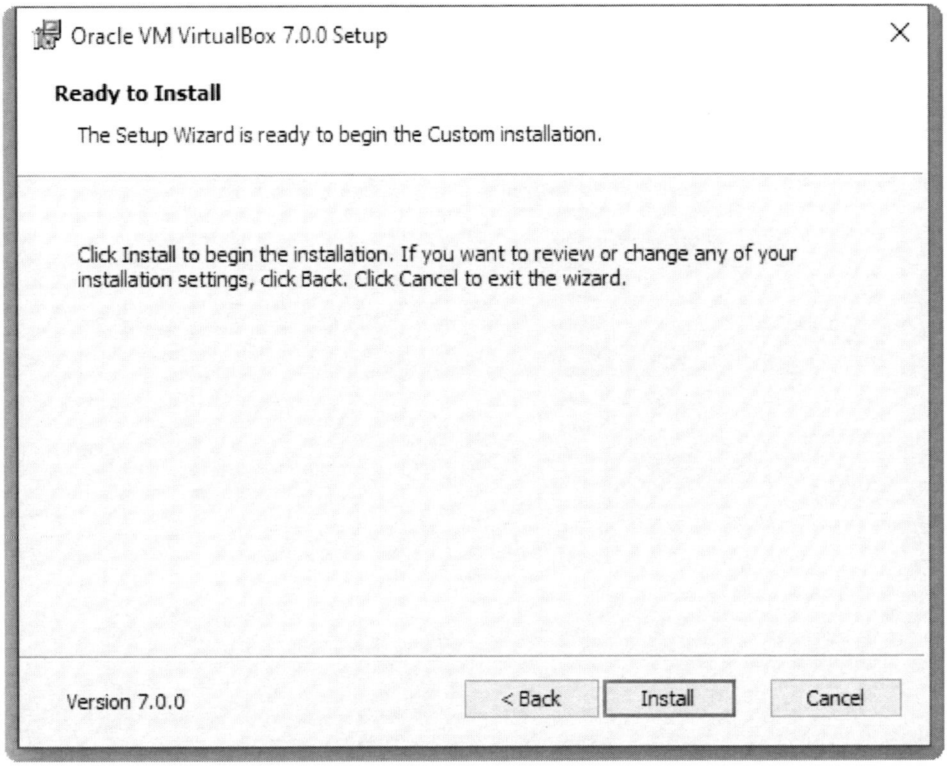

Figure 3.5 VirtualBox 7.0 program installation (Ready to Install).

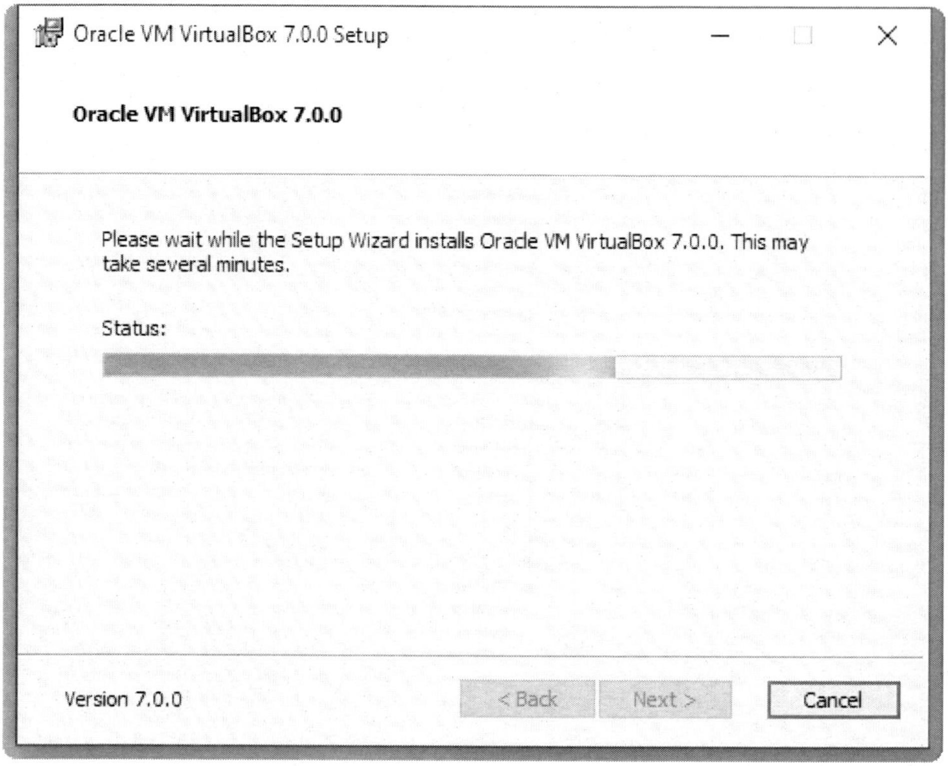

Figure 3.6 VirtualBox 7.0 program installation status.

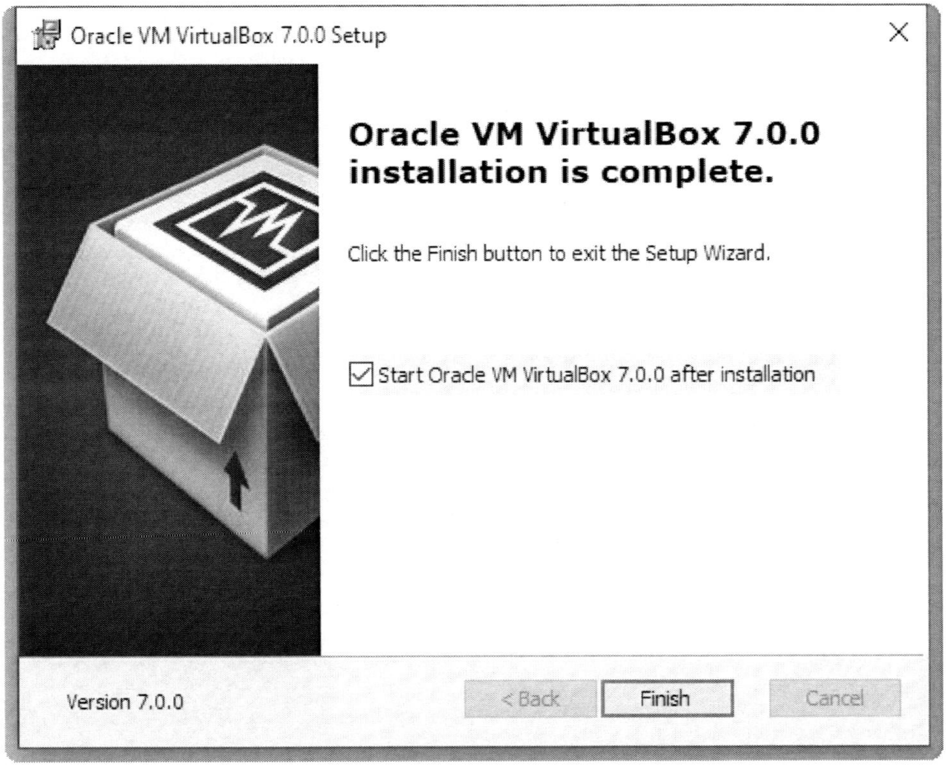

Figure 3.7 VirtualBox 7.0 program installation (Finish and Start).

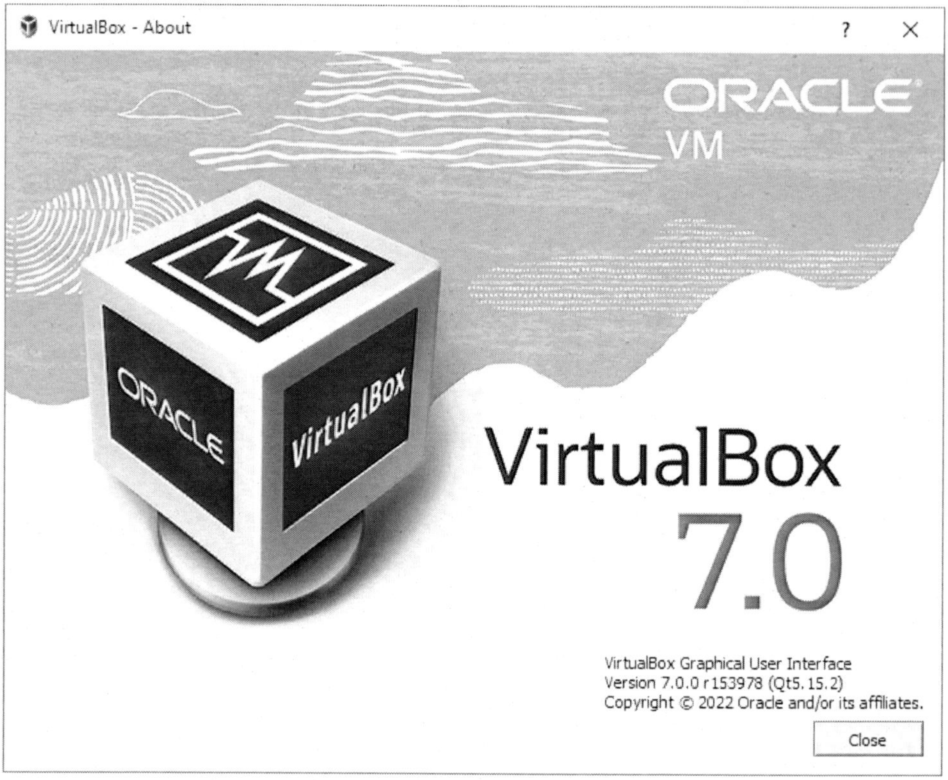

Figure 3.8 VirtualBox 7.0 program (info about the version).

Step 2. Install Extension for VBOX

Download and install **Extension for VirtualBox** from the producer's website.

Source:
https://download.virtualbox.org/virtualbox/Oracle_VM_VirtualBox_Extension_Pack-7.0.0.vbox-extpack

File → Tools → Extension Pack Manager

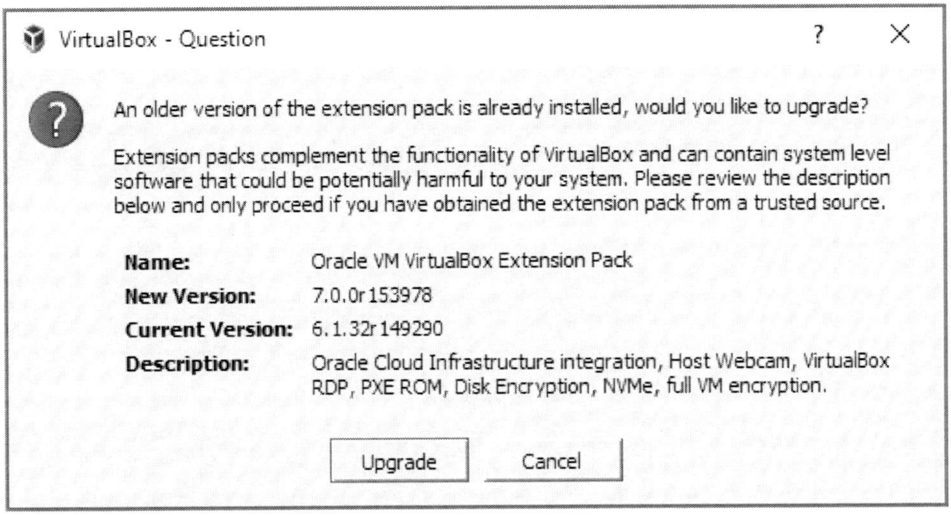

Figure 3.9 Upgrade Extension Pack for the VirtualBox.

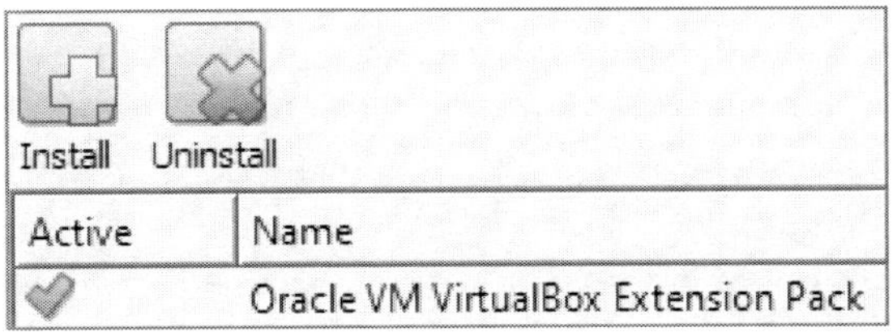

Figure 3.10 Extension for the VirtualBox is upgraded.

Step 3. Download ISO image for ***Ubuntu 20.04.5 LTS.***

From the site **https://releases.ubuntu.com/focal/** select 64-bit PC (AMD64) desktop image and download it.

ISO image file name : **ubuntu-20.04.5-desktop-amd64.iso** [3.7 GB]

Step 4. Run the **VirtualBox**.

Step 5. Create the virtual machine named **UBUNTU_20.04.5** using the menu **Machine→New ...**

Step 6. Specify the name, type and version of the virtual system. Enable option "**Skip Unattended Installation**".

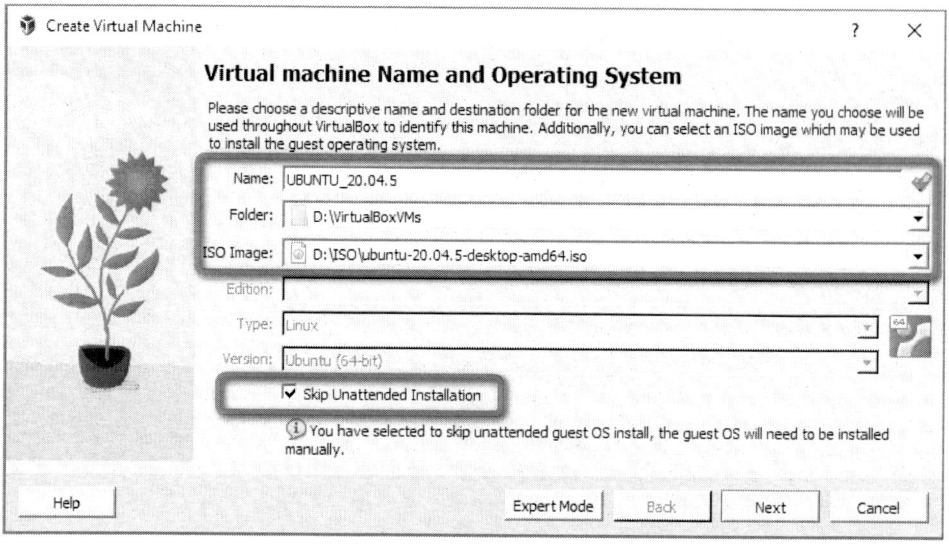

Figure 3.11 Name and location for the virtual machine.

Step 7. Set the Base Memory for the virtual machine.

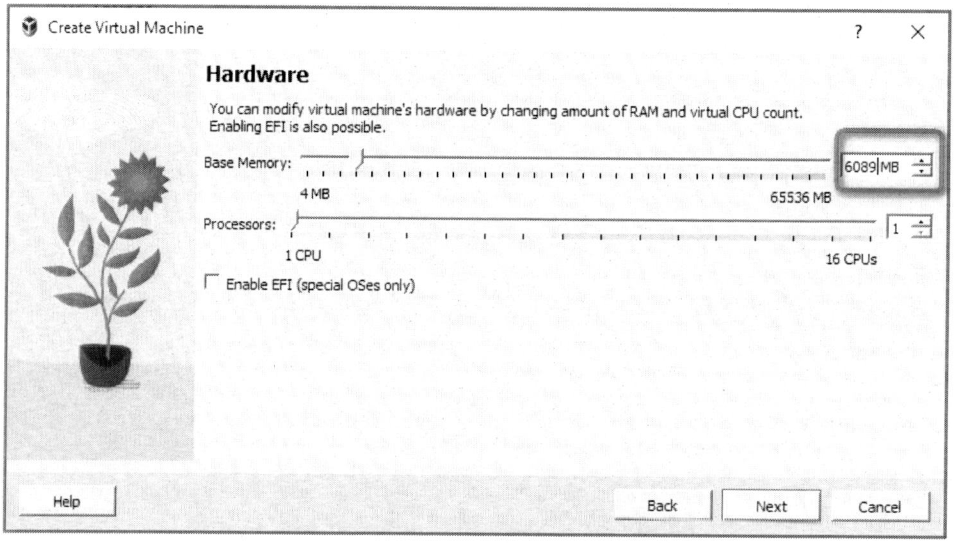

Figure 3.12 Base memory for the virtual machine.

Step 8. Set the Size for the Virtual Hard Disk.

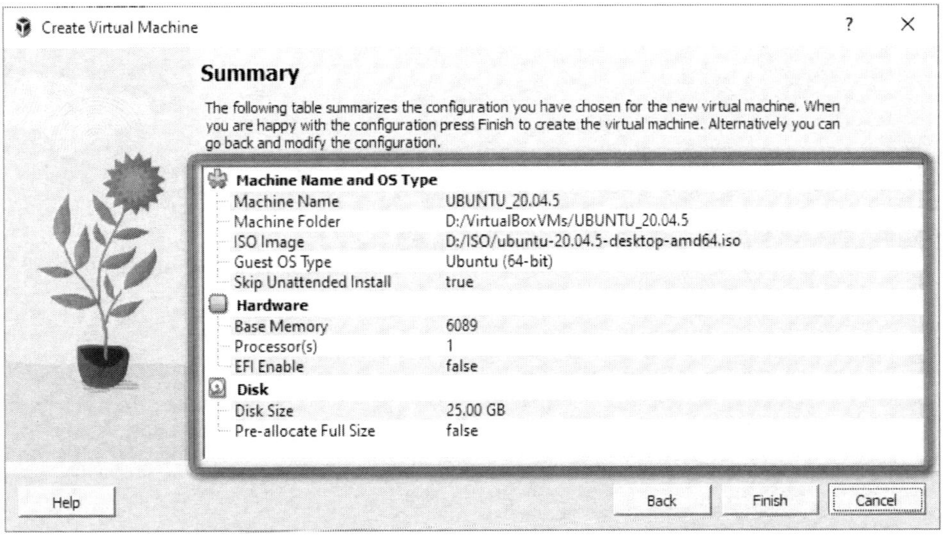

Figure 3.13 Virtual disk for the virtual machine.

Step 9. Read the Summary for the new created virtual machine.

Step 10. Run **UBUNTU** machine.

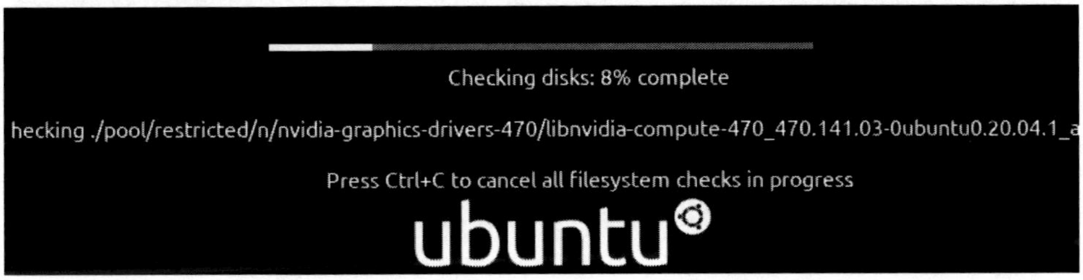

Figure 3.14 Starting Ubuntu Virtual Machine.

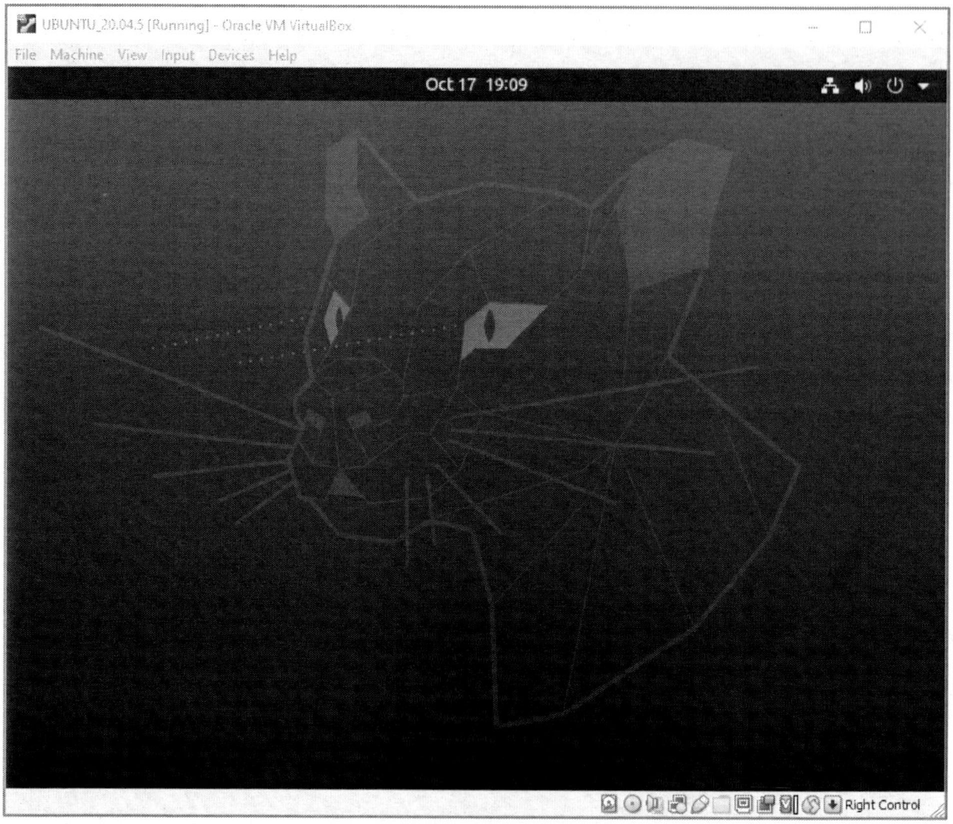

Figure 3.15 Starting Ubuntu Virtual Machine.

Step 11. Click '**Install Ubuntu**' and start installing Linux Ubuntu system according to the following assumptions.

Assumptions:

- Language: **English**
- The host's name **EXERCISES**
- Login **student**
- Password **student**
- Login **root**
- Password **rootmain**

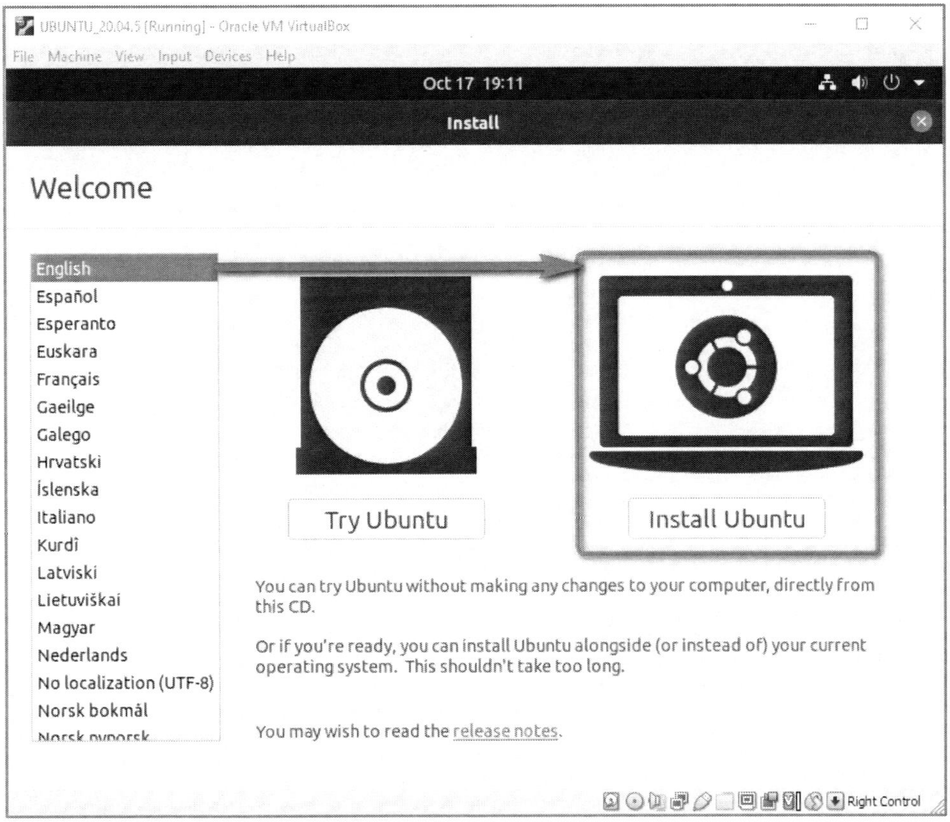

Figure 3.16 Starting of Ubuntu System Installing.

Step 12. Choose the English (US) keyboard layout.

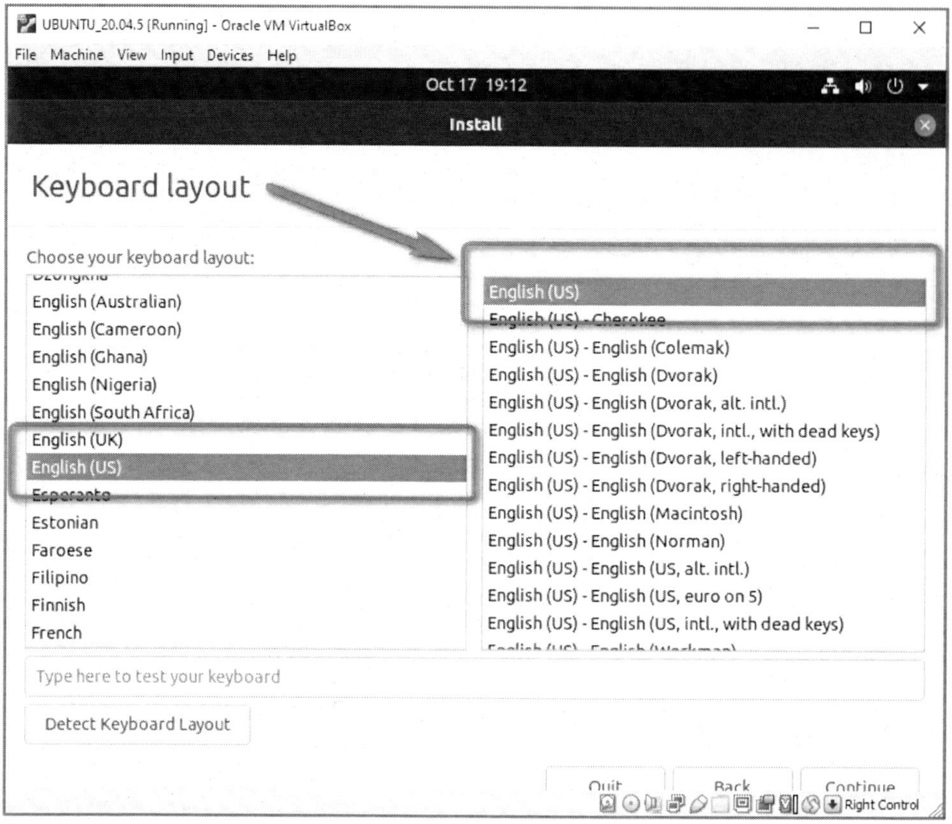

Figure 3.17 Choosing the keyboard layout.

Step 13. Set default values for software and updates. Choose the software for installed machine as **Normal installation**.

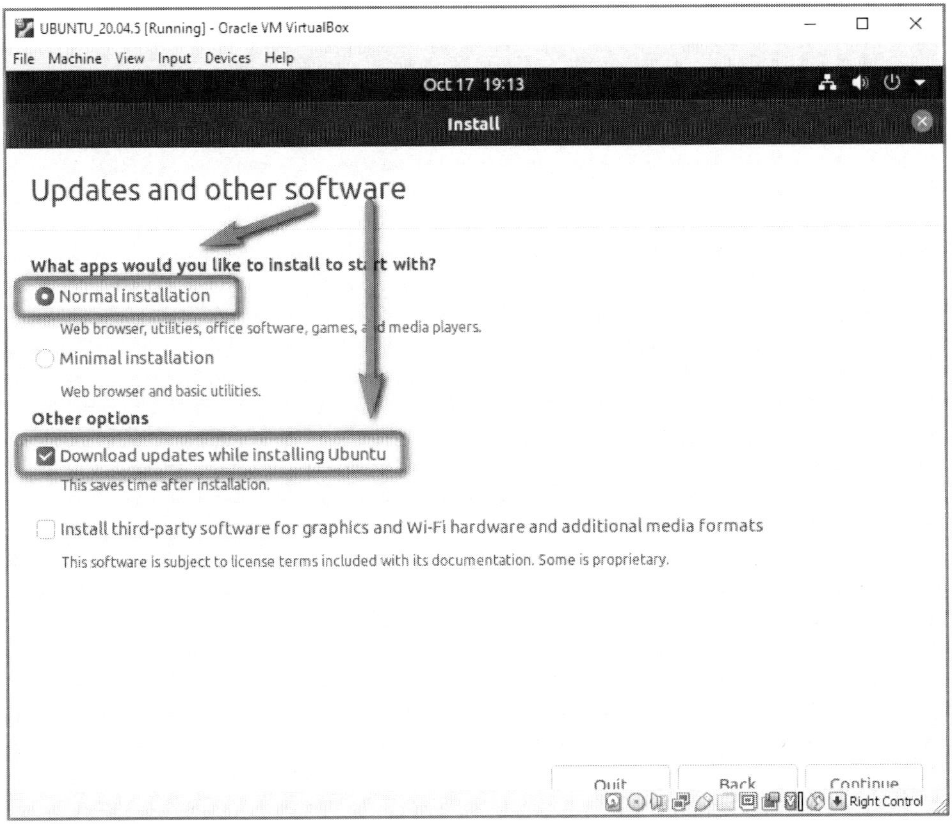

Figure 3.18 Choosing the software.

Step 14. Set default values for installation type – **Erase disk and install Ubuntu** on the entire disk and create the Partition table.

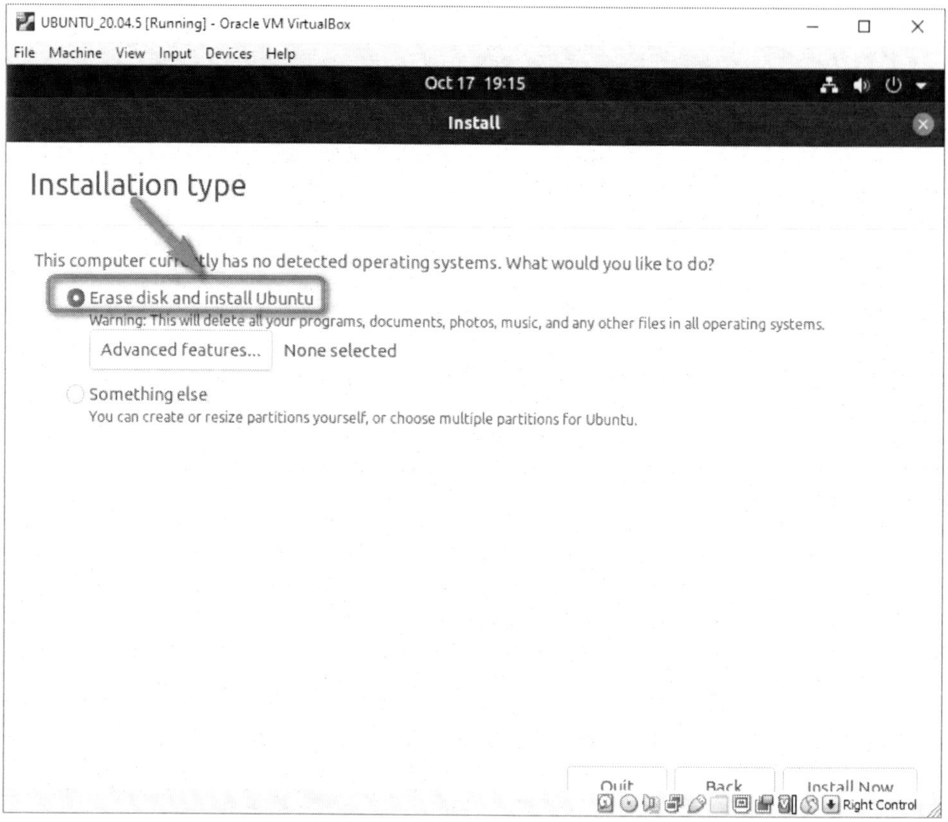

Figure 3.19 Choosing of the installation type.

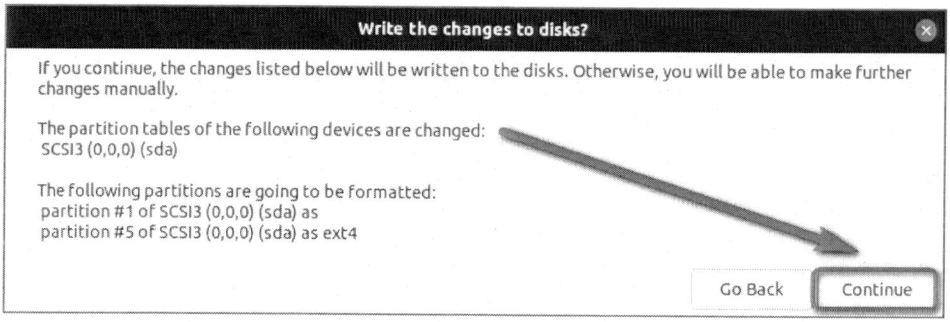

Figure 3.20 Creating the Partition table.

Step 15. Set Your Time zone – e.g. **London**.

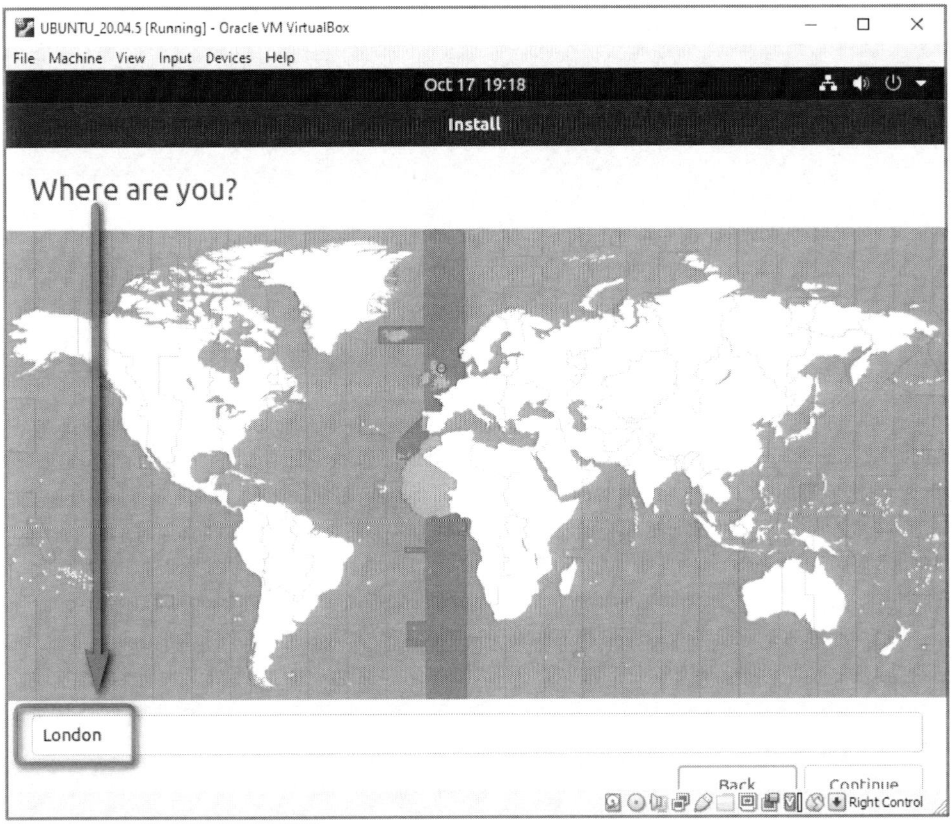

Figure 3.21 Choosing the Time zone.

Step 16. Set the values in the fields for the base account:

- Your name : **student**
- Your computer's name: **EXERCISES**
- Username: **student**
- Password: **student**
- Require my password to log in : **YES**

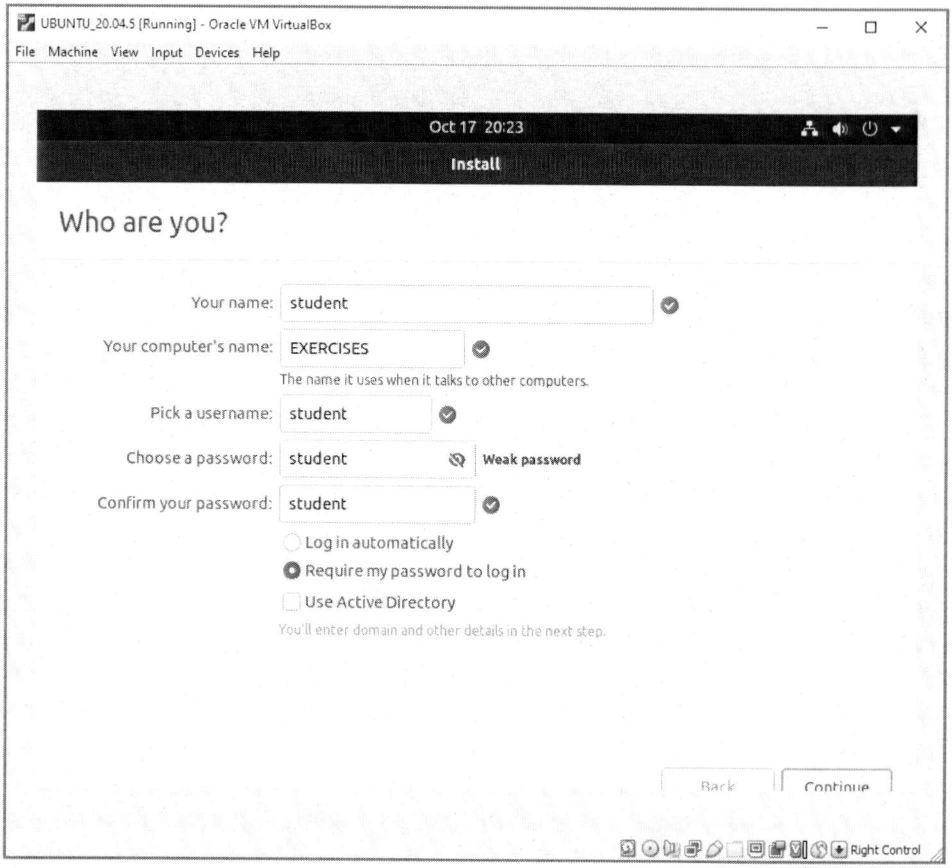

Figure 3.22 Creating the base account.

Step 17. Continue the installation process.

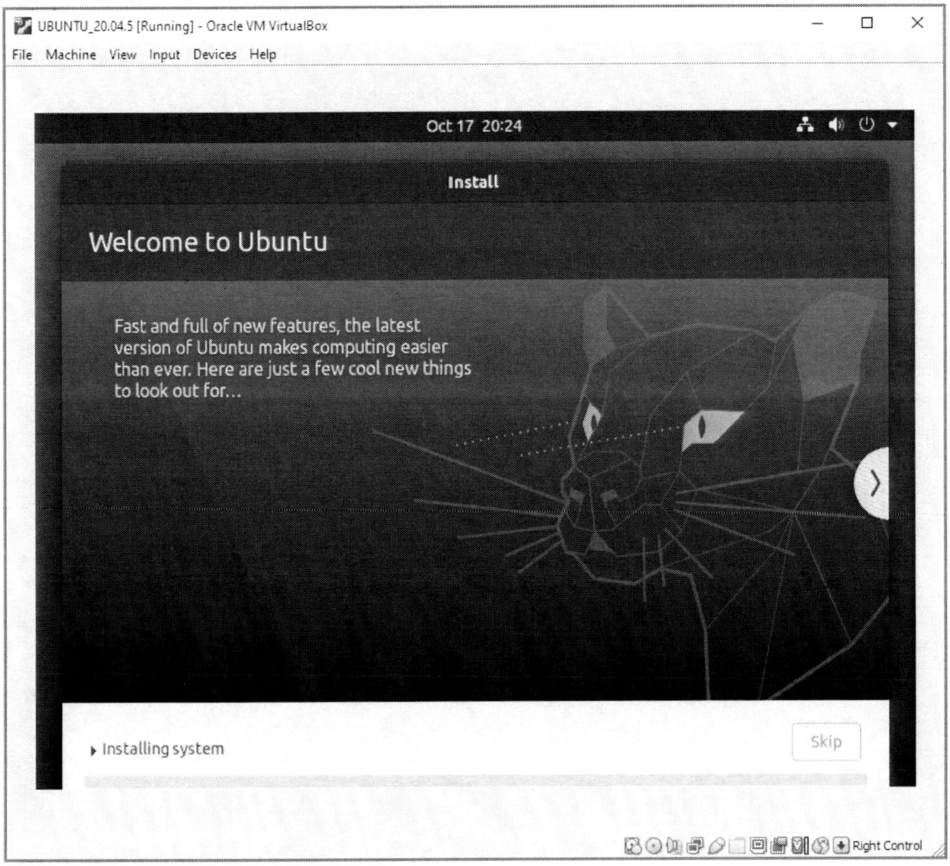

Figure 3.23 Installing Ubuntu – continued installation.

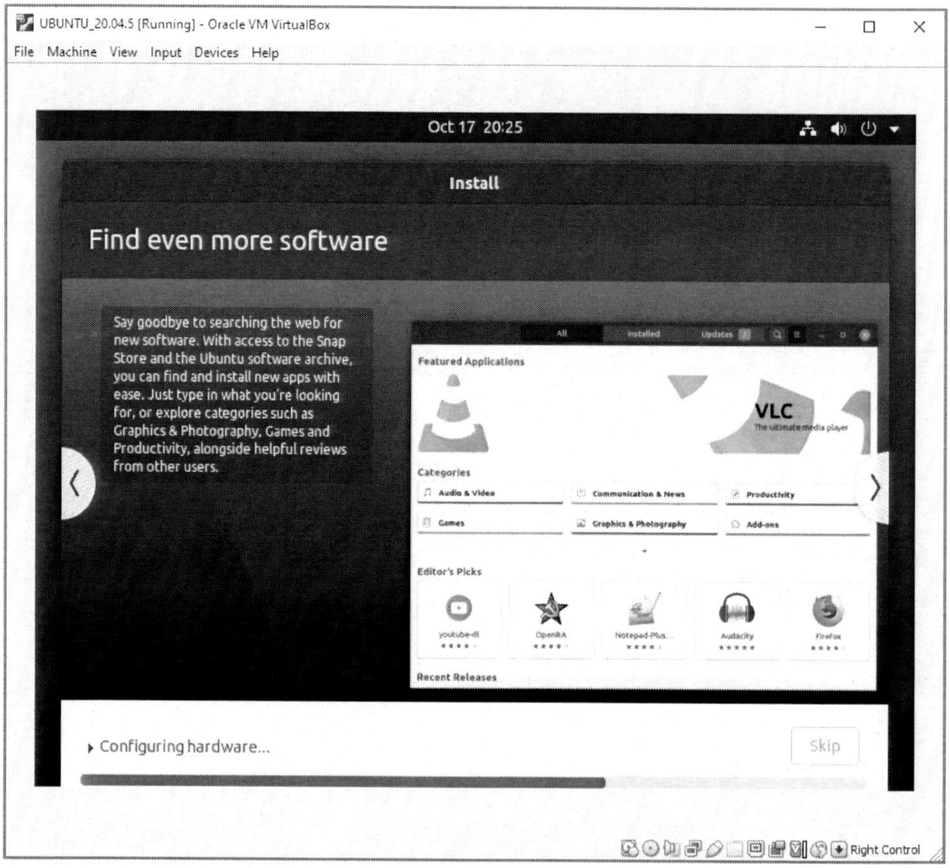

Figure 3.24 Installing the system (continued).

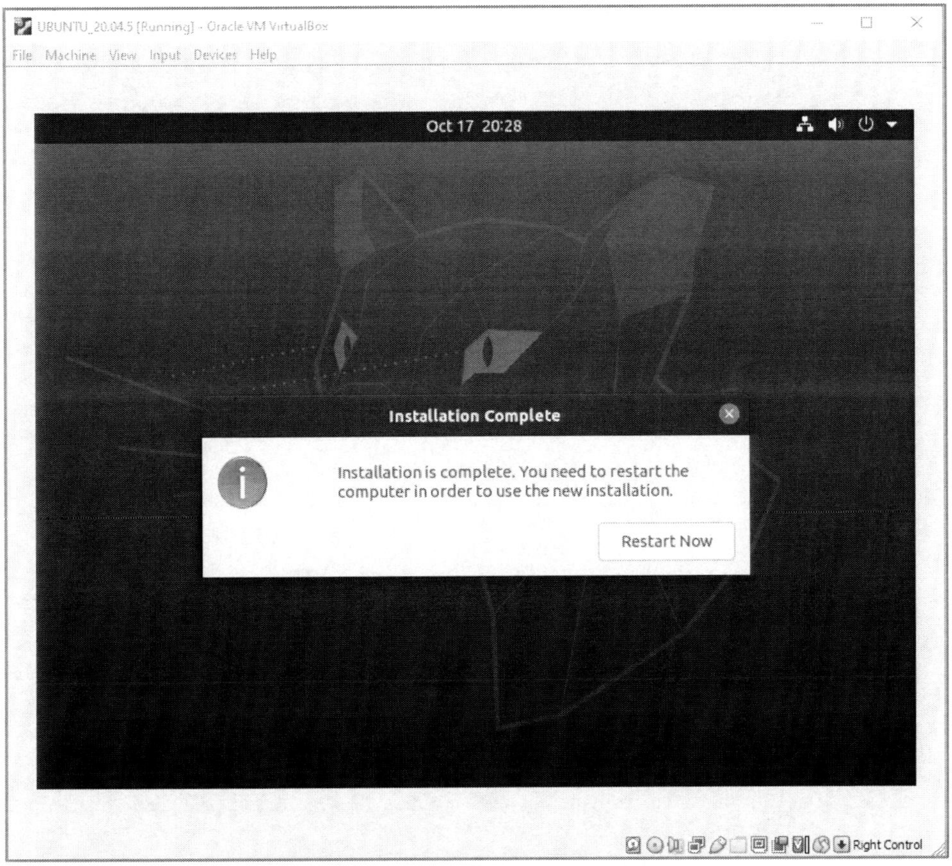

Figure 3.25 Restarting the system.

Figure 3.26 Warning before restarting the system.

Step 18. Before clicking the '**Restart Now**' button, unmount the optical disk.

In order to do it, use **Device → Optical Drives → Remove disk from virtual drive**.

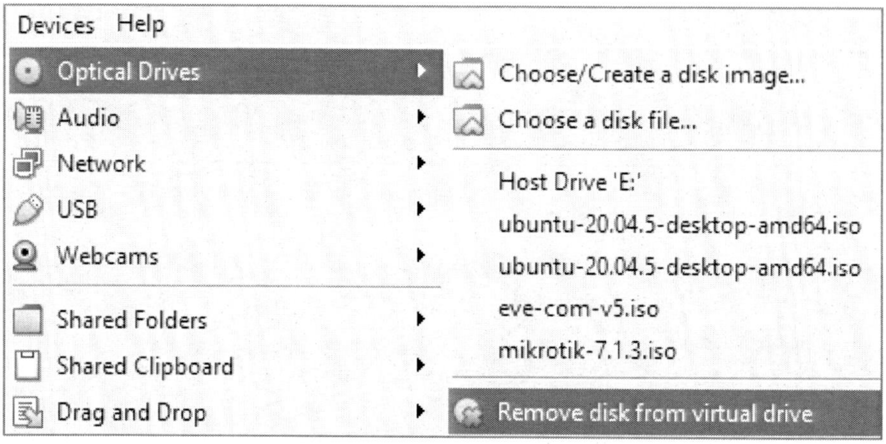

Figure 3.27 Removing the optical disk.

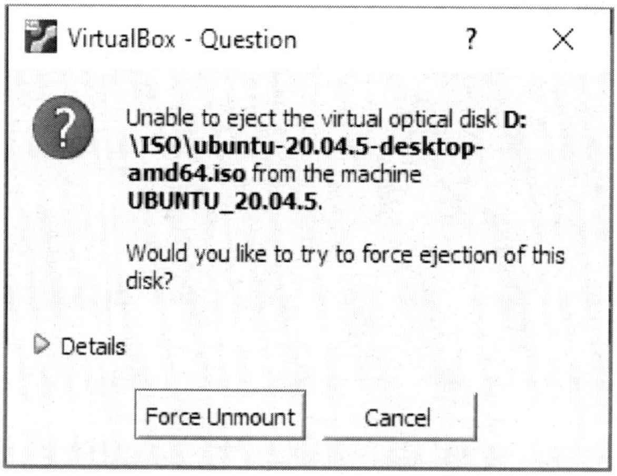

Figure 3.28 Unmounting the optical disk.

Step 19. Restart after installation is completed.

Figure 3.29 Restarting the system.

3.2 First logon to the Ubuntu student account

Step 1. Log into **student** account .

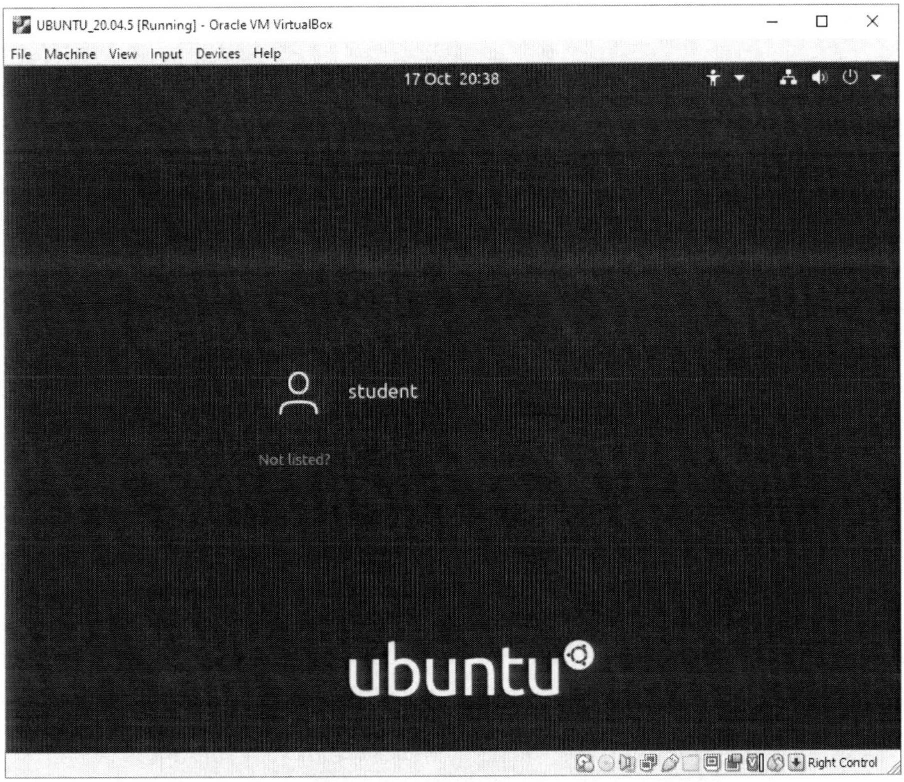

Figure 3.30 Logon screen.

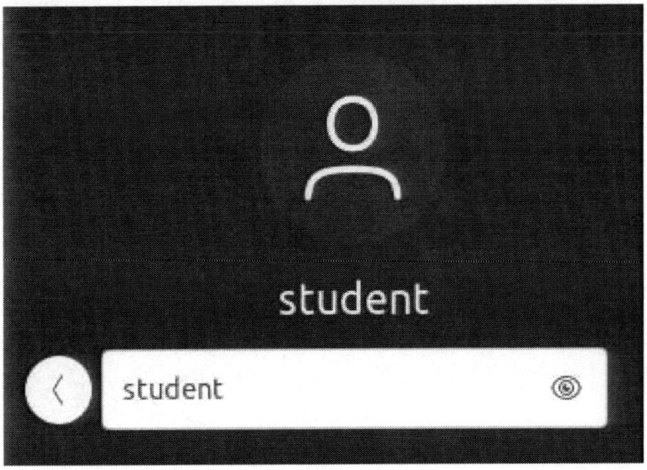

Figure 3.31 Logon as student.

Step 2. Skip the subwindow **Online Accounts**.

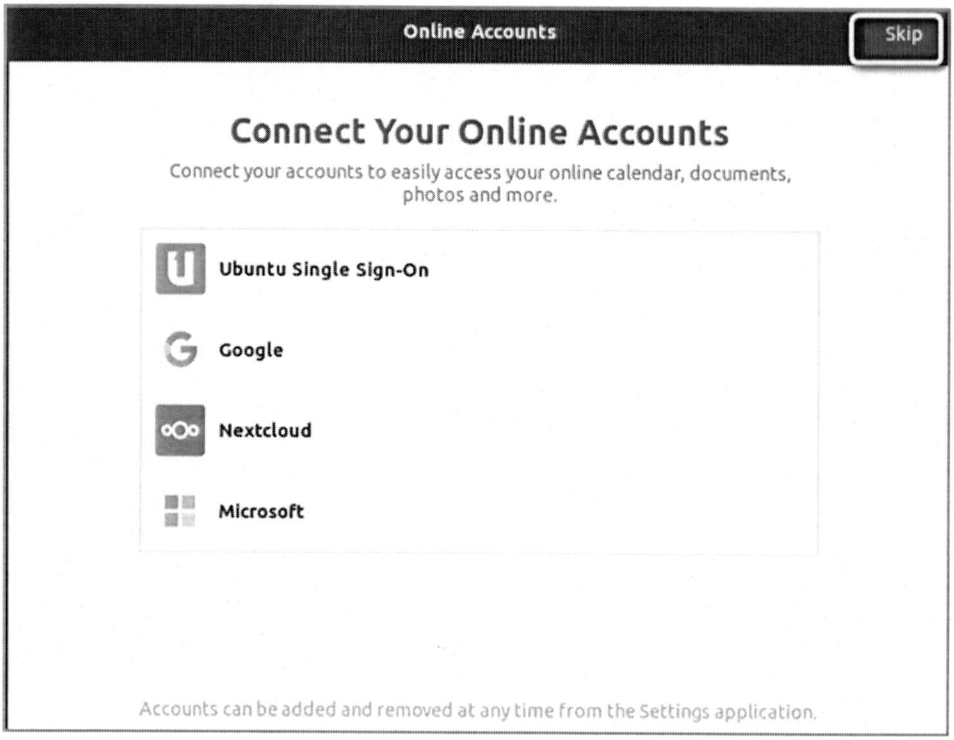

Figure 3.32 Online Accounts subwindow.

Step 3. Enable the option **Yes, Upgrade Now** in the subwindow **Upgrade Available**.

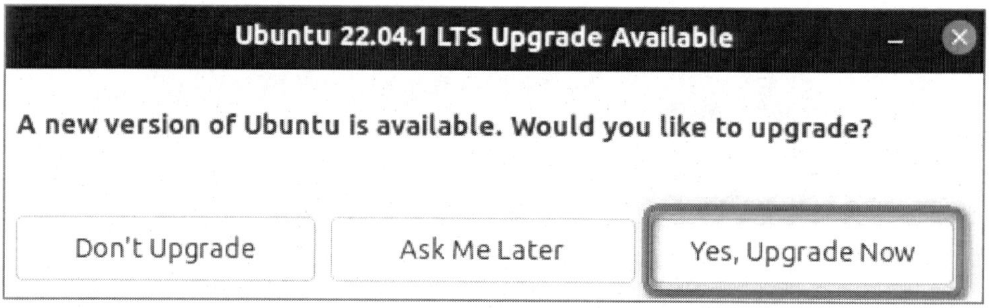

Figure 3.33 Option "Yes, Upgrade Now".

Step 4. Skip the subwindow **Livepatch** by clicking the **Next** button.

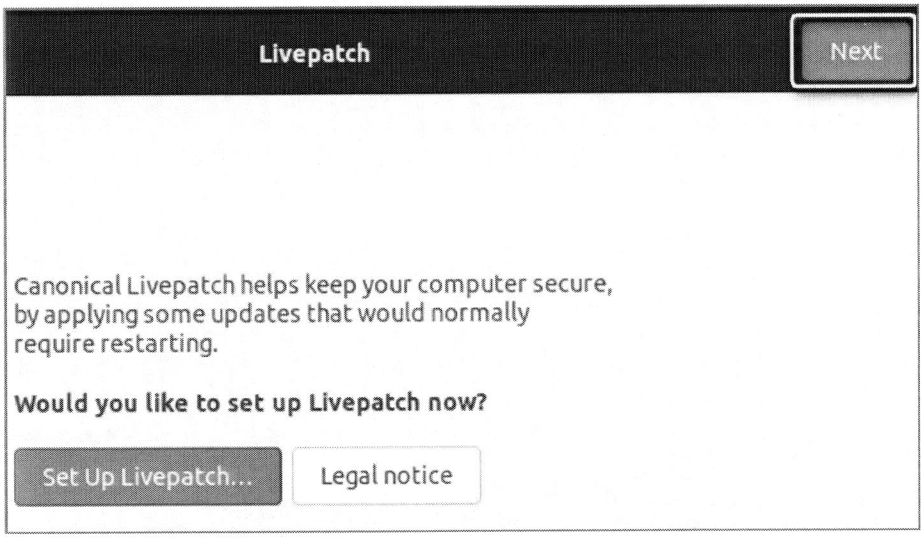

Figure 3.34 Livepatch subwindow.

Step 5. In the subwindow **Help Improve Ubuntu** select the option **No, don't send system info** and click the **Next** button.

Figure 3.35 Help Improve Ubuntu subwindow.

Step 6. In the subwindow **Welcome to Ubuntu** do not enable the option **Location Services** and click the **Next** button.

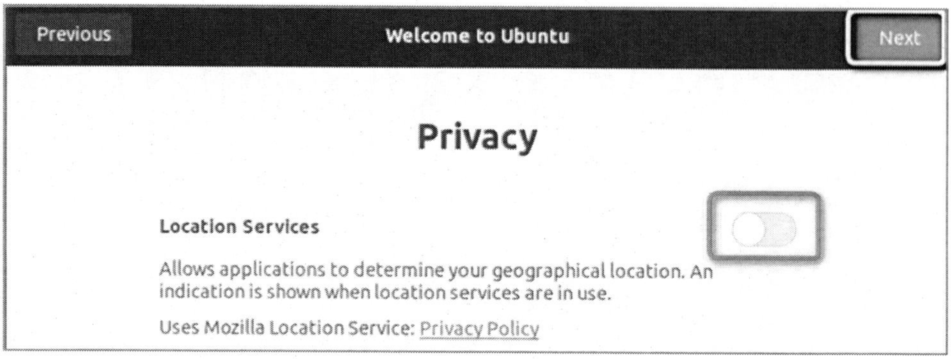

Figure 3.36 Welcome to Ubuntu subwindow.

Step 7. In the subwindow **Ready to go** do not install apps, and click the **Done** button.

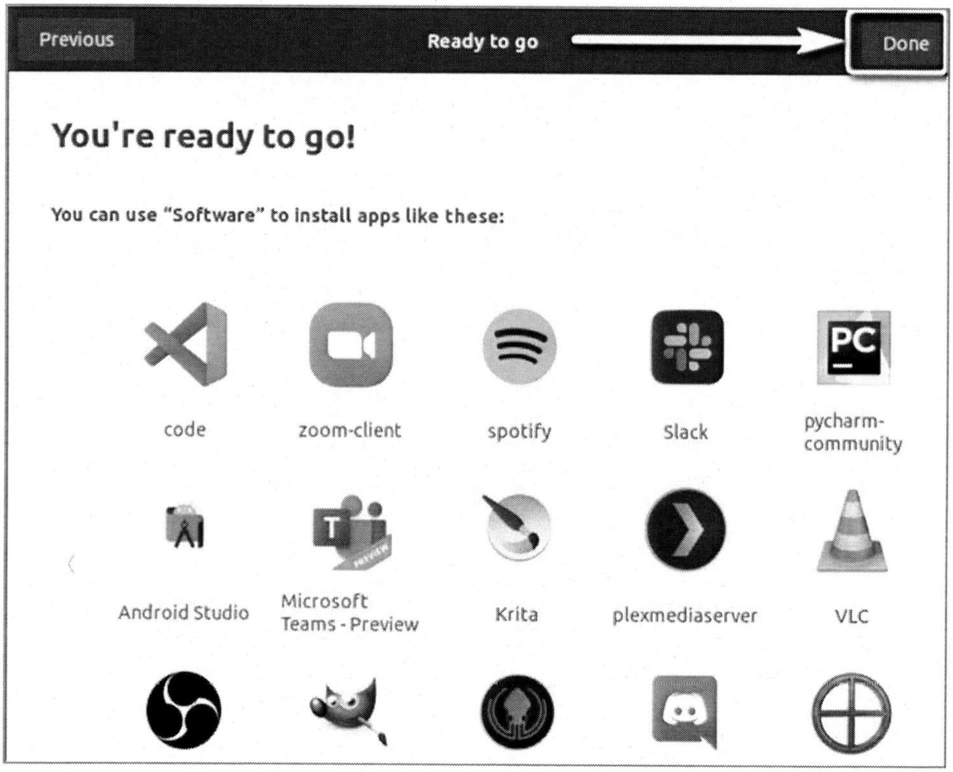

Figure 3.37 Ready to go subwindow.

Step 8. In the subwindow **Software Updater**, click the **Install Now** button.

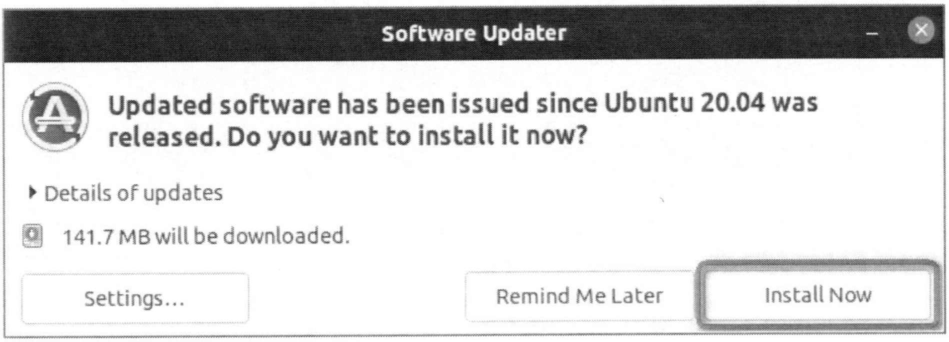

Figure 3.38 Software Updater subwindow.

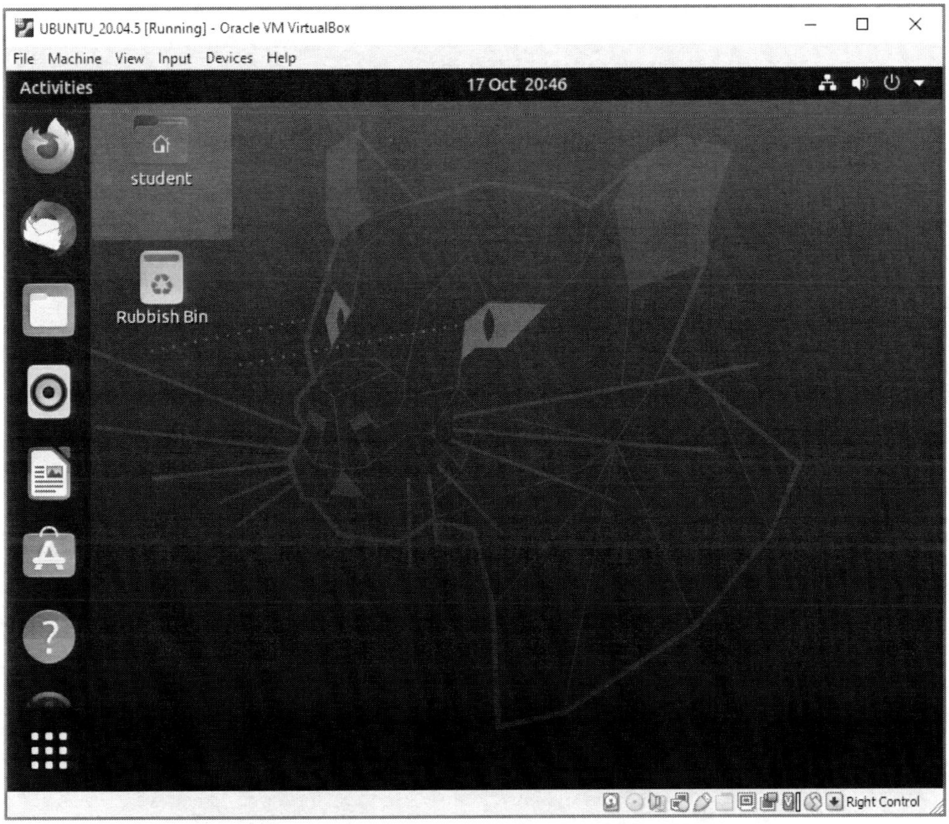

Figure 3.39 The main desktop for student account.

3.3 Unlocking the Ubuntu root account

Root unlocking – assumptions :

- Login **root**

- Password **rootmain**

Step 1. Start the terminal window with the key combination **[Ctrl]+[Alt]+[T]**.

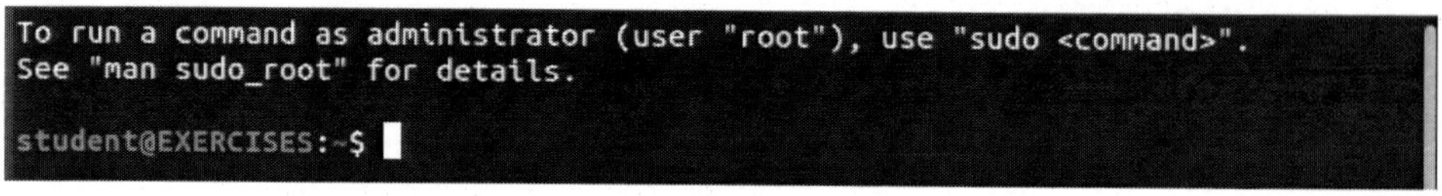

Figure 3.40 Terminal for student account.

Optional method for opening terminal window is as following:

Select **Show Applications** icon

Figure 3.41 Show Applications icon.

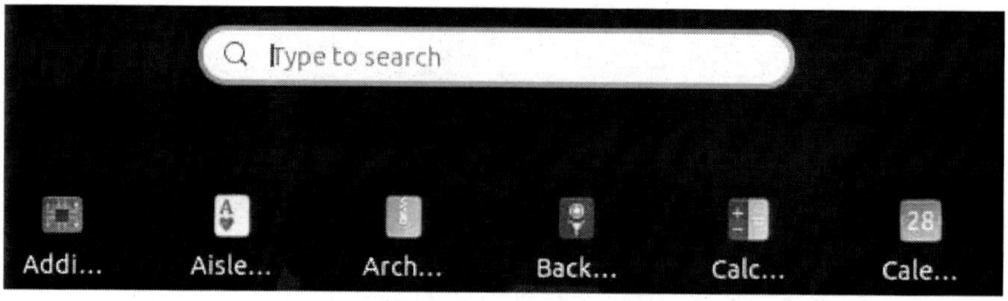

Figure 3.42 Search field.

In the field type word "**terminal**"

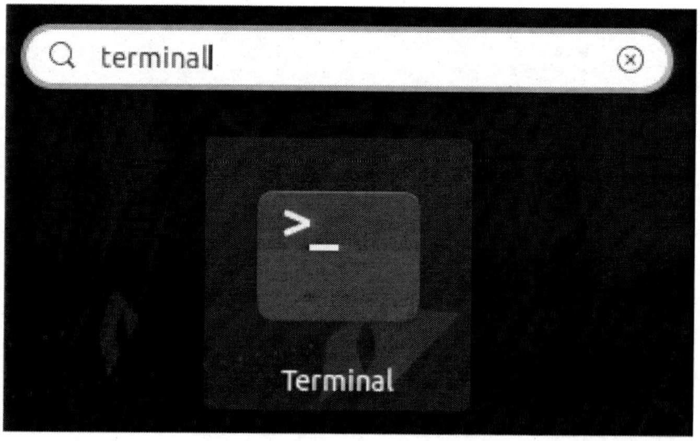

Figure 3.43 Search field.

Click the icon "**Terminal**".

Figure 3.44 Terminal icon.

Step 2. Unlock account **root** and set new password **rootmain** for it.

In order to do it, use command: **`sudo passwd root`**.

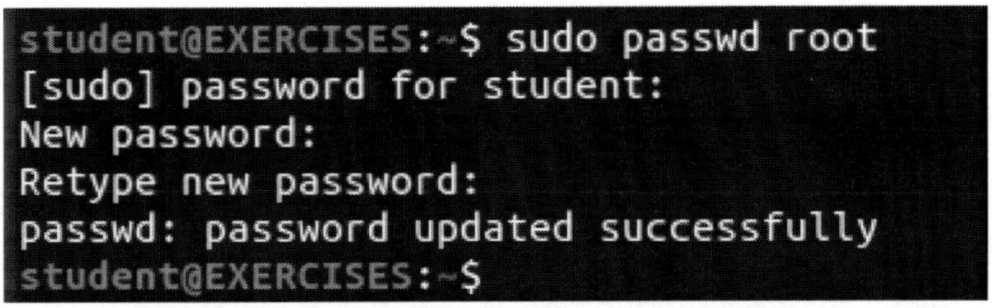

Figure 3.45 Use of command sudo passwd root.

Step 3. Shutdown the system by clicking the **Power Off/Logout** item and then the **Power Off** button.

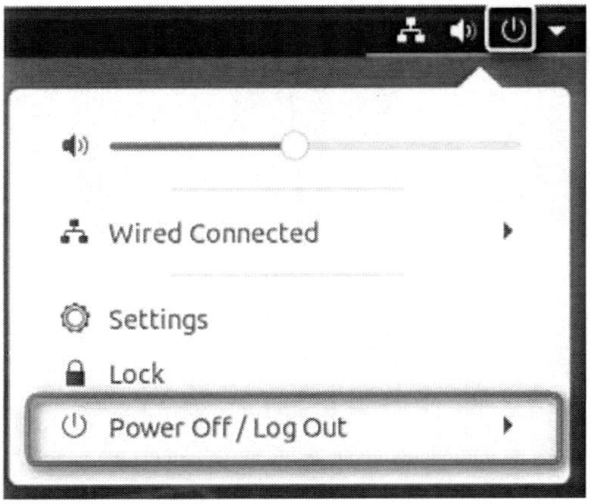

Figure 3.46 Power Off/Log Out item.

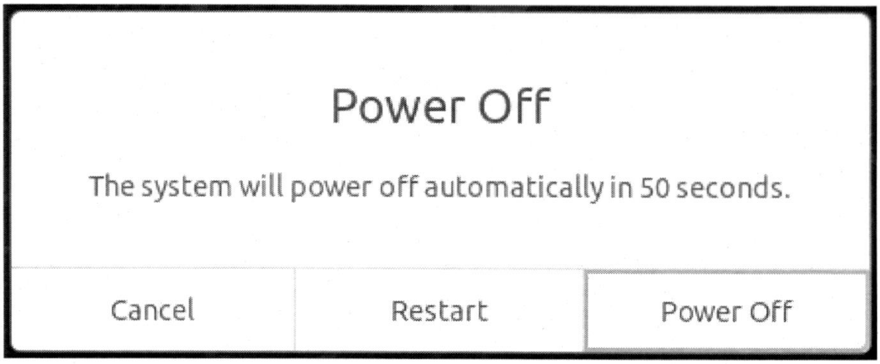

Figure 3.47 Power Off button.

Step 4. After shutdown is completed start the system Ubuntu, activate **the 3rd virtual console** by key combination [**Ctrl+Alt+F3**] and try to log in **root** account with the password **rootmain**.

Figure 3.48 The 3rd console screen.

Figure 3.49 Virtual console for the root account.

Figure 3.50 `apt install net-tools` command.

```
root@EXERCISES:~# apt install net-tools
Reading package lists... Done
Building dependency tree
Reading state information... Done
The following NEW packages will be installed
  net-tools
0 to upgrade, 1 to newly install, 0 to remove and 0 not to upgrade.
Need to get 196 kB of archives.
After this operation, 864 kB of additional disk space will be used.
Get:1 http://gb.archive.ubuntu.com/ubuntu focal/main amd64 net-tools amd64 1.60+git20180626.aebd88
1ubuntu1 [196 kB]
Fetched 196 kB in 2s (101 kB/s)
Selecting previously unselected package net-tools.
(Reading database ... 181790 files and directories currently installed.)
Preparing to unpack .../net-tools_1.60+git20180626.aebd88e-1ubuntu1_amd64.deb ...
Unpacking net-tools (1.60+git20180626.aebd88e-1ubuntu1) ...
Setting up net-tools (1.60+git20180626.aebd88e-1ubuntu1) ...
Processing triggers for man-db (2.9.1-1) ...
root@EXERCISES:~#
```

Figure 3.51 net-tools has been installed.

```
root@EXERCISES:~#
root@EXERCISES:~# logout_
```

Figure 3.52 logout command.

So, we've done installation the Ubuntu system.

3.4 Downloading Packet Tracer in the Ubuntu machine.

Step 1. Log into Ubuntu as a **student**

Step 2. In the browser e.g. FireFox log into Cisco Academy [https://www.netcad.com].

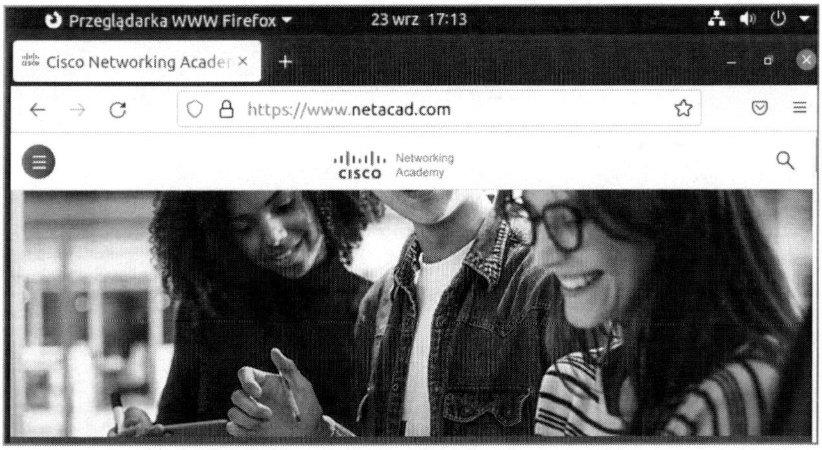

Figure 3.53 Ubuntu – Cisco Networking Academy homepage.

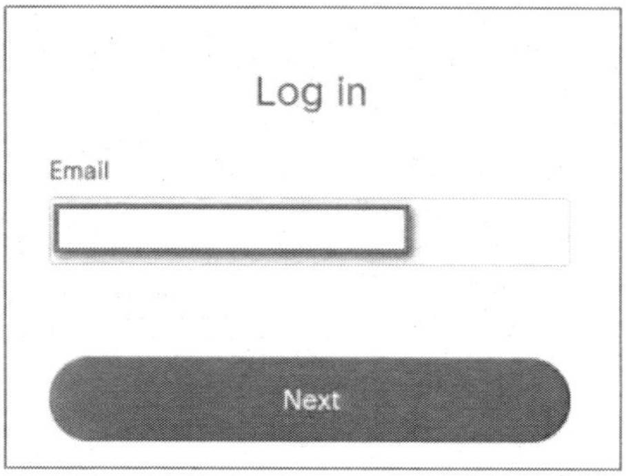

Figure 3.54 Ubuntu – entering login to Cisco Networking Academy.

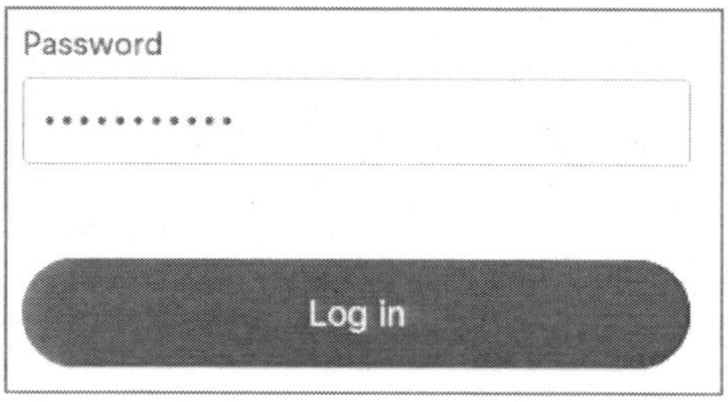

Figure 3.55 Ubuntu – entering password to Cisco Networking Academy.

Step 3. After logging on, choose in the main menu [**Resources**] **→ [Packet Tracer program resources] → [Packet Tracer download page]** and download the file **CiscoPacketTracer_802_Ubuntu_64bit.deb**.

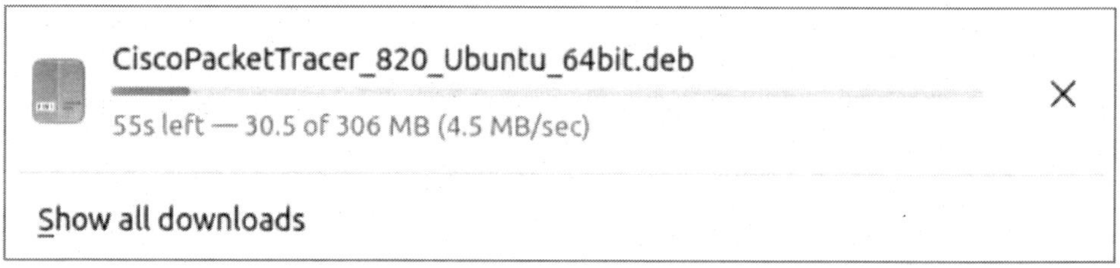

Figure 3.56 Ubuntu – file saving CiscoPacketTracer_802_Ubuntu_64bit.deb.

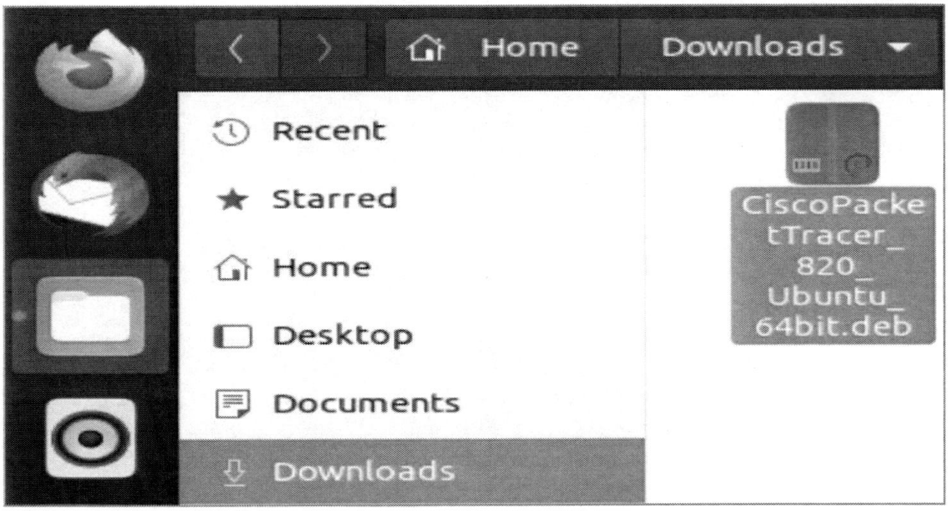

Figure 3.57 File saved in Downloads folder.

Step 4. Log out from NetAcad.com. Alternatively you should enable '**Allow pop-ups for www.netacad.com**.

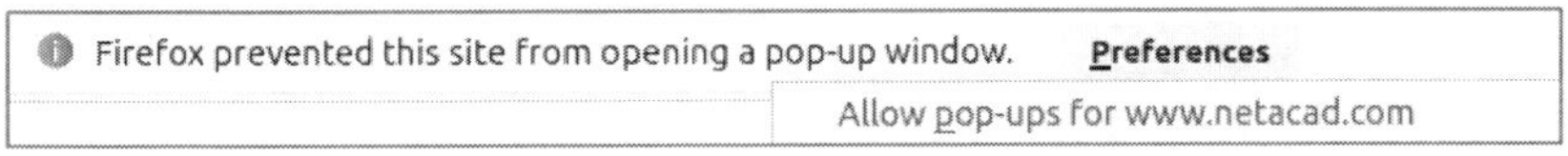

Figure 3.58 Ubuntu – optional deactivation of the option 'Allow pop-ups for www.netacad.com'.

Step 5. Close the browser.

3.5 Installing Packet Tracer in the virtual Ubuntu.

Step 1. Start terminal mode [**Ctrl+Alt+T**] in the virtual **UBUNTU** machine .

Figure 3.59 Ubuntu – terminal mode.

Step 2. Check the contents of the home directory: **/home/student**.

Execute the command: **`ls -la /home/student`**

```
student@EXERCISES:~$ ls -la /home/student
total 92
drwxr-xr-x 18 student student 4096 Oct 17 21:54 .
drwxr-xr-x  3 root    root    4096 Oct 17 20:25 ..
-rw-------  1 student student  511 Oct 25 18:10 .bash_history
-rw-r--r--  1 student student  220 Oct 17 20:25 .bash_logout
-rw-r--r--  1 student student 3771 Oct 17 20:25 .bashrc
drwxr-xr-x 15 student student 4096 Oct 17 21:51 .cache
drwx------ 11 student student 4096 Oct 25 17:11 .config
drwxr-xr-x  2 student student 4096 Oct 17 20:39 Desktop
drwxr-xr-x  2 student student 4096 Oct 17 20:39 Documents
drwxr-xr-x  2 student student 4096 Oct 17 21:21 Downloads
drwx------  3 student student 4096 Oct 17 21:54 .gnupg
drwxr-xr-x  3 student student 4096 Oct 17 20:39 .local
drwx------  4 student student 4096 Oct 17 21:02 .mozilla
drwxr-xr-x  2 student student 4096 Oct 17 20:39 Music
```

Figure 3.60 Ubuntu – Directory with Packet Tracer package is existing.

Step 3. Check the contents of the directory: **/home/student/Downloads**.

Execute the command: **`ls -la /home/student/Downloads`**

```
student@EXERCISES:~$ ls -la /home/student/Downloads
total 313176
drwxr-xr-x  2 student student      4096 Oct 17 21:21 .
drwxr-xr-x 15 student student      4096 Oct 17 21:02 ..
-rw-rw-r--  1 student student 320679542 Oct 17 21:21 CiscoPacketTracer_820_Ubun
tu_64bit.deb
student@EXERCISES:~$
```

Figure 3.61 Ubuntu – Packet Tracer package.

Step 4. Navigate to the Downloads directory.

Execute the command: `cd Downloads`

```
student@EXERCISES:~$ cd Downloads
student@EXERCISES:~/Downloads$
```

Figure 3.62 Ubuntu – Directory with Packet Tracer package is existing.

Step 5. Install the package **CiscoPacketTracer_801_Ubuntu_64bit.deb**

Execute the command:

`sudo dpkg - i CiscoPacketTracer_801_Ubuntu_64bit.deb`

```
student@EXERCISES:~/Downloads$ sudo dpkg -i CiscoPacketTracer_820_Ubuntu_64_bit
.deb
```

Figure 3.63 Ubuntu – Install Packet Tracer package command.

Step 6. Confirm license [**OK**].

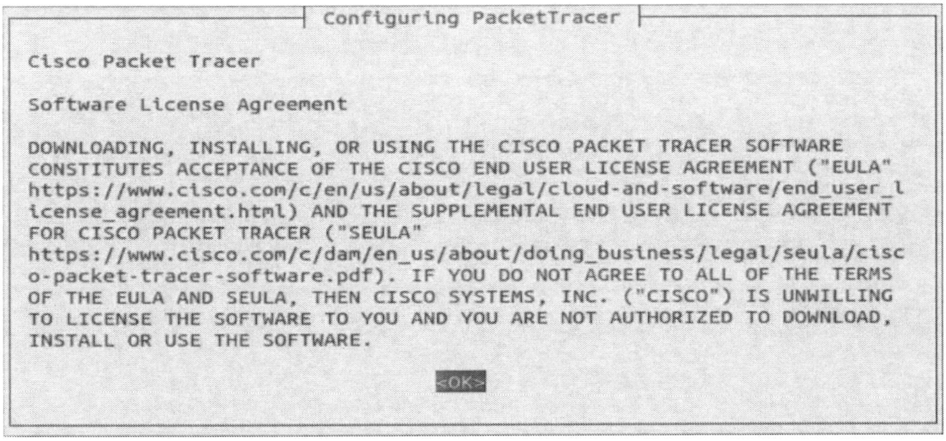

Figure 3.64 Ubuntu – confirmation of the Packet Tracer license.

Step 7. Trust the package configuration [**YES**].

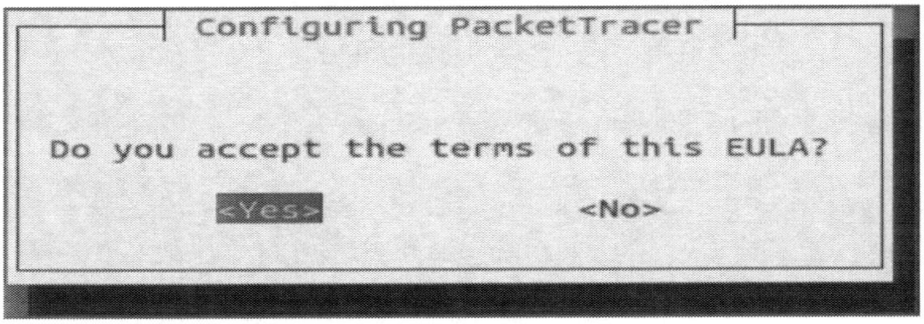

Figure 3.65 Ubuntu – Accepting the installation Packet Tracer license terms.

Step 8. Unpacking and installing.

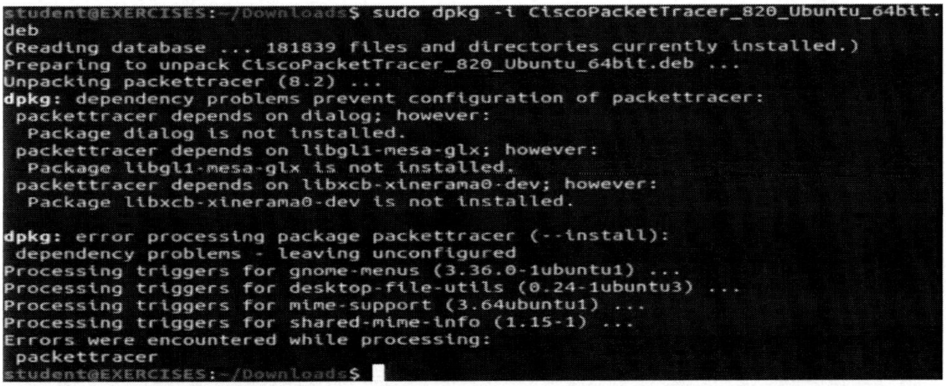

Figure 3.66 Ubuntu – Performing Packet Tracer unpacking and installing.

Step 9. Run the command that installs all package dependencies.

```
sudo apt install -f
```

```
student@EXERCISES:~/Downloads$ sudo apt install -f
```

Figure 3.67 Ubuntu – Package dependency installation command.

```
Selecting previously unselected package libxdmcp-dev:amd64.
Preparing to unpack .../08-libxdmcp-dev_1%3a1.1.3-0ubuntu1_amd64.deb ...
Unpacking libxdmcp-dev:amd64 (1:1.1.3-0ubuntu1) ...
Selecting previously unselected package libxcb1-dev:amd64.
Preparing to unpack .../09-libxcb1-dev_1.14-2_amd64.deb ...
Unpacking libxcb1-dev:amd64 (1.14-2) ...
Selecting previously unselected package libxcb-xinerama0-dev:amd64.
Preparing to unpack .../10-libxcb-xinerama0-dev_1.14-2_amd64.deb ...
Unpacking libxcb-xinerama0-dev:amd64 (1.14-2) ...
Setting up libpthread-stubs0-dev:amd64 (0.4-1) ...
Setting up libxcb-xinerama0:amd64 (1.14-2) ...
Setting up dialog (1.3-20190808-1) ...
Setting up libgl1-mesa-glx:amd64 (21.2.6-0ubuntu0.1~20.04.2) ...
Setting up xorg-sgml-doctools (1:1.11-1) ...
Processing triggers for libc-bin (2.31-0ubuntu9.9) ...
Processing triggers for man-db (2.9.1-1) ...
Processing triggers for sgml-base (1.29.1) ...
Setting up x11proto-dev (2019.2-1ubuntu1) ...
Setting up libxau-dev:amd64 (1:1.0.9-0ubuntu1) ...
Setting up libxdmcp-dev:amd64 (1:1.1.3-0ubuntu1) ...
Setting up x11proto-core-dev (2019.2-1ubuntu1) ...
Setting up libxcb1-dev:amd64 (1.14-2) ...
Setting up libxcb-xinerama0-dev:amd64 (1.14-2) ...
Setting up packettracer (8.2) ...
gtk-update-icon-cache: No theme index file.
student@EXERCISES:~/Downloads$
```

Figure 3.68 Ubuntu – Package dependency installation completed

Step 10. Return to Your home directory and run the Cisco PacketTracer.

```
student@EXERCISES:~$ cd ~
student@EXERCISES:~$ packettracer
```

Figure 3.69 Ubuntu - run the Cisco PacketTracer.

Step 11. During starting the Cisco PacketTracer, You will be asked about "**Multiuser mode**". Answer [**Yes**].

Figure 3.70 Ubuntu – PacketTracer Multiuser mode will be running.

Step 12. Make that after first logging, You cannot require to login for the 3 month's period. So change the option at bottom of screen, as enabled.

Figure 3.71 Ubuntu – Keep me logged in for 3 months option.

Step 13. Log in the `Packet Tracer`.

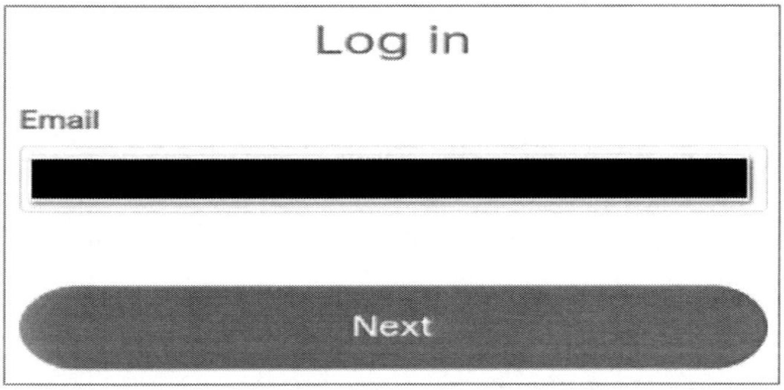

Figure 3.72 Ubuntu – Log in the Packet Tracer window.

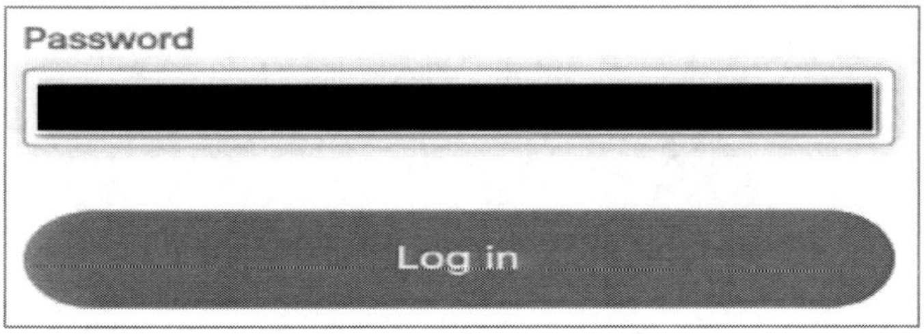

Figure 3.73 Ubuntu – Password for the Packet Tracer window.

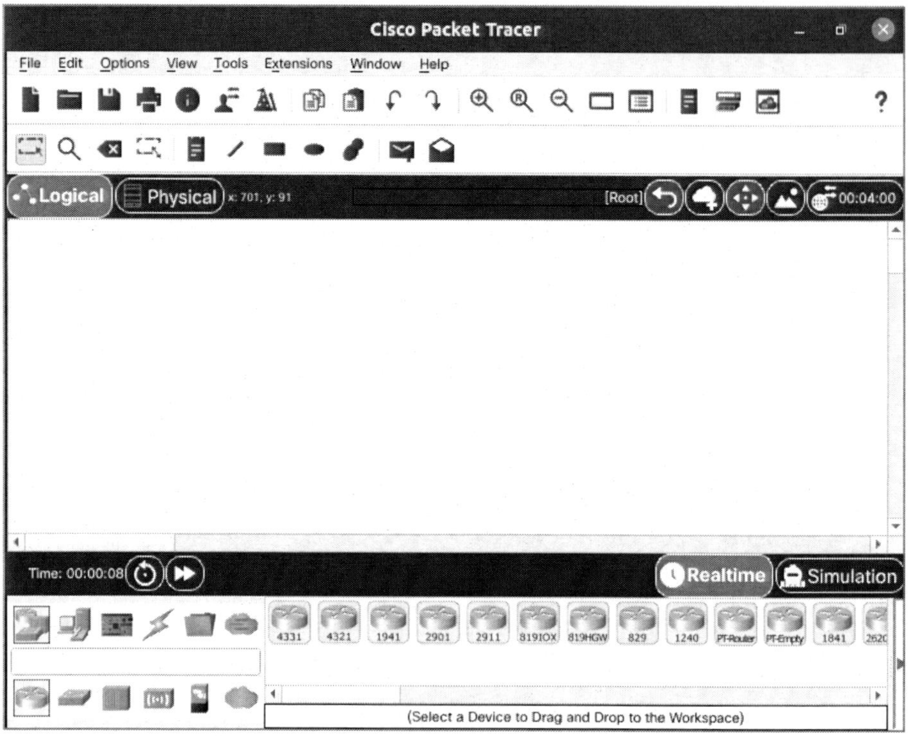

Figure 3.74 Ubuntu – Packet Tracer main view.

3.6 Creating a network in PACKET TRACER IN UBUNTU (Exercise 4)

Part 1. Creating PT network topology in Ubuntu system.

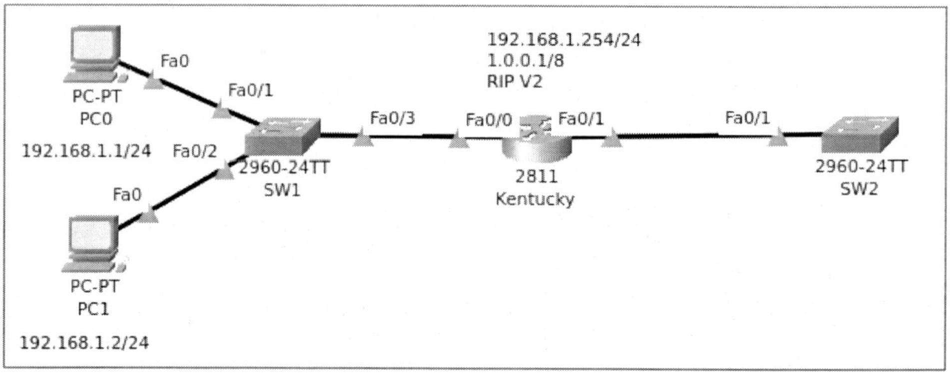

Figure 3.75 Kentucky network topology in Ubuntu.

Part 2. Required equipment:

- PC-PT – 2 pcs
- 296024TT – 2 pcs
- 2811 – 1 pcs

Part 3. Assumptions:

Computers on the 192.168.0.0 network in the PT virtual network in the UBUNTU virtual machine should communicate with computers in the PT on Windows [via the address 172.16.141 port 38000].

RIP V2 protocol should be configured on the **Kentucky** router.

SW2 and **SW3** switches should be connected with appropriate cables.

Part 4. Course of the exercise:

Step 1. Start VirtualBox.

Step 2. Start the UBUNTU machine.

Step 3. Run Packet Tracer in terminal mode.

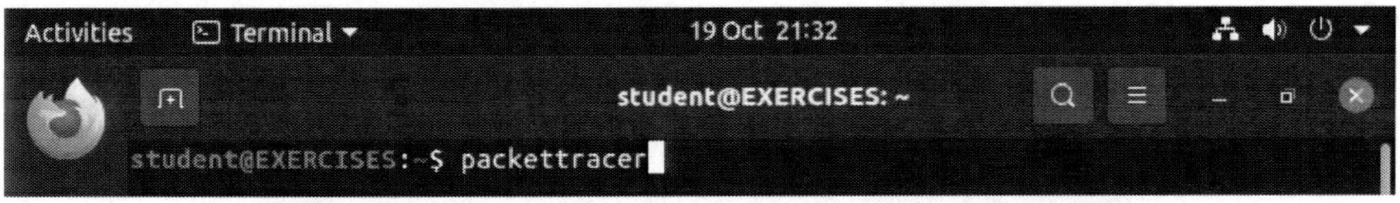

Figure 3.76 Run Packet Tracer in Ubuntu's terminal.

Figure 3.77 Running Packet Tracer in Ubuntu.

Step 4. Create a network topology according to the figure.

Step 5. Configure IP addresses on your network.

For PC0 Fa0:

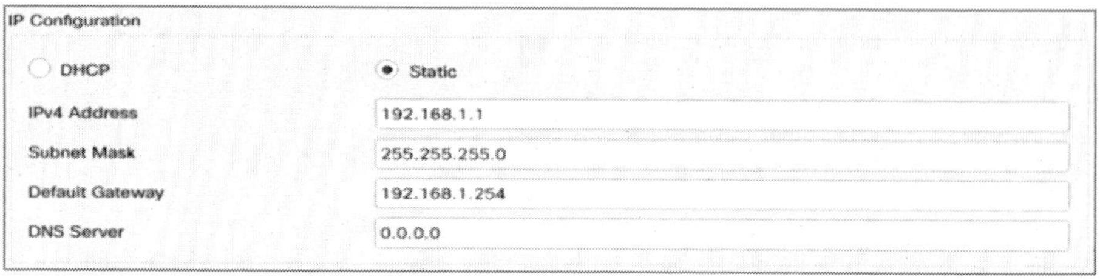

Figure 3.78 Addressing for Fa0 in PC0.

For PC1 Fa0:

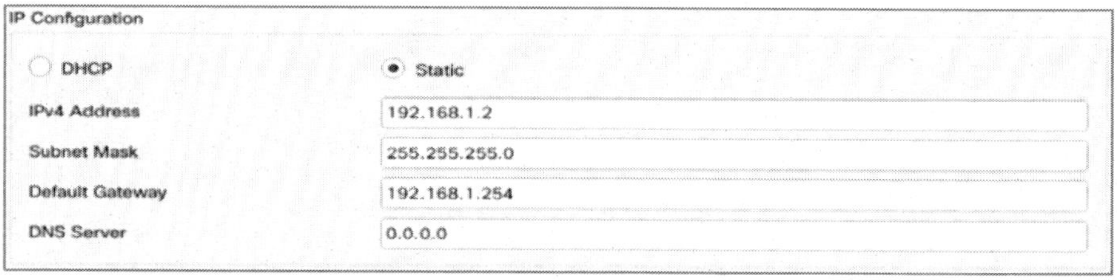

Figure 3.79 Addressing for Fa0 in PC1.

For **Kentucky** Fa0/0:

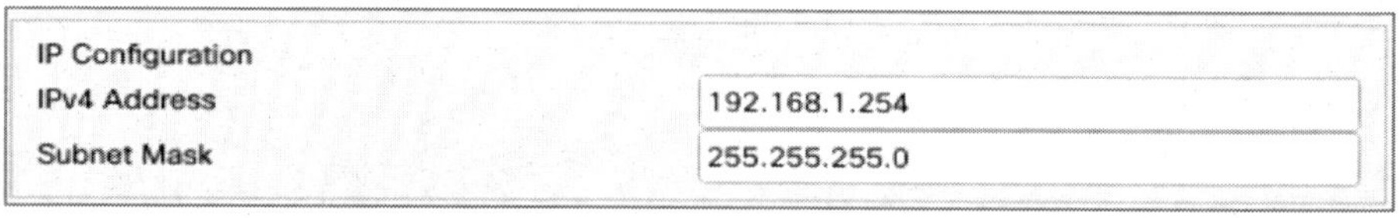

Figure 3.80 Addressing for Fa0/0 in Kentucky.

For **Kentucky** Fa0/1:

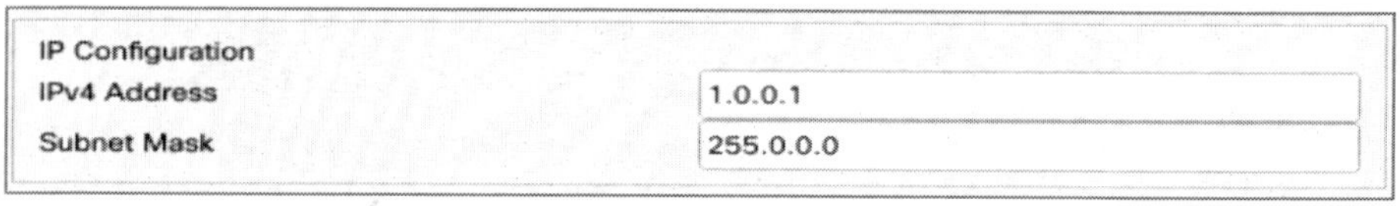

Figure 3.81 Addressing for Fa0/1 in Kentucky.

Step 6. Configure RIPV2.

Commands:

```
router rip
version 2
network 1.0.0.0
network 192.168.1.0
```

```
Kentucky#conf t
Enter configuration commands, one per line.  End with CNTL/Z.
Kentucky(config)#router rip
Kentucky(config-router)#version 2
Kentucky(config-router)#network 1.0.0.0
Kentucky(config-router)#network 192.168.1.0
Kentucky(config-router)#end
Kentucky#
%SYS-5-CONFIG_I: Configured from console by console

Kentucky#
```

Figure 3.82 Configurating the RIPV2 in Kentucky.

Step 7. Save network configurations and topologies.

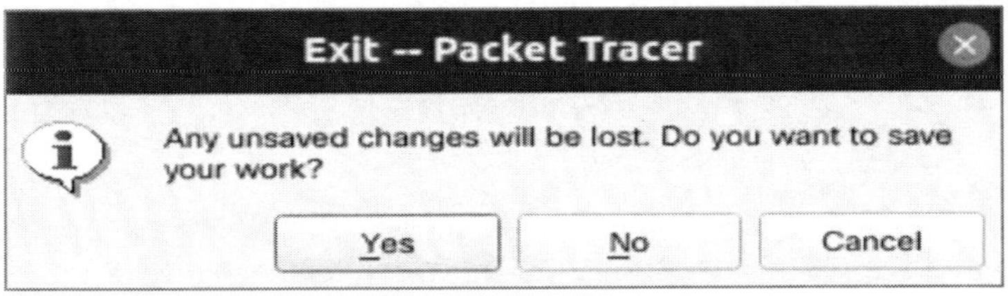

Figure 3.83 Writing the topology in Ubuntu.

Step 8. Terminate Packet Tracer in Ubuntu.

Step 9. Save the topology in a file **exercise4-ubuntu.pkt**

Save the topology in the directory [select catalog **/home/student/pt/saves**].

3.7 Networking in PACKET TRACER IN WINDOWS (Exercise 5)

Part 1. Creating PT network topology in Windows.

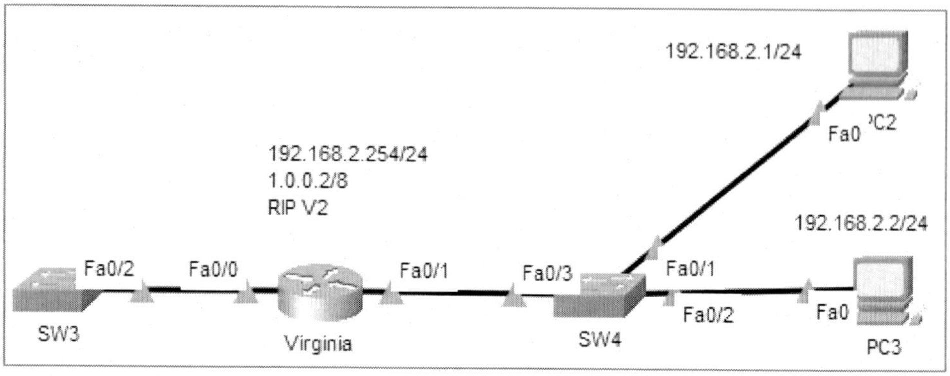

Figure 3.84 Virginia network topology on Windows.

Part 2. Required equipment:

- PC-PT – 2 pcs
- 2960-24TT – 2 pcs
- 2811 – 1 pcs

Part 3. Assumptions:

Computers from the network 192.168.1.0 should communicate with the computers from the network 192.168.0.0. which is located in the Packet Tracer network in the system (in the machine) UBUNTU [see **exercise 3**].

RIP V2 protocol should be configured on **Virginia** router. **SW2** and **SW3** switches should be connected with appropriate cables.

Part 4. Course of the exercise:

Step 1. Run Packet Tracer on Windows.

Step 2. Create a topology according to the figure.

Step 3. Configure IP addresses on the network.

For PC2 Fa0:

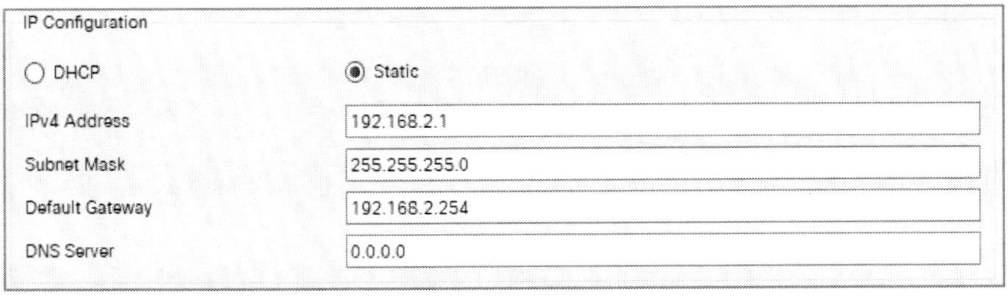

Figure 3.85 Fa0 addressing in PC2.

For PC3 Fa0:

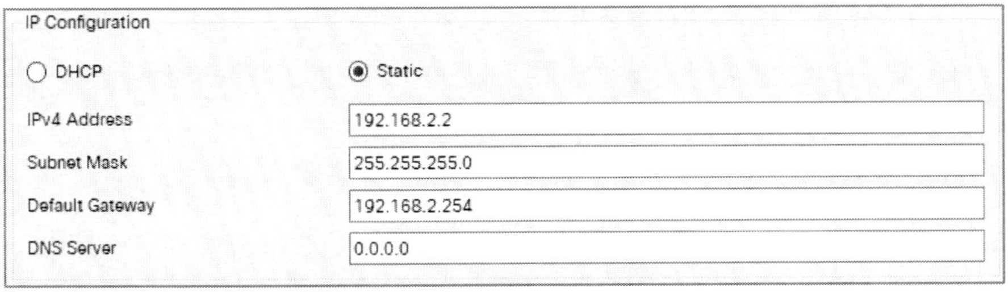

Figure 3.86 Fa0 addressing in PC3.

For **Virginia** Fa0/0:

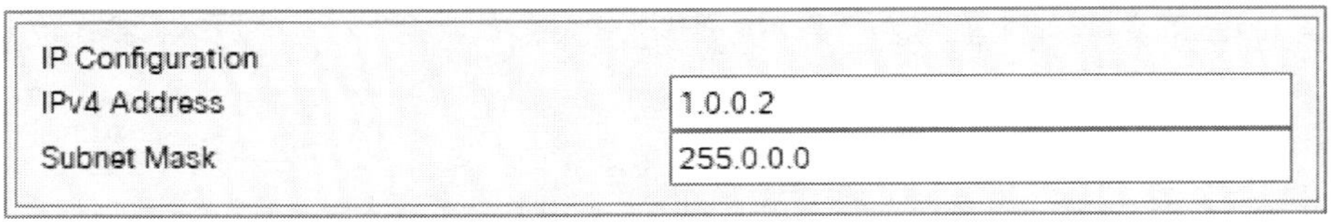

Figure 3.87 Fa0/0 addressing in Virginia.

For **Virginia** Fa0/1:

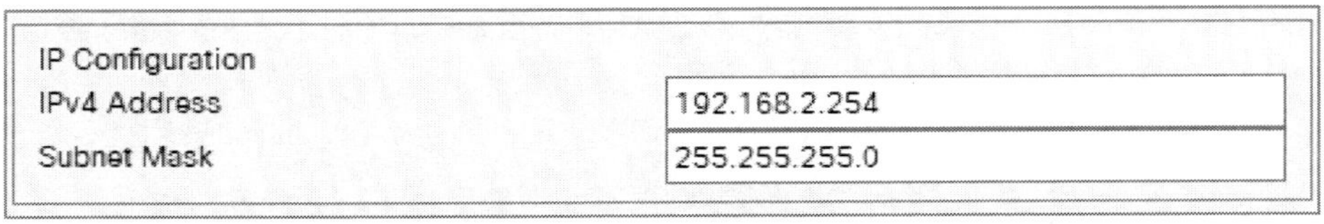

Figure 3.88 Fa0/1 addressing in Virginia.

Step 4. Configure RIPV2.

Commands:

```
router rip
version 2
network 1.0.0.0
```

```
network 192.168.2.0
```

```
Virginia#conf t
Enter configuration commands, one per line.  End with CNTL/Z.
Virginia(config)#router rip
Virginia(config-router)#version 2
Virginia(config-router)#network 1.0.0.0
Virginia(config-router)#network 192.168.2.0
Virginia(config-router)#end
Virginia#
%SYS-5-CONFIG_I: Configured from console by console

Virginia#
```

Figure 3.89 Configurating the RIPV2 in Virginia.

Step 5. Save the topology in a file **exercise5-windows.pkt**

3.8 Connecting networks in UBUNTU PT and WINDOWS PT (Exercise 6)

Part 1. Goal.

Connecting network 192.168.1.0 in the virtual Packet Tracer network in the virtual **UBUNTU** machine with the network 192.168.2.0 in the virtual Packet Tracer network in **Windows**, using SW2 and SW3 switches. The model of the exercise is shown in the figure.

Part 2. Comments.

The exercise assumes that the IP address of the actual real interface on Windows is 172.16.0.141.

In your case, the IP address of your computer may be different. The presented address is an example address. Take this note into account when practicing!

Part 3. Exercise model.

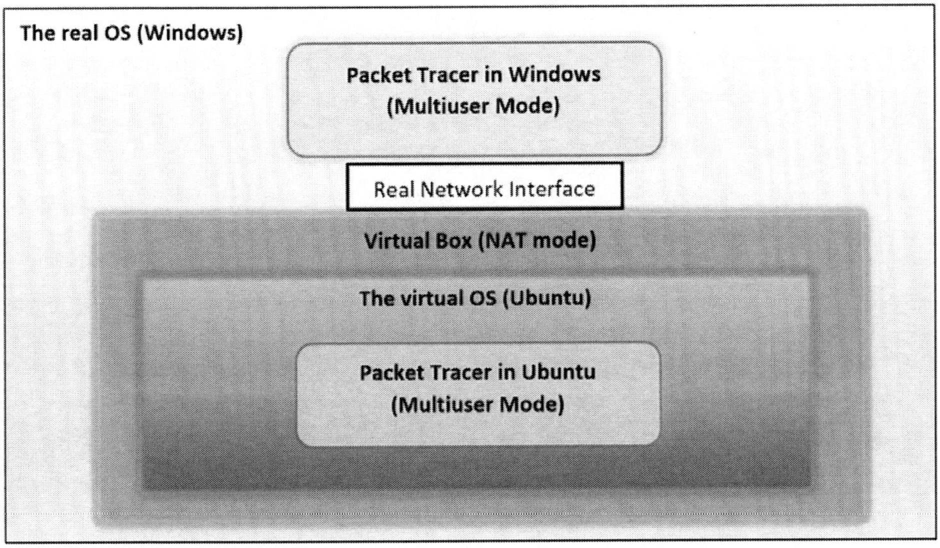

Figure 3.90 Windows real machine and embedded virtual machines.

Part 4. Configuring Multiuser in PT on Windows.

Step 1. **Peer0** cloud creation in PT in Windows.

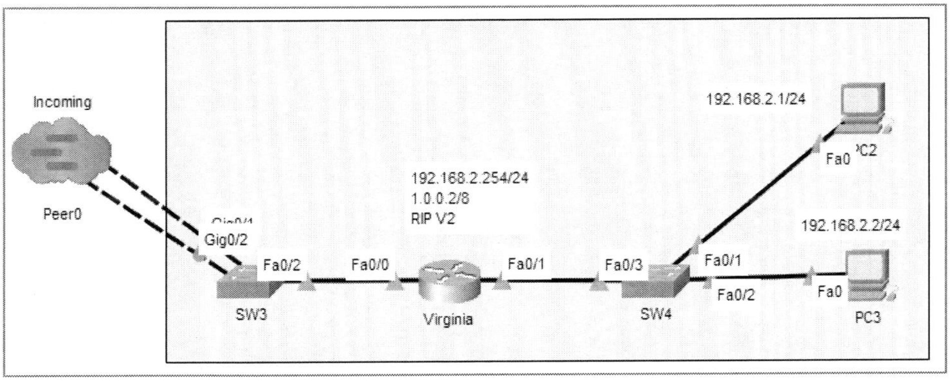

Figure 3.91 Topology in PT on Windows.

Step 2. In **Peer0** cloud in PT on Windows, set **Incoming** mode.

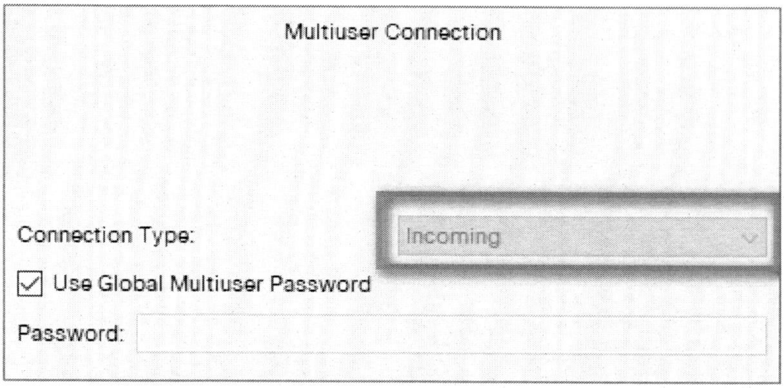

Figure 3.92 'Incoming' connection type in PT in Windows.

Step 3. Set visible ports **GigabitEthernet0/1**, **GigabitEthernet0/2** for **Peer0** cloud in PT in Windows.

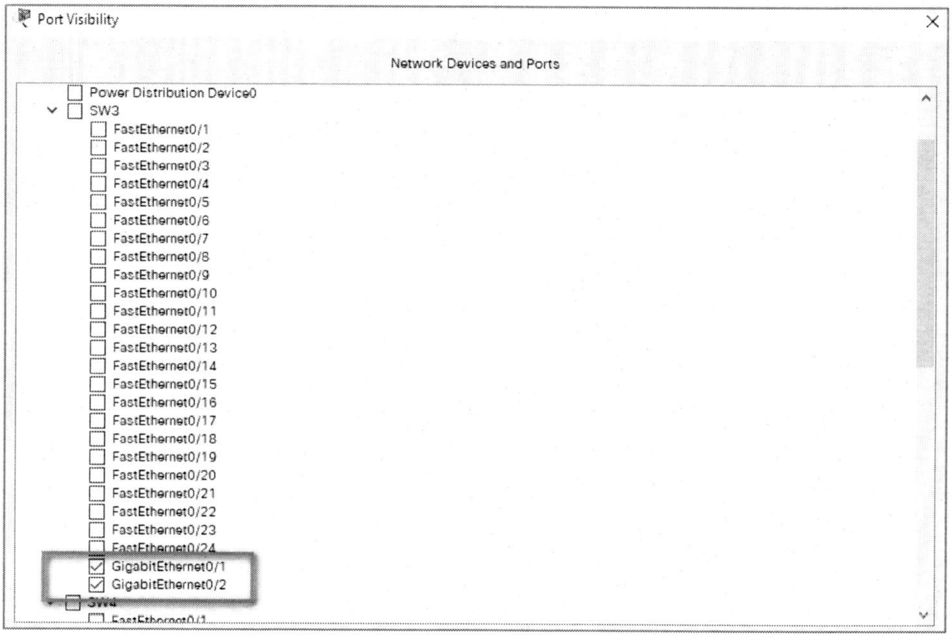

Figure 3.93 Ports visible in cloud 'Incoming' in PT on Windows.

Step 4. In PT in Windows, check if there is an address 172.16.0.141 and if it is set as listening.

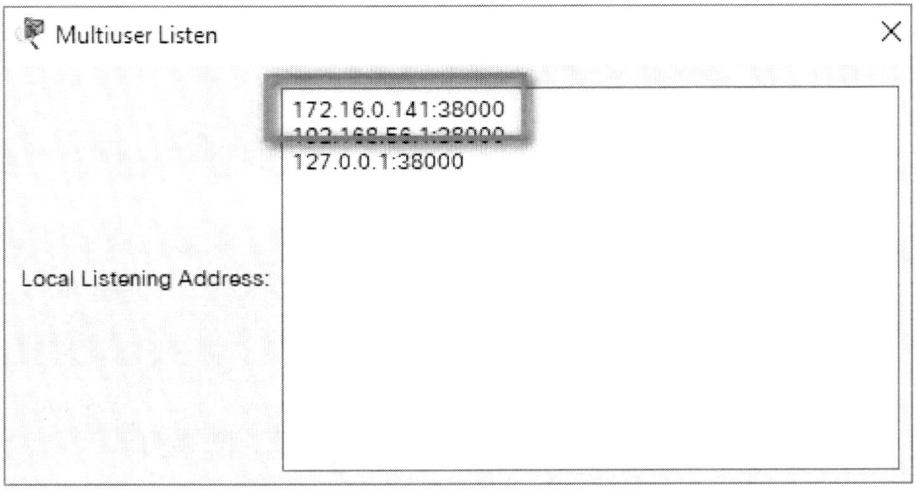

Figure 3.94 Address and port listening in PT on Windows.

Step 5. Now go to the Ubuntu virtual machine.

Part 5. Configuring Multiuser in PT in Ubuntu.

Step 1. Change the network settings of your UBUNTU machine [**NAT, Allow All**].

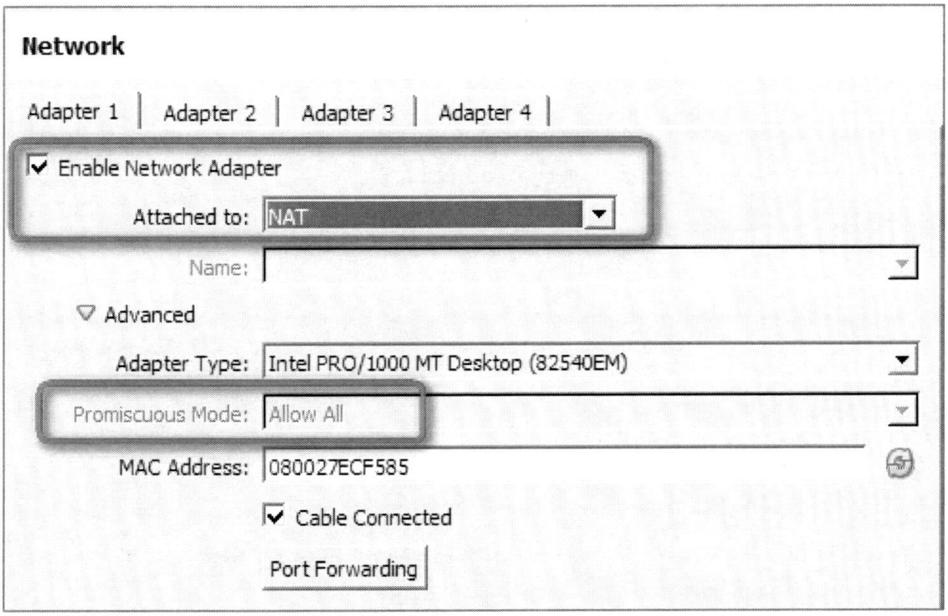

Figure 3.95 Network settings of UBUNTU machine in VirtualBox.

Step 2. Run UBUNTU machine.

Figure 3.96 UBUNTU machine in VirtualBox.

Step 3. On a UBUNTU machine, check the availability of the address 172.16.0.141 on the command line, using the ping command .

```
student@EXERCISES:~$ ping 172.16.0.141
PING 172.16.0.141 (172.16.0.141) 56(84) bytes of data.
64 bytes from 172.16.0.141: icmp_seq=1 ttl=127 time=0.440 ms
64 bytes from 172.16.0.141: icmp_seq=2 ttl=127 time=1.51 ms
^C
--- 172.16.0.141 ping statistics ---
2 packets transmitted, 2 received, 0% packet loss, time 1030ms
```

Figure3.97 The result of the ping command on the UBUNTU machine.

Step 4. Copy the file **/home/student/pt/saves/exercise4-ubuntu.pkt** to the file **/home/student/pt/saves/exercise6-ubuntu.pkt**.

```
student@EXERCISES:~$ cp /home/student/pt/saves/exercise4-ubuntu.pkt /home/stude
nt/pt/saves/exercise6-ubuntu.pkt
student@EXERCISES:~$
student@EXERCISES:~$
student@EXERCISES:~$ ls /home/student/pt/saves
exercise4-ubuntu.pkt  exercise6-ubuntu.pkt
student@EXERCISES:~$
```

Figure 3.98 PKT files in Ubuntu machine.

Step 5. Open network topology **exercise6-ubuntu.pkt**.

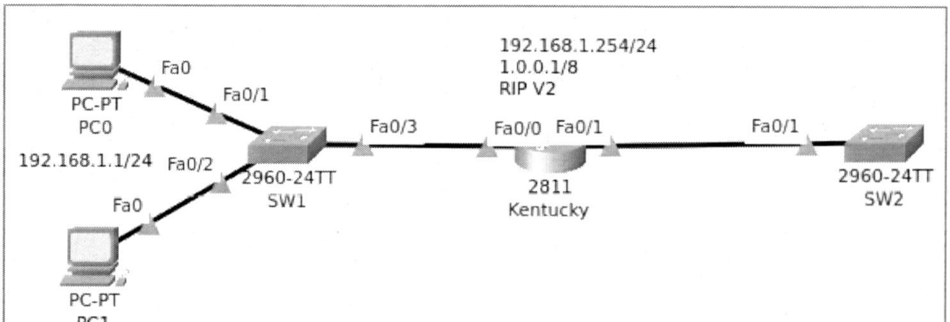

Figure 3.99 Network topology in PT in Ubuntu.

Step 6. Create and configure **Peer0** cloud in PT in Ubuntu.

Step 7. Set **Outgoing** mode.

Step 8. Set **172.16.0.141** address

Step 9. Set the cloud name the same as in PT in Windows: **Peer0**

Step 10. Set the cloud password the same as in PT in Windows: **cisco**

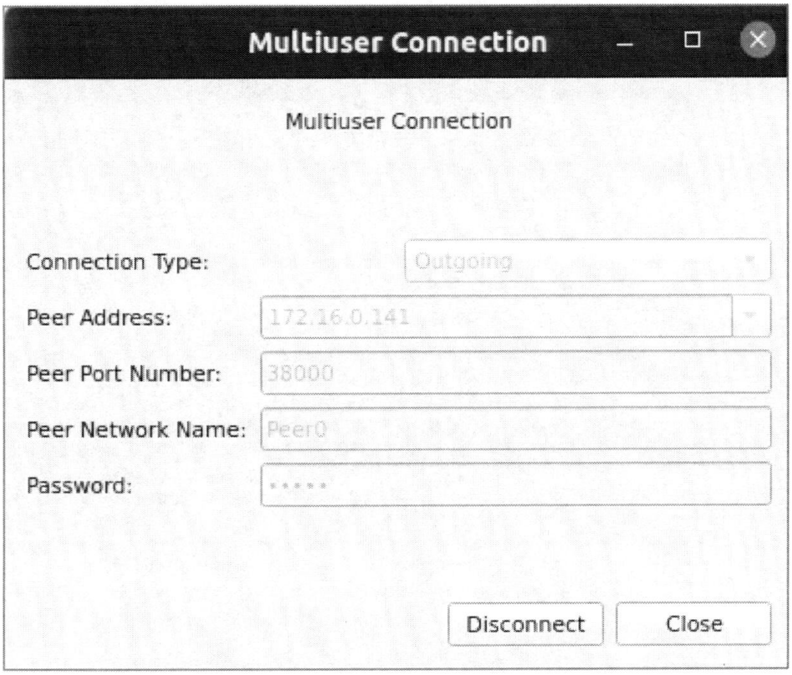

Figure 3.100 'Outgoing' connection type in PT in Ubuntu .

Step 11. Set visible ports **GigabitEthernet0/1**, **GigabitEthernet0/2** for the **Peer0** cloud in PT in Ubuntu (for the **SW2** device).

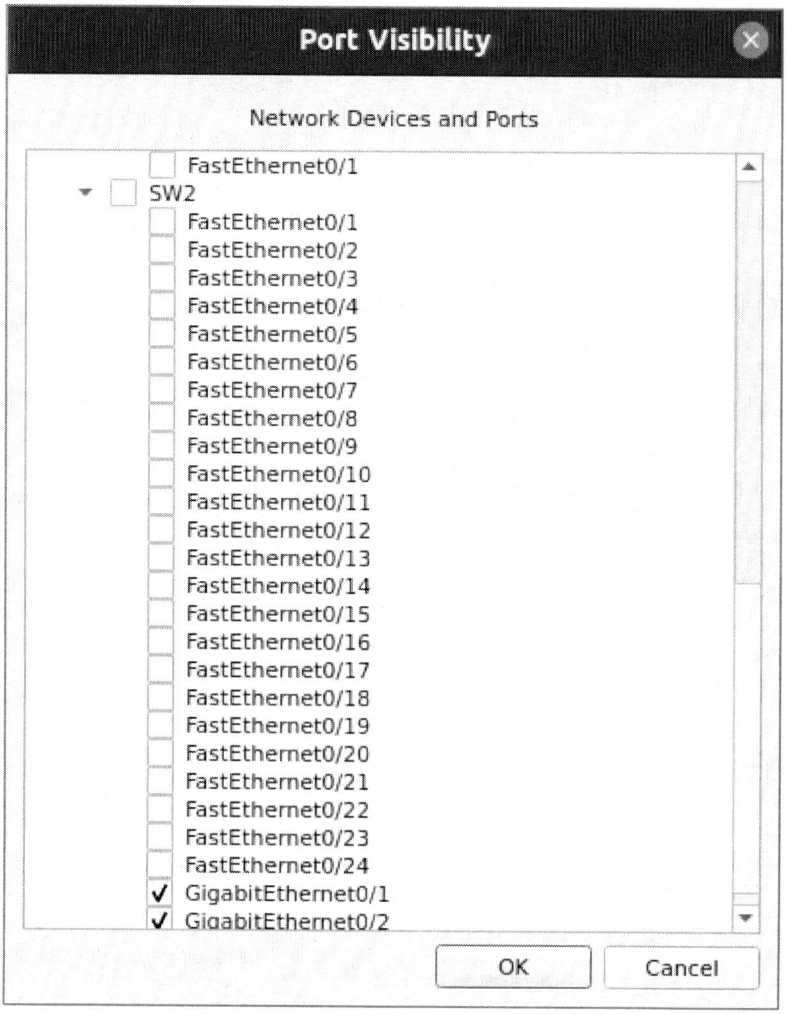

Figure 3.101 Ports visible in cloud 'Outgoing' in PT in Ubuntu.

Step 12. Connect GigabitEthernet0/2 port in SW2 via cloud to port GigabitEthernet0/2 in SW3,using Cooper Cross-Over cable.

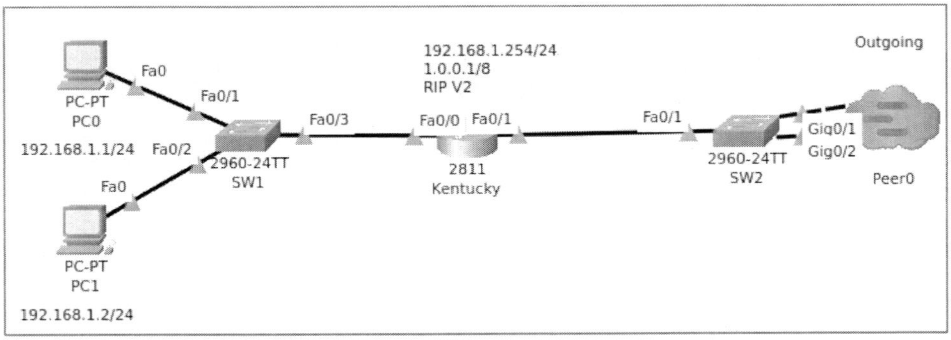

Figure 3.102 Network topology in PT in Ubuntu.

Step 13. Perform communication check between PC0 (192.168.1.1), which is in the topology in PT in Ubuntu in VirtualBox and PC3 (192.168.2.2), which is located in the topology in PT in Windows.

```
C:\>ping 192.168.2.2

Pinging 192.168.2.2 with 32 bytes of data:

Reply from 192.168.2.2: bytes=32 time=11ms TTL=126
Reply from 192.168.2.2: bytes=32 time=13ms TTL=126
Reply from 192.168.2.2: bytes=32 time=18ms TTL=126
Reply from 192.168.2.2: bytes=32 time=8ms TTL=126

Ping statistics for 192.168.2.2:
    Packets: Sent = 4, Received = 4, Lost = 0 (0% loss),
Approximate round trip times in milli-seconds:
    Minimum = 8ms, Maximum = 18ms, Average = 12ms
```

Figure 3.103 The result of the ping command at PC0 in PT in Ubuntu .

Step 14. Perform communication check between PC3 (192.168.2.2), which is in a topology in PT on Windows and PC0 192.168.1.1), which is in the topology in PT in Ubuntu in VirtualBox.

```
C:\>ping 192.168.1.1

Pinging 192.168.1.1 with 32 bytes of data:

Reply from 192.168.1.1: bytes=32 time=14ms TTL=126
Reply from 192.168.1.1: bytes=32 time=12ms TTL=126
Reply from 192.168.1.1: bytes=32 time=13ms TTL=126
Reply from 192.168.1.1: bytes=32 time=13ms TTL=126

Ping statistics for 192.168.1.1:
    Packets: Sent = 4, Received = 4, Lost = 0 (0% loss),
Approximate round trip times in milli-seconds:
    Minimum = 12ms, Maximum = 14ms, Average = 13ms
```

Figure 3.104 The result of the ping PC3 command in PT on Windows.

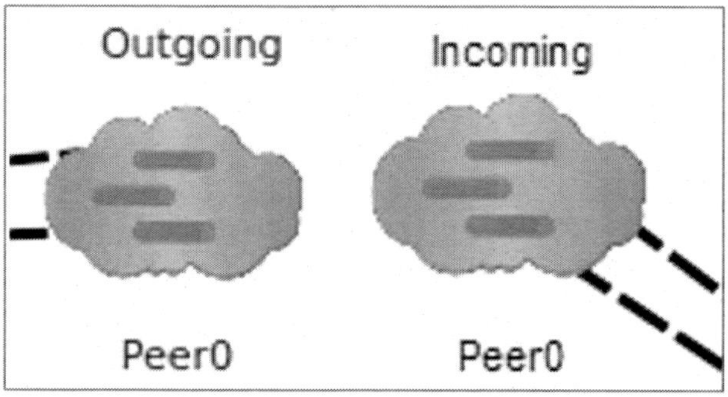

Figure 3.105 Connection between PT on Windows and PT on Ubuntu through Your real LAN was made and works properly.

3.9 List of auxiliary files

- exercise4-ubuntu.pkt
- exercise5-windows.pkt
- exercise6-windows.pkt
- exercise6-ubuntu.pkt

CHAPTER 4

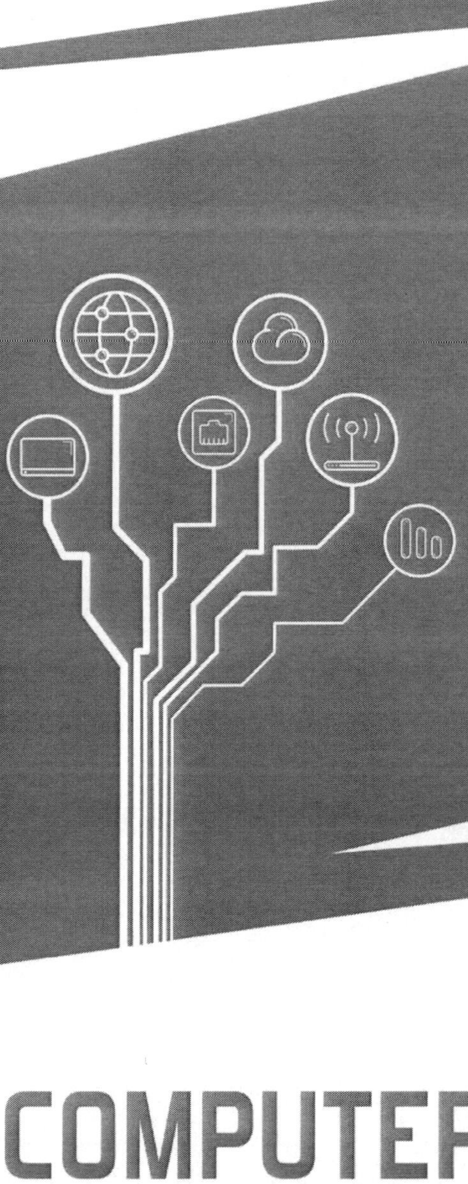

DEVICE PAIRING TECHNOLOGY AND TETHERING

COMPUTER NETWORKS IN PACKET TRACER

FOR ADVANCED USERS

4 Device Pairing Technology and Tethering

4.1 What is Bluetooth device pairing? (Exercise 7)

Bluetooth device pairing (e.g. two smartphones) is a technique of mutual registration of two devices to obtain a connection between them.

Part 1. Creating topology.

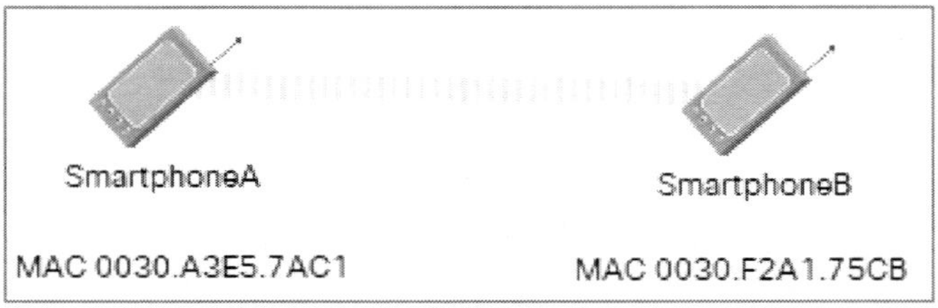

Figure 4.1 Topology of the network using bluetooth.

Part 2. Device addressing

Device	Interface	MAC Address	Range
SmartphoneA	Bluetooth	0030.A3E5.7AC1	10 m
SmartphoneB	Bluetooth	0030.F2A1.75CB	10 m

Table 4.1 MAC addresses of bluetooth interfaces in smartphones.

Part 3. Course of the exercise

Step 1. In both devices under the tab [**Programming**] create JavaScript scripts to test communications.

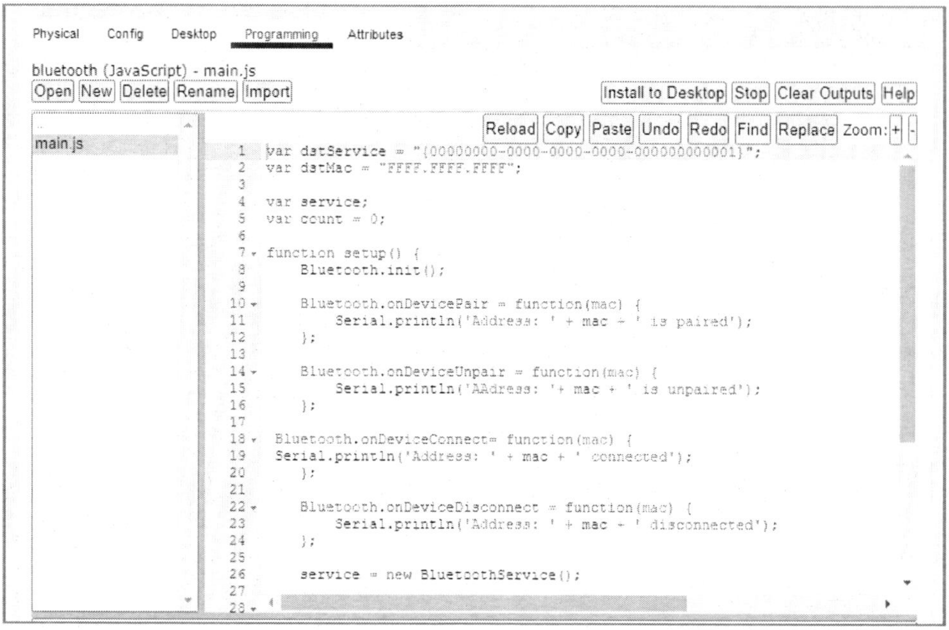

Figure 4.2 [Programming] tab.

main.js script content :

```
var dstService = "{00000000-0000-0000-0000-000000000001}";
var dstMac = "FFFF.FFFF.FFFF";
var service;
var count = 0;

function setup() {
      Bluetooth.init();

      Bluetooth.onDevicePair = function(mac) {
            Serial.println('Address: ' + mac + ' is
paired');
      };

      Bluetooth.onDeviceUnpair = function(mac) {
            Serial.println('Address: '+ mac + ' is
unpaired');
      };

 Bluetooth.onDeviceConnect= function(mac) {
```

```
 Serial.println('Address: ' + mac + ' connected');
        };

        Bluetooth.onDeviceDisconnect = function(mac) {
                Serial.println('Address: ' + mac + '
disconnected ');
        };

        service = new BluetoothService();

        service.onReceive = function(srcMac, srcService,
dstMac, dstService, data) {
                Serial.println("Received from address "
                        + srcMac + ":" + data);
        };

        Serial.println(service.start(dstService));
}

function loop() {
        service.send(dstMac, dstService, "Hello " +
(count++));
        delay(5000);
}
```

Step 2. On both devices, run the scripts using the button [**Run**].

Step 3. Turn on Bluetooth on both smartphones.

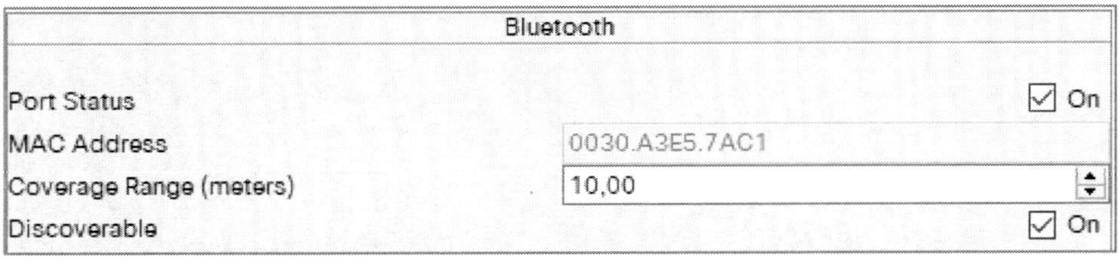

Figure 4.3 [Bluetooth] interface parameters.

Step 4. Go to the physical topology and adjust the location of the smartphones so that their ranges allow them to connect.

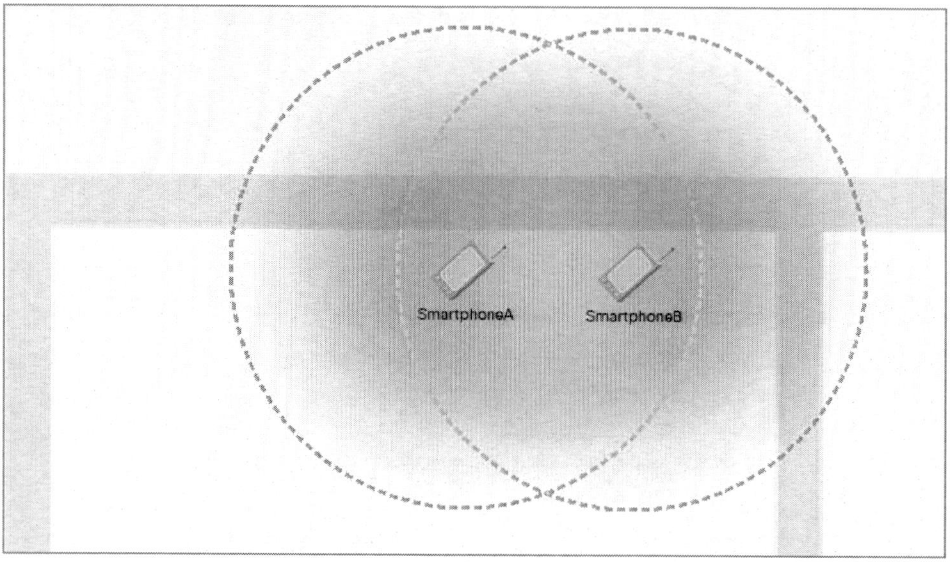

Figure 4.4 Smartphone coverage in physical topology.

Step 5. Go to logical topology and in Smartphone A select the tab [**Config**].

Step 6. Select [**Bluetooth**] and click [**Discover**] button. The SmartphoneB name and MAC address will appear in the list of recognized devices.

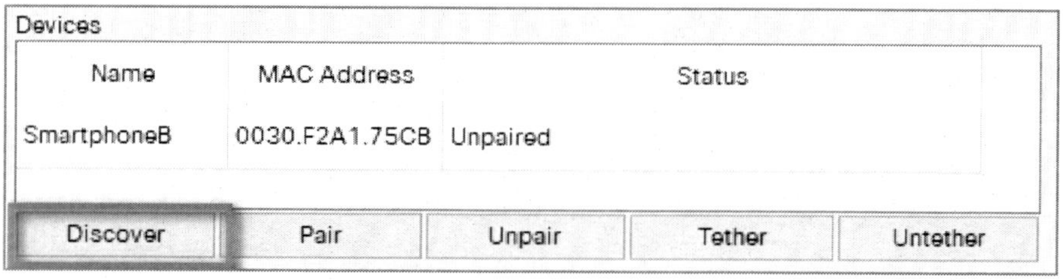

Figure 4.5 [Discover] button.

Step 7. Click [**Pair**] button.

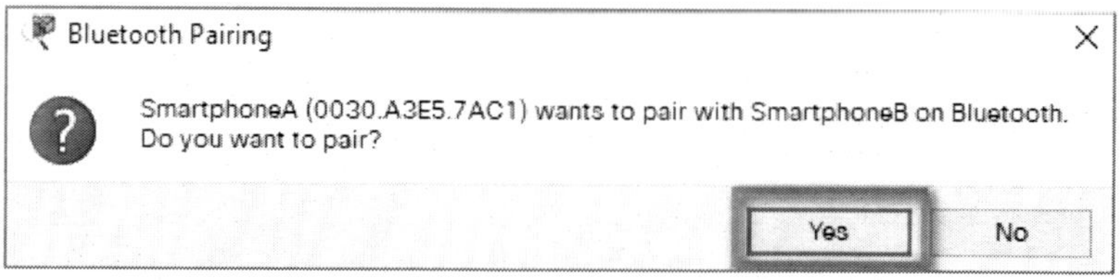

Figure 4.6 Pairing smartphones.

A message will appear, in which you click the button [**Yes**]. In the list of recognized devices, the status for SmartphoneB will change to '**Paired, Connected**.'

Figure 4.7 Status for SmartphoneB [Paired, Connected].

Step 8. Observe test script messages - tab [**Programming**].

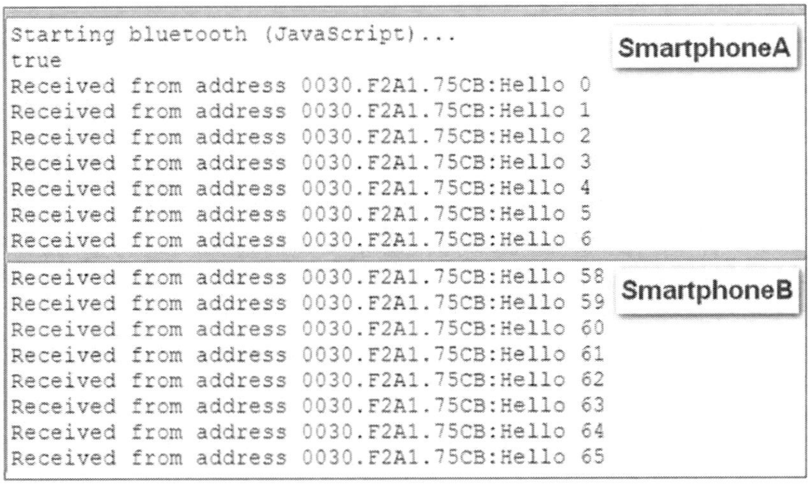

Figure 4.8 Test script messages on both smartphones during data exchange.

Alternate between disabling and enabling device pairing and watch the script messages on both smartphones.

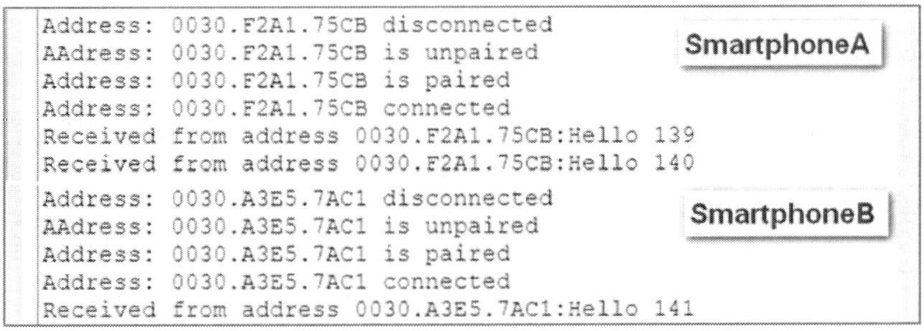

Figure 4.9 Test script messages on both smartphones after enabling pairing.

4.2 Setting up tethering (Exercise 8)

What is tethering?

Tethering is a technique for accessing the Internet using an access point on a cell phone.

Part 1. Preparing topology.

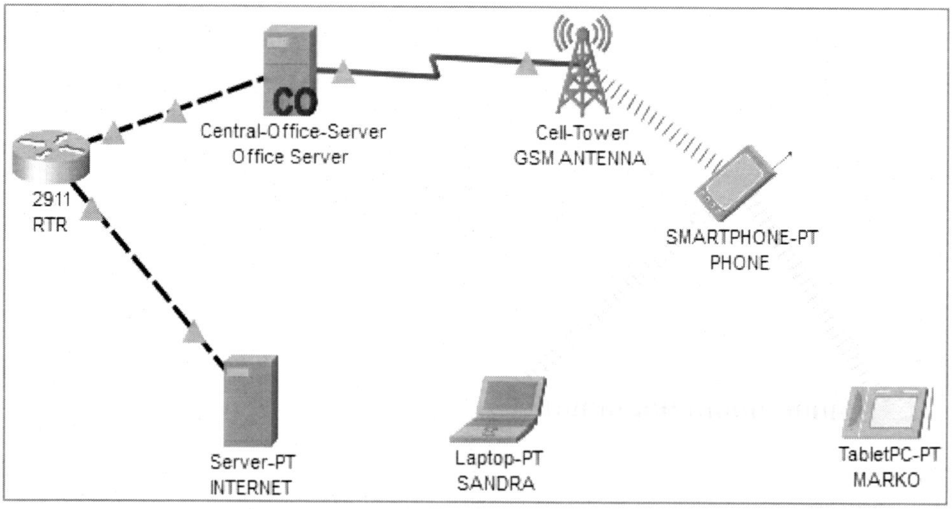

Figure 4.10 Topology of the network using tethering.

Part 2. Device addressing.

Device	Interface	IP Address	Mask	Gateway	DNS
INTERNET	Fa0	100.100.100.100	/8	100.100.100.200	100.100.100.100
RTR	Gi/1	100.100.100.200	/8	*)	*)
RTR	Gi0/0	10.1.1.1	/8	*)	*)
Office Server	Backbone	10.1.1.2	/8	10.1.1.1	100.100.100.100
Office Server	Cellular	172.16.1.1	/24	*)	*)
PHONE	3G/4G	DHCP	-	172.16.0.1	-
PHONE	Bluetooth	DHCP	-	-	-
SANDRA	Bluetooth	DHCP	-	172.20.10.1	
MARKO	Bluetooth	DHCP	-	172.20.10.1	

Table 4.2 Device addressing

*) – not applicable

Part 3. Doing the exercise.

Step 1. Wait for Smartphone **PHONE** to connect to Cell Tower **GSM ANTENNA**.

Step 2. On the **PHONE**, go to the tab **[Config] - [Settings] – [Cellurar Tethering] – [Bluetooth] – [On]**

Step 3. Go to **SANDRA** laptop

Step 4. Go to **Desktop → Bluetooth**

Step 5. Perform **Discover**

Step 6. Select the **PHONE** device and perform **Tether**

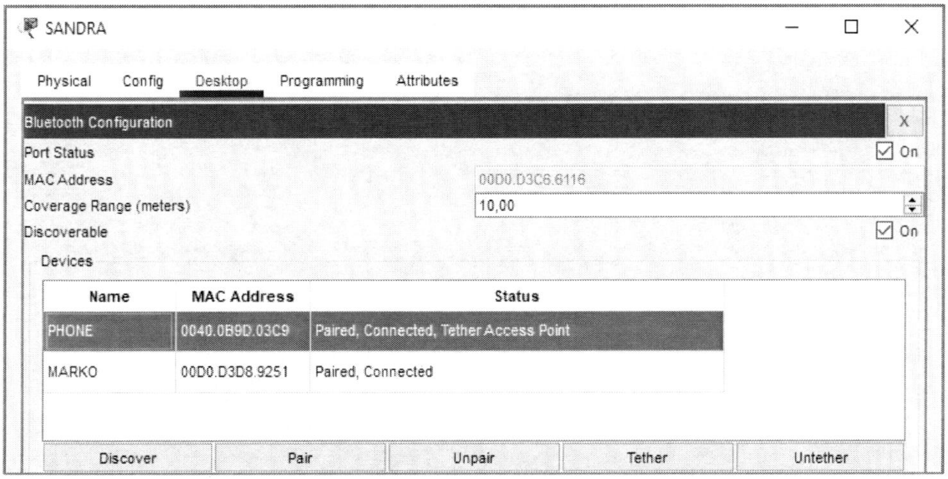

Figure 4.11 Thetering from SANDRA to PHONE.

Step 7. Go to **MARKO** tablet

Step 8. Go to **Desktop → Bluetooth**

Step 9. Perform **Discover**

Step 10. Select the **PHONE** device and perform **Tether**

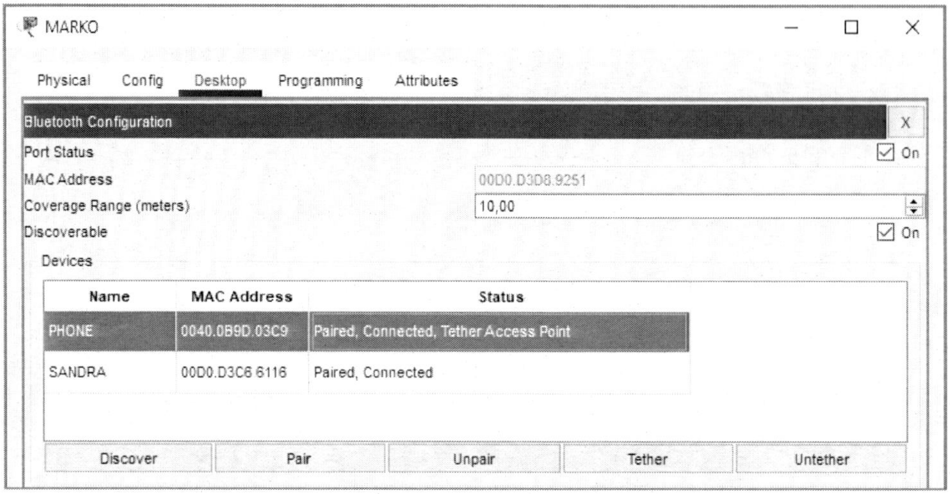

Figure 4.12 Thetering from MARKO to PHONE.

Step 11. Try from your **SANDRA** Laptop to view a page with the address **100.100.100.100.100**, using Web Browser.

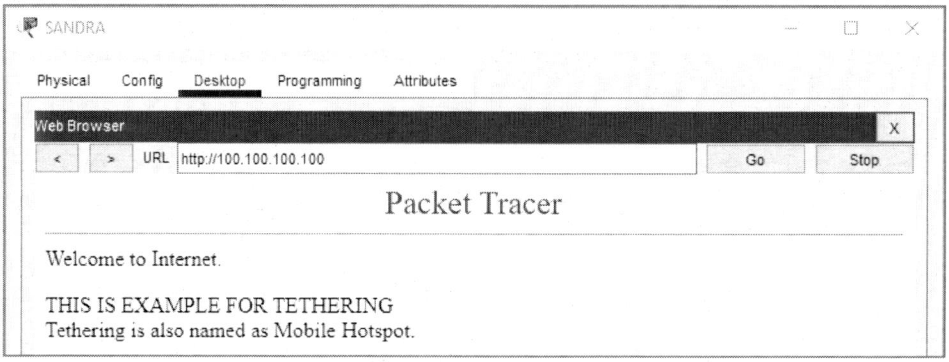

Figure 4.13 Access to Internet from SANDRA laptop.

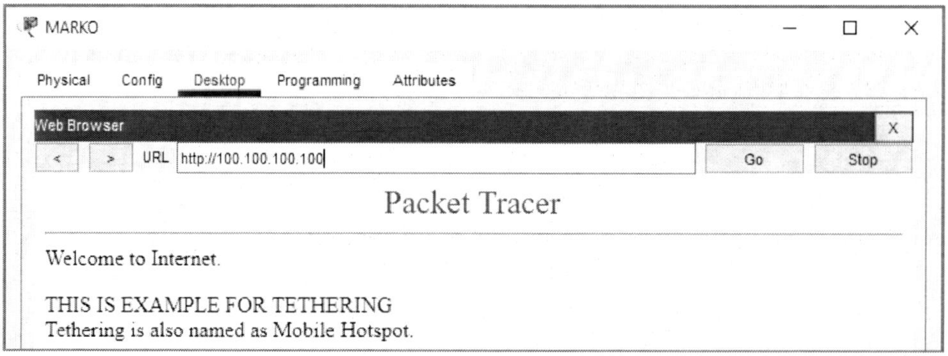

Figure 4.14 Access to Internet from MARKO laptop.

4.3 List of auxiliary files

- exercise7-bluetooth-pairing.pkt
- exercise8-tethering-in-smartphone.pkt

CHAPTER 5

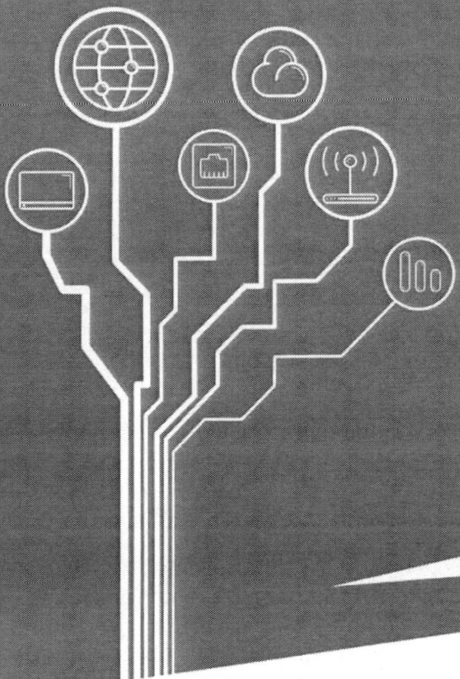

MOBILE GSM TELEPHONY

COMPUTER NETWORKS IN PACKET TRACER

FOR ADVANCED USERS

5 Mobile GSM Telephony

5.1 Communication between two GSM mobile networks (Exercise 9)

Part 1. Assumptions.

Smartphone-DAVID communicates with Smartphone-BARBARA on two different GSM networks, using the ping command.

GSM networks are connected through a network consisting of routers RTR-PLUS, RTR-INTERNET, RTR-PLAY.

EIGRP 100 routing and static routes to GSM networks should be configured in the routers.

Part 2. Plan of the exercise.

Step 1. Build a logic topology according to the figure.

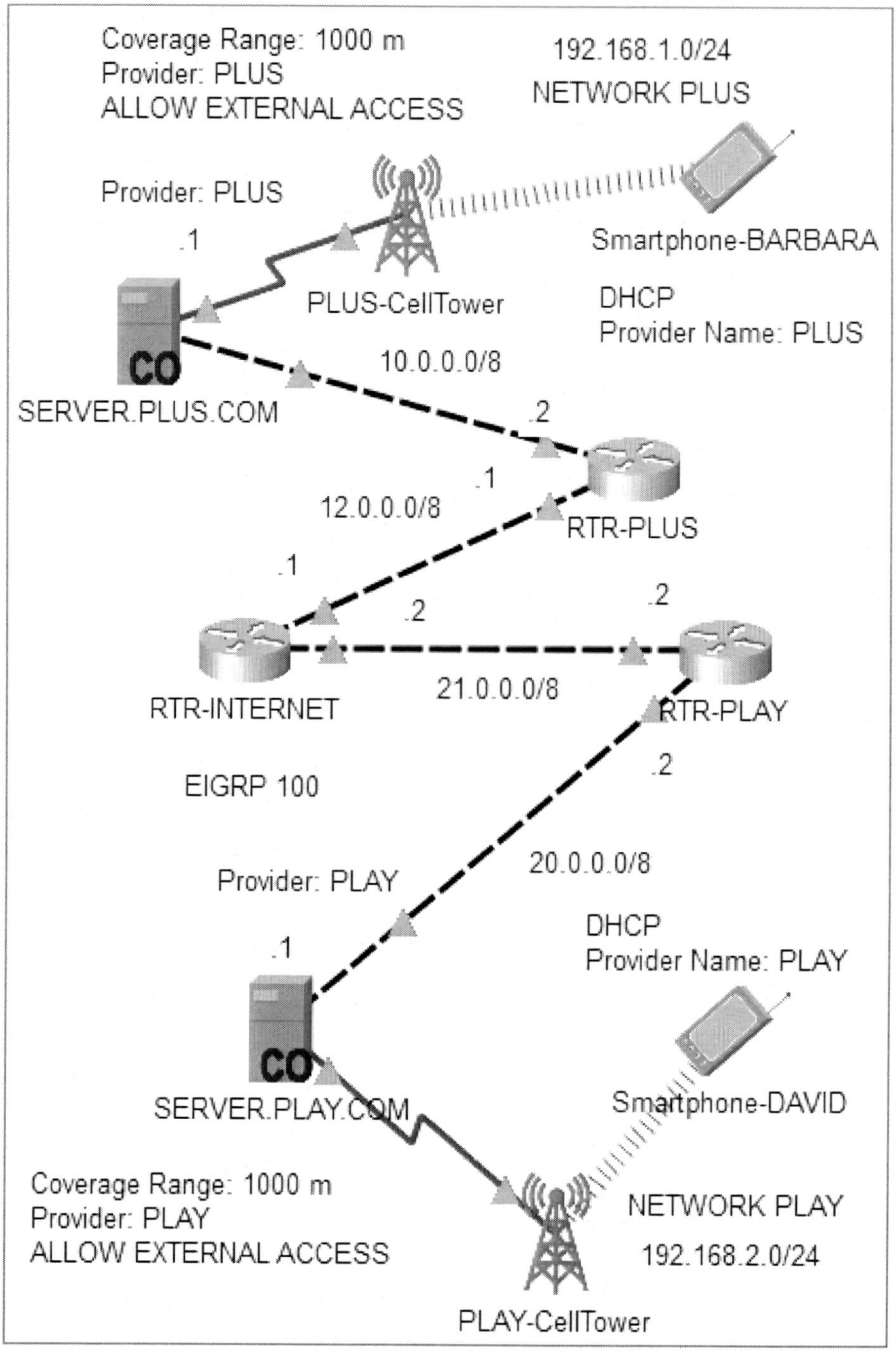

Figure 5.1 Logical topology with two GSM networks.

Step 2. Build the physical topology according to the drawings.

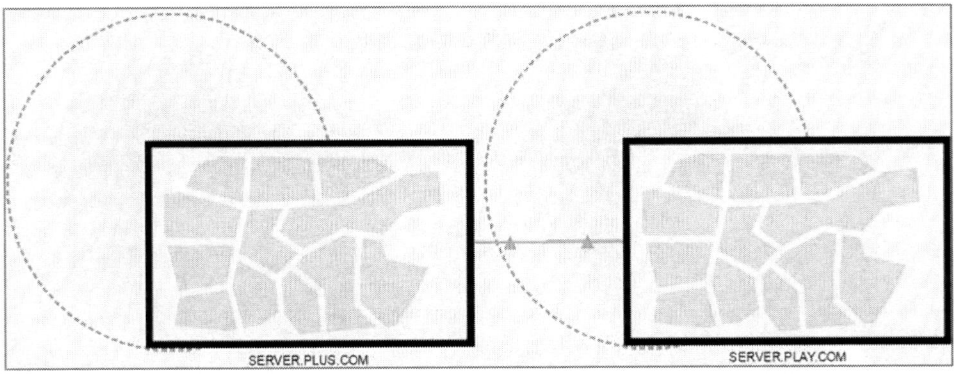

Figure 5.2 Resulting physical topology - Intercity level.

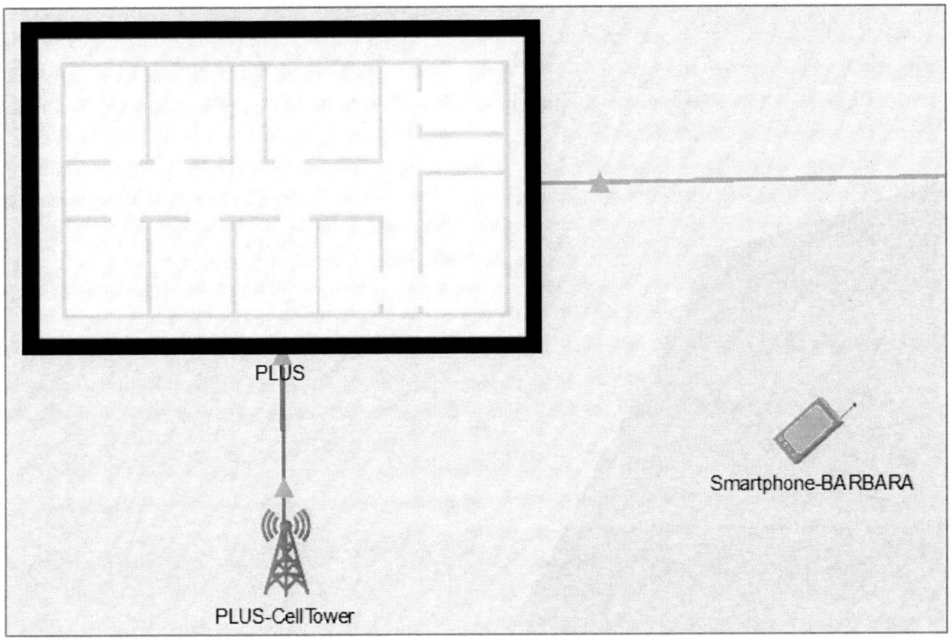

Figure 5.3 Resulting physical topology - SERVER.PLUS.COM level.

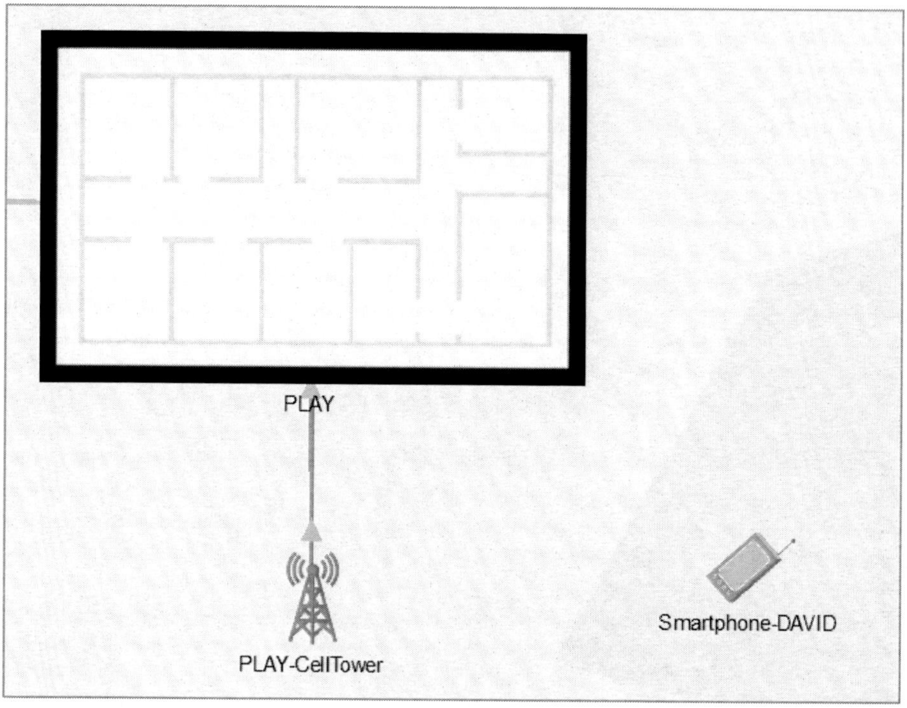

Figure 5.4 Resulting physical topology - SERVER.PLAY.COM level .

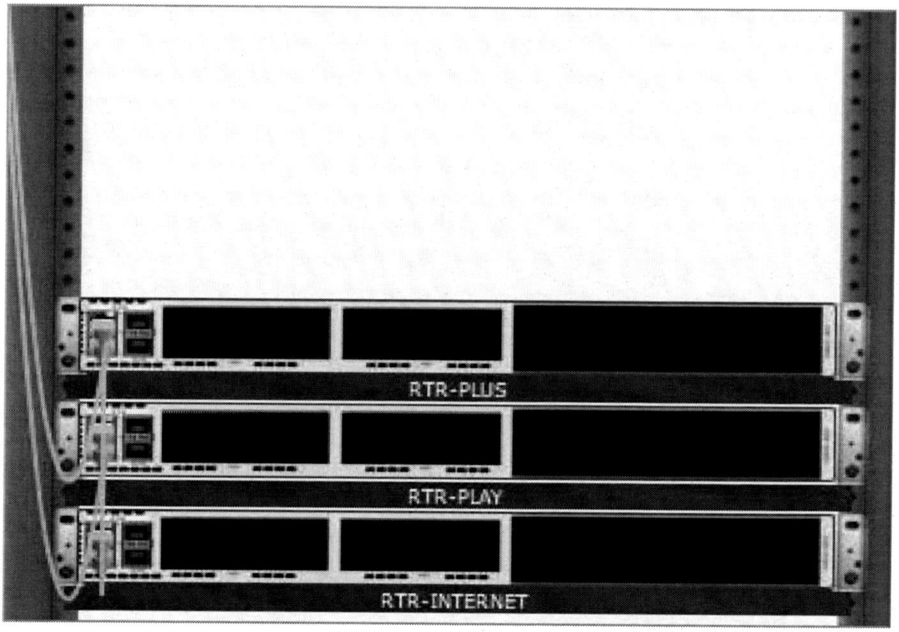

Figure 5.5 Resulting physical topology - Main Wiring Closet level .

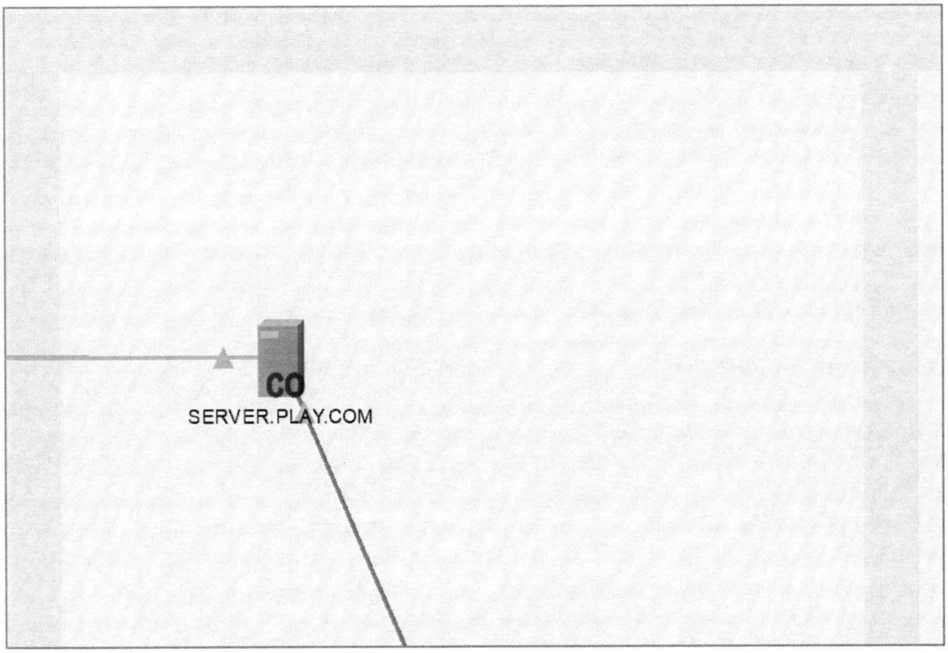

Figure 5.6 Resulting physical topology - PLAY level

Step 3. Configure the logical network topology (host names and IP addressing and EIGRP routing and static routes) for RTR-PLUS, RTR-INTERNET, RTR-PLAY.

RTR-PLUS router configuration

```
hostname RTR-PLUS
interface GigabitEthernet0/0/0
ip address 10.0.0.2 255.0.0.0
interface GigabitEthernet0/0/1
ip address 12.0.0.2 255.0.0.0
router eigrp 100
network 10.0.0.0
network 12.0.0.0
ip route 192.168.1.0 255.255.255.0 10.0.0.1
ip route 192.168.2.0 255.255.255.0 12.0.0.1
```

RTR-INTERNET router configuration

```
hostname RTR-INTERNET
interface GigabitEthernet0/0/0
ip address 12.0.0.1 255.0.0.0
```

```
interface GigabitEthernet0/0/1
ip address 21.0.0.1 255.0.0.0
router eigrp 100
network 12.0.0.0
network 21.0.0.0
ip route 192.168.2.0 255.255.255.0 21.0.0.2
ip route 192.168.1.0 255.255.255.0 12.0.0.2
```

RTR-PLAY router configuration

```
hostname RTR-PLAY
interface GigabitEthernet0/0/0
ip address 20.0.0.2 255.0.0.0
interface GigabitEthernet0/0/1
ip address 21.0.0.2 255.0.0.0
router eigrp 100
network 21.0.0.0
network 20.0.0.0
ip route 192.168.2.0 255.255.255.0 20.0.0.1
ip route 192.168.1.0 255.255.255.0 21.0.0.1
```

Step 4. Configure CO server for PLUS network.

Display Name	SERVER.PLUS.COM
Domain Name	SERVER.PLUS.COM
Provider	PLUS
Allow External Access	Yes
BACKBONE IP	10.0.0.1
BACKBONE Subnet Mask	255.0.0.0
BACKBONE Default Gateway	10.0.0.2
CELL TOWER IP	192.168.1.1
CELL TOWER Subnet Mask	255.255.255.0

Table 5.1 SERVER.PLUS.COM configuration

Step 5. Configure PLUS-Cell Tower.

Display Name	PLUS-Cell Tower
Coverage Range	1000 m
Provider	PLUS
Allow External Access	Yes

Table 5.2 PLUS-CellTower configuration

Step 6. Configure CO server for PLUS network.

Display Name	SERVER.PLAY.COM
Domain Name	SERVER.PLAY.COM
Provider	PLAY
Allow External Access	Yes
BACKBONE IP	20.0.0.1
BACKBONE Subnet Mask	255.0.0.0
BACKBONE Default Gateway	20.0.0.2
CELL TOWER IP	192.168.2.1
CELL TOWER Subnet Mask	255.255.255.0

Table 5.3 SERVER.PLAY.COM configuration

Step 7. Configure PLAY-CellTower .

Display Name	PLAY-CellTower
Coverage Range	1000 m
Provider	PLAY
Allow External Access	Yes

Table 5.4 PLAY-CellTower configuration

Step 8. Check communication between smartphones.

Check that the ping from Smartphone-BARBARA to Smartphone-DAVID (192.168.2.100) completes successfully.

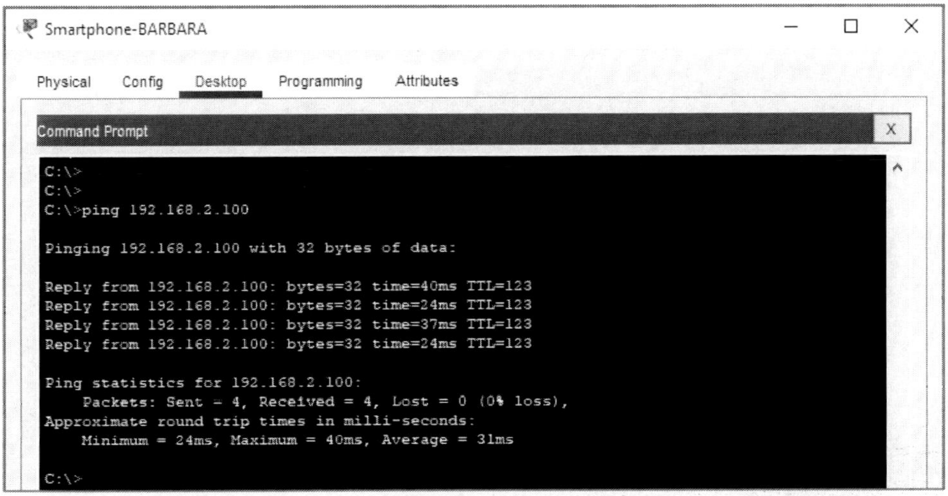

Figure 5.7 The result of the ping command from Smartphone-BARBARA to Smartphone-DAVID.

Step 9. Check communication between smartphones.

Check that the ping from Smartphone-DAVID to Smartphone-BARBARA (192.168.1.100) completes successfully.

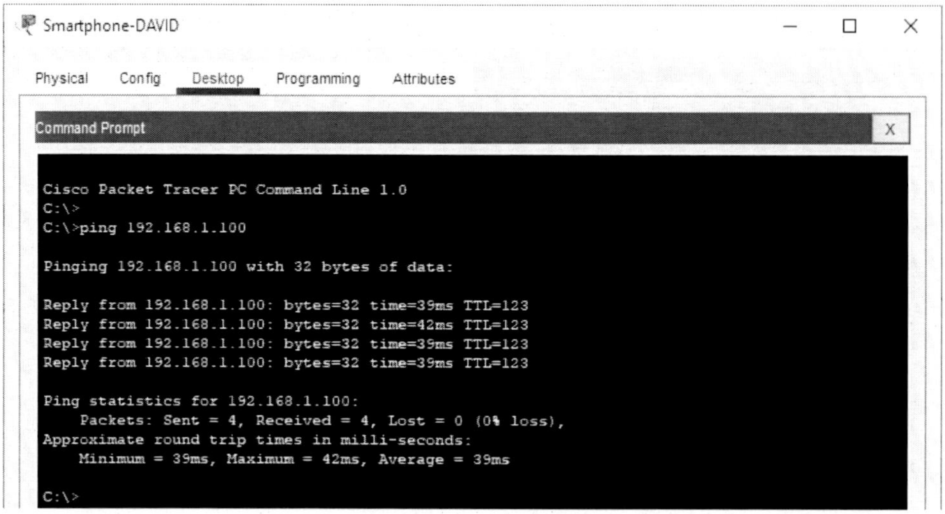

Figure 5.8 The result of the ping command from Smartphone-DAVID to Smartphone-BARBARA.

5.2 Communication between three GSM mobile networks (Exercise 10)

Part 1. Assumptions.

Configure OSPF 1 AREA 100 and subnets on the RTR router:

- Fa0/0 - NET10: 172.16.10.0/24
- Fa0/1 - NET20: 172.16.20.0/24
- Fa0/2 - NET30: 172.16.30.0/24

Configure static routes to the GSM network on the RTR router:

- GSM1 (172.16.1.0/24)
- GSM1 (172.16.2.0/24)
- GSM3 (172.16.3.0/24)

Part 2. Physical topologies.

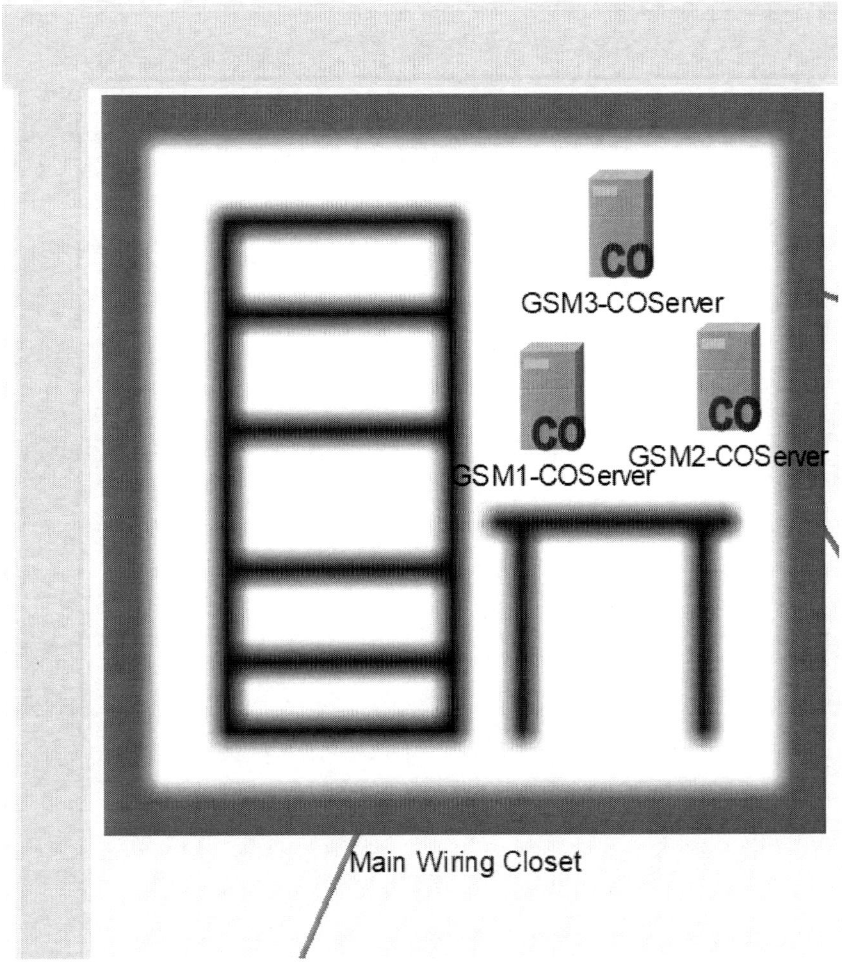

Figure 5.9 Resulting physical topology - Corporate Office level .

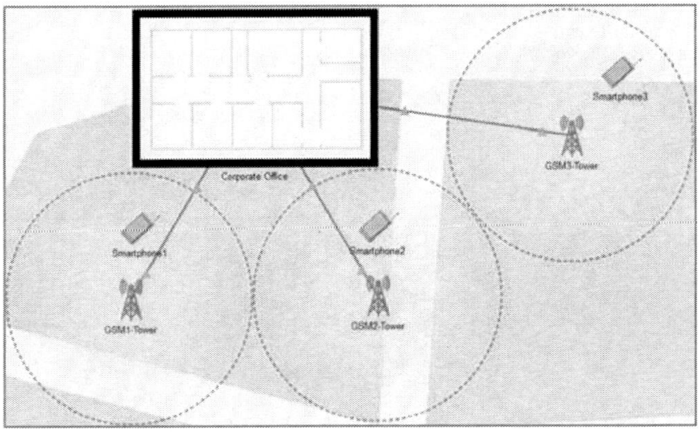

Figure 5.10 Resulting physical topology - Home City level.

Part 3. Logical topologies.

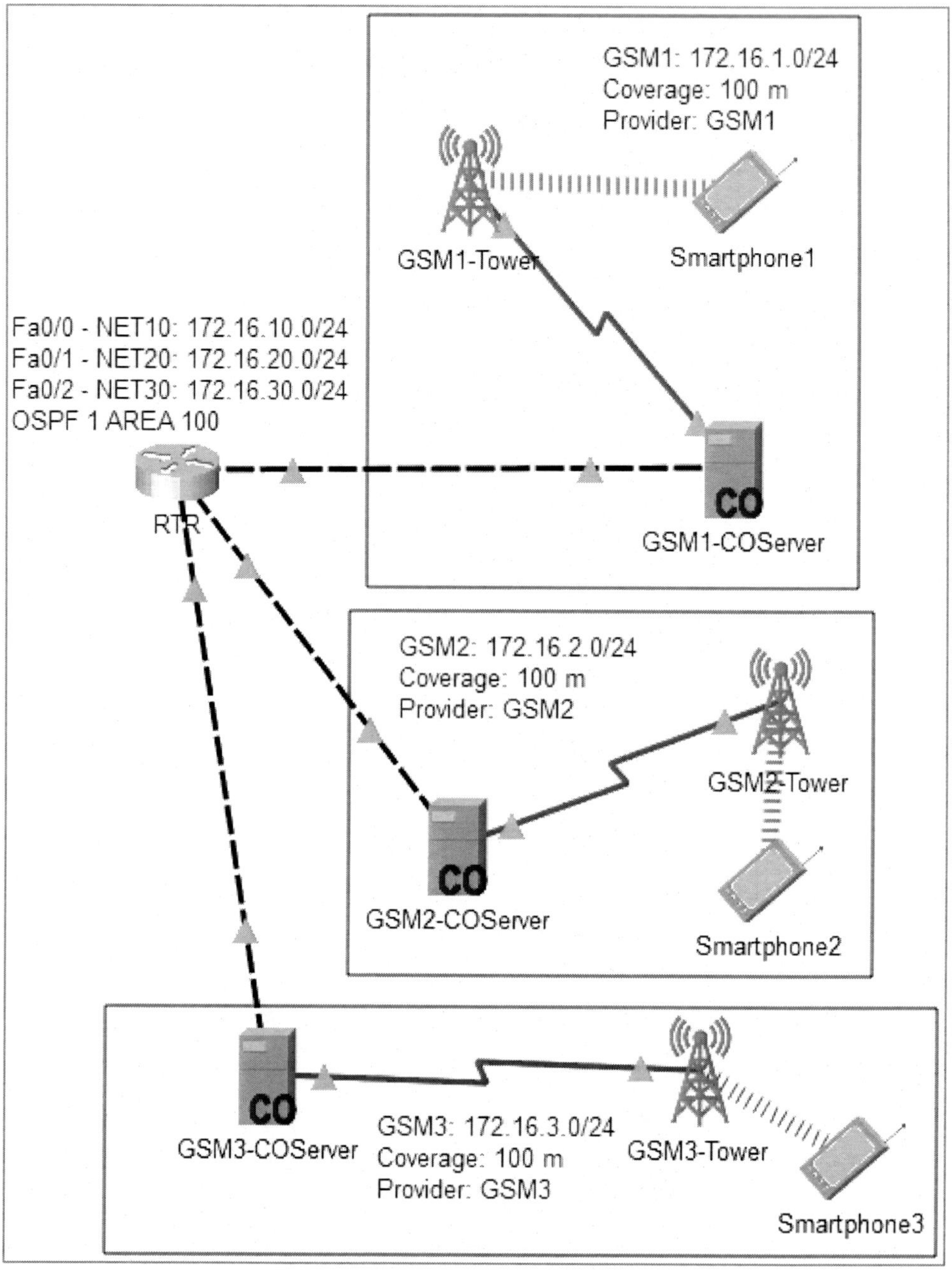

Figure 5.11 Logical topology.

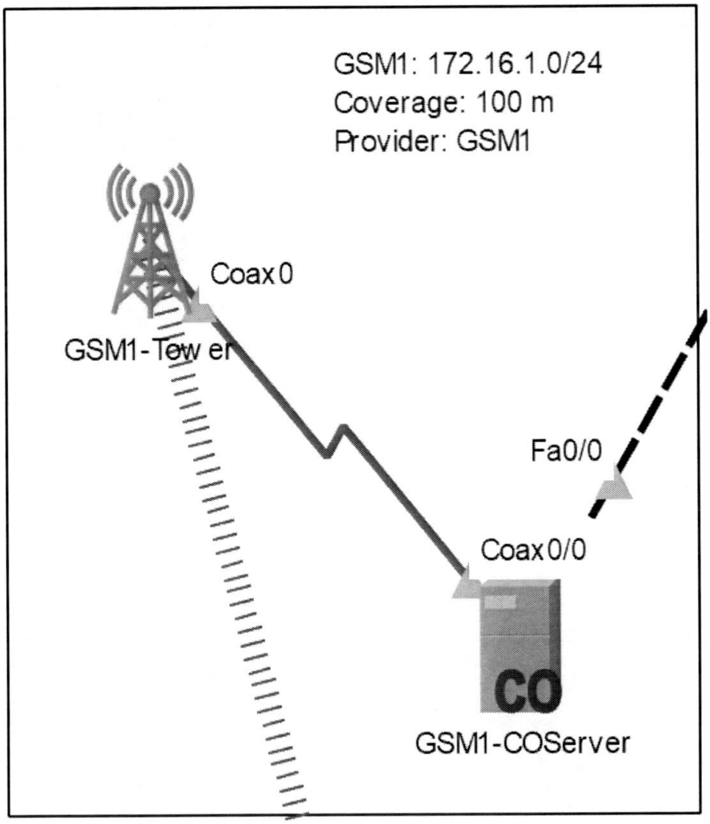

Figure 5.12 Logical topology of GSM1 network.

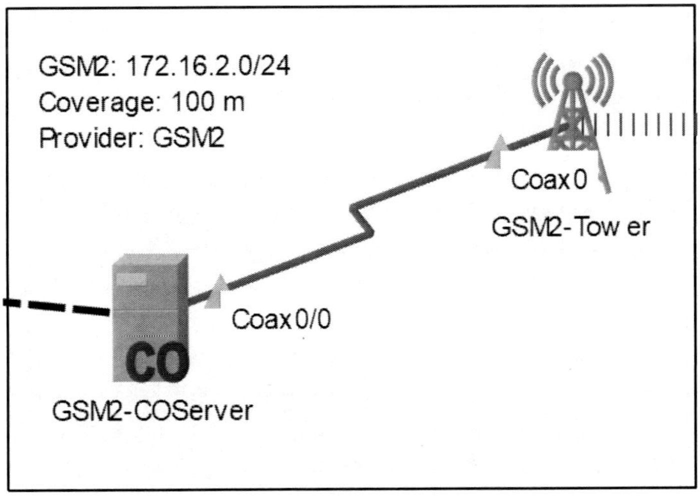

Figure 5.13 Logical topology of GSM2 network.

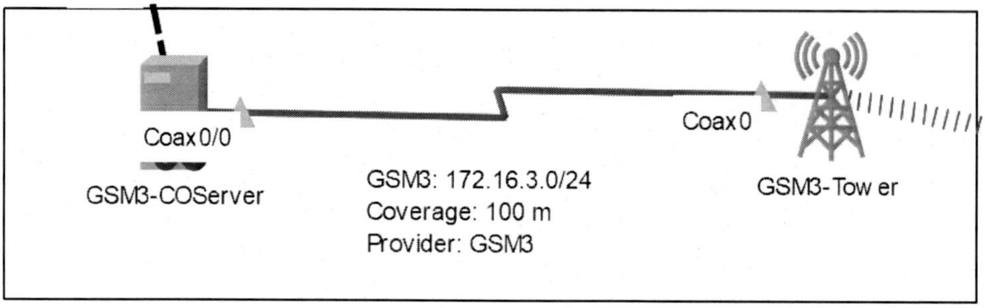

Figure 5.14 Logical topology of GSM3 network.

Part 4. Plan of the exercise.

Step 1. Configure GSM networks according to the drawings of logical topologies and physical topologies.

Step 2. Configure RTR.

RTR router configuration:

```
hostname RTR
interface FastEthernet 0/0
ip address 172.16.10.1 255.255.255.0
interface FastEthernet 1/0
ip address 172.16.20.1 255.255.255.0
interface FastEthernet 2/0
ip address 172.16.30.1 255.255.255.0
router ospf 1
network 172.16.10.0 0.0.0.255 area 100
network 172.16.20.0 0.0.0.255 area 100
network 172.16.30.0 0.0.0.255 area 100
ip route 172.16.1.0 255.255.255.0 172.16.10.2
ip route 172.16.2.0 255.255.255.0 172.16.20.2
ip route 172.16.3.0 255.255.255.0 172.16.30.2
```

Step 2. Check the communication (using the ping command) between Smartphone1 and Smartphone2.

```
C:\>ping 172.16.2.100

Pinging 172.16.2.100 with 32 bytes of data:

Reply from 172.16.2.100: bytes=32 time=31ms TTL=125
Reply from 172.16.2.100: bytes=32 time=24ms TTL=125
Reply from 172.16.2.100: bytes=32 time=26ms TTL=125
Reply from 172.16.2.100: bytes=32 time=26ms TTL=125

Ping statistics for 172.16.2.100:
    Packets: Sent = 4, Received = 4, Lost = 0 (0% loss),
Approximate round trip times in milli-seconds:
    Minimum = 24ms, Maximum = 31ms, Average = 26ms
```

Figure 5.15 The result of the ping command from Smartphone1 Smartphone2

Step 3. Check the communication (using the ping command) between Smartphone2 and Smartphone3.

```
C:\>ping 172.16.3.101

Pinging 172.16.3.101 with 32 bytes of data:

Reply from 172.16.3.101: bytes=32 time=26ms TTL=125
Reply from 172.16.3.101: bytes=32 time=26ms TTL=125
Reply from 172.16.3.101: bytes=32 time=33ms TTL=125
Reply from 172.16.3.101: bytes=32 time=16ms TTL=125

Ping statistics for 172.16.3.101:
    Packets: Sent = 4, Received = 4, Lost = 0 (0% loss),
Approximate round trip times in milli-seconds:
    Minimum = 16ms, Maximum = 33ms, Average = 25ms
```

Figure 5.16 The result of the ping command from Smartphone2 Smartphone3

5.3 List of auxiliary files

- exercise9-two-mobile-gsm-networks.pkt
- exercise10-three-mobile-gsm-networks.pkt

CHAPTER 6

NETWORK CONTROLLER

COMPUTER NETWORKS IN PACKET TRACER

FOR ADVANCED USERS

6 Network Controller

6.1 Introduction to network controllers

What is Cisco DNA?

Cisco DNA (ang. ***Digital Network Architecture***) is an architecture that provides centralized management, control and analysis for networks.

What is SDN?

SDN (ang. ***Software-Defined Network***) is a network defined by software, and the network virtualization approach aims to optimize controlled network resources, by means of separating the network control level from the network data level.

What is Network Controller?

Network controller, managed by Web GUI or using APIs provides a centralized dashboard for viewing network status, quickly identify devices and approve configuration changes to all managed devices simultaneously. In addition, you can access the network controller from the actual network (using a browser).

Network controller - a brief description of the device in PT

The new **NETWORK CONTROLLER** device in the Packet Tracer program, that is ***Network Controller***, created in Packet Tracer 8.0.0, is a device that simulates similar devices - actual controllers in SDN.

In the current version of Packet Tracer, you can only practice a limited approach to network management using the Network Controller model, so this chapter includes exercises on the following topics only:

- Creating an administrator account.
- Configure administrator authentication.
- Search and identification of devices.
- Display of network topology.
- Access to the controller from the real network.
- Remote configuration change of devices.

Source: Cisco Packet Tracer electronic help. [C:\Program Files\Cisco Packet Tracer 8.0.1\help\default\index.htm]. (Academy, Online help for the program Cisco Packet Tracer, 2022) [2]

6.2 Create an administrator account (Exercise 11)

Part 1.Required equipment.

- Server-PT – 2 pcs
- PC-PT – 2 pcs
- Switch 2960-24TT –3 pcs
- Router 2811 –2 pcs

Part 2. Network addressing and topology.

Device	Model	Interface	IP/Mask	Default gate	DNS
PC0	PC-PT	Fa	1.1.1.2/8	1.1.1.1	-
PC1	PC-PT	Fa	192.168.1.1/24	192.168.1.254	-
PC2	PC-PT	Fa	192.168.1.2/24	192.168.1.254	-
SVR1	Server-PT	Fa	192.168.2.1/24	192.168.2.254	-
SVR2	Server-PT	Fa	192.168.2.2/24	192.168.2.254	-
SW1	2960-24TT	VLAN1	1.1.1.253/8	1.1.1.1	-
SWA	2960-24TT	VLAN1	192.168.1.253/24	192.168.1.254	-
SWB	2960-24TT	VLAN1	192.168.2.253/24	192.168.2.254	-
RTR1	2811	Fa0/0	1.1.1.1/8	-	-
RTR1	2811	Se0/0/0	172.16.0.1/16	-	-
RTR2	2811	Se0/0/0	172.16.0.2/16	-	-
RTR2	2811	Fa0/0	192.168.1.254/24	-	-
RTR2	2811	Fa0/1	192.168.2.254/24	-	-

Table 6.1 Assumptions - Managed network addressing

[2] Cisco Packet Tracer electronic help

Version	2
Domain	ssh.server
RSA key length	1024
Username	admin
Password	admin123

Table 6.2 SSH configuration parameters.

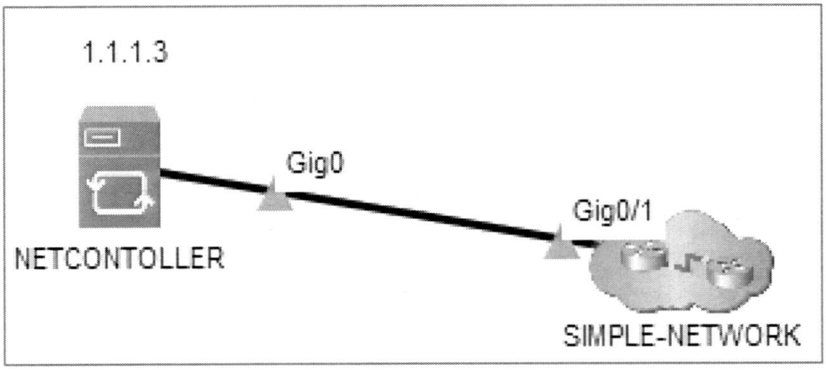

Figure 6.1 General cloud topology (Exercise 11).

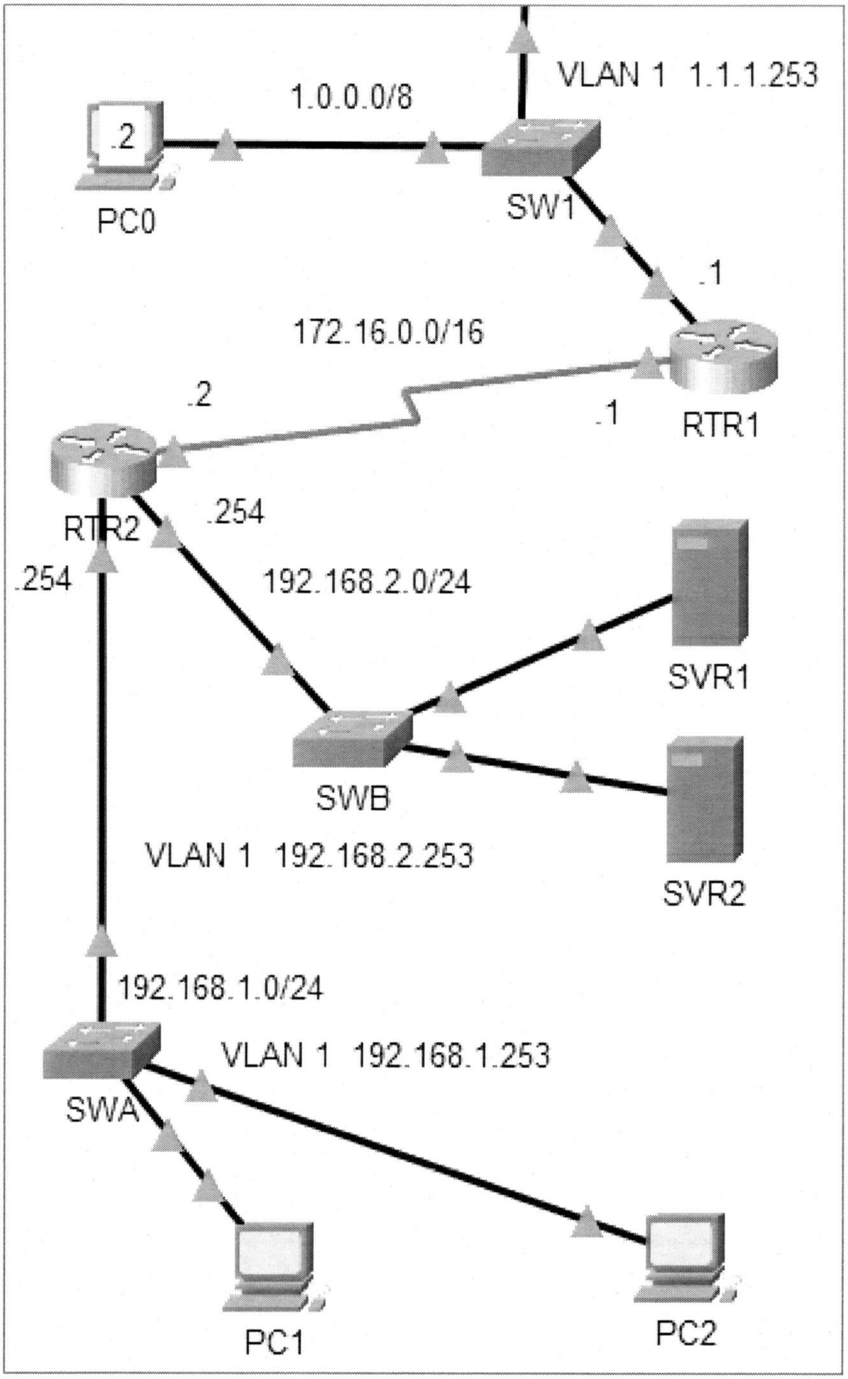

Figure 6.2 Logical topology of a managed network (Exercise 11).

Part 3. Plan of the exercise.

Note: in case of problems, open the file **exercise11-network-controller.pkt** and analyze the solution to the exercise.

Step 1. To begin with, in order to manage the network, create a network that will be managed.

Very important: In order for the network controller to work properly, **each device** on the managed network **must have** the following security configured:

SSH security - VTY lines – commands:

```
line vty 0 4
login local
```

Security - encrypted password for privileged mode (ENABLE SECRET PASSWORD) – commands:

```
enable secret cisco
```

Step 2. Insert a managed network into the cloud named '**SIMPLE-NETWORK**'.

Step 3. Insert the controller **NETCONTROLLER** and connect it with the interface Gig0/1 in SW1.

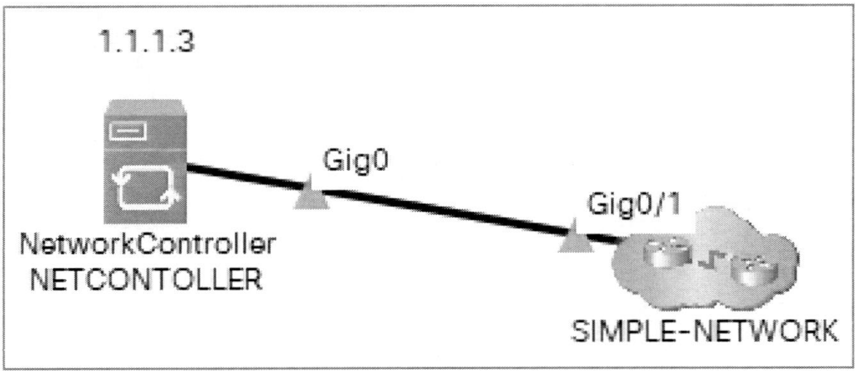

Figure 6.3 Logical topology (Exercise 11).

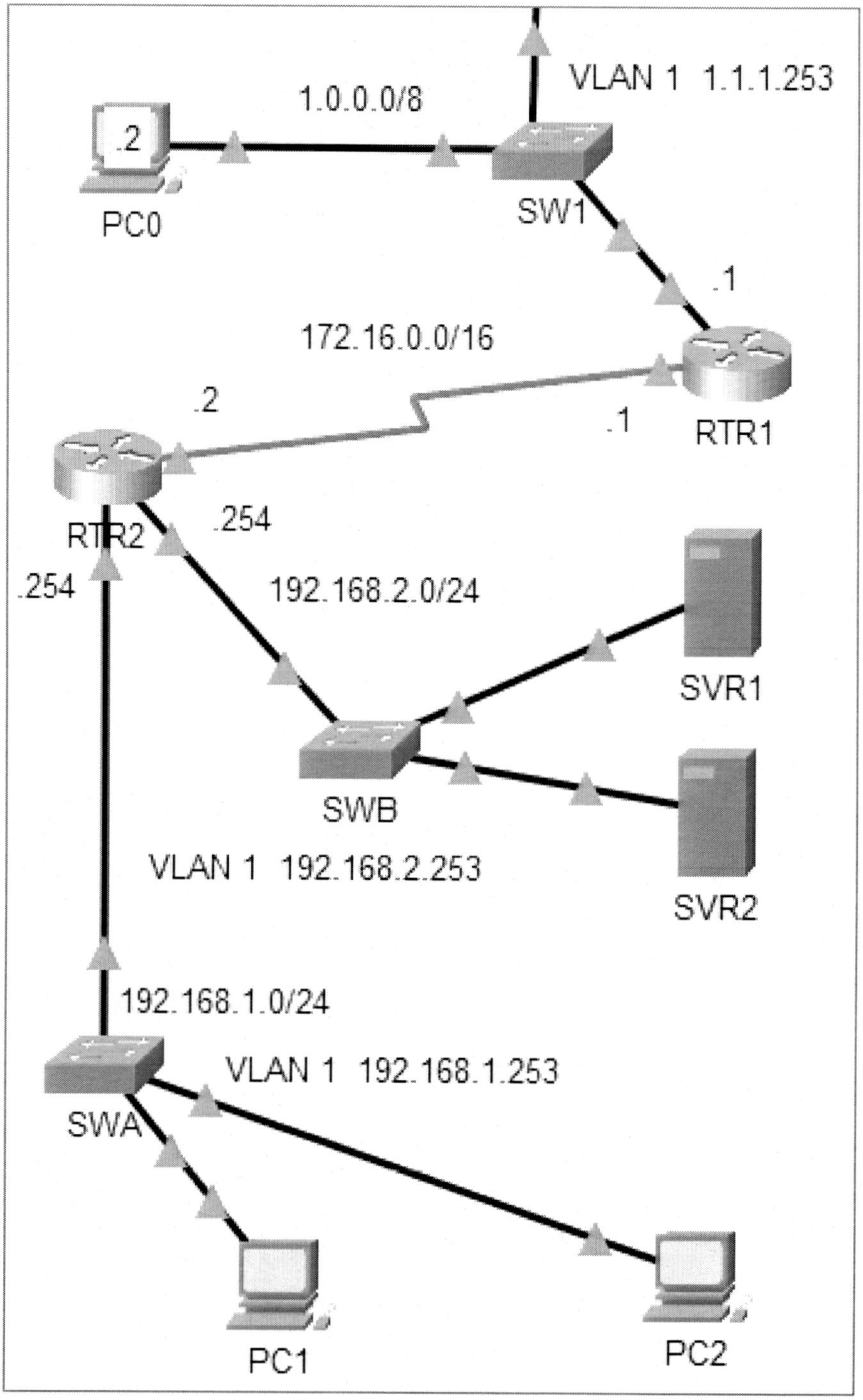

Figure 6.4 Cloud topology (Exercise 11).

Step 4. Perform basic controller interface configuration.

Note: When a message appears - warning '**PT will use the default gateway of the fastest functional port**', then it should be confirmed.

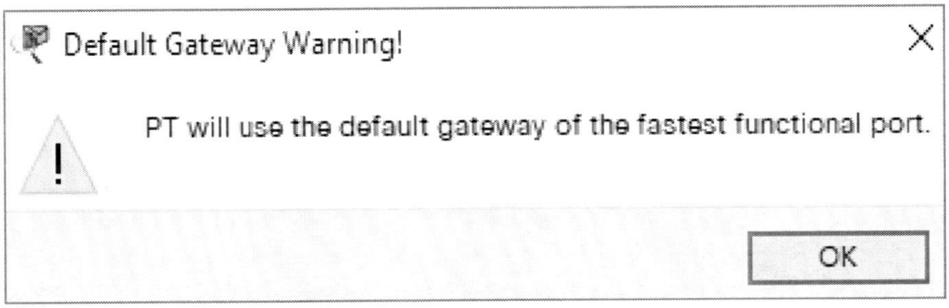

Figure 6.5 Message 'Default Gateway Warning'.

Step 5. Configure NETCONTROLLER interface according to data given in the table.

Name	NETCONTOLLER
Interface	Gi0
IP address	1.1.1.3
Mask	255.0.0.0
Default gate	1.1.1.1

Table 6.3 Controller interface configuration parameters

Step 6. Perform access configuration from the actual network.

Note: If the **Server Status** field says "**Disabled in Preferences**," then go to Packet Tracer's "**Options →Preferences→ Miscellaneous→ Enable External Network for Network Controller REST API"** and enable it.

Then return to the tab **Config → Controller** in the controller and enable the option [**Access Enabled**].

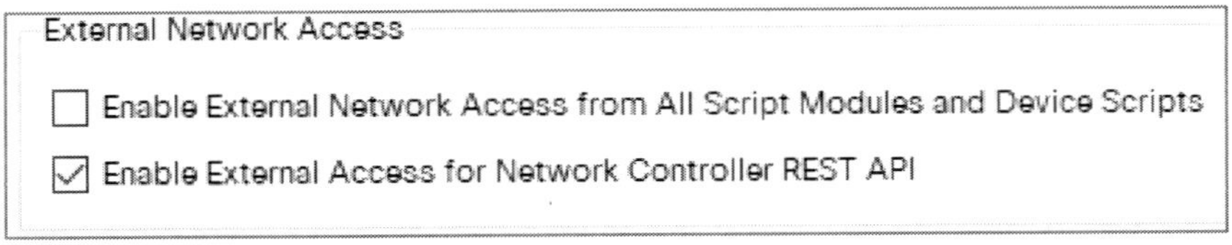

Fig. 6.6 Enable External Network for Network Controller REST API option.

Option	Config → Controller
Access Enabled	YES
HTTP Port	58000
Server Status	Disabled in Preferences/Listening on port 58000

Table 6.4 Parameters for access from the actual network.

An additional option in PT to access the network controller from the actual network is [**Real World Controller Settings**].

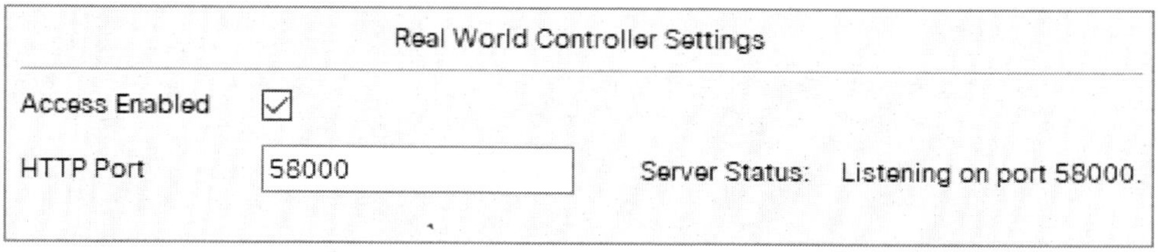

Figure 6.7 Enabling the option [Real World Controller - HTTP Port].

Step 7. Create a master administrator account in the NETCONTROLLER controller.

Username	admin
Password	admin123

Table 6.5 Administrator account details in the controller.

Step 8. Go to the Web Browser in PC0, enter the address 1.1.1.3, create an administrator account.

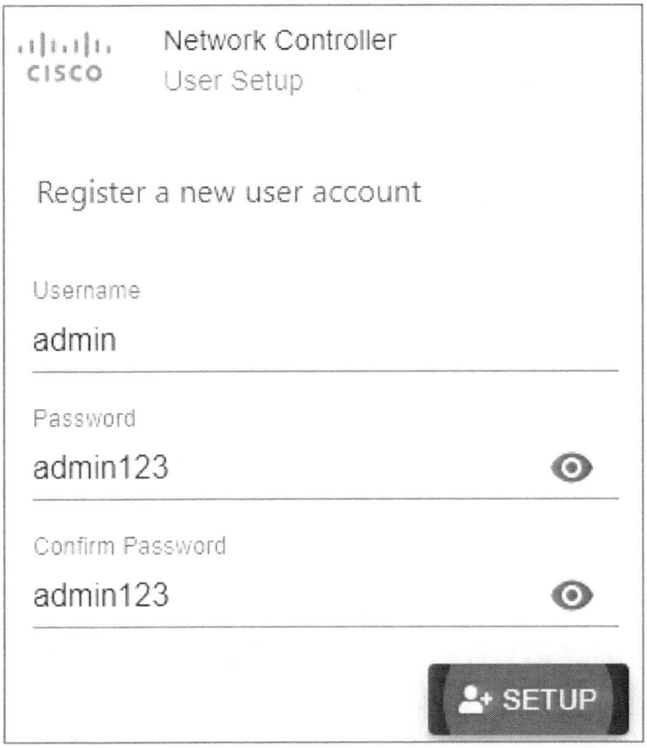

Figure 6.8 Creating an administrator account on the controller.

6.3 CONFIGURATION OF AUTHORIZATION (Exercise 12)

This exercise is a continuation of **exercise 11**. To configure authentication, follow the steps described below.

Step 1. Log in to the administrator account on the **NETCONTROLLER** controller.

Figure 6.9 Login screen for administrator account in controller

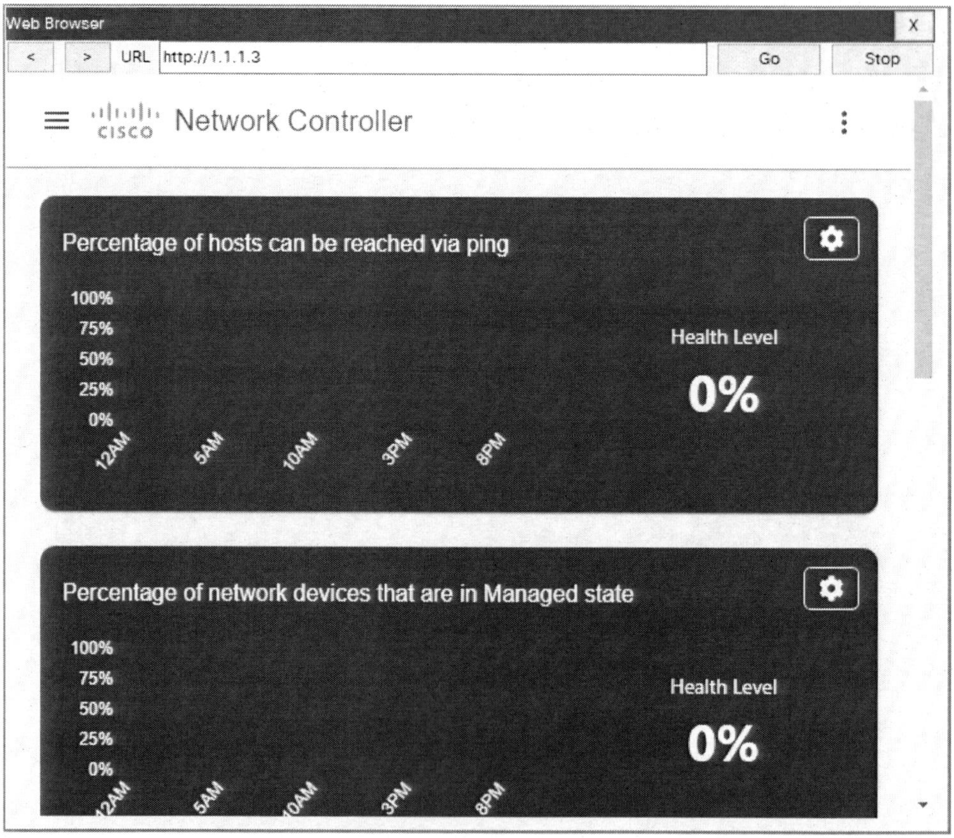

Figure 6.10 The main screen on the controller after logging in

Step 2. Configure global authentication in the controller.

Username	admin
Password	admin123
Enable Password	cisco
Description	AUTHENTICATION

Table 6.6 Global authentication data

Step 3. Go to the main menu and select [**Provisioning**].

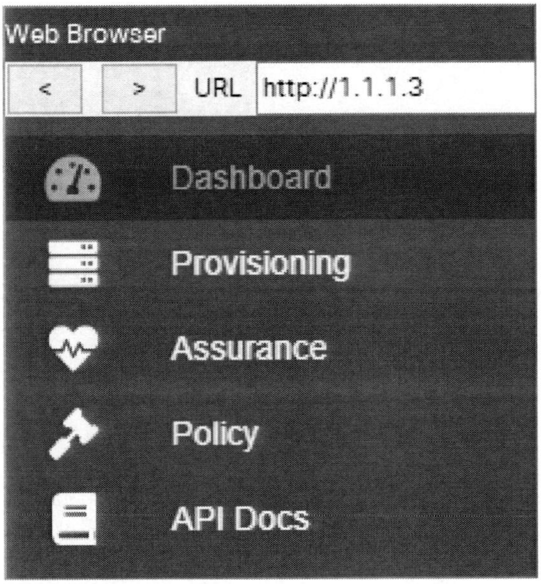

Figure 6.11 Main menu in the controller

Step 4. Next select [**CREDENTIALS**] position.

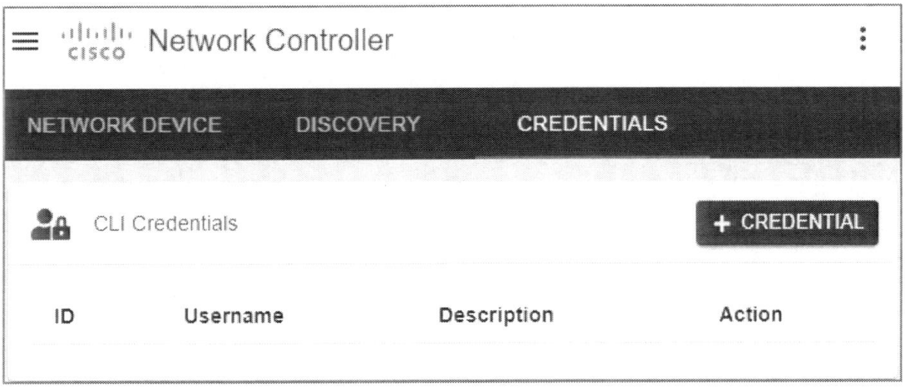

Figure 6.12 Menu [Provisioning-CREDENTIALS]

Step 5. Next click [+**CREDENTIALS**] button.

Step 6. In the dialog box, enter the data and confirm it with the button [**OKEY**].

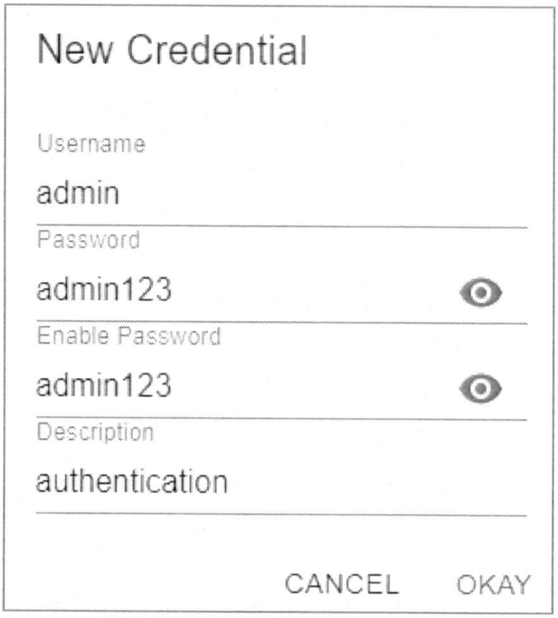

Figure 6.13 Introducing CREDENTIALS authentication data

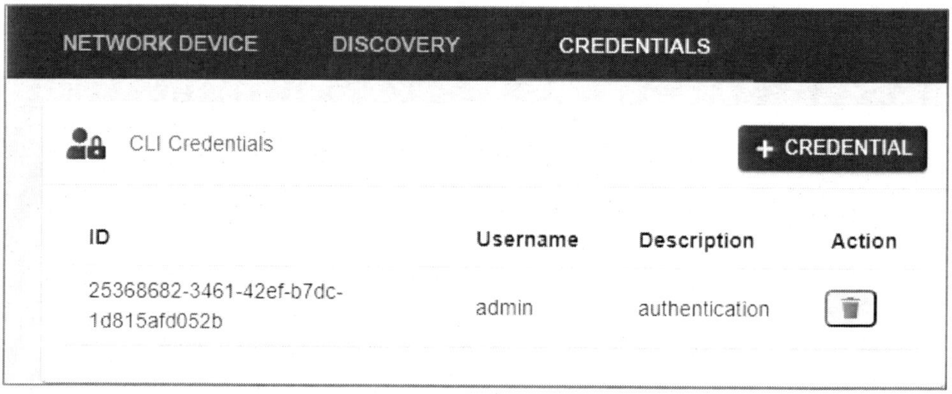

Figure 6.14 CREDENTIALS authentication performed

6.4 IDENTIFICATION OF DEVICES (Exercise 13)

This exercise is a continuation of **exercise 12**. To configure network device recognition and identification, follow the steps described below.

Step 1. On the main menu, select [**Provisioning**].

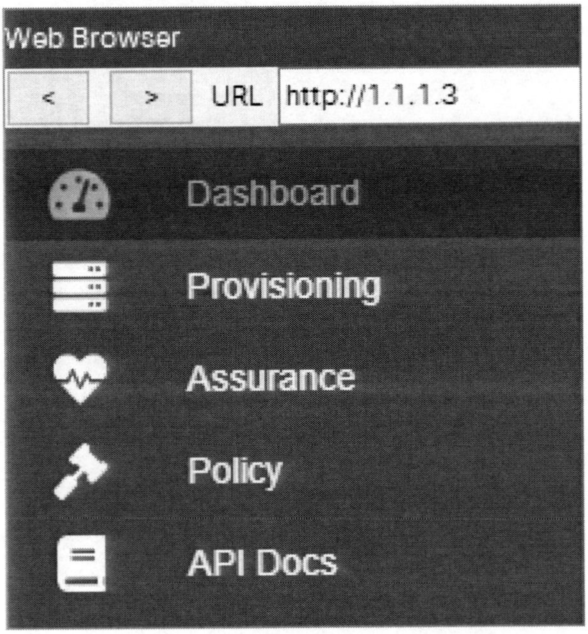

Figure 6.15 Main menu in the controller

Step 2. Select [**DISCOVERY**] position.

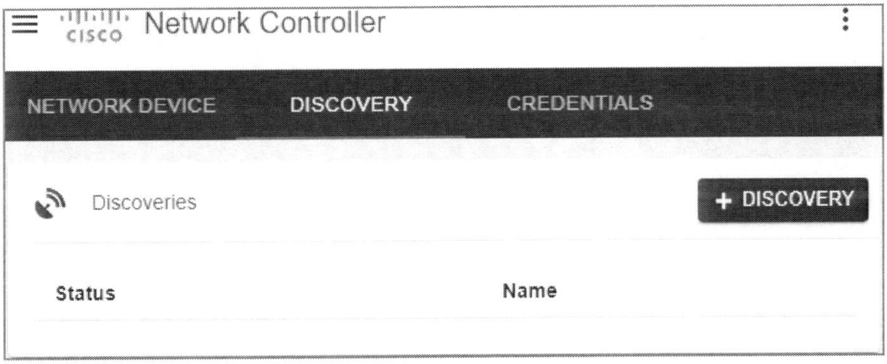

Figure 6.16 [DISCOVERY] position

Step 3. Next click [**+DISCOVERY**] button.

Step 4. Configure search parameters.

Set up a search using **CDP** (Cisco Discovery Protocol) for the devices. Include common parameters according to the following table.

Discovery Type	CDP
Timeout	5
Retry	3

CDP Level	16
CLI Credential List	**admin-authentication**

Table 6.7 Search parameters.

Name	IP Address
RTR1	1.1.1.1
RTR2	172.16.0.2
SW1	1.1.1.253
SWA	192.168.1.253
SWB	192.168.2.253
PC1	192.168.1.1
PC2	192.168.1.2
SVR1	192.168.2.1
SVR2	192.168.2.2

Table 6.8 Additional search data.

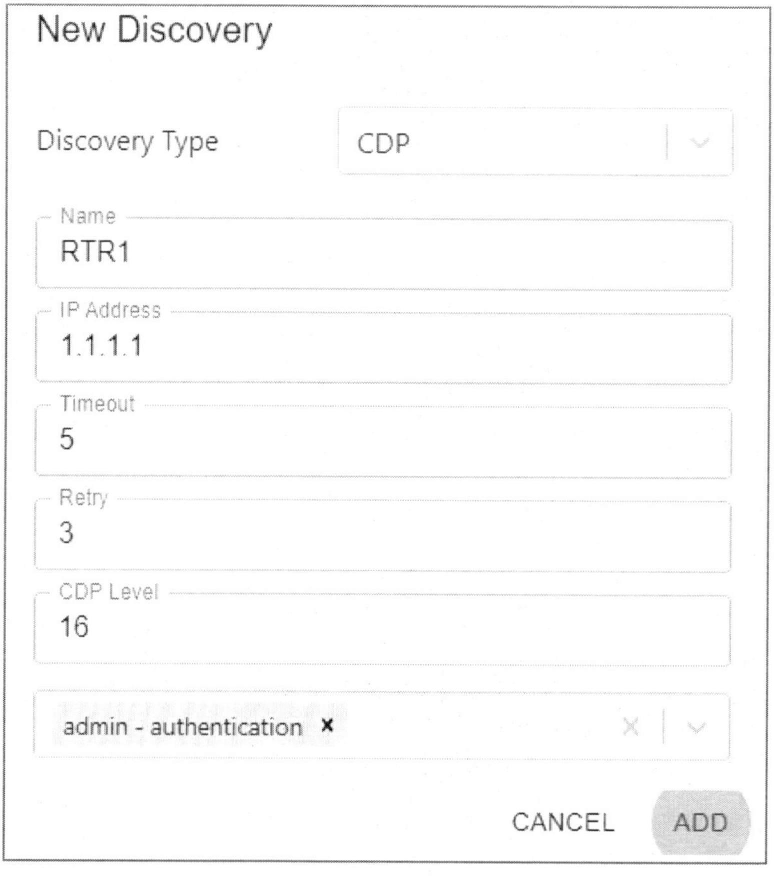

Figure 6.17 Searching for an RTR1 device using CDP

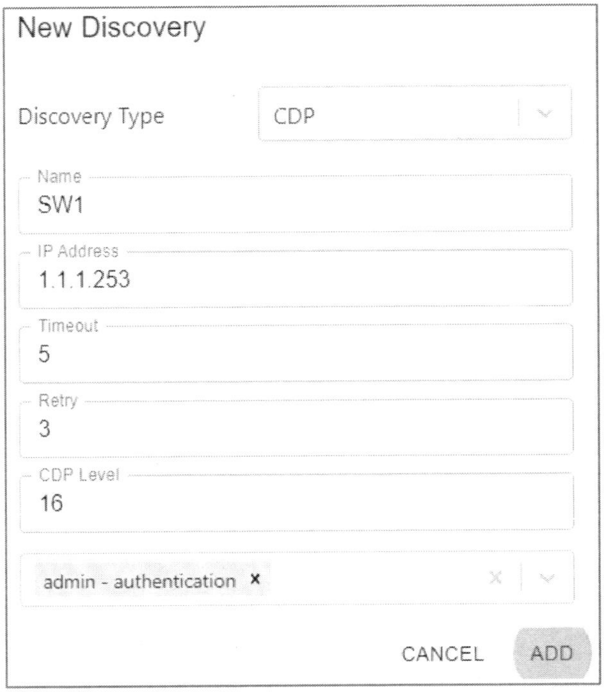

Figure 6.18 Searching for an SW1 device using CDP

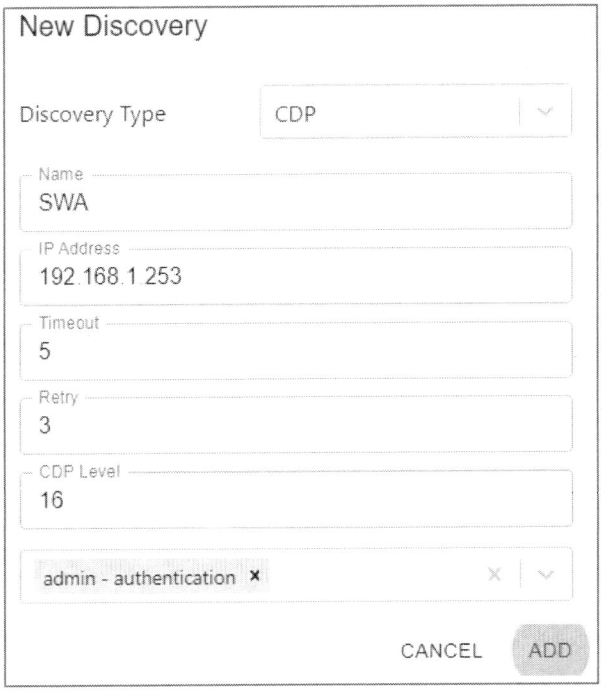

Figure 6.19 Searching for an SWA device using CDP

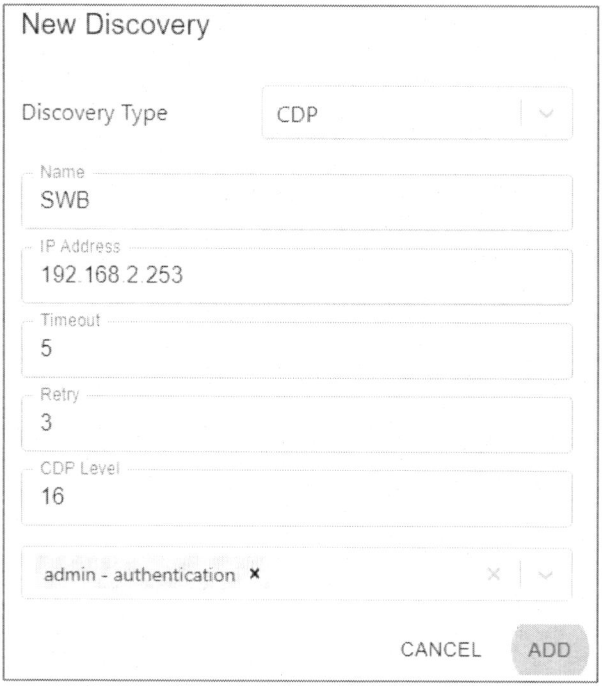

Figure 6.20 Searching for an SWB device using CDP

Figure 6.21 Searching for a PC1 device using CDP

Figure 6.22 Searching for a PC2 device using CDP

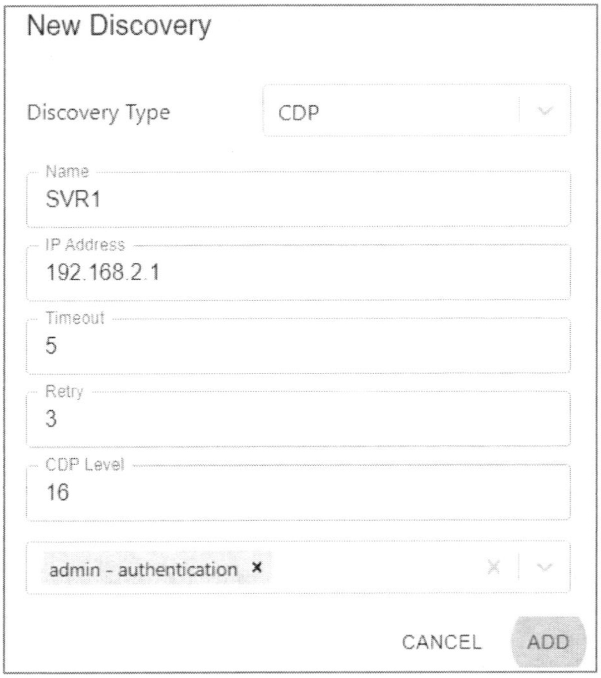

Figure 6.23 Searching for SVR1 device using CDP

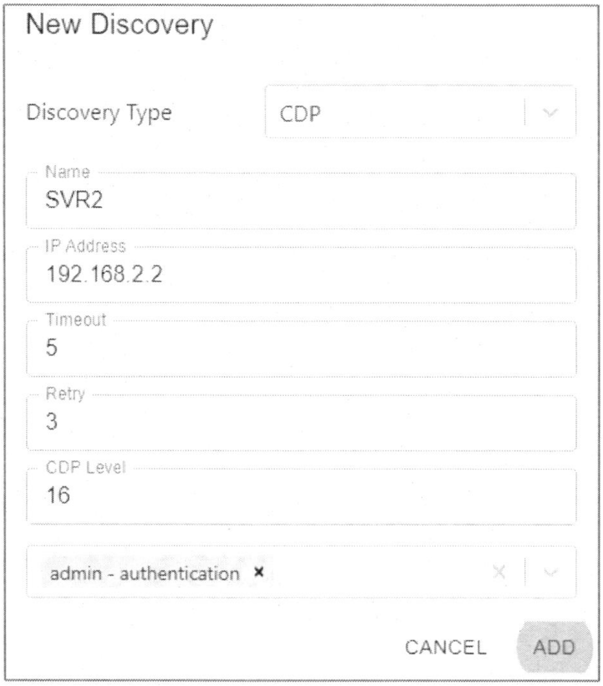

Figure 6.24 Searching for SVR2 device using CDP

Note: You have to wait, sometimes for several minutes, to get the 'Complete' status

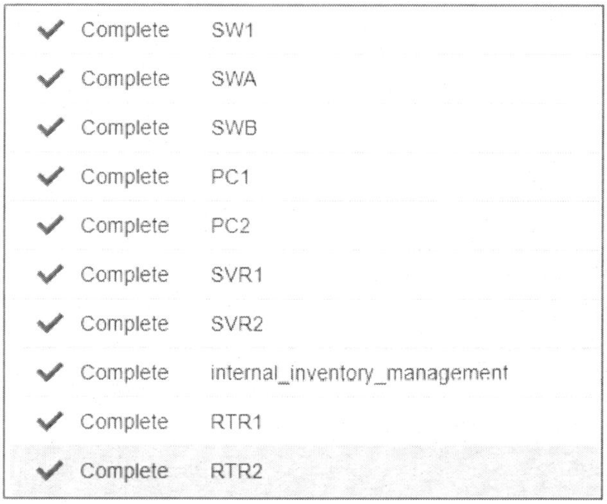

Figure 6.25 Device search result

Step 5. View identified hosts.

From the main menu, select [**Assurance**].

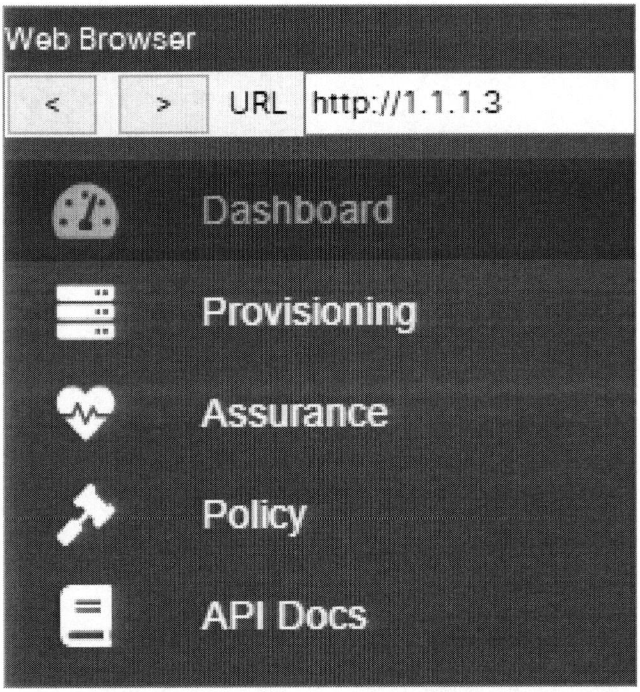

Figure 6.26 Main menu in the controller

Step 6. Select [**HOST**] position.

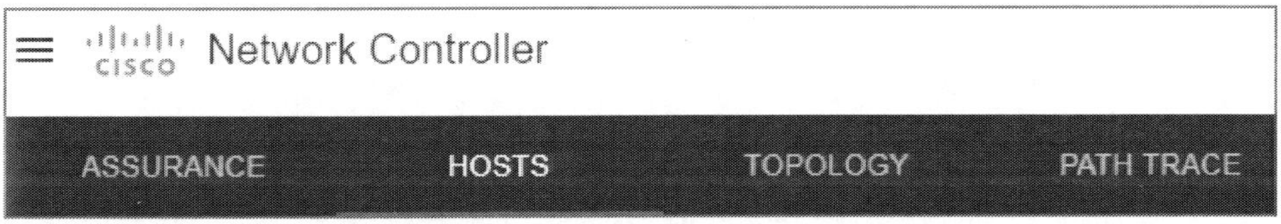

Figure 6.27 Selecting the [HOSTS] item.

Host

Host Device				Connected Network Device		
MAC	IP	Hostname	Type	IP	Hostname	Port
00E0.A313.7D46	1.1.1.2	PC0	Pc	1.1.1.253	SW1	FastEthernet0/1
0060.3E3B.C2D6	192.168.2.1	SVR1	Server	192.168.2.253	SWB	FastEthernet0/2
0001.9783.3BB8	192.168.2.2	SVR2	Server	192.168.2.253	SWB	FastEthernet0/3
00D0.D347.EEB1	192.168.1.1	PC1	Pc	192.168.1.253	SWA	FastEthernet0/2
00D0.BC2D.DC1A	192.168.1.2	PC2	Pc	192.168.1.253	SWA	FastEthernet0/3

Figure 6.28 List of hosts and their connections

Step 7. Select [**HOST**] position.

Step 8. You will find the finished solution in the file **exercise13-network-controller.pkt.** Open it and test the configurations described in the previous steps.

6.5 Displaying the network topology (Exercise 14)

Part 1. Required security features in the equipment

```
enable password cisco
ssh version 2
domain-name ssh.server
username admin password admin123
```

Part 2. Required devices

- PC-PT – 4 pts
- Switch 2960-24TT –2 pts
- Router ISR4331 – 1 pts
- NetworkController –1 pts

Part 3. Network addressing

Device	Model	Interface	IP/Mask	Default gate
NET-CONTROLLER	Network Controller	Gig0	1.0.0.4/8	1.0.0.2
admin	PC-PT	Fa0	1.0.0.1/8	1.0.0.2
SW-admin	2960-24TT	VLAN1	1.0.0.3/8	1.0.0.2
RTR-LAN	ISR4331	Gig0/0/0	1.0.0.2/8	-
RTR-LAN	ISR4331	Gig0/0/1	192.168.1.1/24	-
SW-LAN	2960-24TT	VLAN1	192.168.1.3/24	192.168.1.1
PC4	PC-PT	Fa0	192.168.1.4/24	192.168.1.1
PC5	PC-PT	Fa0	192.168.1.5/24	192.168.1.1
PC6	PC-PT	Fa0	192.168.1.6/24	192.168.1.1

Table 6.9 Managed network addressing.

Version	2
Domain	ssh.server
RSA key length	1024
Username	admin
Password	admin123

Table 6.10 SSH configuration parameters.

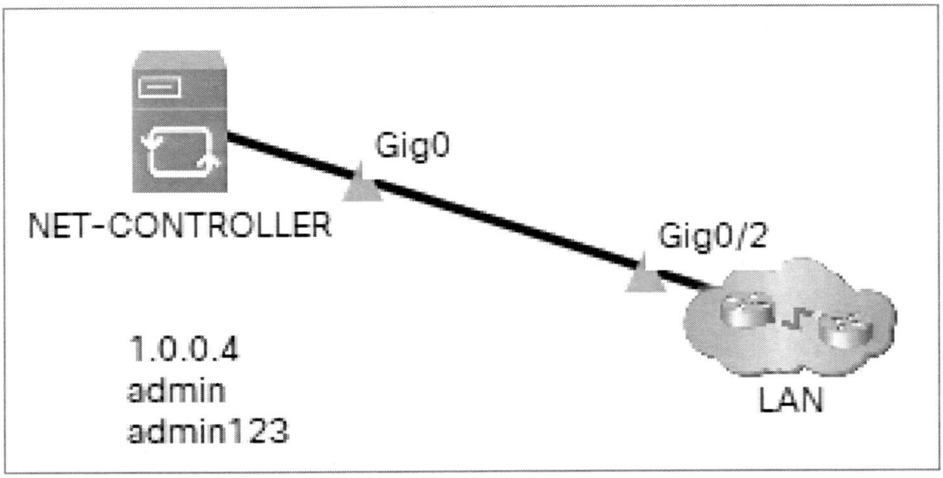

Figure 6.29 Logical topology of a managed network (Exercise 14)

Part 4. Plan of the exercise.

The solution to the exercise can be found in the file **exercise14-network-controller.pkt**.

Step 1. Open the network topology file **exercise14-network-controller.pkt**.

Step 2. From the **admin** computer, log into the network controller (address **1.0.0.4**).

Login: **admin** password : **admin123**

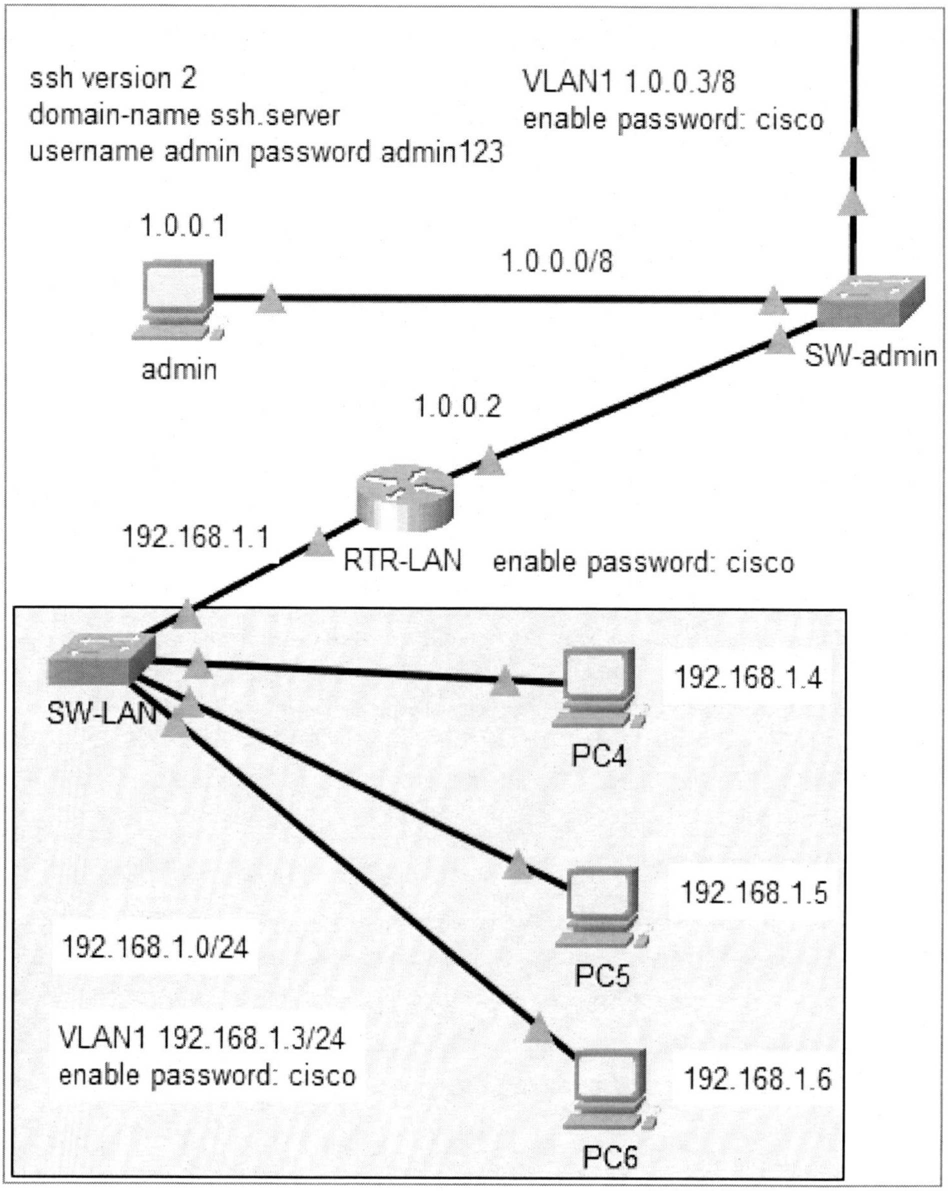

Figure 6.30 LAN topology (Exercise 14)

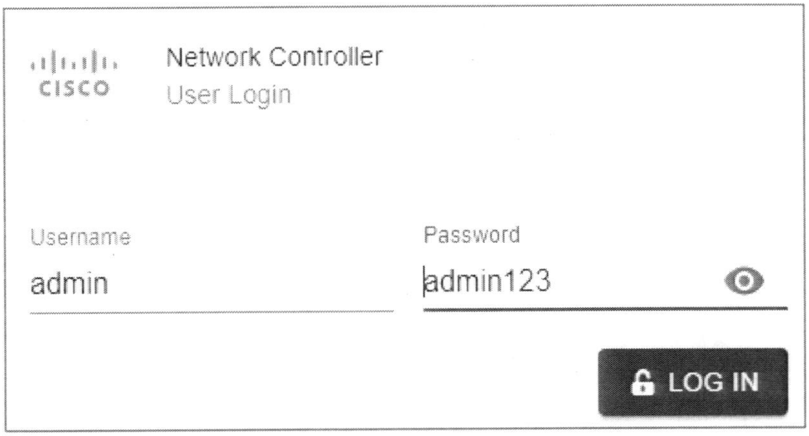

Figure 6.31 Login to the controller

Step 3. To view the topology, select the menu icon.

Figure 6.32 Menu icon in Network Controller

Step 4. Select [**Assurance**] position.

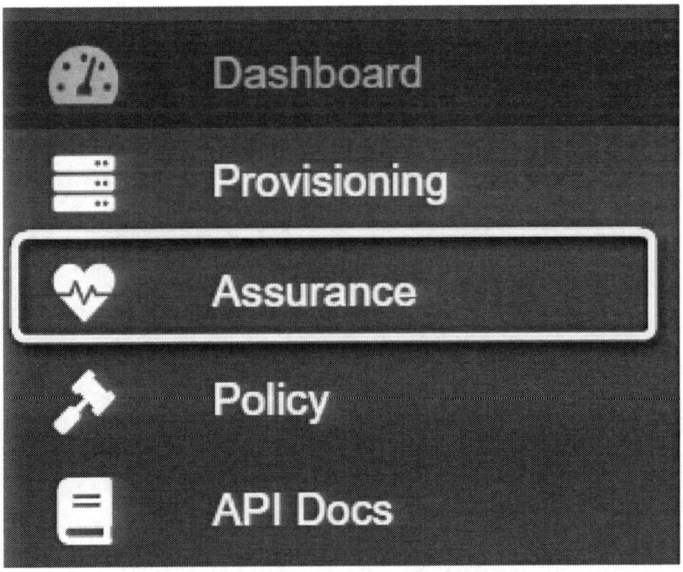

Figure 6.33 Assurance position

Step 5. Select [**TOPOLOGY**] position.

Figure 6.34 TOPOLOGY position

Step 6. Select [**TOPOLOGY**] position.

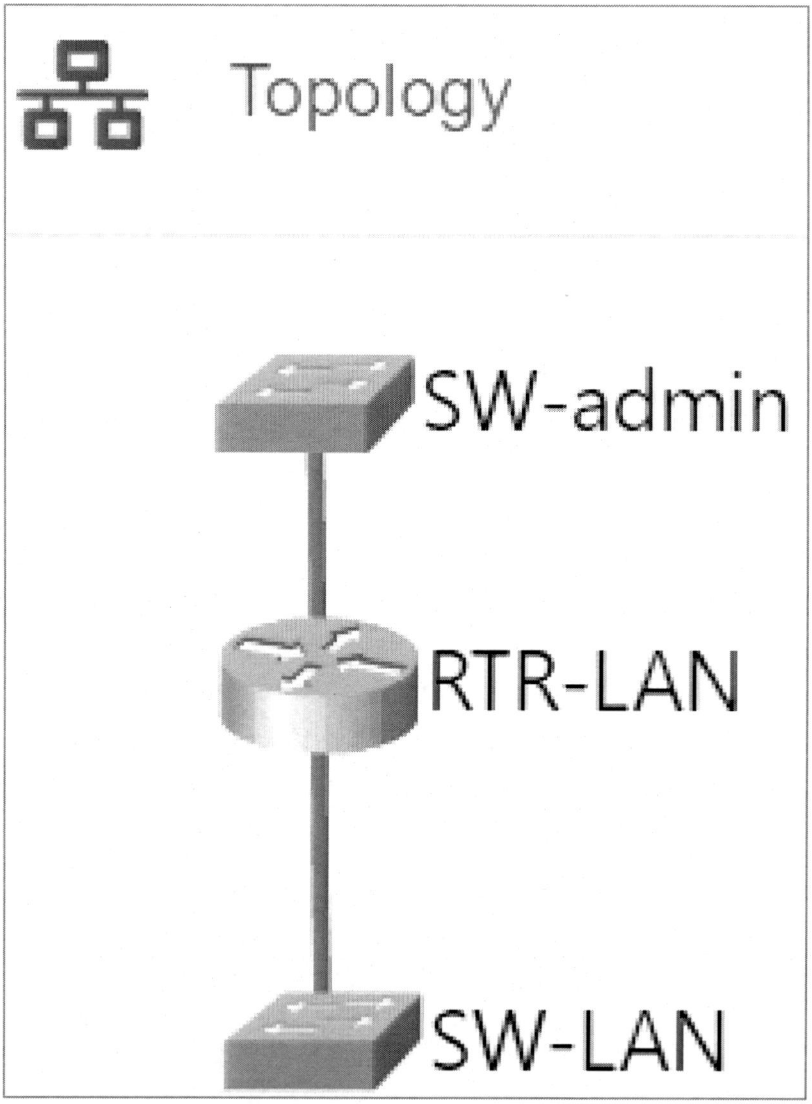

Figure 6.35 Display of network topology

6.6 Accessing the Net Controller from the real network (Exercise 15)

Part 1. Required settings in the controller.

[NET-CONTROLLER]→[Config] → [Controller] → [HTTP Port]

Figure 6.36 Activation of port 58000.

Part 2. Required devices.

- PC-PT – 4 pts
- Switch 2960-24TT – 2 pts
- Router ISR4331 – 1 pts
- NetworkController – 1 pts

Part 3. Plan of the exercise.

Step 1. Open file **exercise15-network-controller.pkt**.

Step 2. When the message appears '**Network Controller External Access**', click [**Yes**].

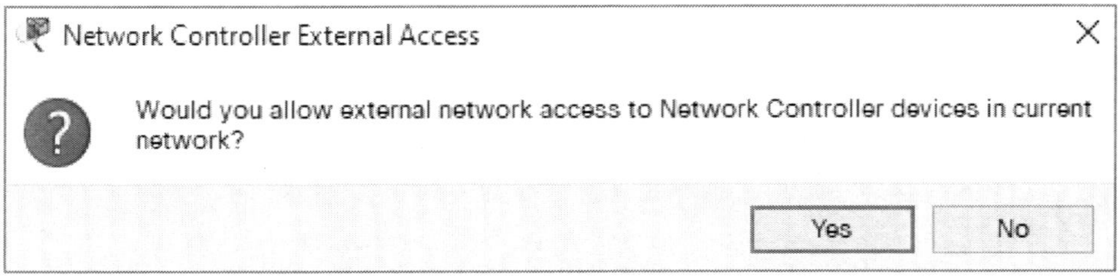

Figure 6.37 Activation of port 58000 - Confirmation

Step 3. Check the following Packet Tracer options:

'Options→Preferences→Miscellaneous→Enable External Network for Network Controller REST API' – turn it on.

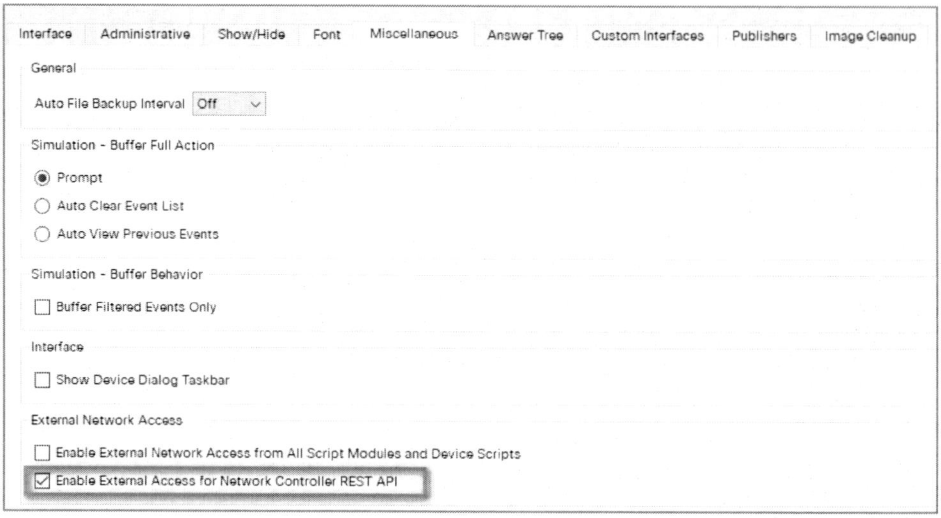

Figure 6.38 Enable External Access for Network Controller REST API

Step 4. Connect from a real IP address (e.g., FireFox browser) to NET CONTROLLER, using port**.**

Start the **Fire Fox** browser and type in the address you are looking for: **http://localhost:58000/**

Figure 6.39 Address line in the browser

Step 5. A login window will appear. Login to NETCONTROLLER.

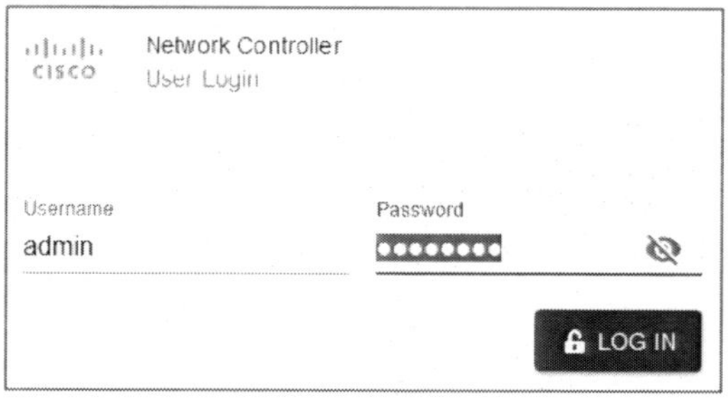

Figure 6.40 Browser login window

Step 6. Go to the main menu and select [**ASSURANCE**]→[**HOSTS**].

Host

	Host Device				Connected Network Device		
	MAC	IP	Hostname	Type	IP	Hostname	Port
⚙	0001.C722.5703	1.0.0.1	admin	Pc	1.0.0.3	SW-admin	FastEthernet0/1
⚙	00E0.B0BE.B47B	192.168.1.4	PC4	Pc	192.168.1.3	SW-LAN	FastEthernet0/1
⚙	0090.2163.7D57	192.168.1.5	PC5	Pc	192.168.1.3	SW-LAN	FastEthernet0/2
⚙	0001.9729.22CA	192.168.1.6	PC6	Pc	192.168.1.3	SW-LAN	FastEthernet0/3

Figure 6.41 The result of selecting [ASSURANCE]→[HOSTS].

Step 7. Go to the main menu and select [**ASSURANCE**]→[**TOPOLOGY**].

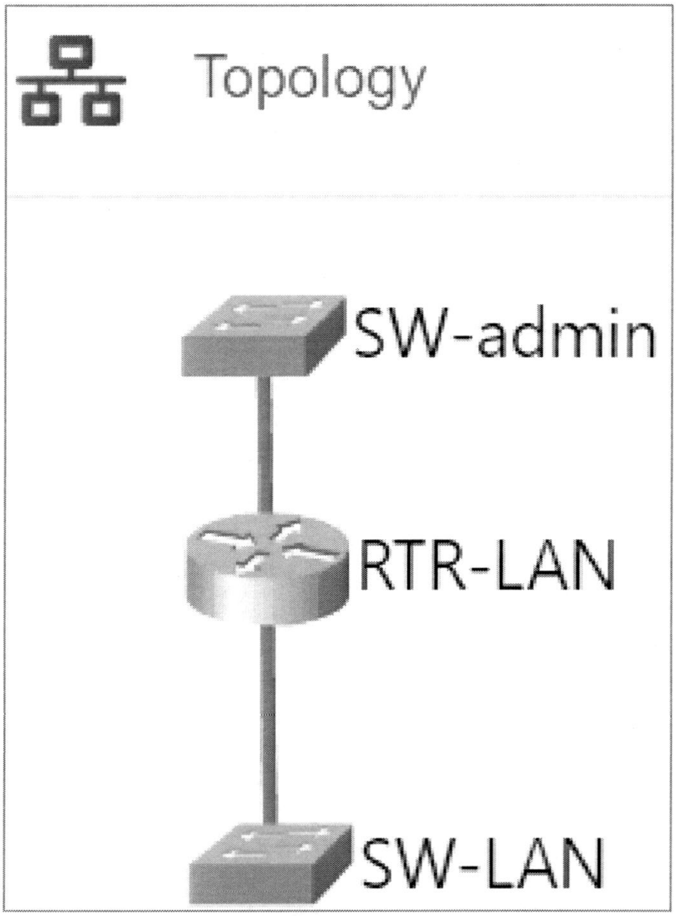

Figure 6.42 The result of selecting [ASSURANCE]→[TOPOLOGY].

6.7 Remote reconfiguration of devices (Exercise 16)

Part 1. Required devices:

- PC-PT – 4 pts
- Switch 2960-24TT – 2 pts
- Router ISR4331 –1 pts
- Network Controller – 1 pts
- Server-PT – 1 pts

Part 2. Network topology.

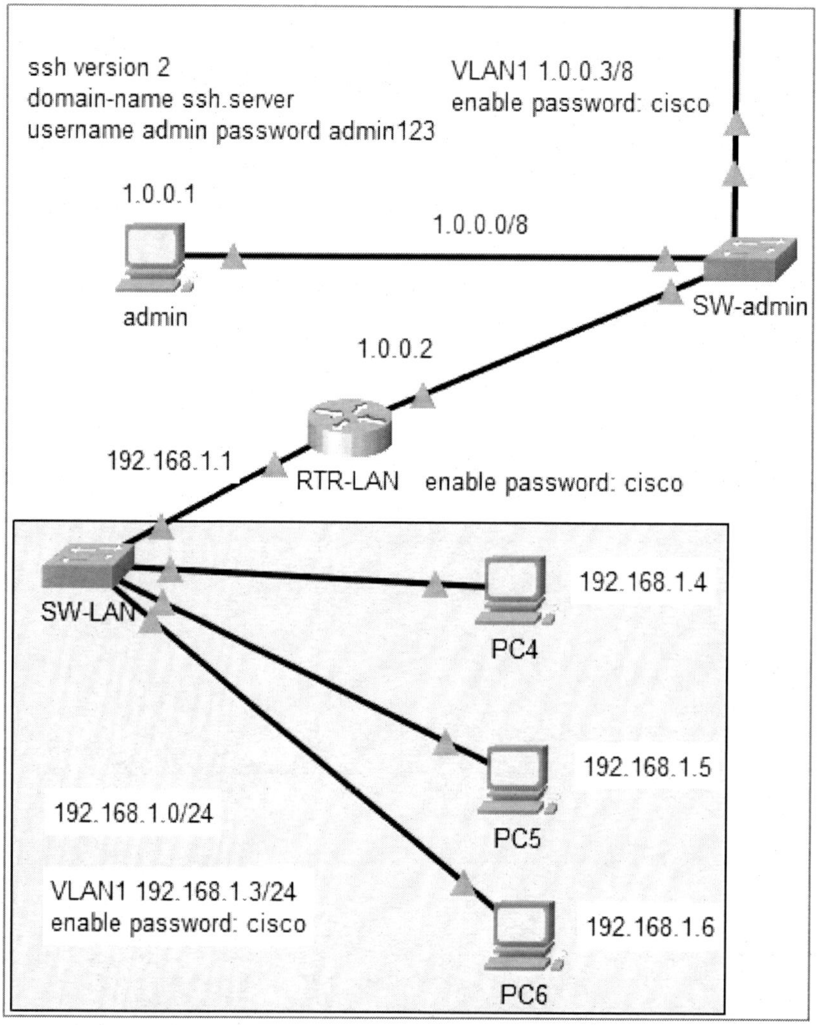

Figure 6.43 Logical topology of a managed network (Exercise 16)

Part 3. Assumptions.

The topology includes a configured DNS and NTP service at **server.com** (address 1.0.0.254).

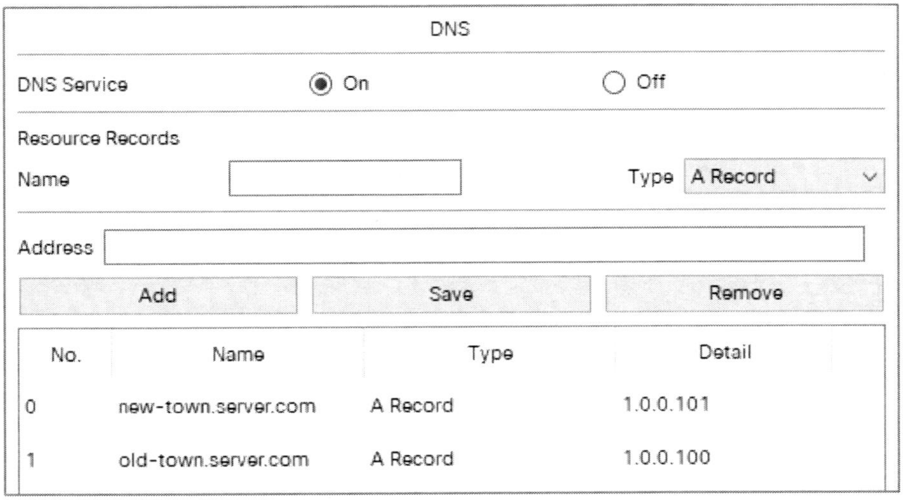

Figure 6.44 Confguration of DNS service at server.com .

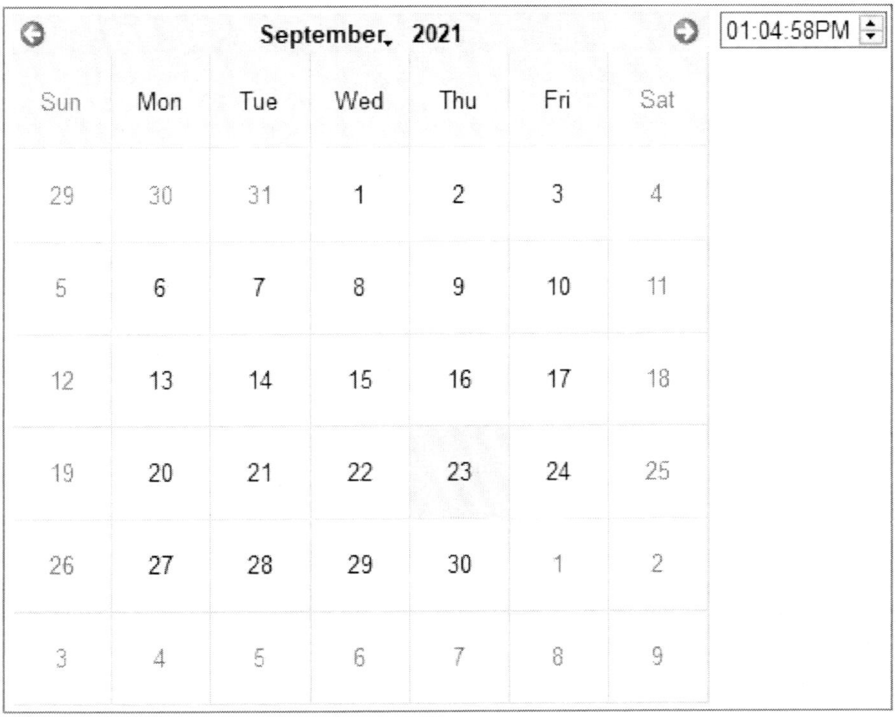

Figure 6.45 Configuration of NTP service at server.com.

Part 4. Plan of the exercise.

Step 1. Open the network topology file **nc-exercise4.pkt.**

Step 2. From the **admin** computer, log into the network controller (address **1.0.0.4**).

Login: **admin** password: **admin123**

Remote configuration modification in devices: SW-admin, SW-LAN, RTR-LAN.

Step 3. Go to the main menu and select [**POLICY**]→[**NETWORK SETTINGS**].

Step 4. Select [**DNS**] position.

Step 5. In the **Domain Name** field, type **'server.com'**. In the **Ip Address** field, type **'1.0.0.254'**. Click the **[SAVE]** button.

Note: This operation is possible only for devices with ISO-XE operating system and for the 2960-24TT switch.

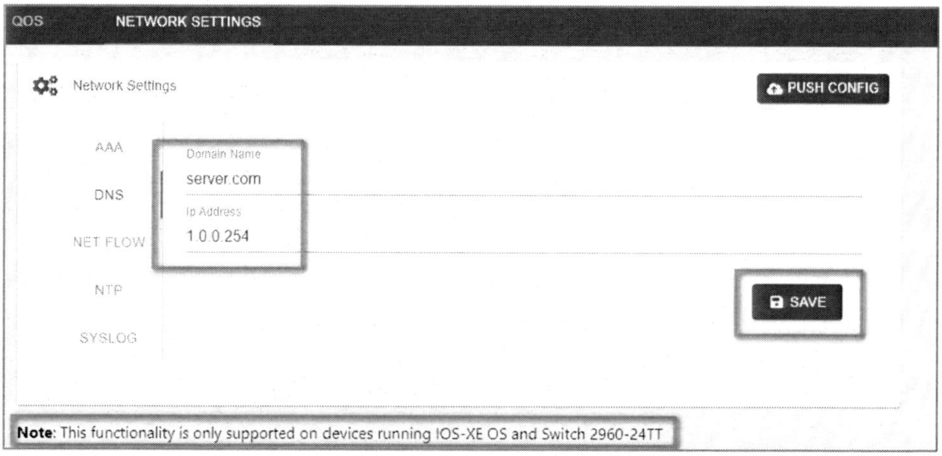

Figure 6.46 Confguration of remote change of device configurations .

Step 6. To execute and approve the remote configuration change, click the [**PUSH CONFIG]** button and then the **[OKEY]** button.

Figure 6.47 Remote change of confguration in devices.

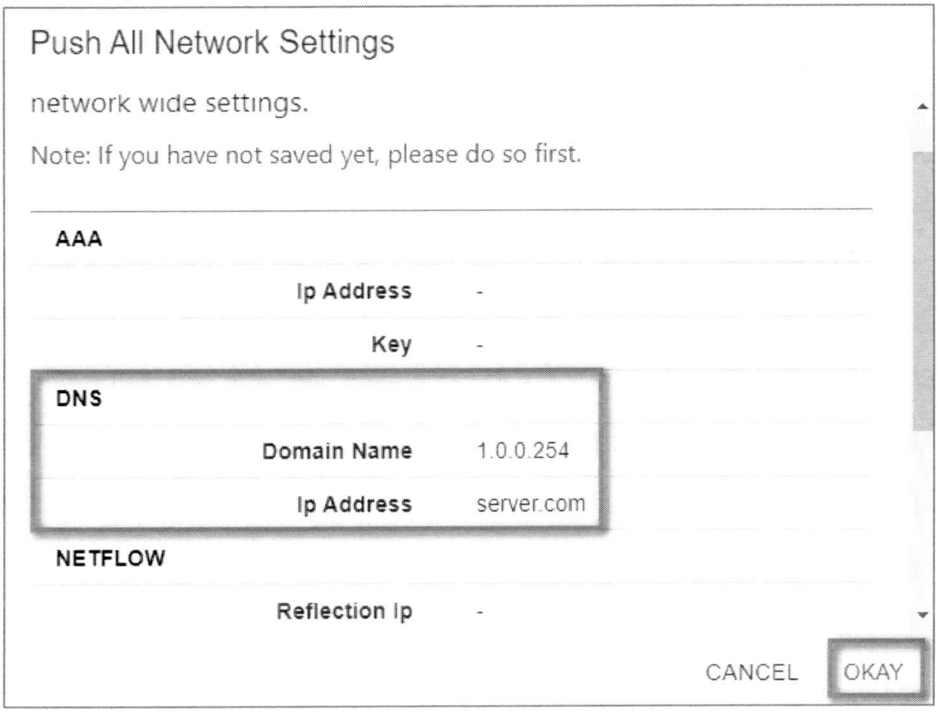

Figure 6.48 Approval of remote confguration change in devices.

Step 7. Go to the main menu and select [**POLICY**]→[**NETWORK SETTINGS**].

Step 8. Select [**NTP**] position.

Step 9. In the **Server Ip** field type **'1.0.0.254'**. Click [**SAVE**] button and then [**PUSH CONFIG**].

Figure 6.49 Remote change of confguration in devices.

Note: This operation is possible only for devices with ISO-XE operating system and for the 2960-24TT switch.

Step 10. To approve the remote configuration change, click the button [**OKEY**].

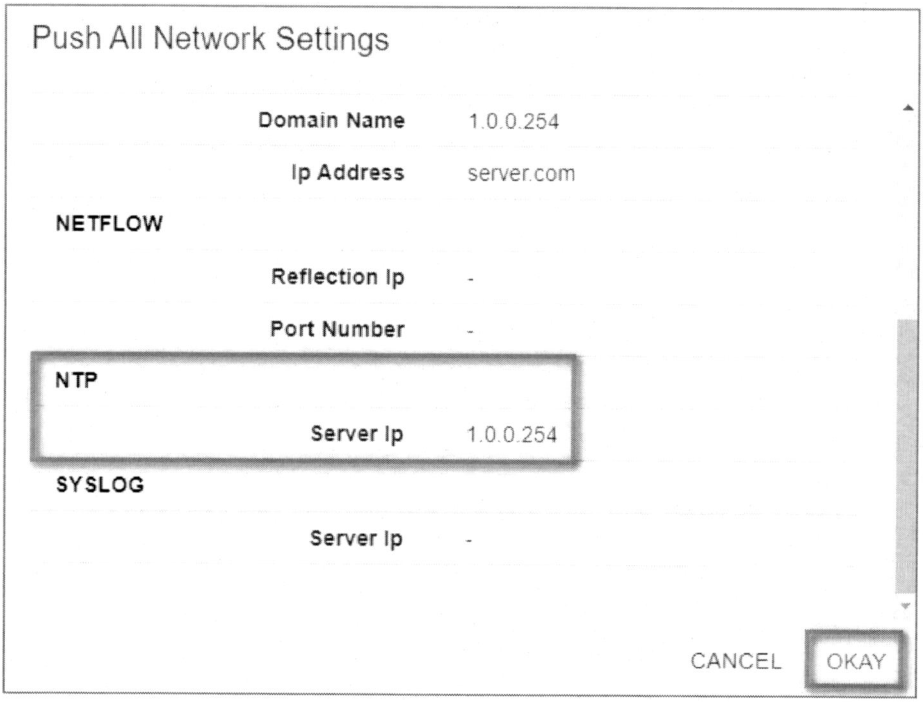

Figure 6.50 Approval of remote confguration change in devices .

Step 11. Check the current configuration in **RTR-LAN**.

Use the command: **`sh r | include ip name-server`**.

```
RTR-LAN#sh r | include ip name-server
ip name-server 1.0.0.254
RTR-LAN#
```

Figure 6.51 Result of the command sh r | ip name-server

Use the command: **`sh r | include ntp`**.

```
RTR-LAN#sh r | include ntp
ntp server 1.0.0.254
RTR-LAN#
```

Figure 6.52 Result of the command sh r | include ntp

You can also check that in the following topology, the device clock times have been synchronized with the time in the **server.com server**.

Figure 6.53 Network topology and remotely managed devices.

6.8 List of auxiliary files

- exercise11-network-controller.pkt
- exercise12-network-controller.pkt
- exercise13-network-controller.pkt
- exercise14-network-controller.pkt
- exercise15-network-controller.pkt
- exercise16-network-controller.pkt

CHAPTER 7

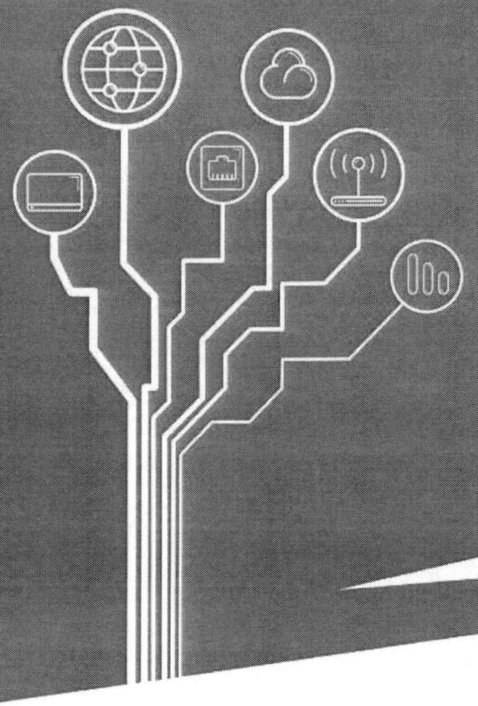

WIRELESS NETWORK CONTROLLERS

COMPUTER NETWORKS IN PACKET TRACER

FOR ADVANCED USERS

7 Wireless Network Controllers

7.1 Description of WLAN and CAPWAP network controllers

Part 1 Brief description of the LAP-PT device

The **LAP-PT** device belongs to the group of wireless access point devices and is used exclusively for WiFi networks. It can configure static addresses, possibly dynamic ones via DHCP: gateway address, DNS address and radio signal access range in meters (**maximum 1000 m**).

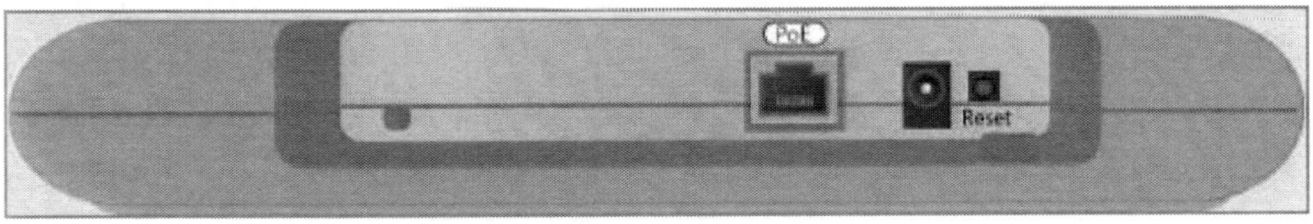

Figure 7.1 View of the LAP-PT device

The device LAP-PT has got:

- **Gigabit Ethernet** port
- **Dot11Radio** module for radio communication.

Part 2. Brief description of 3702i device

It is used to operate the Wi-Fi network in which the **WLC** controllers are located. It can be used to configure the static address of the **WLC (Wireless Controller)**. For the internal network, you can configure the following static addresses, possibly dynamic (via DHCP): gateway address, DNS address and radio signal access range in meters (**maximum 1000 m**).

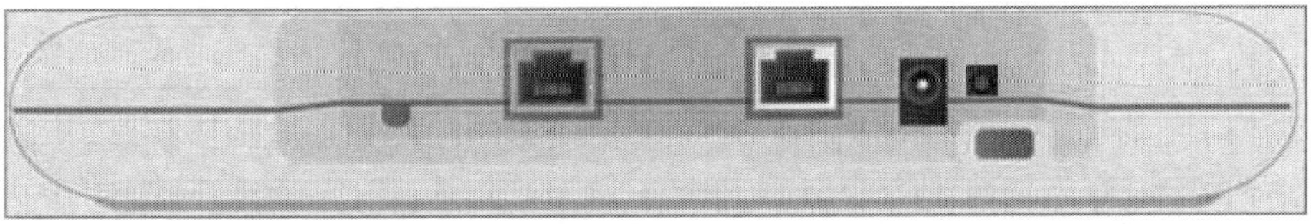

Figure 7.2 View of the 3702i device

The device has got:

- **Gigabit Ethernet** port
- **Dot11Radio** module for radio communication.

Part 3. Brief description of WLC-PT device.

The **WLC-PT** device belongs to a group of wireless access point controller (aka **Wireless LAN Controller**) devices.

Figure 7.3 View of the WLC-PT device

The device is equipped with interfaces and modules:

- **GigabitEthernet0** (without being able to configure it)
- **Management**
- **Dot11Radio** for radio communication
- **Wireless LAN**
- **AP Groups**

For the internal network in the **Management** interface, the following static addresses can be configured: IP address, subnet mask, default gateway address, DNS address.

Wireless LAN module allows you to configure, among other things: authentication type, RADIUS server configuration, encryption type.

The **AP Groups** module allows you to configure, among other things: LAN groups, SSID names belonging to groups.

You can also freely configure the DHCP addressing pool on the device.

The **WLC-2504** device belongs to a group of wireless access point controller (aka **Wireless LAN Controller**) devices, where only the **Management** interface can be configured.

Figure 7.4 View of WLC-2504 device

The device is equipped with:

- 4 interfaces Gigabit Ethernet 1000 Mb/s (**GigabitEthernet0 – GigabitEthernet3**)
- 1 interface **Management** in which the following static addresses can be configured: IP address, subnet mask, default gateway address, DNS address.

Part 5. Brief description of CAPWAP protocol.

CAPWAP (Control And Provisioning of Wireless Access Points protocol) is a protocol for controlling and sharing wireless access points (Access Points).

CAPWAP enables the **WLC**'s central controller to access the wireless WLAN and manage a collection of wireless access points (APs).

The protocol specification is described in RFC 5415. (Calhoun, Montemurro i Stanley, 2022)[3]

For an example WLC configuration, see the document titled "VLANs on Wireless LAN Controllers Configuration Example." (www.cisco.com) [4]

7.2 Configuring access points using WLC-PT (Exercise 17)

This exercise is introductory in nature to the configuration of more advanced WLC-type controllers.

Part 1 Network Topology

[3] Calhoun, Montemurro i Stanley. RFC 5415.
[4] Cisco. VLANs on Wireless LAN Controllers Configuration Example.

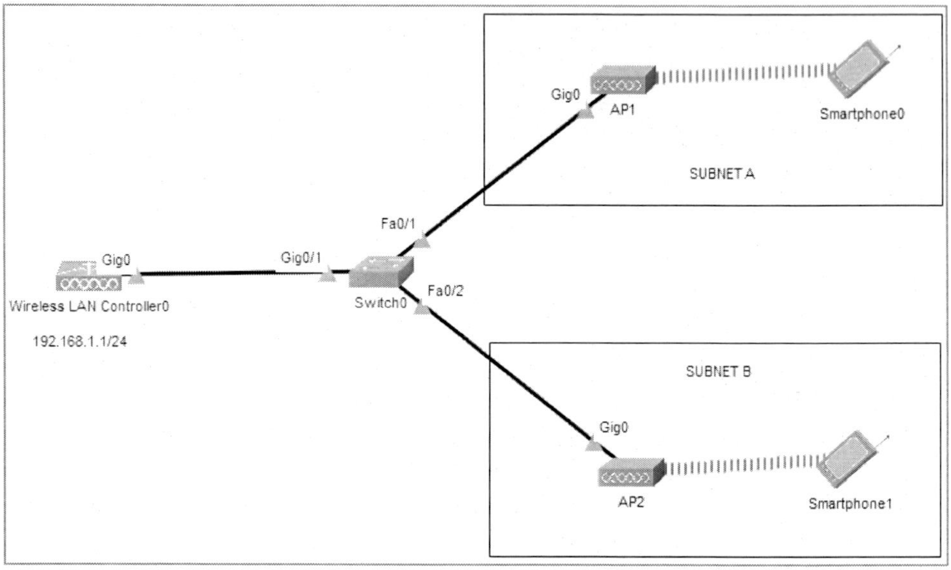

Figure 7.5 Logical topology of the WLC-PT network

Part 2. Assumptions.

Wireless LAN Controler0 controller's address: 192.168.1.1/24

Default gate: 192.168.1.1

Light Weight Access Point0 serves subnet A where Smartphone0 is located.

Light Weight Access Point1 serves subnet B in which Smartphone1 is located.

Part 3. Plan of the exercise.

Step 1. Create a topology according to the figure.

Step 2. Connect the power supply (ACCCESS_ POINT_POWER_ADAPTER module) to both acccss points.

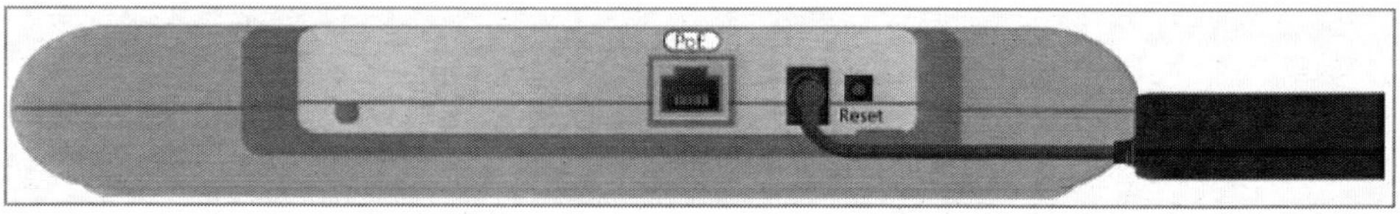

Figure 7.6 Connecting power to the access point

Step 3. Rename the access points to AP1 and AP2, respectively.

Figure 7.7 Changing the name of the AP1 access point

Figure 7.8 Changing the name of the AP2 access point

Step 4. Configure IP addressing for **Wireless LAN Controler0**.

Go to [**Config→INTERFACE→Management**] and set the appropriate addressing.

The DNS server address in this exercise is not required because in this topology the DNS server does not exist.

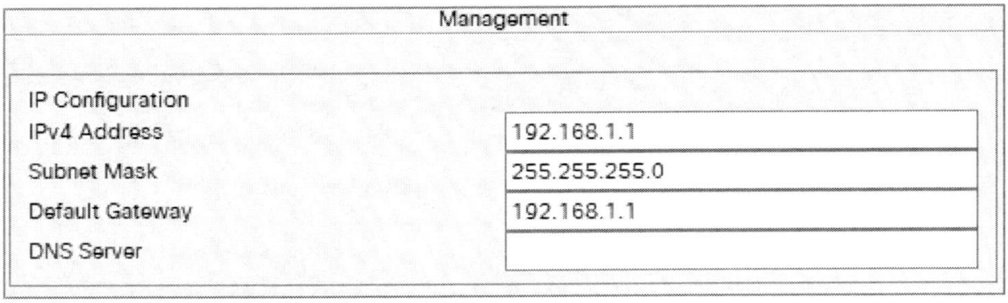

Figure 7.9 Addressing the Management interface in the WLC

Step 5. Add and configure the first subnet in the wireless subnet database.

Go to [**Config→Wireless LANs**] and insert the first subnet (A).

Set the appropriate fields for the subnet A:

- Name: **netA**
- SSID: **FIRST**
- VLAN: **0**
- Authentication: **Disable**

Next, use the [**Save**] button.

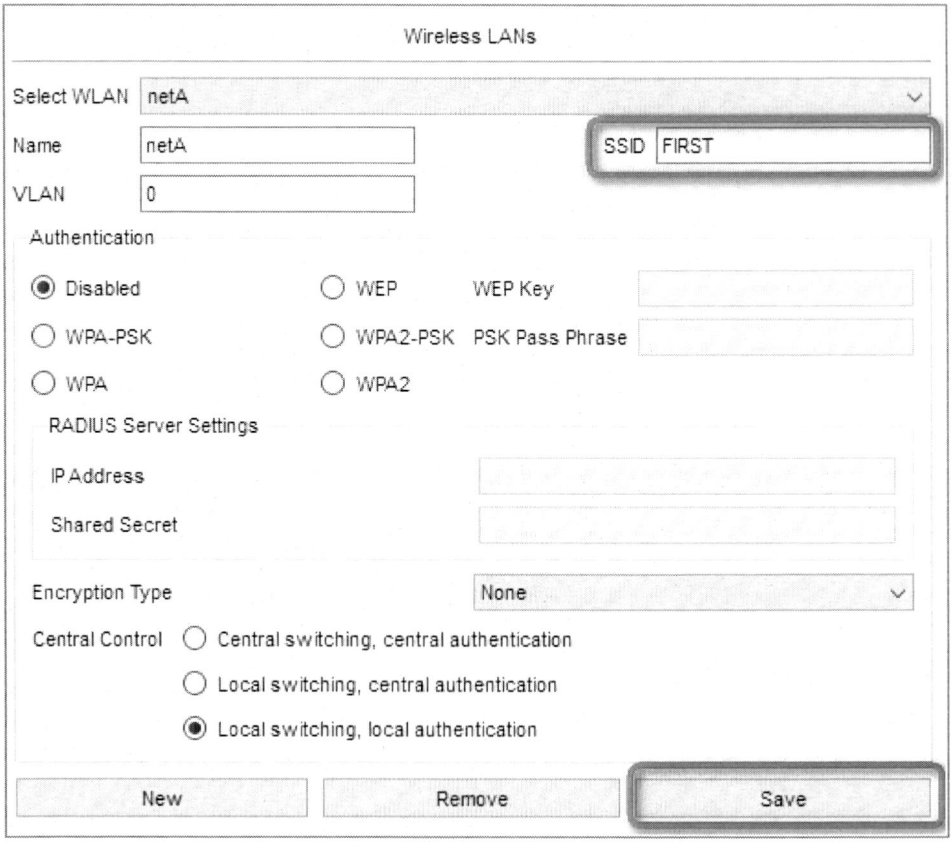

Figure 7.10 Adding the first subnet in the WLC

Step 6. Add and configure a second subnet in the wireless subnet database.

Click [**New**] button to insert the second subnet (B).

Figure 7.11 Adding the second subnet in the WLC

Set the appropriate fields for the subnet B:

- Name: **netB**
- SSID: **SECOND**
- VLAN: **0**
- Authentication: **Disable**

Next, use the [**Save**] button.

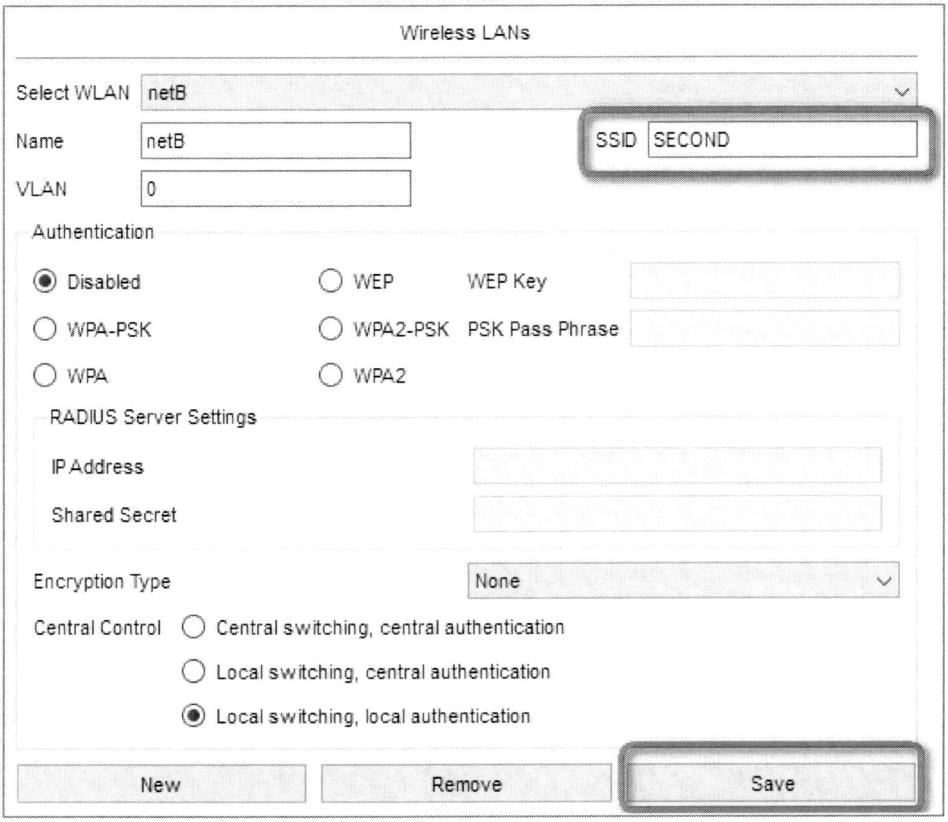

Figure 7.12 Configuring a second subnet in the WLC

Step 7. Configure the DHCP service pool.

Go to [**Config→ DHCP**] and insert the first subnet (A).

Set the appropriate fields:

- Pool Name: **WLC-POOL**
- Default Gateway: **192.1681.1.1**
- Start IP Address: **192.168.1.200**
- Subnet Mask: **255.255.255.0**
- Maximum Number of Users: **50**
- WLC Address: **192.1681.1.1**

NOTE: In the DNS Server field, enter any IP address.

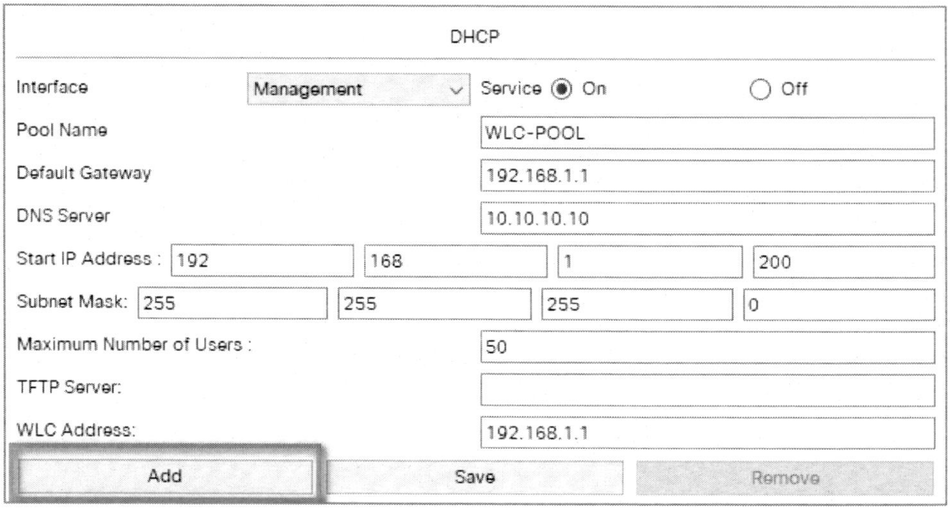

Figure 7.13 Configuring a DHCP pool in the WLC

Click [**Add**] button.

The DHCP service in the WLC has been configured.

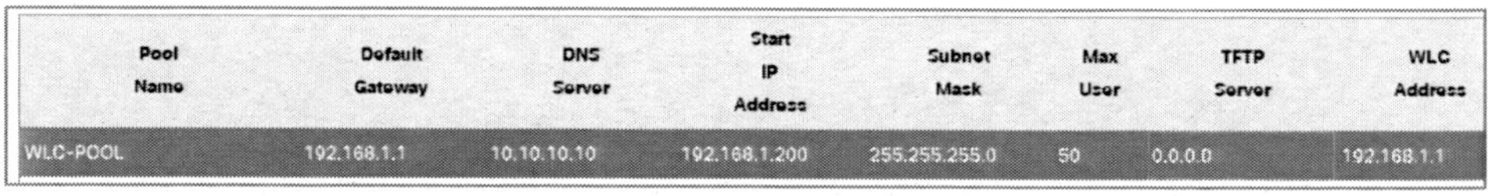

Pool Name	Default Gateway	DNS Server	Start IP Address	Subnet Mask	Max User	TFTP Server	WLC Address
WLC-POOL	192.168.1.1	10.10.10.10	192.168.1.200	255.255.255.0	50	0.0.0.0	192.168.1.1

Figure 7.14 Parameters of DHCP service in WLC

Step 8. Check the current parameters of the wireless subnet group.

Go to [**Config→AP Groups**].

Figure 7.15 Current default-group parameters in the WLC

Step 9. Create a new wireless subnet group **GROUP1** and associate only the **netA** subnet and **AP1** access point with it.

Go to [**Config→AP Groups**] and click [**New**] button.

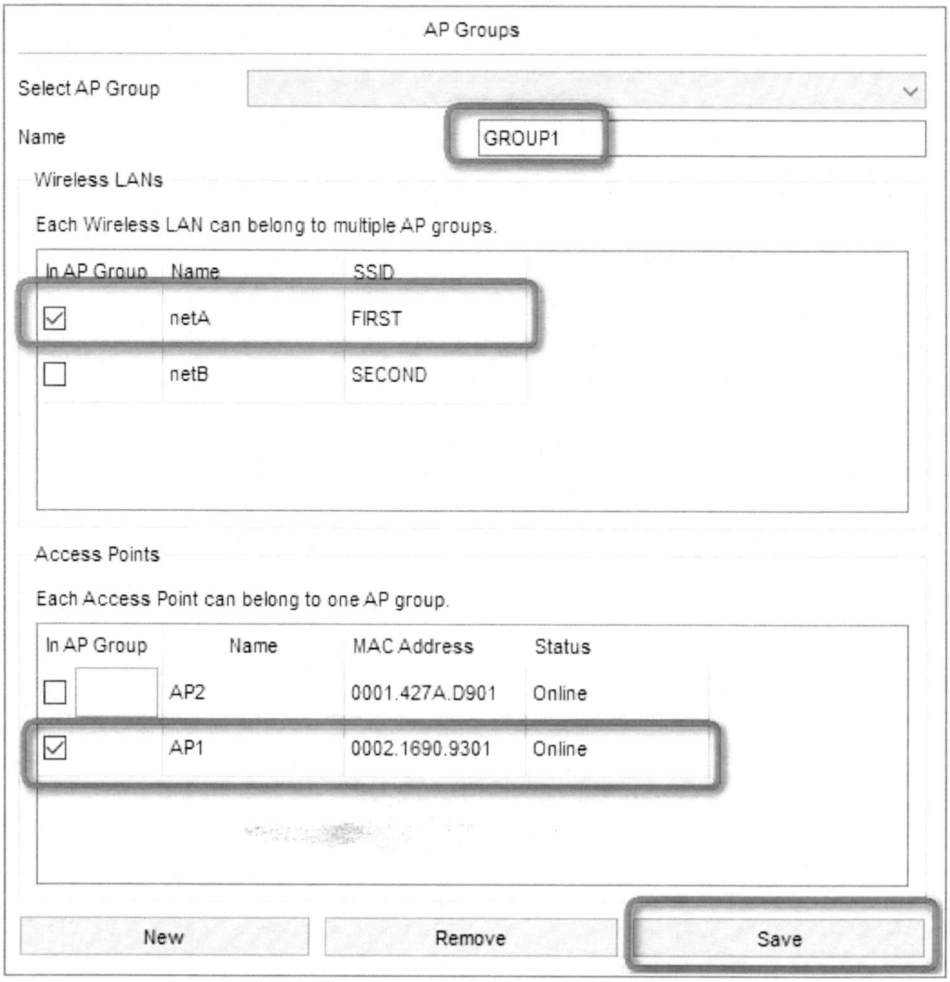

Figure 7.16 Creating a new GROUP1 in WLC

Select the appropriate options and click the [**Save**] button.

Step 10 Create a new wireless subnet **GROUP2** and associate only the **netB** subnet and **AP2** access point with it.

Go to [**Config→AP Groups**] and click [**New**] button.

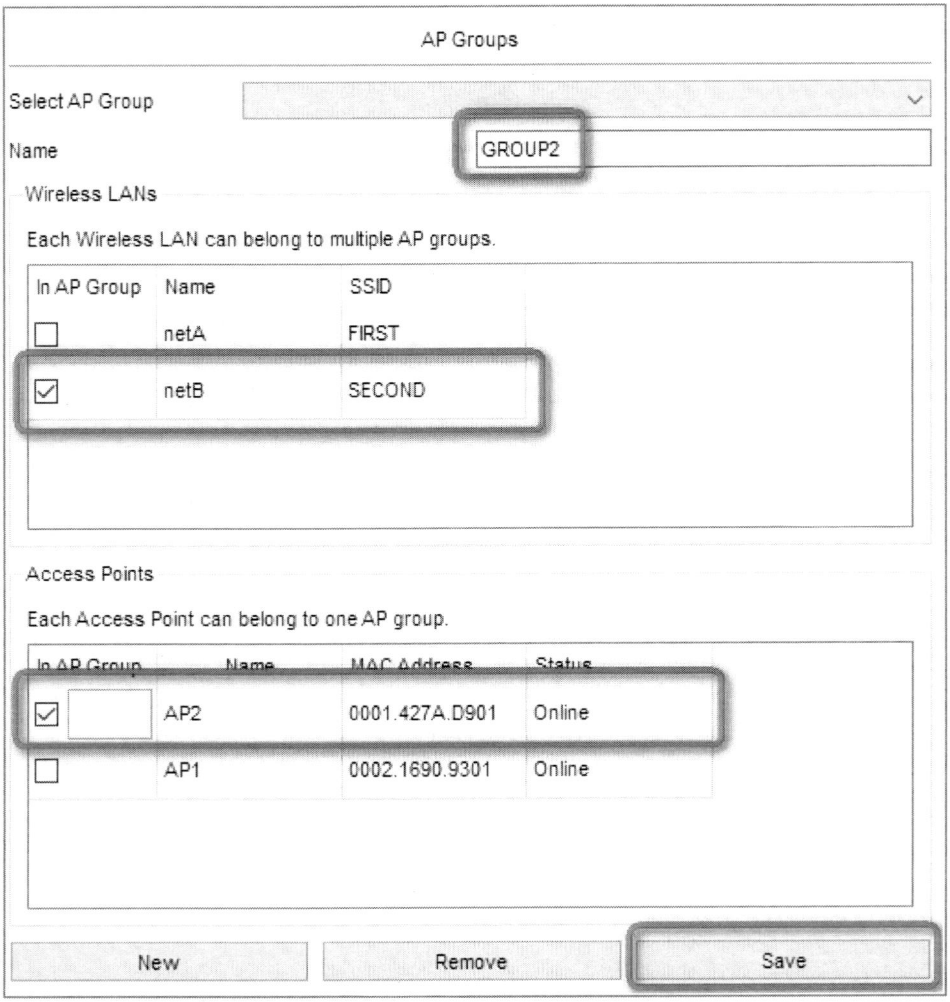

Figure 7.17 Creating a new GROUP2 in WLC

Select the appropriate options and click [**Save**].

Step 11. Configure the operating parameters of the wireless card in the **Smartphone0**.

Go to [**Config→INTERFACE→Wireless0**].

In the **SSID** field insert name **FIRST**.

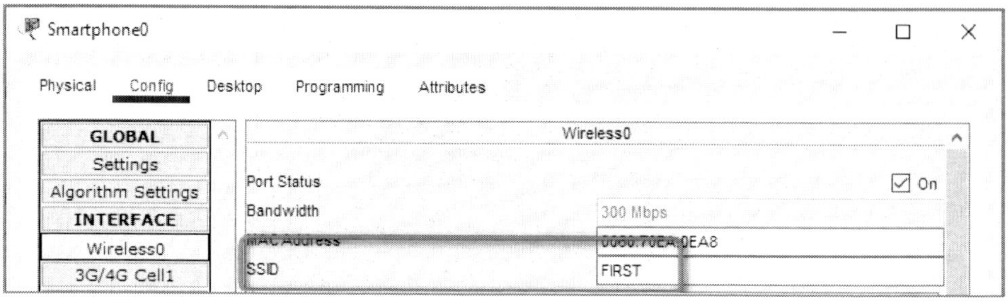

Figure 7.18 Parameters of the wireless card in Smartphone0

Step 12. Configure the operating parameters of the wireless card in **Smartphone1**.

Go to [**Config→INTERFACE→Wireless0**].

In the **SSID** field insert name **SECOND**.

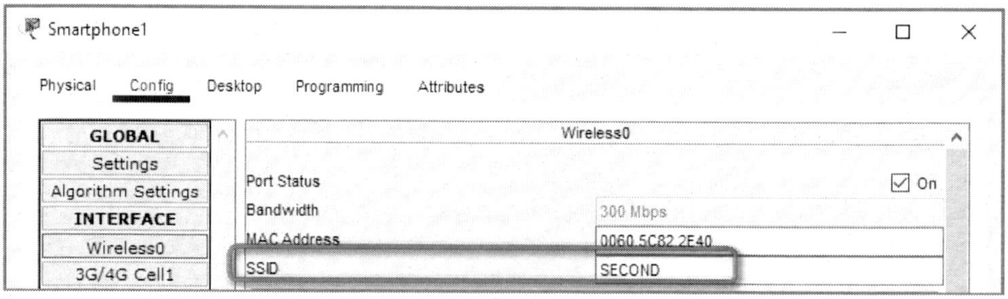

Figure 7.19 Parameters of wireless card in Smartphone1

NOTE: On both devices: **Smartphone0** and **Smartphone1,** on the wireless interfaces, DHCP must be set.

Step 13. Check which access points the devices have connected to: **Smartphone0** and **Smartphone1**.

Part 4. Resulting topology

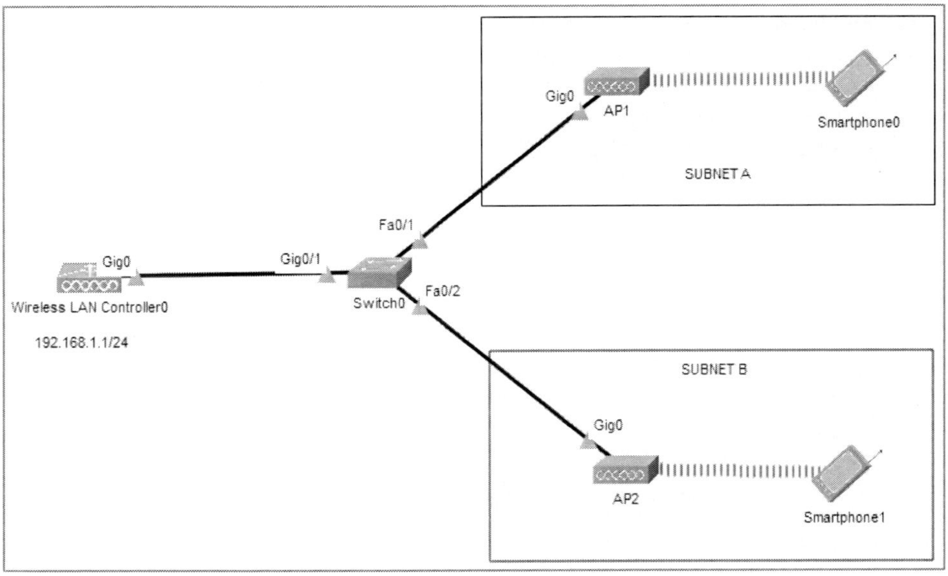

Figure 7.20 Resulting logical network topology

7.3 Managing local networks with WLC-PT (Exercise 18)

Part 1. Introduction and assumptions for wireless network design.

This exercise is an expanded version of the previous exercise. The exercise integrates logical topology configuration activities with physical topology creation.

Files required for physical topology:

- biology.jpg
- biotechnology.png
- building.png
- campus.png

and for logical topology:

- www.institute.com-index.html
- biology.html
- biotechnology.html
- biology.jpg
- biotechnology.jpg

Required equipment:

- WLC-PT controller – 1 pts
- Router 1941 – 1 pts
- Switch 2960 – 1 pts
- Switch 3560-24PS – 1 pts
- Access point LAP-PT – 2 pts
- PC-PT computer equipped with the card Linksys-WMP300N – 4 pts
- Server-PT – 1 pts

Part 2. General assumptions.

- PC0, PC1 computers are located in the Biology Department building,
- Biology-AP access point is located in the server room of the Biology Department building,
- Biotechnology-AP access point is located in the building of the Department of Biotechnology,
- PC2, PC3 are located in the Biotechnology Department building,

with the following conditions:

- PC0, PC2 are assigned to network ID1 and VLAN 10,
- PC1, PC3 are assigned to ID2 network and VLAN 20,

In the WLC controller, networks ID1 and ID2 are assigned to a group named **default-group.**

Part 3. Logical topology.

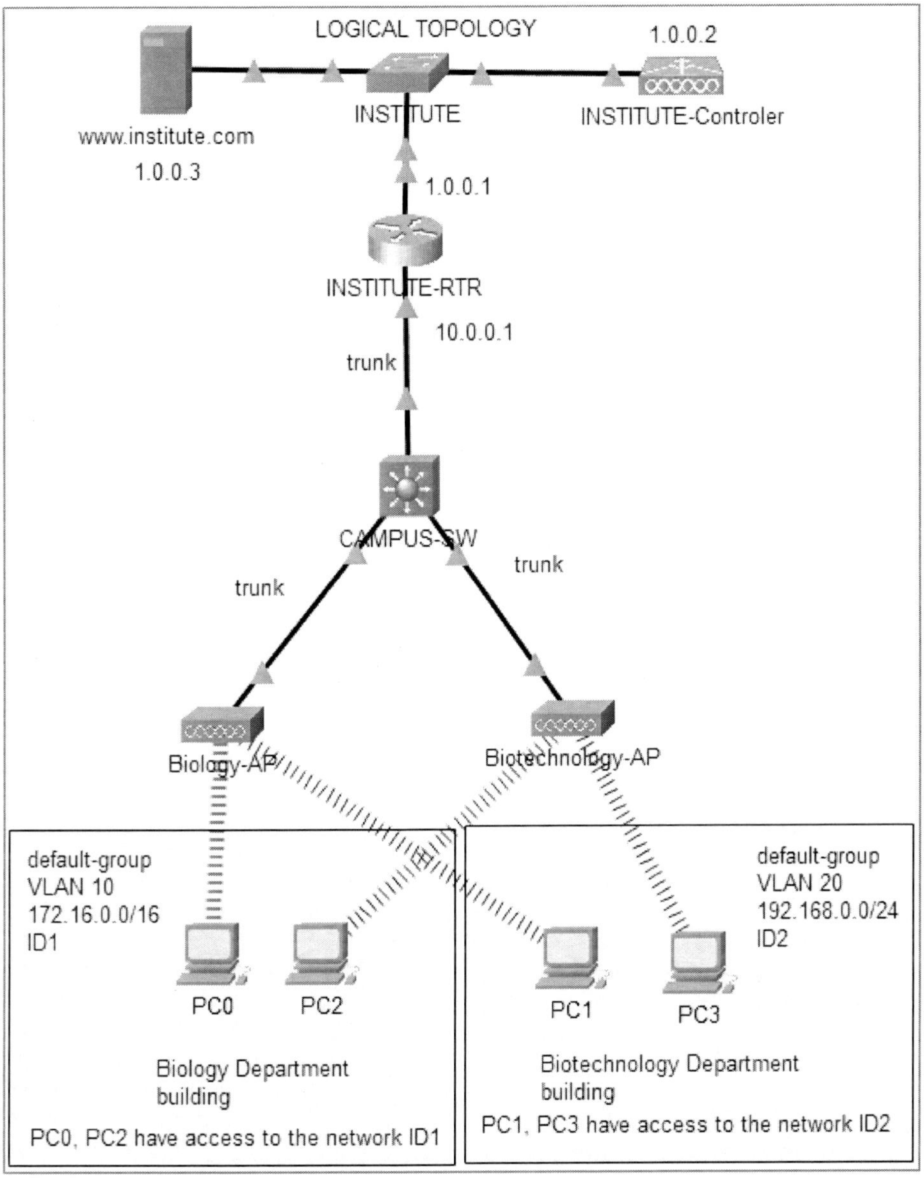

Figure 7.21 Logical topology of the network

DEVICE	INTERFACE	IP	MASK	GATE	VLAN
INSTITUTE-Controller	Management	1.0.0.2	255.0.0.0	1.0.0.1	*)
www.institute.com-index.html	Fa0	1.0.0.3	255.0.0.0	1.0.0.1	*)
INSTITUTE-	Gi0/0	10.0.0.1	255.0.0.0	*)	*)

RTR					
INSTITUTE-RTR	Gi0/0.10	172.16.0.1	255.255.0.0	*)	10
INSTITUTE-RTR	Gi0/0.20	192.168.0.1	255.255.255.0	*)	20
INSTITUTE-RTR	Gi0/1	1.0.0.1	255.0.0.0	*)	*)
CAMPUS-SW	Gi0/2	*)	*)	*)	Trunk
CAMPUS-SW	Fa0/1	*)	*)	*)	Trunk
CAMPUS-SW	Fa0/2	*)	*)	*)	Trunk
Biology-AP	Gi0	DHCP	255.0.0.0	10.0.0.1	10,20
Biotechnology-AP	Gi0	DHCP	255.0.0.0	10.0.0.1	10,20
PC0	Wireless0	DHCP	255.255.0.0	172.16.0.1	10
PC1	Wireless0	DHCP	255.255.255.0	192.168.0.1	20
PC2	Wireless0	DHCP	255.255.0.0	172.16.0.1	10
PC3	Wireless0	DHCP	255.255.255.0	192.168.0.1	20

Table 7.1 Logical addressing of devices

*) Not applicable

Name WLAN	VLAN	SSID	Authentication	Key	Encryption
Wlan1	10	ID1	WEP	1234567890	40/64-bits (10 HEX digits)
Wlan2	20	ID2	WPA2-PSK	12345678	AES

Table 7.2 VLANS' configuration

Local switching
Local authentication

Table 7.3 Configuring Central Control options

Each wireless network belongs to a common group named **default-group**.

Group	WLAN	SSID
default-group	Wlan1	ID1
default-group	Wlan2	ID2

Table 7.4 Assigning WLANs to groups

Device	Physical location	Access point	Group	WLAN	VLAN
PC0	Biology Department building	Biology-AP	default-group	Wlan1	10
PC1	Biotechnology Department building	Biology-AP	default-group	Wlan2	20
PC2	Biology Department building	Biotechnology-AP	default-group	Wlan1	10
PC3	Biotechnology Department building	Biotechnology-AP	default-group	Wlan2	20

Table 7.5 Physical location of terminal equipment

Part 4. Physical topology.

- The range of the access points is 50 meters.
- The physical topologies of each building are shown in the figures below.

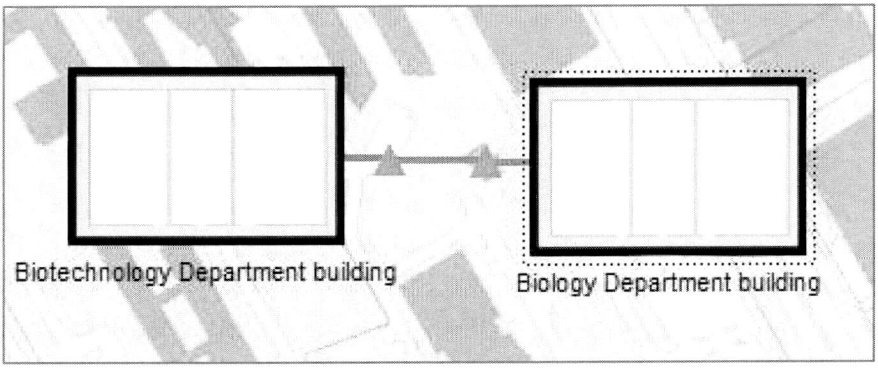

Figure 7.22 Physical topology of the network (campus)

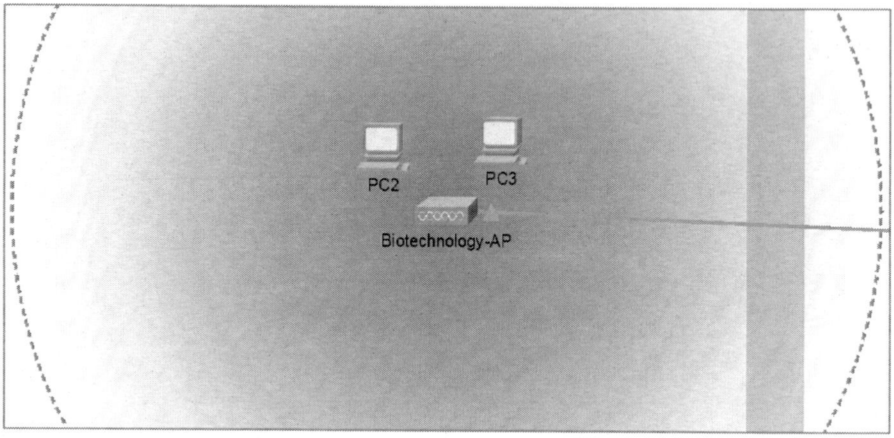

Figure 7.23 Physical topology of the Department of Biotechnology

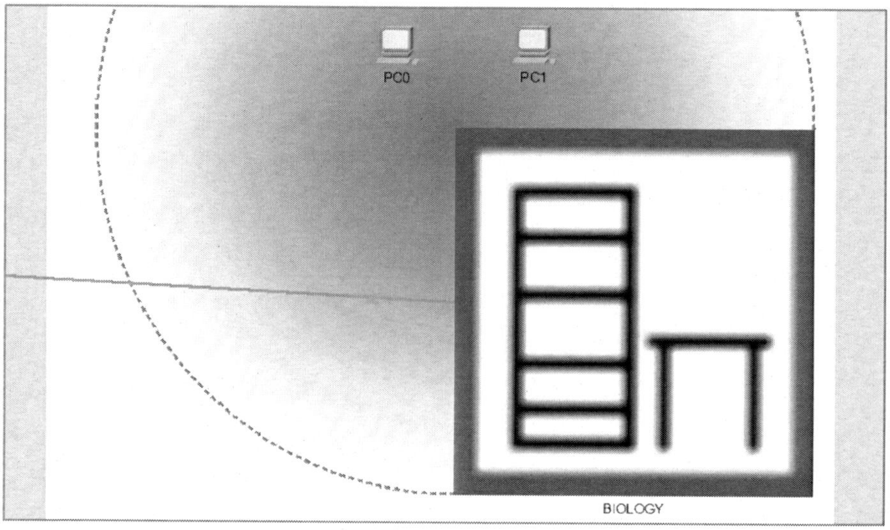

Figure 7.24 Physical topology of the Department of Biology

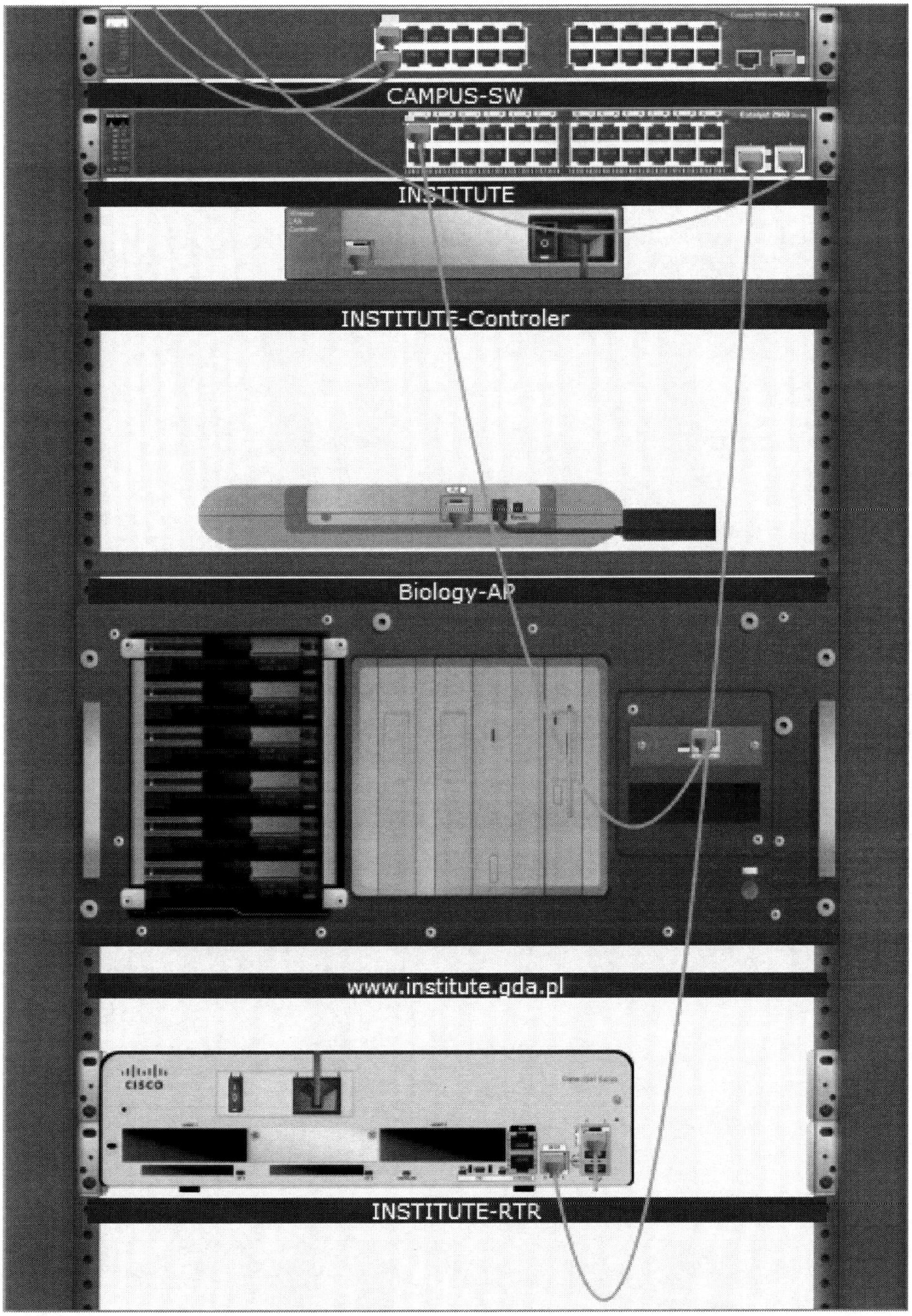

Figure 7.25 Cabinet in the Department of Biology

Part 5. Plan of the exercise – Creating and configuring a wireless network.

Step 1. Create a physical topology.

At the Intercity level, insert an image from the campus.png file.

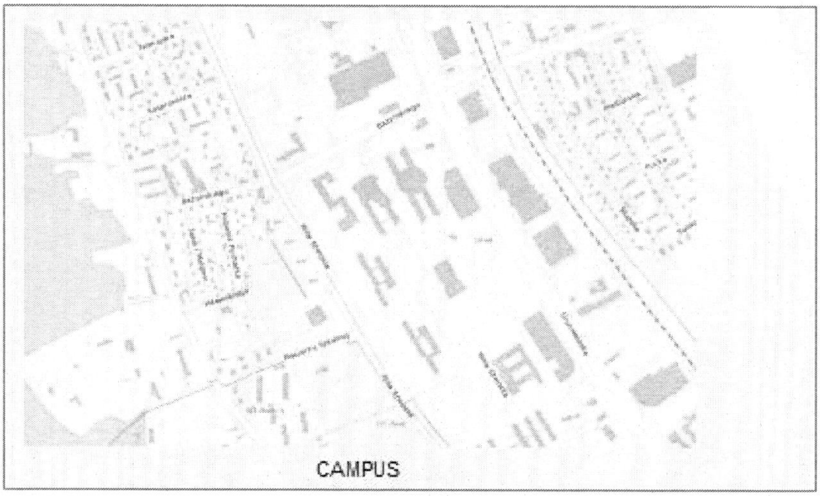

Figure 7.26 Intercity level topology

Go to CAMPUS level, insert two buildings with names:

- Department of Biology
- Department of Biotechnology

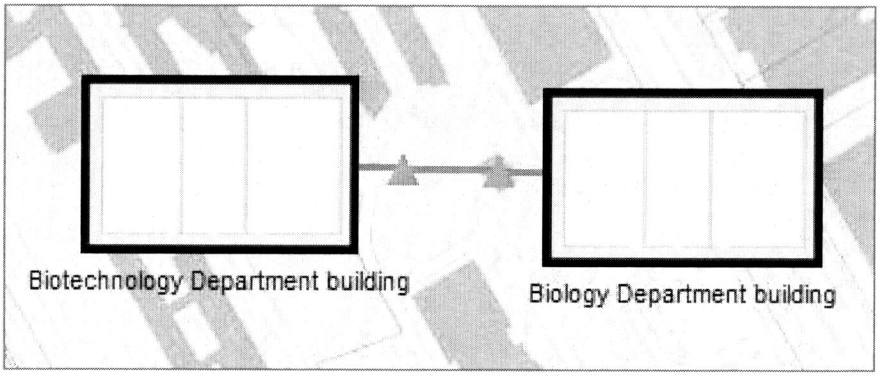

Figure 7.27 Topology at the CAMPUS level

Go to the Biology Faculty level. On the level of the Faculty of Biology, insert the image from the file building.png

At the Biology Department level, change the name of the Main Wiring Closet to BIOLOGY.

Go to the level of the Faculty of Biotechnology. On the level of the Faculty of Biotechnology, insert the image from the file building.png

Go to the BIOLOGY level and insert the following devices:

- CAMPUS-SW
- INSTITUTE
- INSTITUTE-Controller
- Biology-AP
- www.institute.com-index.html
- INSTITUTE-RTR

Go to the Biology Department level and insert the following devices:

- PC0
- PC1

Go to the Biotechnology Department level and insert the following devices:

- Biotechnology-AP
- PC2
- PC3

Step 2. Configure WWW server.

Use the files to configure the server:

- index.html
- biology.html
- biology.jpg
- biotechnology.html
- biotechnology.jpg

Configure http pages and subpages:

```
<html>
<body>
<center><font size='+2' color='blue'>Biology</font></center>
<p><img src="/biology.jpg"/></p>
<br><a href='index.html'>Back</a>
</body>
</html>
```

[Services]-[HTTP]-[biology.html]-[Edit]

```
<html>
<body>
<center><font size='+2'
color='red'>Biotechnology</font></center>


<p><img src="/biotechnology.jpg"/></p>
<br><a href='index.html'>Back</a>
</body>
</html>
```

[Services]-[HTTP]-[biotechnology.html]-[Edit]

```
<html>
<center><font size='+2' color='blue'>Cisco Packet Tracer
8.0</font></center>
<hr>Welcome to Interdisciplinary Institute - biology and
biotechnology.
<br><a href='biology.html'>Biology</a>
<br><a href='biotechnology.html'>Biotechnology</a>
</html>
```

Services]-[HTTP]-[index.html]-[Edit]

Step 3. Configure DNS server.

Go to the server **<u>www.institute.com</u>**, to the DNS service and add a Type A record.

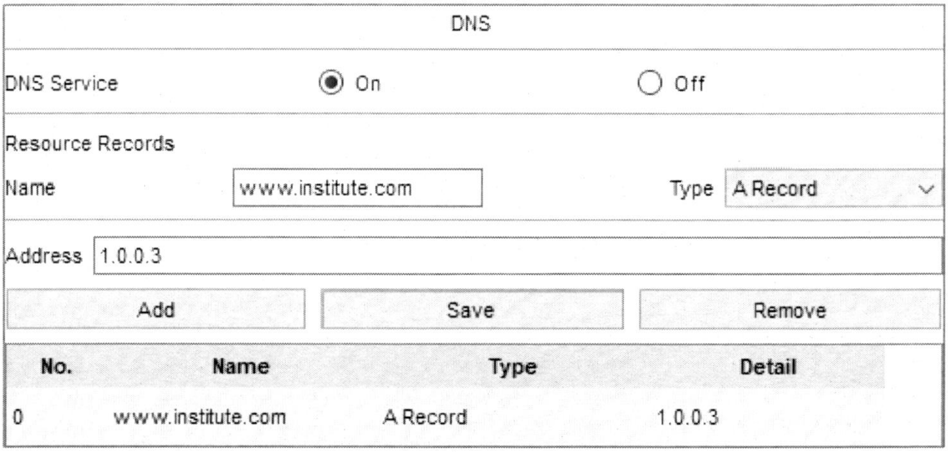

Figure 7.28 DNS server configuration

Step 4. Configure Management interface in INSTITUTE-Controller.

On the INSTITUTE-Controller, configure the **Management** interface.

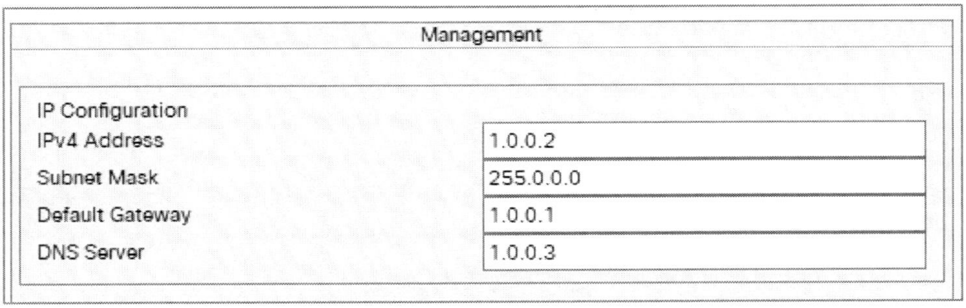

Figure 7.29 Management interface configuration

Step 5. Configure the interfaces in INSTITUTE-RTR

On the **INSTITUTE-RTR**, configure the following interfaces:

- Gi0/0
- Gi0/0.10
- Gi0/0.20
- Gi0/1

IOS commands :

```
interface GigabitEthernet0/0
ip address 10.0.0.1 255.0.0.0
no shutdown

interface GigabitEthernet0/0.10
encapsulation dot1Q 10
ip address 172.16.0.1 255.255.0.0
no shutdown

interface GigabitEthernet0/0.20
encapsulation dot1Q 20
ip address 192.168.0.1 255.255.255.0
no shutdown

interface GigabitEthernet0/1
ip address 1.0.0.1 255.0.0.0
```

```
no shutdown
```

Step 6. Configure DHCP in INSTITUTE-RTR

On the **INSTITUTE-RTR** device, configure three DHCP pools.

IOS commands:

```
ip dhcp excluded-address 10.0.0.0 10.0.0.10
ip dhcp excluded-address 172.16.0.0 172.16.0.10
ip dhcp excluded-address 192.168.0.0 192.168.0.10

ip dhcp pool  NET10
network 10.0.0.0  255.0.0.0
default-router 10.0.0.1
option 43 ip 1.0.0.2

ip dhcp pool  NET172
network 172.16.0.0 255.255.0.0
default-router 172.16.0.1
dns-server 1.0.0.3

ip dhcp pool  NET192
network 192.168.0.0 255.255.255.0
default-router 192.168.0.1
dns-server 1.0.0.3
```

Step 7. Configure the interfaces in CAMPUS-SW

On the CAMPUS-SW, configure the following interfaces in trunk mode:

- Fa0/1
- Fa0/2
- Gi0/2

IOS commands :

```
interface FastEthernet0/1
switchport trunk encapsulation dot1q
switchport mode trunk

interface FastEthernet0/2
```

```
switchport trunk encapsulation dot1q
switchport mode trunk

interface GigabitEthernet0/2
switchport trunk encapsulation dot1q
switchport mode trunk
```

Step 8. Check network communications.

Go to PC3, then in your browser type **www.institute.com** and check that the home page and subpages are displayed.

Figure 7.30 www.institute.com

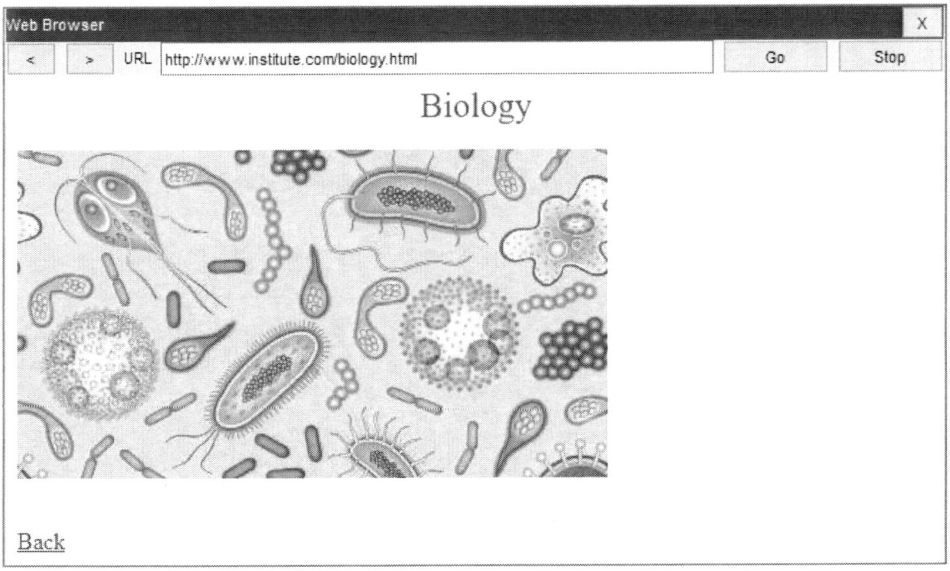

Figure 7.31 Subpage biology.html

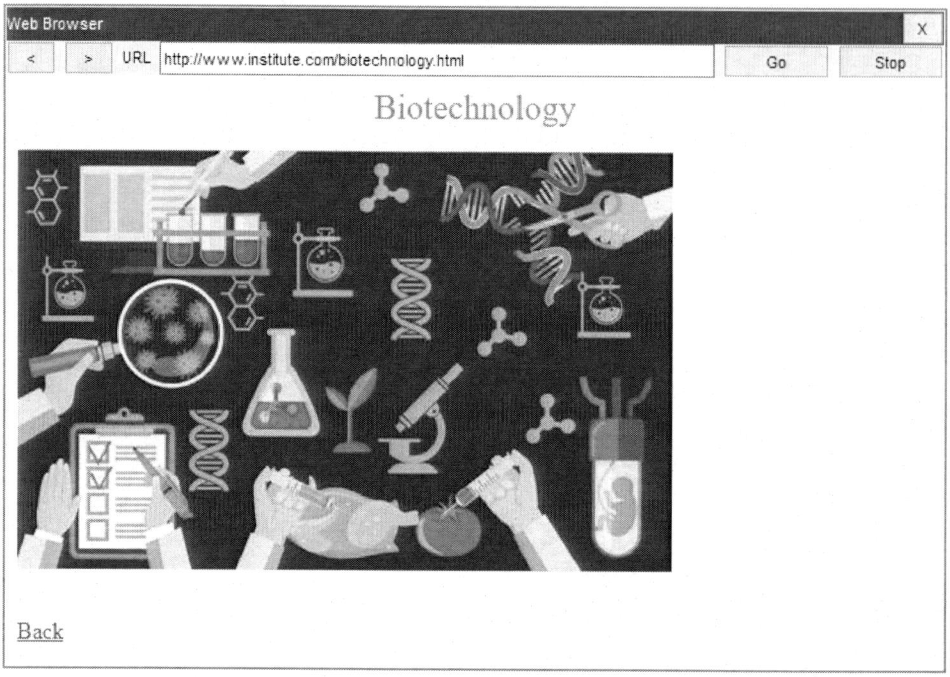

Figure 7.32 Subpage biotechnology.html

7.4 Initializing the WLC-2504 using the GUI (Exercise 19)

This exercise is introductory to the basic configuration of WLC-2504 type controllers.

Part 1. Initial topology.

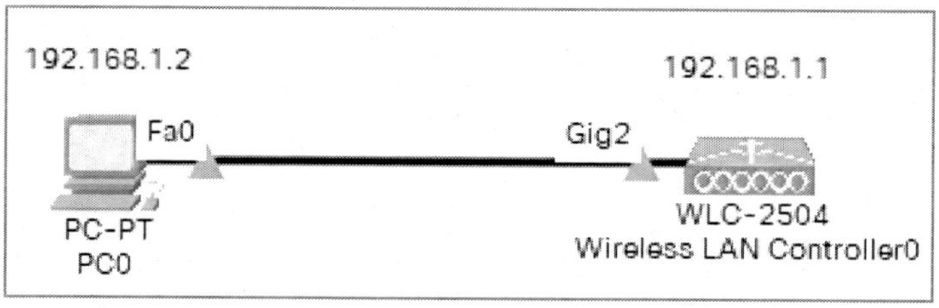

Figure 7.33 Initial topology

Part 2. Required equipment.

- WLC-2504 controller – 1 pts
- PC-PT – 1 pts

Part 3. Plan of the exercise.

Step 1. Create initial topology

Assign a static IP address to PC0 such as. 192.168.1.2

Step 2. Check if the address 192.168.1.1 is available

From PC0, ping 192.168.1.1

```
C:\>ping 192.168.1.1

Pinging 192.168.1.1 with 32 bytes of data:

Reply from 192.168.1.1: bytes=32 time<1ms TTL=255
Reply from 192.168.1.1: bytes=32 time<1ms TTL=255
Reply from 192.168.1.1: bytes=32 time<1ms TTL=255
Reply from 192.168.1.1: bytes=32 time<1ms TTL=255

Ping statistics for 192.168.1.1:
    Packets: Sent = 4, Received = 4, Lost = 0 (0% loss),
Approximate round trip times in milli-seconds:
    Minimum = 0ms, Maximum = 0ms, Average = 0ms
```

Figure 7.34 The result of the ping 192.168.1.1 command

Step 3. In PC0 in Web Browser, type 192.168.1.1.

A page to create an administrator account will appear, after a few seconds.

Step 4. Create an administrator account

Username	**admin**
Password	**Admin123**

Table 7.6 An administrator account

The password must be strong (uppercase, lowercase characters and numbers), and contain min. 6 characters.

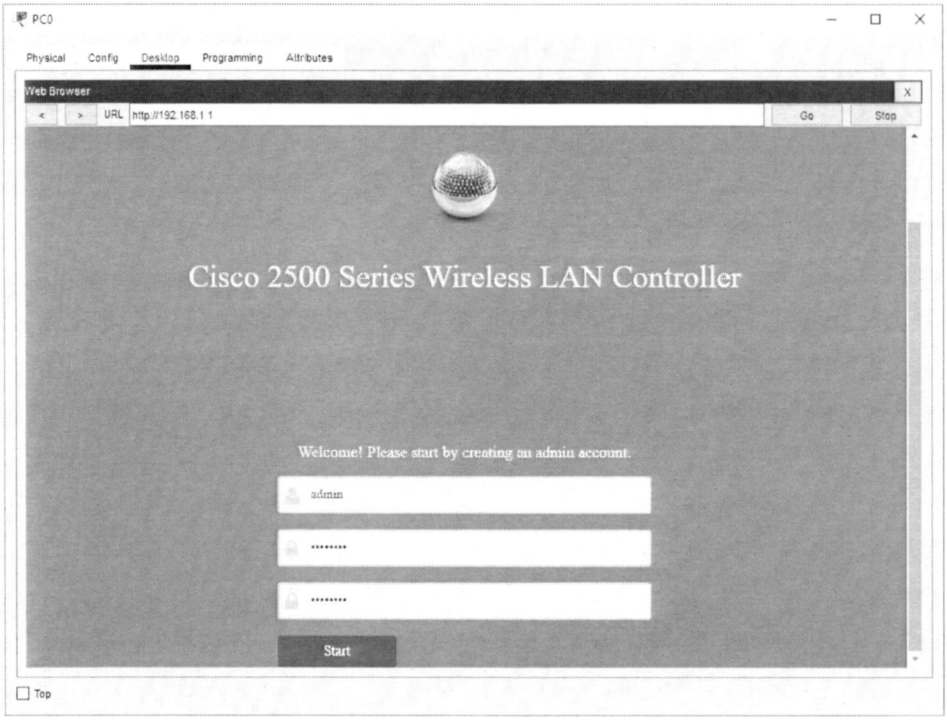

Figure 7.35 A page to create an administrator account

Step 5. Set basic configuration parameters

System Name	**UNIVERSITY**
Country	(optional)
Time zone	(optional)
NTP Server	(optional)
Management IP Address	**192.168.100.10**
Subnet Mask	**255.255.255.0**
Default Gateway	**192.168.100.1**
Management VLAN ID	0

Table 7.7 Configuration parameters for UNIVERSITY

Type basic data and click [Next].

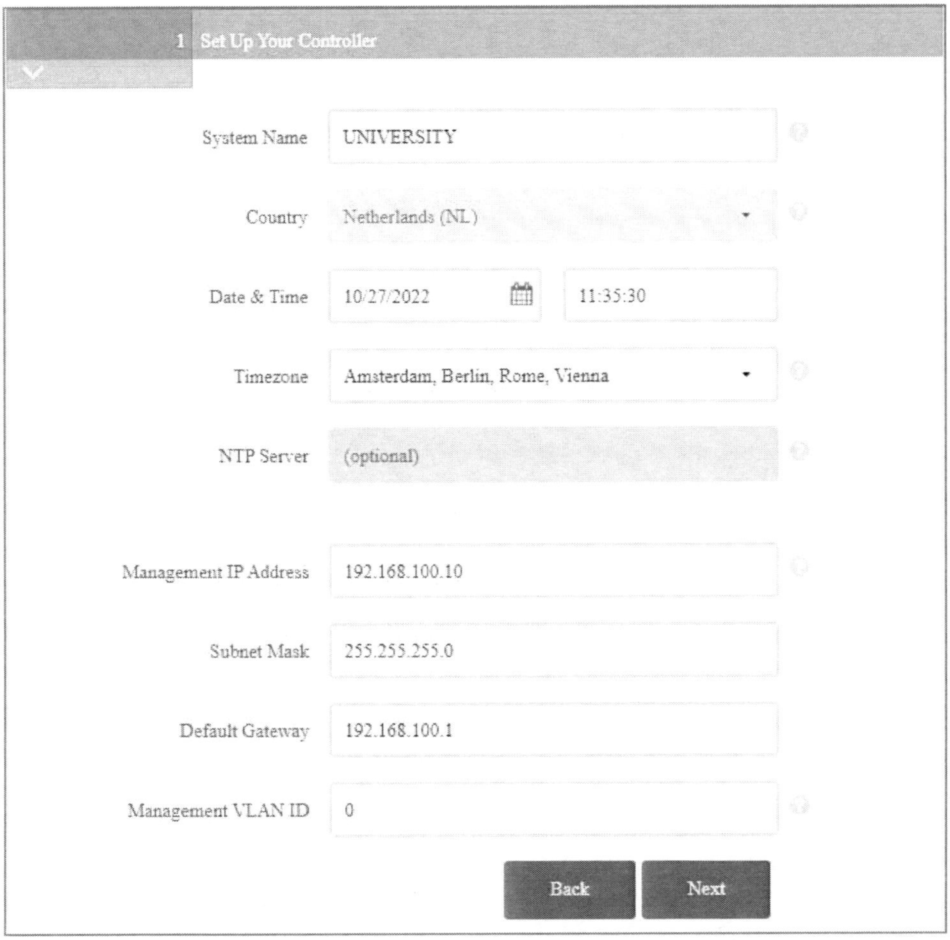

Figure 7.36 Basic configuration parameter settings

Step 6. Set up Employee Network wireless network for employees.

Network Name	**EMPLOYEE**
Security	**WPA2 Personal**
Passphrase	**1234567890**
VLAN	**Management VLAN**
DHCP Server Address	0.0.0.0 (optional)

Table 7.8 Configuration parameters for EMPLOYEE

NOTE: **Passphrase** must have at least 8 characters ASCII.

Step 7. Type appropriate data and click [**Next**].

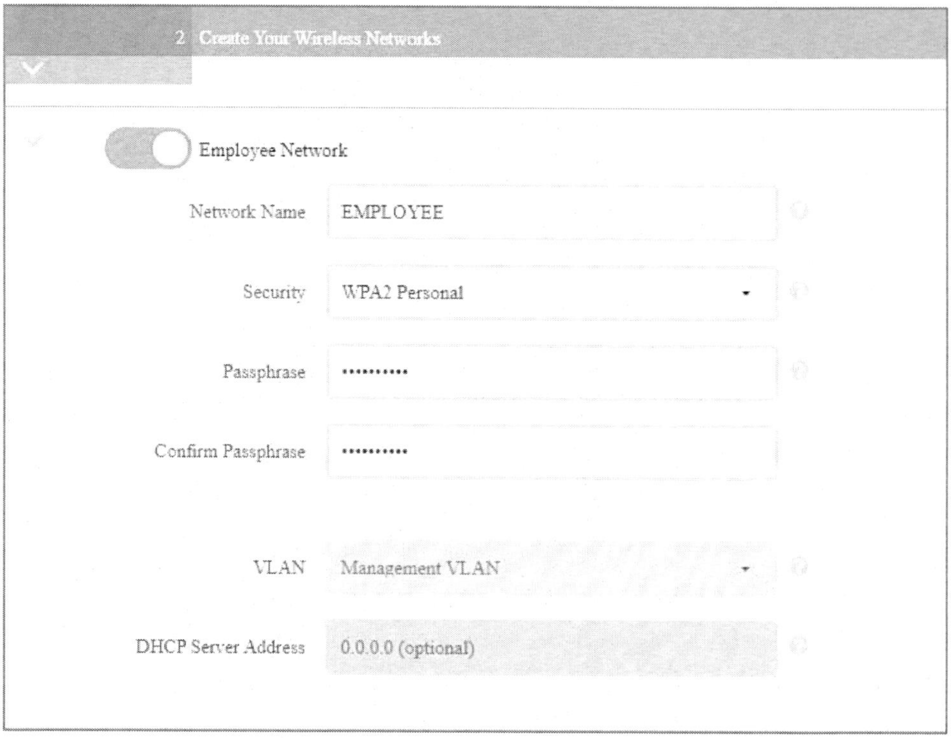

Figure 7.37 Configuring the Employee Network

Leave the **DHCP Server Address** field of unchanged and don't change the rest options.

Step 8. Save the configuration with the [**Apply**] button.

Figure 7.38 Configuring the Employee Network (continuation)

Confirm the entry with [**OK**].

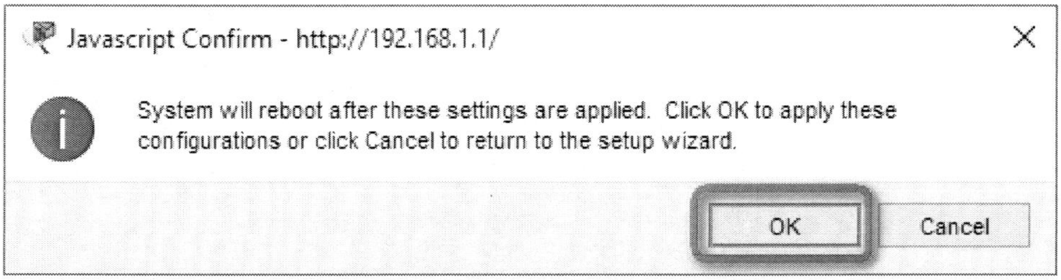

Figure 7.39 Saving configurations

Step 9. Wait until the controller has performed a saving and reboot.

It could take a several minutes.

Figure 7.40 Waiting for configuration record to complete

Current topology:

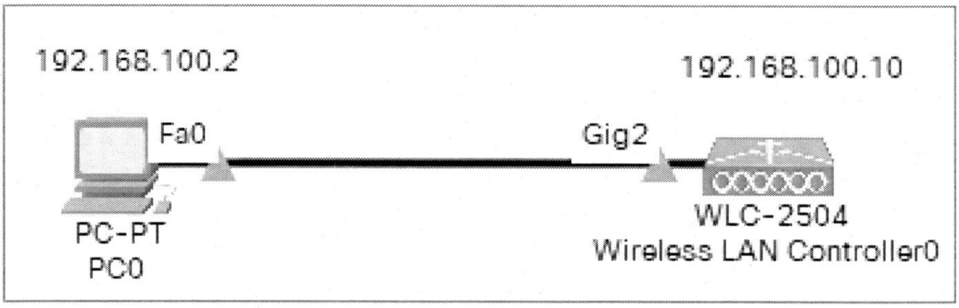

Figure 7.41 Current network topology

Step 10. Check that the management interface address on the WLC-2504 has changed to **192.168.100.10**

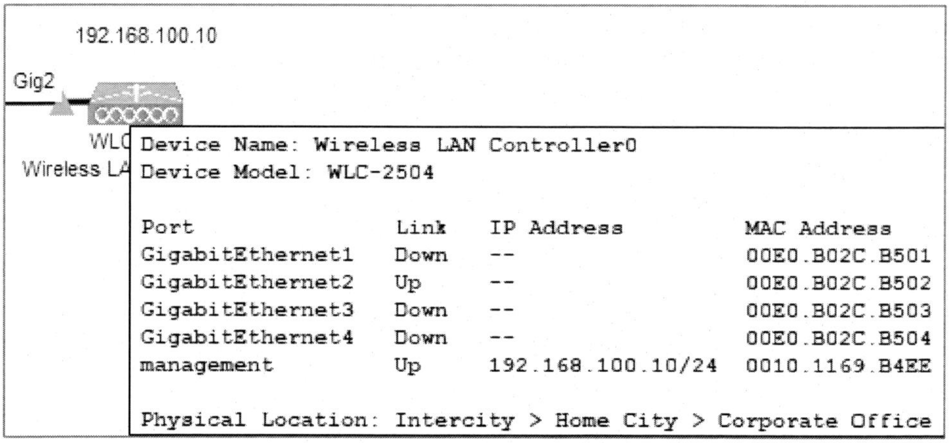

Figure 7.42 The Management Address

Since you are now on the 192.168.100.0/24 network, change the static address in PC0 to, for example: **192.168.100.2**

Figure 7.43 PC0 static addressing

Step 11. Check if the address 192.168.100.10 is available.

From PC0, ping 192.168.100.10

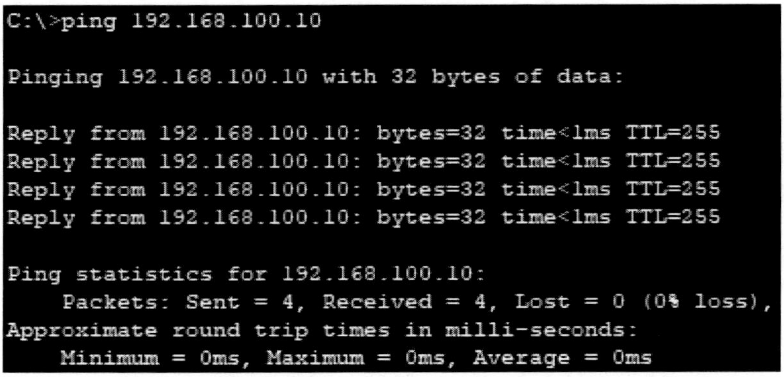

```
C:\>ping 192.168.100.10

Pinging 192.168.100.10 with 32 bytes of data:

Reply from 192.168.100.10: bytes=32 time<1ms TTL=255
Reply from 192.168.100.10: bytes=32 time<1ms TTL=255
Reply from 192.168.100.10: bytes=32 time<1ms TTL=255
Reply from 192.168.100.10: bytes=32 time<1ms TTL=255

Ping statistics for 192.168.100.10:
    Packets: Sent = 4, Received = 4, Lost = 0 (0% loss),
Approximate round trip times in milli-seconds:
    Minimum = 0ms, Maximum = 0ms, Average = 0ms
```

Figure 7.44 The result of the ping 192.168.100.10 command

Step 12. Log in to the WLC-2504 and check the configuration data.

On PC0 in the Web Browser, type the https://192.168.100.10 address

Do not forget about **HTTPS** protocol!

Figure 7.45 WLC-2504 controller home page

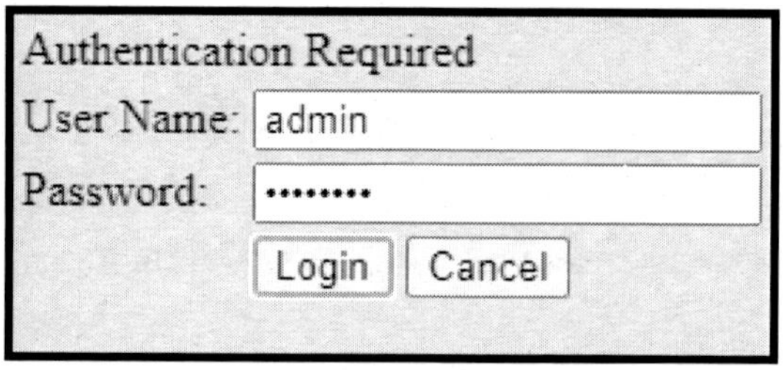

Figure 7.46 Logging into the WLC-2504 controller

After logging in, the controller's main panel appears along with a horizontal menu.

Figure 7.47 Main menu of the WLC-2504 controller

Step 13. Familiarize yourself with the main data (parameters) in the MONITOR menu.

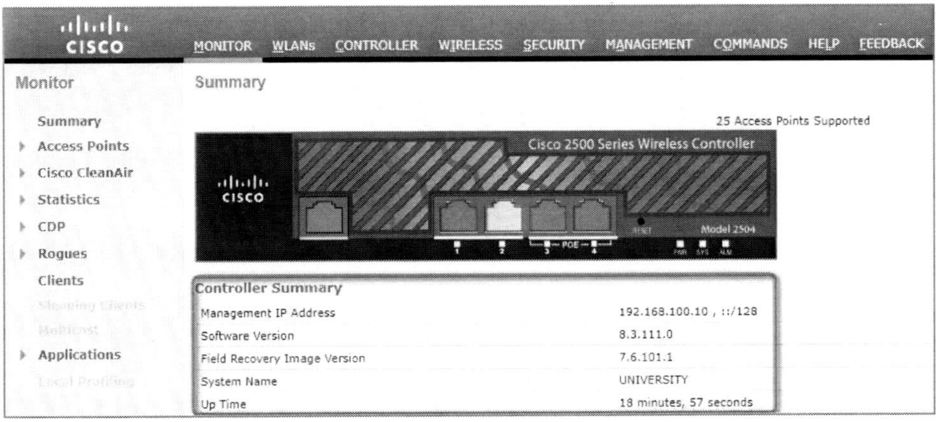

Figure 7.48 Main panel of the WLC-2504 controller

Step 14. Familiarize yourself with the main data (parameters) in the WLANs menu.

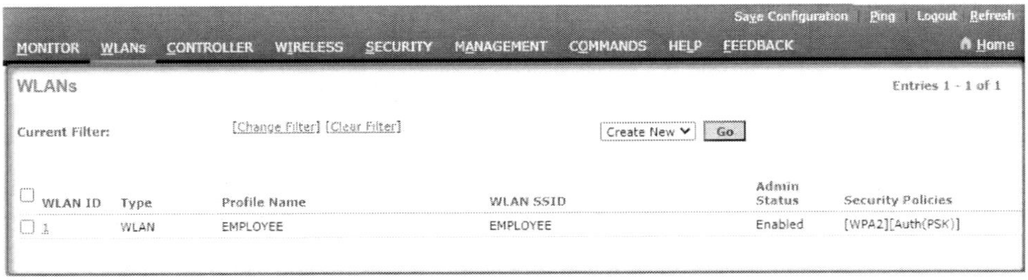

Figure 7.49 Data in the WLANs section

Step 15. Read the procedure for creating new networks in the WLANs section.

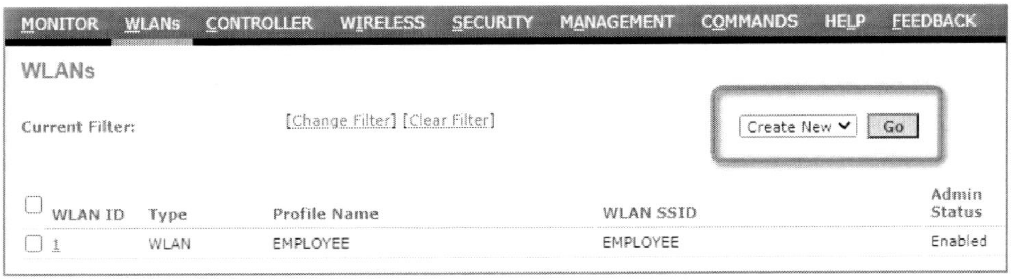

Figure 7.50 GO button

In the WLANs section, click the [**Go**] button to the right of the [**Create New**] item.

Enter the name of the new network, profile name, SSID of the network, and select the network ID.

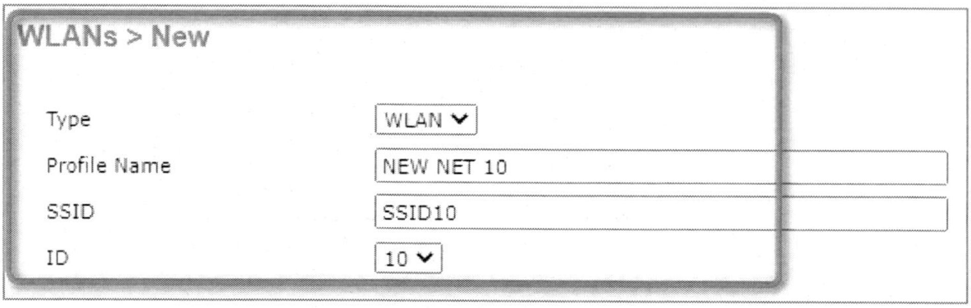

Figure 7.51 Example data for the new network

To approve the above configuration, click the [**Apply**] button.

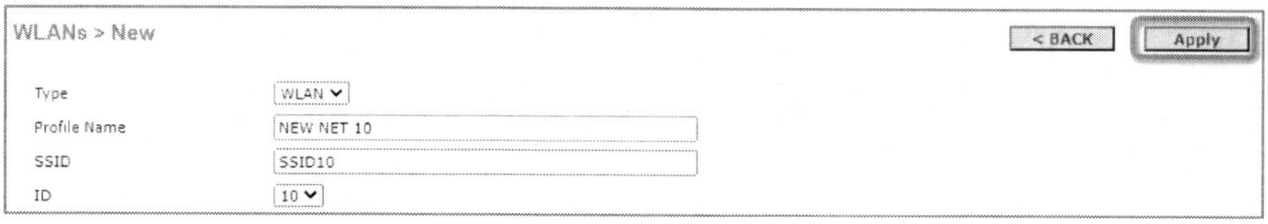

Figure 7.52 Validation of data for the new network

In the [**General**] tab, enable the [**Status**] option.

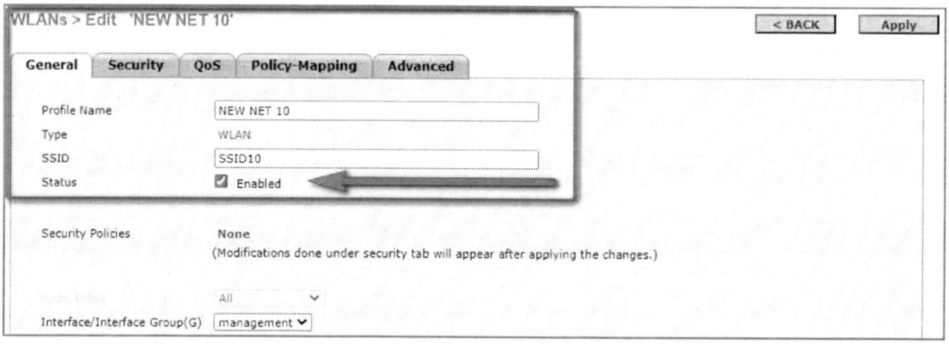

Figure 7.53 [General] tab

In the [**Security**] tab and [**Layer2**] sub-tab, enable [**Static WEP**].

In the [**Encription Key**] field, enter a key such as 0123456789.

Next click [**Apply**] button,

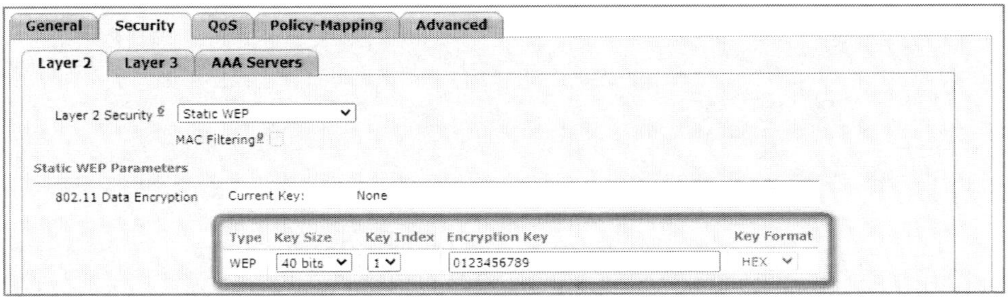

Figure 7.54 [Security] tab and [Static WEP] option

Or, in the [**Security**] tab and [**Layer2**] sub-tab, enable [**WPA+WPA2**] check WPA Encryption: **AES**

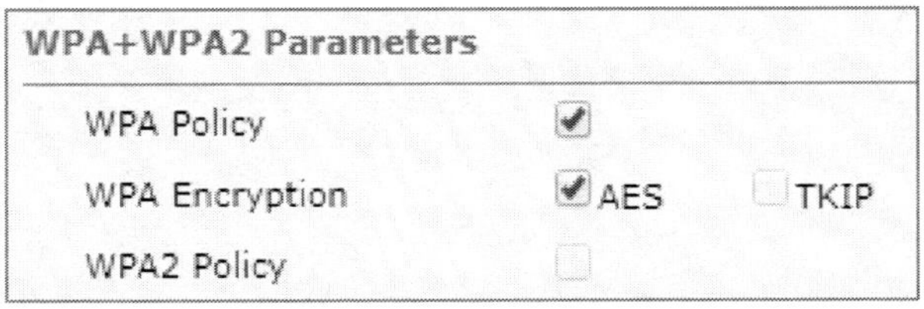

Figure 7.55 Encryption algorithm selection [WPA+WPA2].

Check the [**PSK**] option.

In the [**PSK Format**] field, enter the key, e.g. 12345678.

Next click [**Apply**] button.

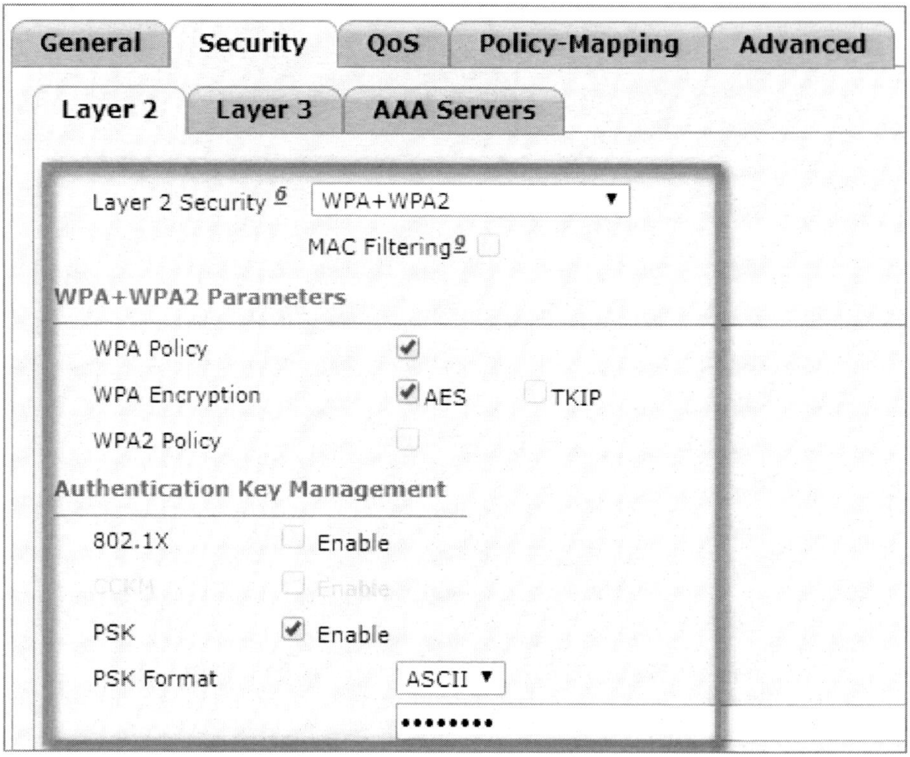

Figure 7.56 [Security] tab and [WPA+WPA2] option

View the network and security summary.

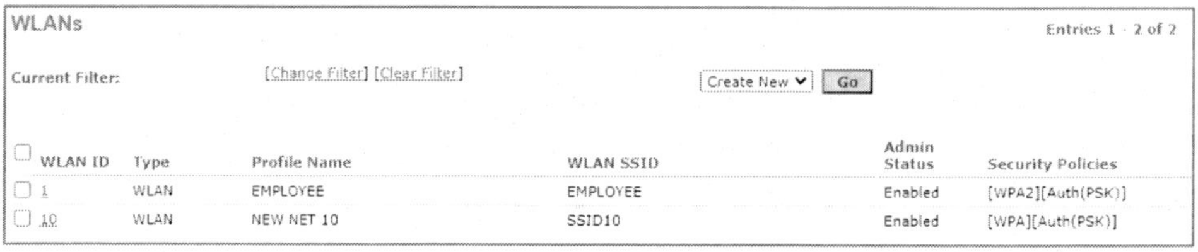

Figure 7.57 List of networks in the WLC-2504

Step 16. Familiarize yourself with the main parameters in the CONTROLLER menu (section).

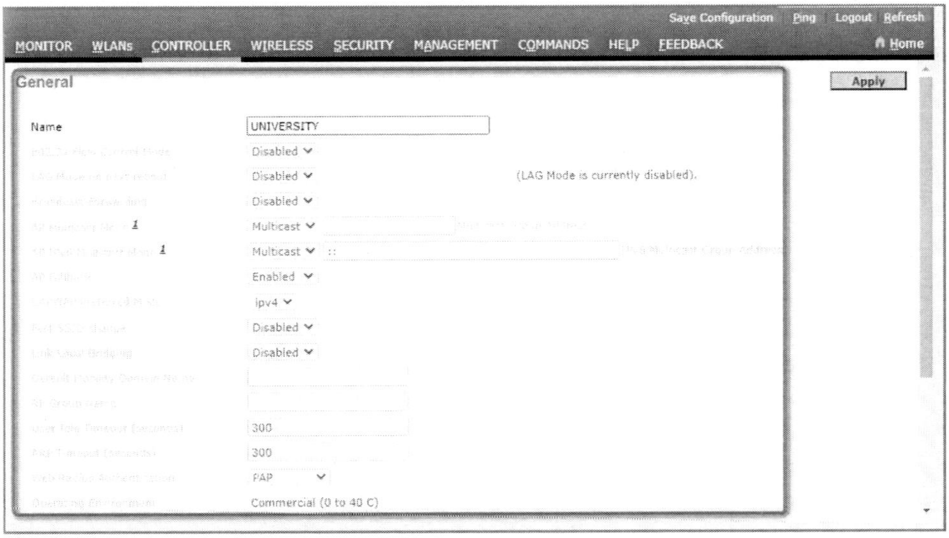

Figure 7.58 Data in CONTROLLER section

Step 17 Review the main parameters in the WIRELESS menu (section).

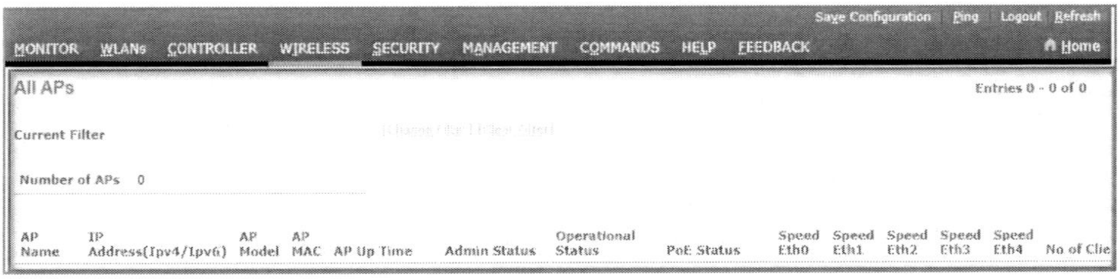

Figure 7.59 Data in the WIRELESS section

Step 18. Familiarize yourself with the main parameters in the SECURITY menu (section)

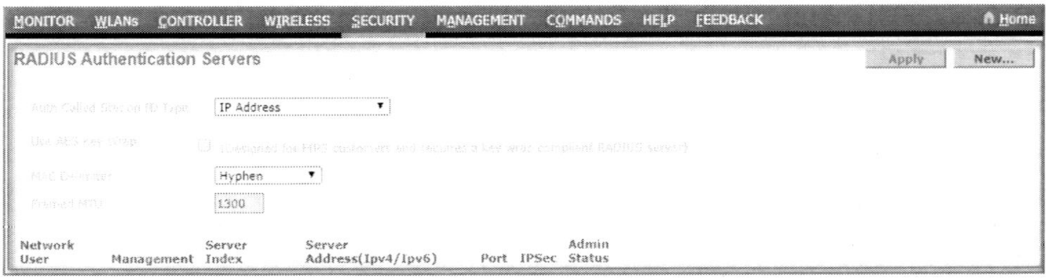

Figure 7.60 Data in the SECURITY section

Step 19 Review the main parameters in the MANAGEMENT menu (section).

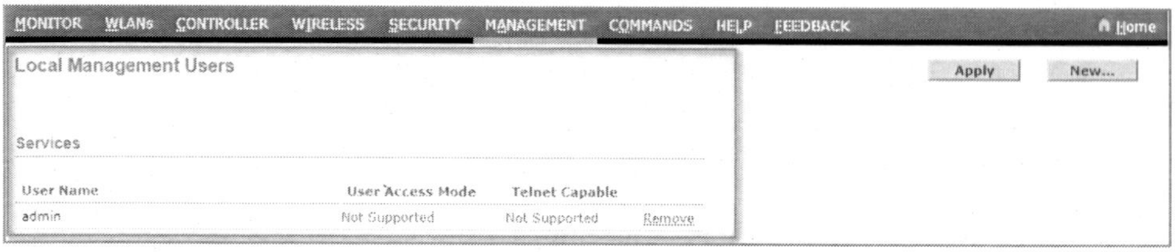

Figure 7.61 Data in the MANAGEMENT section

Step 20 Review the main parameters in the COMMANDS menu (section).

Figure 7.62 Data in the COMMANDS section

Note: HELP and FEEDBACK menu support is not implemented in PT.

Step 21. Log out from WLC-2504.

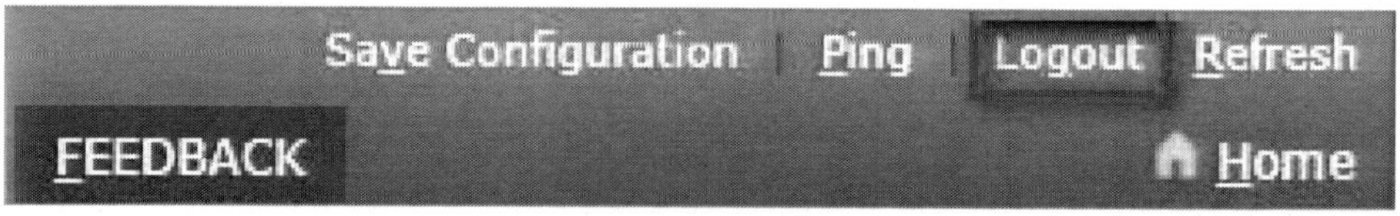

Figure 7.63 Logout button

7.5 Managing WLANs in WLC-2504 (Exercise 20)

Part 1 Assumptions for the exercise and required equipment.

- The RTR router acts as a **router on a stick** and a DHCP server.
- The management interface address of the WLC-2504: **10.0.0.2/8**.
- WLC-2504 management address: **https://10.0.0.2**.
- Login to WLC-2504: **admin**
- Password to WLC-2504: **admin**
- Two WLANs operating in different VLANs
- VLAN10 belongs to ssid1 wireless network **ssid1**.
- VLAN20 belongs to the wireless network **ssid2**.
- The **10.0.0.0/8** management network is in VLAN 1 and is for communication between the WLC and the AP.
- WLAN data communication takes place in VLANs **10** and **20**.
- Building A is served by one AP named **BUILDING A**, with two wireless networks: **ssid1** and **ssid2**.
- Building B is served by one AP named **BUILDING B**, with two wireless networks: **ssid1 and ssid2**.
- AP range: 249 meters.
- Network security **wlan1**: (SSID=**ssid1** + authentication)
  - Security Policies: WEP, WEP Key=**1234567890**
- Network security **wlan2**: (SSID=**ssid2** + authentication)
  - Security Policies: WPA2-PSK, PSK Pass Phrase=**12345678**

- WLC-2504 controller – 1 pcs
- Router 1941 (router on a stick, DHCP server, and routing) – 1 pcs
- 3560-24PS switcher – 1 pcs
- PC-PT (as AdminPC) – 1 pcs
- Access point LAP-PT – 2 pcs
- PC-PT (PC0-PC3) equipped in Linksyss-WMP300N card – 4 pcs

Part 2. Network topology.

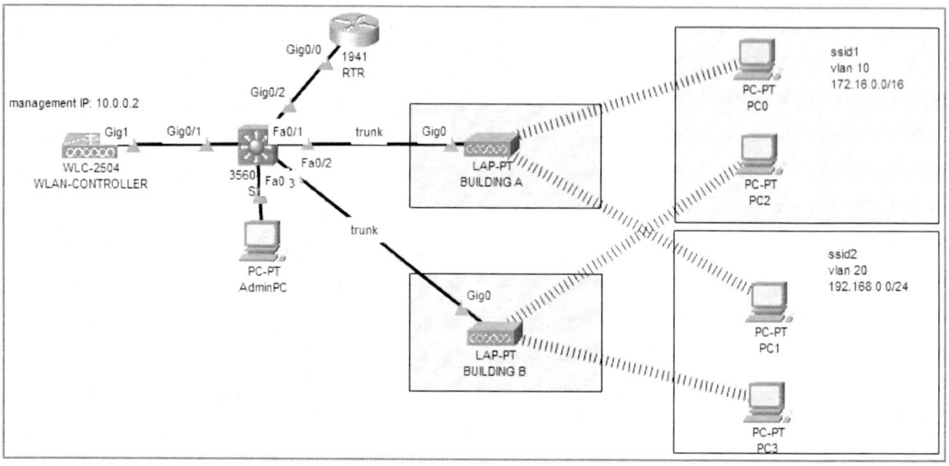

Figure 7.64 Network topology

Part 3. Plan of the exercise – configuring wireless networks.

Step 1. Change hostnames (where possible) and descriptive names to those in the table below.

Type of device	Description	Host name
1941	RTR	RTR
WLC-2504	WLAN-CONTROLLER	-
3560-24PS	SW	SW
LAP-PT	BUILDING A	-
LAP-PT	BUILDING B	-

Table 7.9 Host names and descriptive names

Step 2. Create two WLANs and verify that they match the ones listed in the table below.

WLAN	WLAN SSID	Security Policies	Key/PSK Pass Phrase
wlan1	ssid1	WEP	1234567890
wlan2	ssid2	WPA2-PSK	12345678

Table 7.10 WLAN and SSID names and security

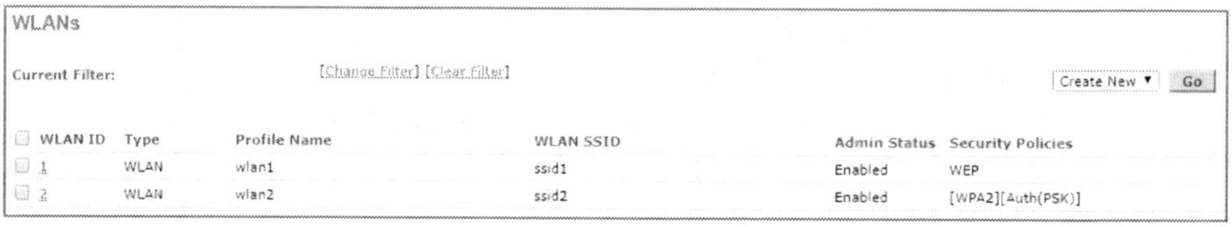

Figure 7.65 WLAN and SSID names and their security types

Step 3. Configure the RTR router using the following commands.

```
enable
conf t
hostname RTR

interface GigabitEthernet0/0
ip address 10.0.0.1 255.0.0.0

interface GigabitEthernet0/0.10
encapsulation dot1Q 10
ip address 172.16.0.1 255.255.0.0
no shutdown

interface GigabitEthernet0/0.20
encapsulation dot1Q 20
ip address 192.168.0.1 255.255.255.0
no shutdown

ip dhcp excluded-address 10.0.0.0 10.0.0.10
ip dhcp excluded-address 172.16.0.0 172.16.0.10
ip dhcp excluded-address 192.168.0.0 192.168.0.10

ip dhcp pool net10
network 10.0.0.0 255.0.0.0
default-router 10.0.0.1

ip dhcp pool net172
network 172.16.0.0 255.255.0.0
default-router 172.16.0.1

ip dhcp pool net192
network 192.168.0.0 255.255.255.0
default-router 192.168.0.1
```

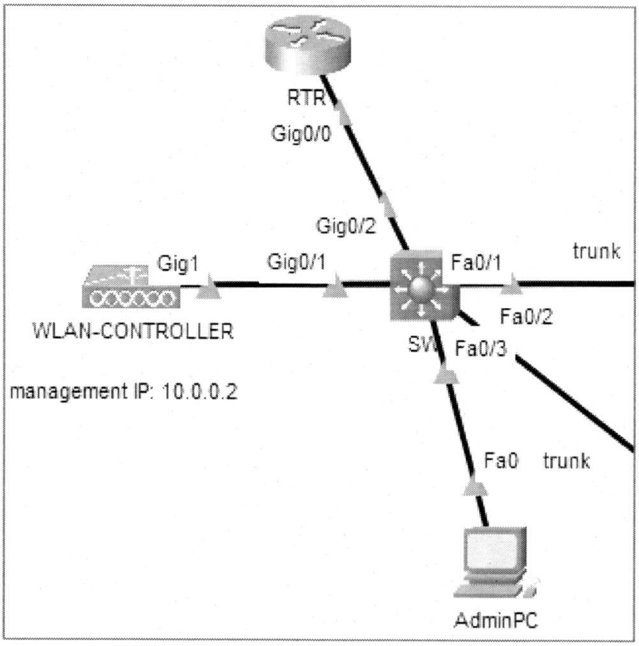

Figure 7.66 Fragment of the network topology

Step 4. Configure the switch (trunk connections and encapsulation) using the following commands.

```
enable
conf t
hostname SW

interface FastEthernet0/1
switchport trunk encapsulation dot1q
switchport mode trunk

interface FastEthernet0/2
switchport trunk encapsulation dot1q
switchport mode trunk

interface GigabitEthernet0/2
switchport trunk encapsulation dot1q
switchport mode trunk
```

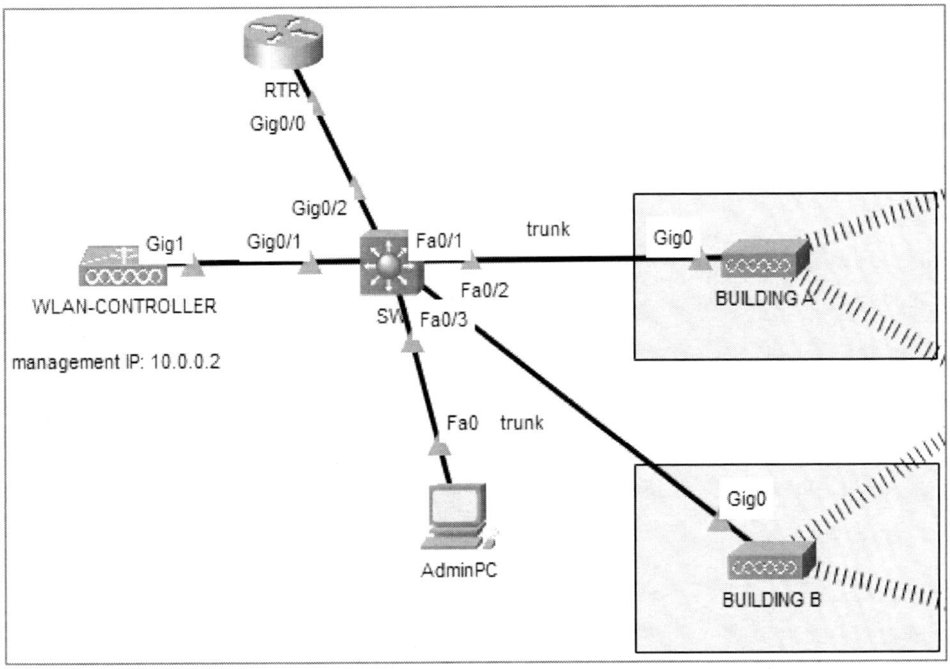

Figure 7.67 Fragment of the network topology

Step 5. Configure end devices on **ssid1** network.

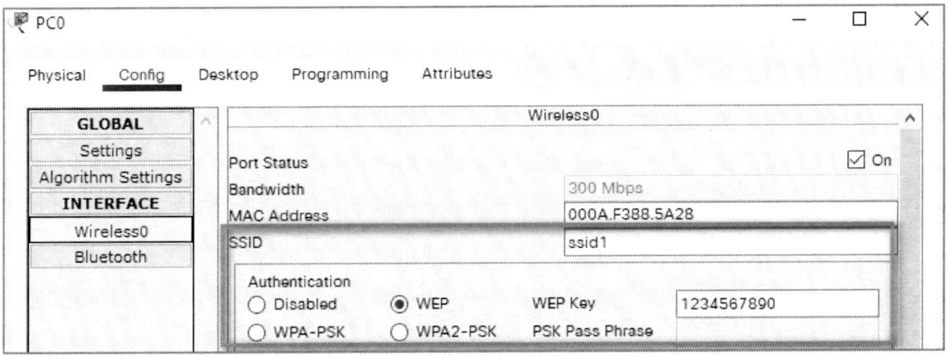

Figure 7.68 PC0 configuration

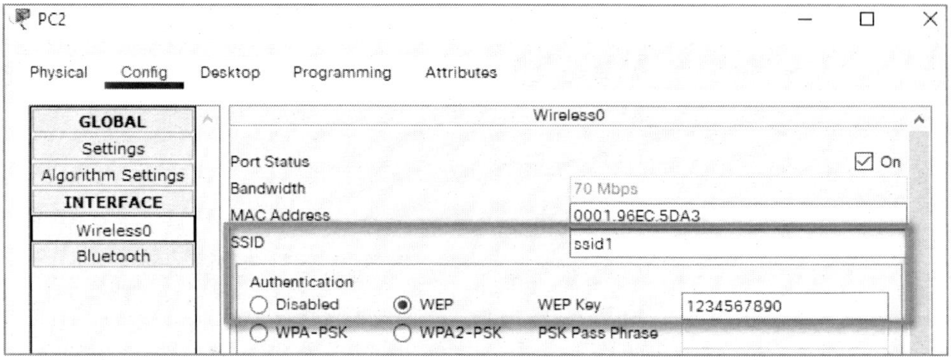

Figure 7.69 PC2 configuration

Step 6. Configure end devices on **ssid2** network.

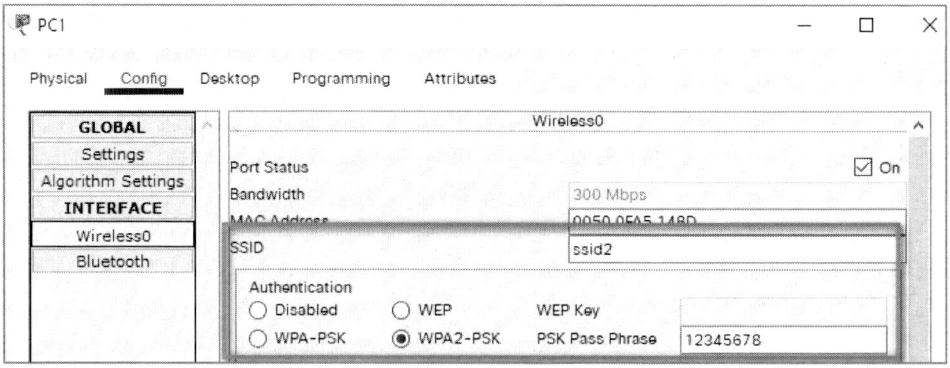

Figure 7.70 PC1 configuration

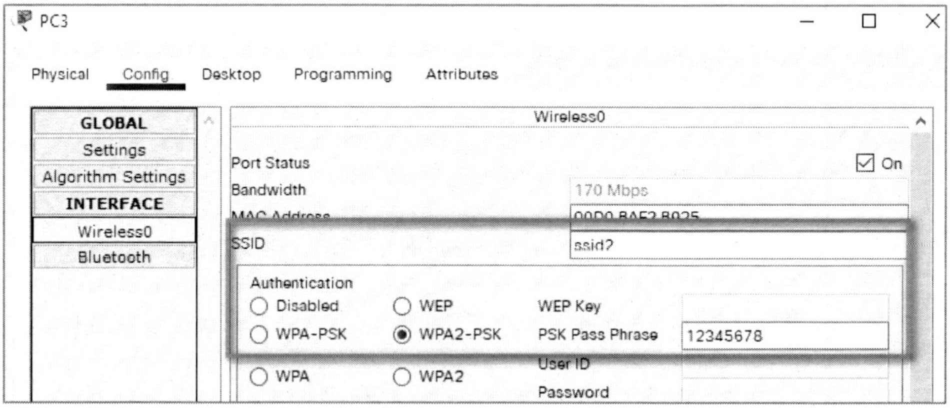

Figure 7.71 PC3 configuration

7.6 List of auxiliary files

- biology.html
- biology.jpg
- biology.png
- biotechnology.html
- biotechnology.jpg
- biotechnology.png
- building.png
- campus.png
- exercise17-wlc-pt.pkt
- exercise18-wlc-pt.pkt
- exercise19-wlc-2504.pkt
- exercise20-wlc-2504.pkt
- www.institute.com-index.html

CHAPTER 8

INTEGRATED INDUSTRIAL ROUTERS

8 Integrated Industrial Routers

8.1 DESCRIPTION OF INTEGRATED ROUTERS

Industrial integrated routers, in addition to supporting Wi-Fi, wired networks, also have support for fourth-generation integrated wireless WANs (4G LTE) and also support Machine-to-Machine (M2M) applications.

Part 1. A brief description of the Cisco IOx environment.

The Cisco IOx application environment is a combination of Cisco IOS and Linux OS to provide higher network security.

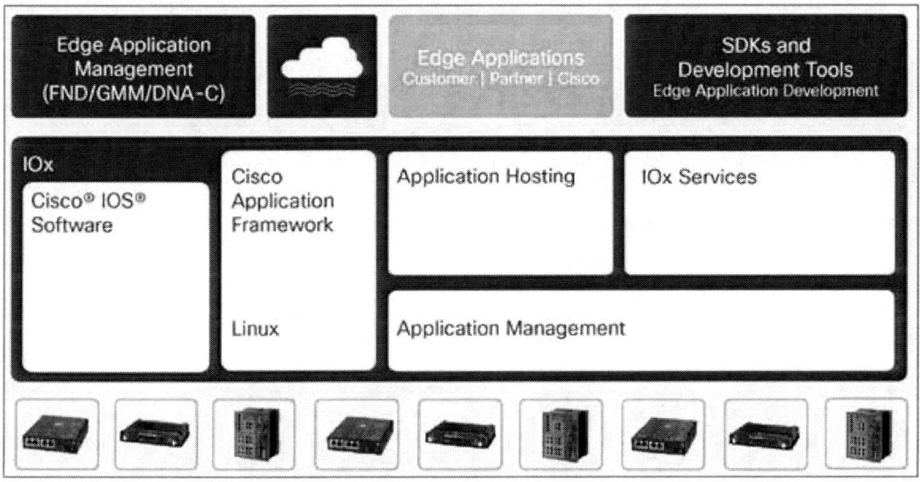

Figure 8.1 Cisco IOx application environment - source (Cisco.live, 2019) [5]

Part 2. A brief description of fog computing.

Fog computing is a decentralized computing framework placed between the cloud and end devices. It allows users to place resources, including applications and the data they generate, in physical locations to increase performance.

[5] Presentation Cisco.live. Las Vegas. 2019.

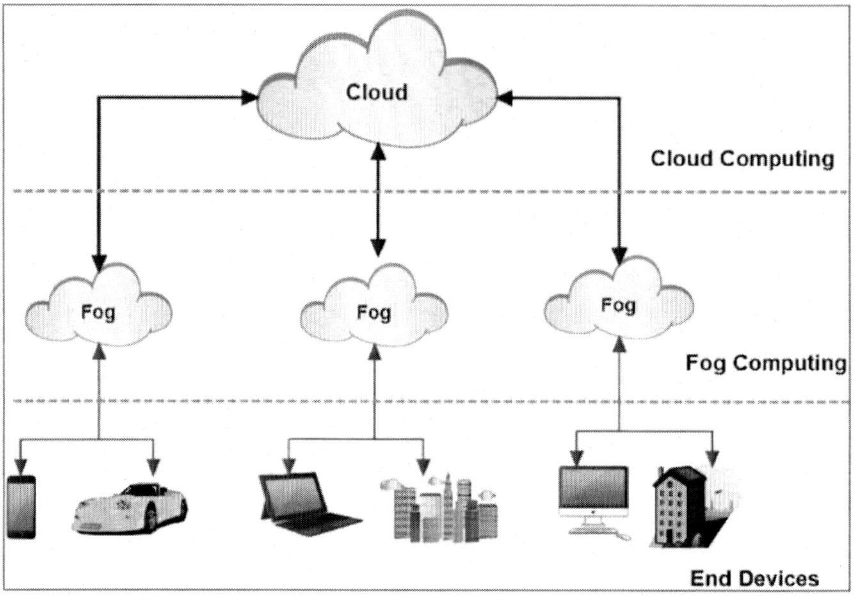

Figure 8.2 Fog computing IOx - source (Cisco.live, 2019) [6]

Part 3. A brief description of the 819 routers software.

In the 819 series routers, individual software components run in two CPU cores:

- in core 0 (Core 0) runs IOS,
- Core 1 runs the so-called Host OS, the so-called hypervisor, and applications.

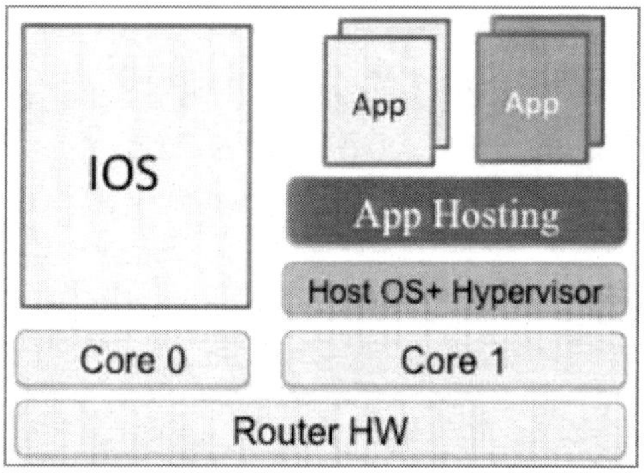

Figure 8.3 Placement of systems and applications in the 819 IOx series router - source (Cisco.live, 2019) [7]

[6] Presentation Cisco.live. Las Vegas.2019.
[7] Presentation Cisco.live. Las Vegas.2019.

The industrial integrated router models implemented in Packet Tracer are:

- Router 819HG-4G-IOX
- Router 819HGW

Part 4. A brief description of the 819HG-4G-IOX router.

The **819HG-4G-IOX** router supports Machine-to-Machine (M2M) applications and cellular network services.

Figure 8.4 View of 819HG-4G-IOX

The **819IOX** router comes standard with two antennas and non-replaceable MODULES:

- one **GigabitEthernet0** interface,
- four (**FastEthernet0 – FastEthernet3**) interfaces,
- one **Serial0** serial communication interface,
- one **Ethernet1** interface,
- one **VirtualPortGroup0**,
- one **Cellular0 interface**.

Part 5. Brief description of the 819HGW router.

The **Cisco 819HGW** (Integrated Services Router), is a variation of the **819** router model that supports Machine-to-Machine (M2M) applications and cellular network services.

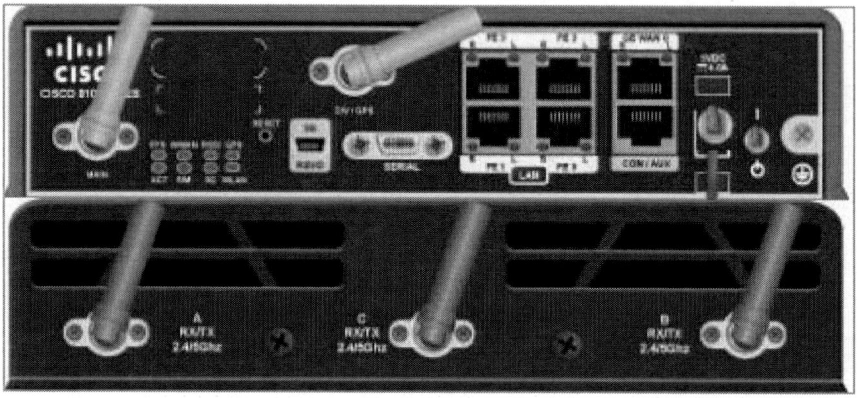

Figure 8.5 View of 819HGW

The **819HGW** router comes standard with five antennas and non-replaceable:

- one **GigabitEthernet0** interface,
- four (**FastEthernet0 – FastEthernet3**) interfaces,
- one **Serial0** serial communication interface,
- one **Ethernet1** interface,
- one **Wlan-Gigabitethernet0** wireless interface,
- one **Cellular0** interface,
- one internal module acting as **wlan-ap0** access point.

Part 6. Main commands of the IOX service configuration mode.

To enter **IOX** mode, follow the commands:

```
enable
conf t
iox
```

Command	Brief description
`host ip address`	IP address and mask for Ethernet interface1
`host ip default-gateway`	IP address of the default gateway for the Ethernet interface1
`exit`	Exit from IOX mode

Table 8.1 IOx commands

Source: (Cisco800, 2022), (IOx-Application-Hosting, 2022) [8]

[8] Cisco 800 Series Integrated Services Routers Software Configuration Guide.

Part 7. Initial configuration setup commands.

Note: addresses are examples.

NAT settings on the inside.

```
enable
conf t
interface Ethernet1
ip address 192.168.3.1 255.255.255.0
ip nat inside
no shutdown
exit
```

IOx host addressing settings

```
enable
conf t
iox
host ip address 192.168.3.2 255.255.255.0
host ip default-gateway 192.168.3.1
exit
```

NAT settings on the external side

```
enable
conf t
interface GigabitEthernet0
ip address 1.100.30.113 255.255.255.0
ip nat outside
no shutdown
exit
```

Settings of address ranges, subject to translation by NAT

```
enable
conf t
ip access-list standard NAT_ACL
permit 192.168.0.0 0.0.255.255
exit
```

Association of an external interface with a NAT_ACL list

```
enable
conf  t
ip nat inside source list NAT_ACL interface GigabitEthernet0
overload
exit
```

Association of external interface with IOx TCP port 8443

```
enable
conf  t
ip nat inside source static tcp 192.168.3.2 8443 interface
GigabitEthernet0 8443
exit
```

Part 8. Local management interface components.

The **Local Management UI** consists of the following components, shown in the figure.

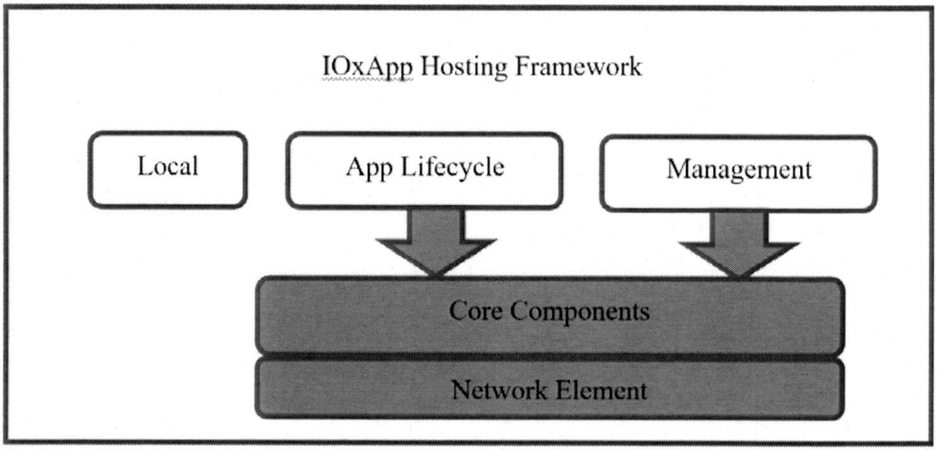

Fig. 8.6 Local Management UI components

Local Management UI is available via **8332** port.

8.2 Basic configuration for 819HG-4G-IOX (Exercise 21)

Part 1.Network topology.

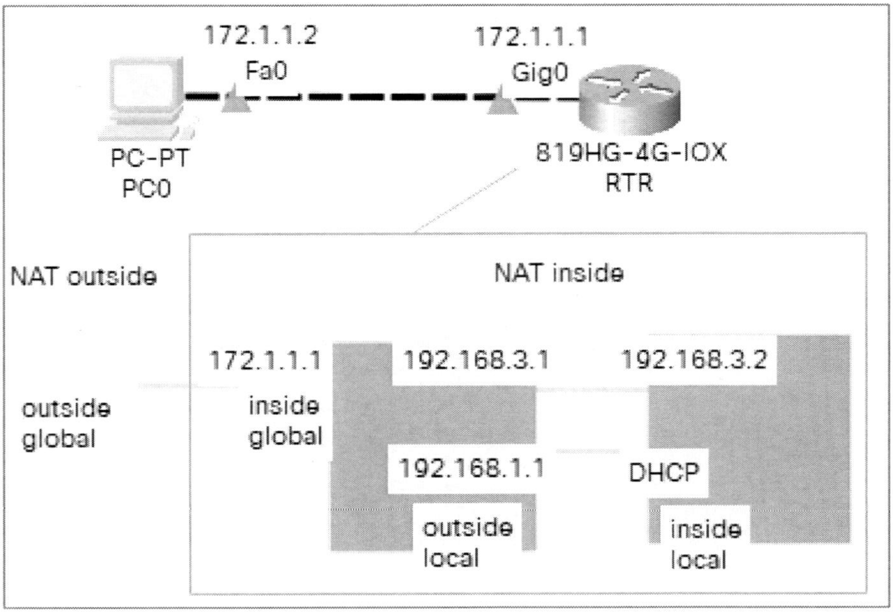

Figure 8.7 Network topology

Part 2. Required equipment.

- PC-PT – 1 pcs
- 819HG-4G-IOX router – 1 pcs

Device	Model	Interface	IP/Mask	Default gateway
PC0	PC-PT	Fa0	172.1.1.2/24	172.1.1.1
RTR	819HG-4G-IOX	Gi0	172.1.1.1/24	-

Table 8.2 Network addressing

Part 3. Plan of the exercise.

Configure the RTR router according to the following steps:

Step 1. Create a password-protected account

Commands:

```
username cisco privilege 15
password 0 cisco
```

Step 2. Configure DHCP.

Commands:

```
enable
conf  t
hostname  RTR
ip dhcp excluded-address 192.168.1.0 192.168.1.1

ip dhcp pool iox-apps
network 192.168.1.0 255.255.255.0
default-router 192.168.1.1
```

Step 3. Configure NAT and host IOx addressing.

Commands:

```
interface GigabitEthernet0
ip address 172.1.1.1 255.255.255.0
ip nat outside

interface Ethernet1
ip address 192.168.3.1 255.255.255.0
ip nat inside

interface VirtualPortGroup0
ip address 192.168.1.1 255.255.255.0
ip nat inside

iox
host ip address 192.168.3.2 255.255.255.0
host ip default-gateway 192.168.3.1

ip nat inside source list NAT_ACL inteface  Gi0  overload
ip nat inside source static  tcp  192.168.3.2  8443
172.1.1.1  8443

ip access-list standard NAT_ACL
permit 192.168.0.0   0.0.255.255
```

Step 4. Check NAT addressing.

Commands:

show ip nat translations

```
RTR#show  ip  nat  translations
Pro  Inside global      Inside local        Outside local       Outside global
tcp 172.1.1.1:8443      192.168.3.2:8443    ---                 ---
```

Figure 8.8 NAT addressing in RTR router

Step 5. Check access to the site https://172.1.1.1:8443 and log in.

In PC0, open the page https://172.1.1.1:8443 (log into Cisco Application Management. User: **cisco** Password: **cisco**).

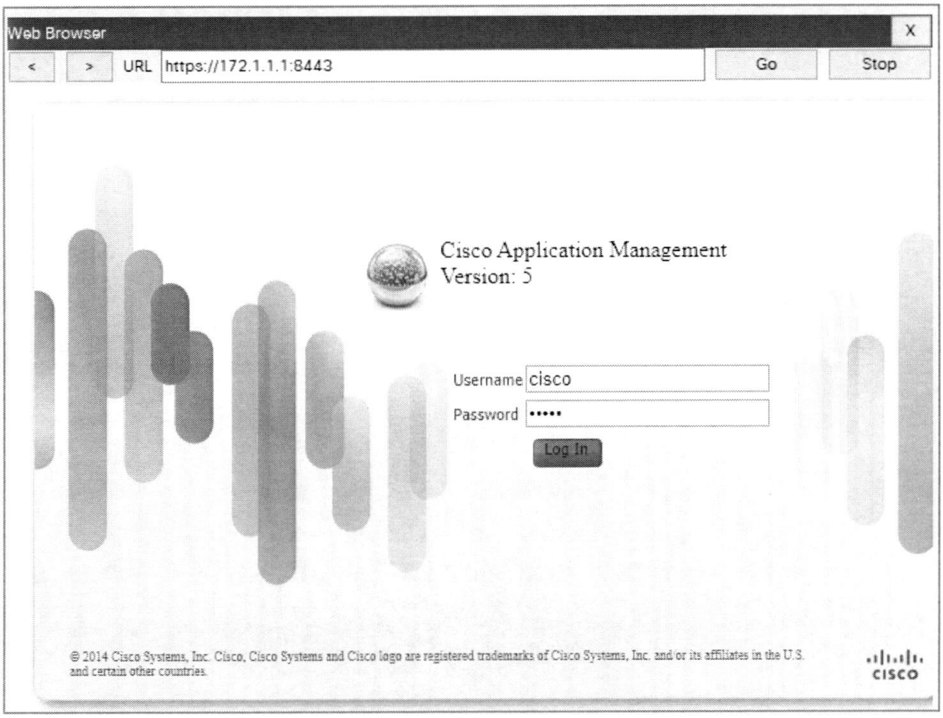

Figure 8.9 https://172.1.1.1:8443

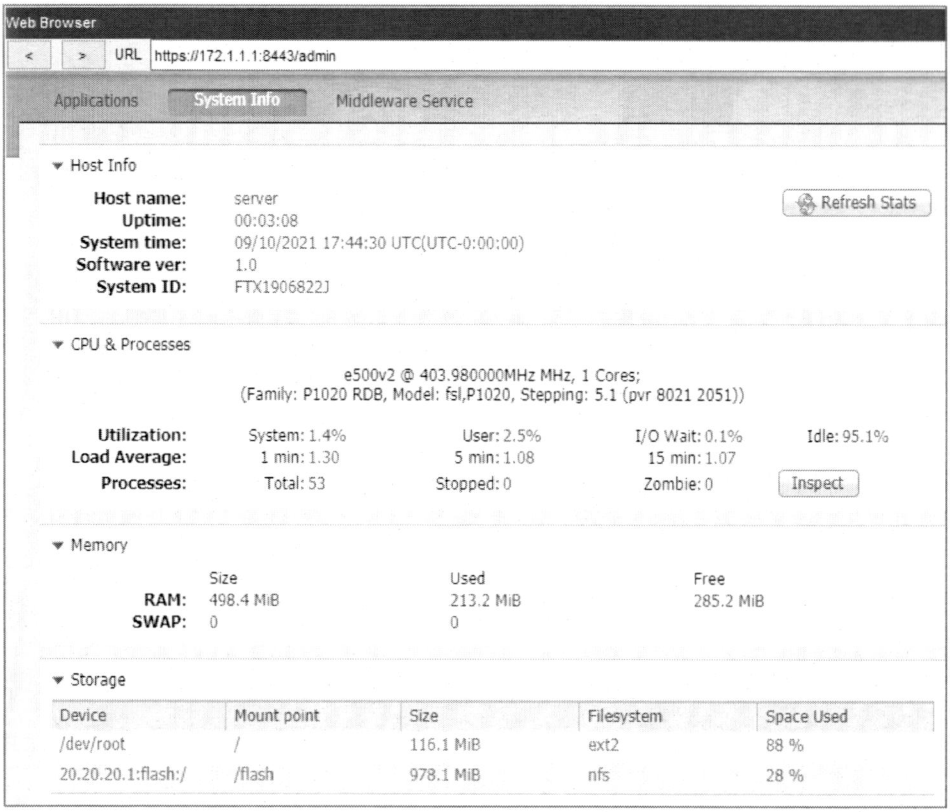

Figure 8.10 https://172.1.1.1:8443/admin

8.3 Running a virtual machine in 819HG-4G-IOX (Exercise 22)

Part 1. Network topology.

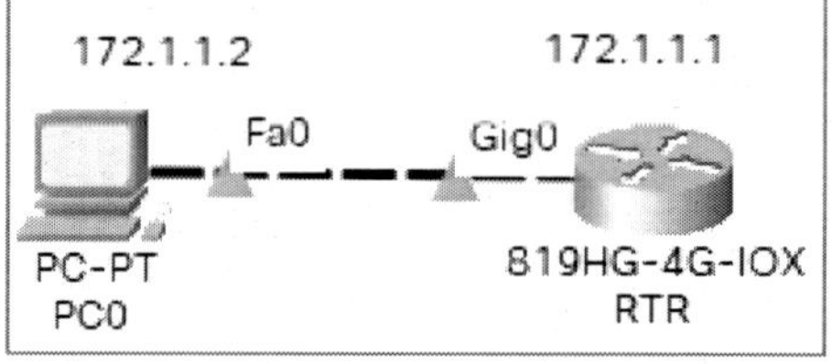

Figure 8.11 Network topology

Part 2. Required equipment:

- PC-PT – 1 pcs
- 819HG-4G-IOX – 1 pcs

Part 3. **Assumptions:**

The RTR router has configured addressing, NAT, and:

- Cisco Application Management listening on port 8443,
- access to Cisco Application Management is configured (login: cisco, password: cisco).
- The virtual machine is located on PC0 in the vm1 directory.

Part 3. Plan of the exercise – method 1 – using GUI.

Configure RTR router according to the given steps:

Step 1. Log into Cisco Application Management

From PC0 log into Cisco Application Management (address https://172.1.1.1:8443).

Figure 8.12 Cisco Application Management login page

Step 2. Add new virtual machine.

Using [**Add/Deploy**] button add virtual machine.

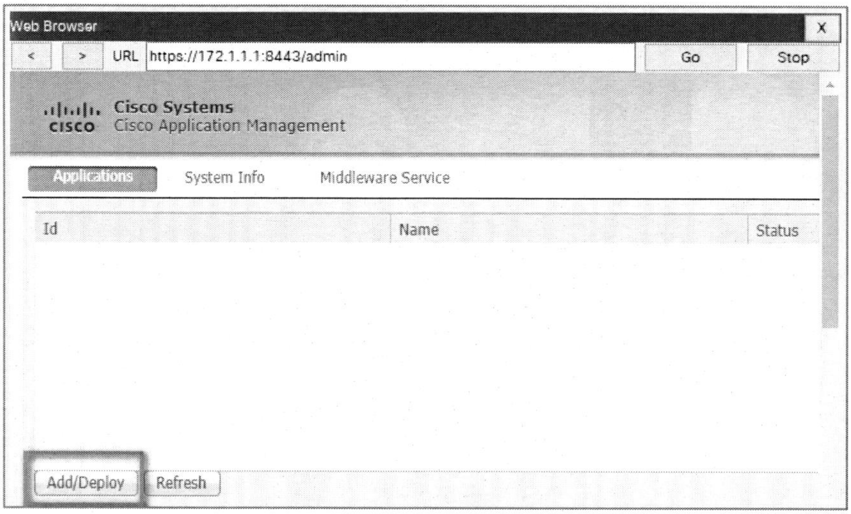

Figure 8.13 Adding a virtual machine

In **Application Id** field type 1.

Select the file (**Project Name**) **vm1**.

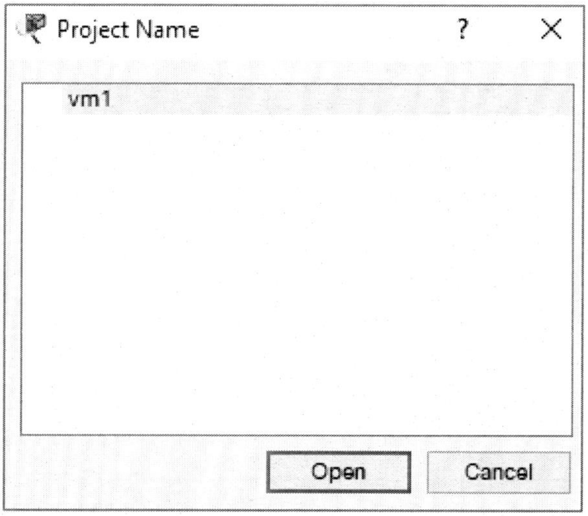

Figure 8.14 Selecting a virtual machine

Step 3. Start and stop the virtual machine.

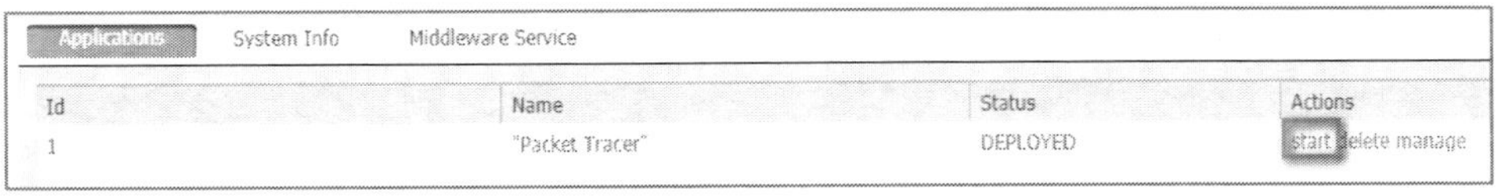

Figure 8.15 Running a virtual machine

Figure 8.16 Stopping the virtual machine

Figure 8.17 Status of the virtual machine

Part 4. Course of the exercise – method 2 – using CLI.

Step 1. On your computer, go to the **vml** directory and check its contents.

Use the commands : **`cd, dir.`**

```
C:\>
C:\>cd vml
C:\vml>dir

 Volume in drive C has no label.
 Volume Serial Number is 5E12-4AF3
 Directory of C:\vml

5/13/2015    14:11 PM          205         app_manifest.yaml
5/13/2015    14:11 PM          0           e500v2-linux-guest.uImage
5/13/2015    14:11 PM          554         imgb_cb_script.sh
5/13/2015    14:11 PM          148         vml.js
5/13/2015    14:12 PM          240         vml.ova
5/13/2015    14:11 PM          3           vml.ver
5/13/2015    14:11 PM          406         vml.xml
                 1556 bytes          7 File(s)
C:\vml>
```

Figure 8.18 Checking the contents of the C:\vlm directory

Step 2. On the router RTR and transfer the **vml.ova** file from PC0 to the flash memory on the router.

Use the commands: **`enable, copy`**

```
RTR#
RTR#copy tftp flash
Address or name of remote host []? 172.1.1.2
Source filename []? vml.ova
Destination filename [vml.ova]?

Accessing tftp://172.1.1.2/vml.ova...
Loading vml.ova from 172.1.1.2: !
[OK - 240 bytes]

240 bytes copied in 0 secs
```

Figure 8.19 Uploading the vml.ova file to flash memory on the router

Step 3. On the router, check the contents of the flash memory.

Use the command : **`dir`**

```
RTR#dir
Directory of flash:/

    4  -rw-     33591768          <no date>  c800-universalk9_iox-mz.SPA.155-1.T.bin
    2  -rw-        28282          <no date>  sigdef-category.xml
    1  -rw-       227537          <no date>  sigdef-default.xml
    5  -rw-          240          <no date>  vml.ova

255744000 bytes total (221896173 bytes free)
```

Figure 8.20 Checking the contents of flash memory:/

Step 4. Install a virtual machine on the router.

Use the commands :

`enable, virtual-service install name vm1 package flash:/vm1.ova`

```
RTR#
RTR#virtual-service install name vml package flash:/vml.ova
Installing package 'flash:/vml.ova' for virtual service 'vml'. Once the install has
finished, the VM may be activated. Use 'show virtual-service list' for progress.
*mar 1 00:42:23.657: %VIRT_SERVICE-5-INSTALL_STATE: Successfully installed virtual
service vml
RTR#
```

Figure 8.21 Installing the virtual machine

Step 5. On the router, go to global configuration mode and start vm1.

Use the commands :

`conf t, virtual-service vm1, activate`

```
RTR#
RTR#conf t
Enter configuration commands, one per line.  End with CNTL/Z.
RTR(config)#virtual-service vm1
RTR(config-virt-serv)#activate
% Activating virtual-service 'vm1', this might take a few minutes. Use 'show virtual-
service list' for progress.
*mar 1 00:46:47.249%VIRT_SERVICE-5-ACTIVATION_STATE: Successfully activate virtual
service vm1
RTR(config-virt-serv)#
```

Figure 8.22 Running the virtual machine

Step 6. On the router, stop vm1

Use the commands :

`conf t, virtual-service vm1, no activate`

```
RTR(config-virt-serv)#
RTR(config-virt-serv)#no activate
*mar 1 00:48:48.652%VIRT_SERVICE-5-ACTIVATION_STATE: Successfully deactivate virtual
service vm1
RTR(config-virt-serv)#
```

Figure 8.23 Stopping the virtual machine

8.4 List of auxiliary files

- exercise21-isr819hg-4g-iox-basic-configuration.pkt
- exercise22-isr819hg-4g-iox-running-virtual-machine.pkt

CHAPTER 9

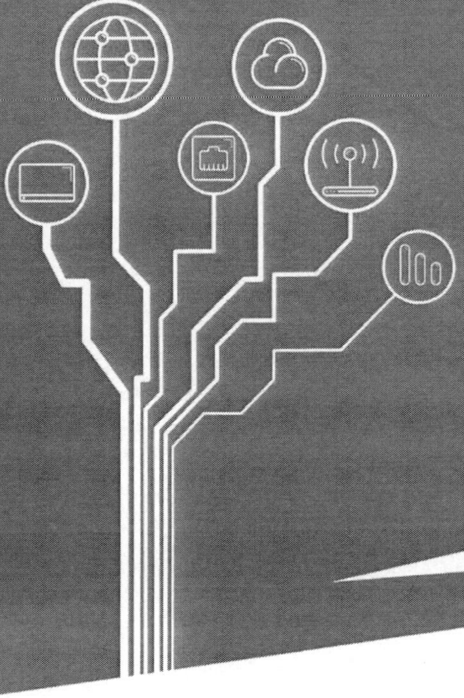

HOT SWAPPING DEVICES

COMPUTER NETWORKS IN PACKET TRACER

FOR ADVANCED USERS

9 Hot Swapping Devices

9.1 What is Hot Swapping ?

What is **hot swapping**?

Hot swapping is a feature of a device that allows modules (components) to be replaced or added to the device without shutting down, stopping or rebooting the system. An example of such a device is the **3650-24PS** multilayer switch model.

9.2 Adding power modules (Exercise 23)

In this exercise, we will look at adding **AC-POWER-SUPPLY** power modules.

Step 1. Insert 3650-24PS multilayer switch into logical topology

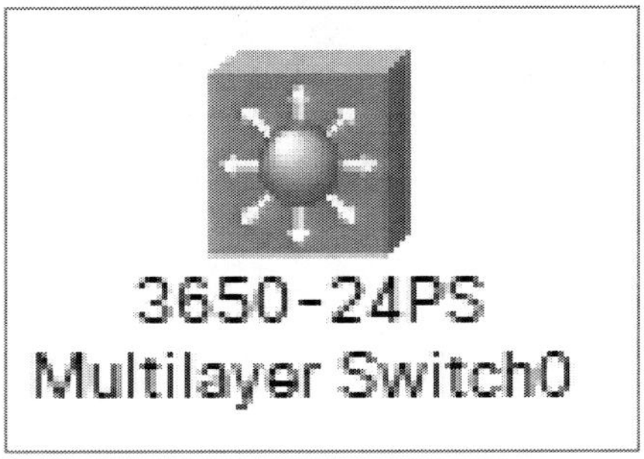

Figure 9.1 View of 3650-24PS symbol (logical topology)

Step 2 Familiarize yourself with the bays designated for power modules.

The 3650-24PS multilayer switch has two empty bays (slots) for power.

Fig. 9.2 View of 3650-24PS device (spaces for power supply modules)

The power supply of the switch is provided by one or **AC-POWER-SUPPLY** modules

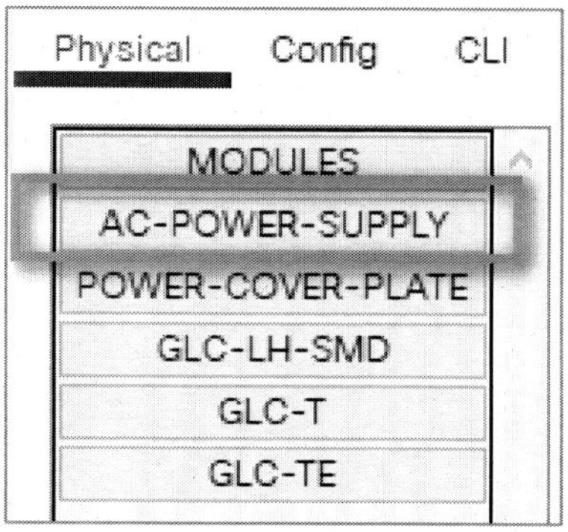

Figure 9.3 AC-POWER-SUPPLY power supply module

Step 3. Go to the [**Physical**] tab and use the mouse to move the **AC-POWER-SUPPLY** module to the first empty slot.

Figure 9.4 Appearance of the 3650-24PS (one power module)

Step 4. Using the appropriate IOS commands, check the power consumed by the device and the various interfaces.

Commands:

```
show environment power
show power inline
```

```
Switch>en
Switch#
Switch#show environment power
SW  PID                 Serial#     Status           Sys Pwr  PoE Pwr  Watts
--  ------------------  ----------  ---------------  -------  -------  -----
1A  PWR-C2-640WAC       8G8MWVES90W  OK              Good     Good     640
1B  Not Present
```

Figure 9.5 The result of executing the show environment power command

```
Switch#show power inline
Available:390.0(w)  Used:0.0(w)  Remaining:390.0(w)

Interface Admin  Oper       Power   Device              Class Max
                            (Watts)
--------- ------ ---------- ------- ------------------- ----- ----
Gig1/0/1  auto   off        0.0     n/a                 n/a   30.0
Gig1/0/2  auto   off        0.0     n/a                 n/a   30.0
Gig1/0/3  auto   off        0.0     n/a                 n/a   30.0
Gig1/0/4  auto   off        0.0     n/a                 n/a   30.0
Gig1/0/5  auto   off        0.0     n/a                 n/a   30.0
Gig1/0/6  auto   off        0.0     n/a                 n/a   30.0
Gig1/0/7  auto   off        0.0     n/a                 n/a   30.0
Gig1/0/8  auto   off        0.0     n/a                 n/a   30.0
Gig1/0/9  auto   off        0.0     n/a                 n/a   30.0
Gig1/0/10 auto   off        0.0     n/a                 n/a   30.0
Gig1/0/11 auto   off        0.0     n/a                 n/a   30.0
Gig1/0/12 auto   off        0.0     n/a                 n/a   30.0
Gig1/0/13 auto   off        0.0     n/a                 n/a   30.0
Gig1/0/14 auto   off        0.0     n/a                 n/a   30.0
Gig1/0/15 auto   off        0.0     n/a                 n/a   30.0
Gig1/0/16 auto   off        0.0     n/a                 n/a   30.0
Gig1/0/17 auto   off        0.0     n/a                 n/a   30.0
Gig1/0/18 auto   off        0.0     n/a                 n/a   30.0
Gig1/0/19 auto   off        0.0     n/a                 n/a   30.0
Gig1/0/20 auto   off        0.0     n/a                 n/a   30.0
Gig1/0/21 auto   off        0.0     n/a                 n/a   30.0
Gig1/0/22 auto   off        0.0     n/a                 n/a   30.0
Gig1/0/23 auto   off        0.0     n/a                 n/a   30.0
Gig1/0/24 auto   off        0.0     n/a                 n/a   30.0
```

Figure 9.6 The result of executing the show power inline command

Step 5. Go to the **[Physical]** tab and use the mouse to move the **AC-POWER-SUPPLY** module to the second empty slot.

Figure 9.7 Appearance of the 3650-24PS (two power modules)

Step 6. Using the appropriate IOS commands, check the power consumed by the device.

Commands:

```
show environment power
show power inline
```

```
Switch#
Switch#show environment power
SW  PID                 Serial#     Status           Sys Pwr  PoE Pwr  Watts
--  ------------------  ----------  ---------------  -------  -------  -----
1A  PWR-C2-640WAC       8G8MWVES90W  OK              Good     Good       640
1B  PWR-C2-640WAC       M5F2K90YTZ2  OK              Good     Good       640
Switch#
```

Figure 9.8 The result of executing the show environment power command

```
Switch#show power inline
Available:780.0(w)  Used:0.0(w)  Remaining:780.0(w)

Interface Admin  Oper       Power   Device              Class Max
                            (Watts)
--------- ------ ---------- ------- ------------------- ----- ----
Gig1/0/1  auto   off        0.0     n/a                 n/a   30.0
Gig1/0/2  auto   off        0.0     n/a                 n/a   30.0
Gig1/0/3  auto   off        0.0     n/a                 n/a   30.0
Gig1/0/4  auto   off        0.0     n/a                 n/a   30.0
Gig1/0/5  auto   off        0.0     n/a                 n/a   30.0
Gig1/0/6  auto   off        0.0     n/a                 n/a   30.0
Gig1/0/7  auto   off        0.0     n/a                 n/a   30.0
Gig1/0/8  auto   off        0.0     n/a                 n/a   30.0
Gig1/0/9  auto   off        0.0     n/a                 n/a   30.0
Gig1/0/10 auto   off        0.0     n/a                 n/a   30.0
Gig1/0/11 auto   off        0.0     n/a                 n/a   30.0
Gig1/0/12 auto   off        0.0     n/a                 n/a   30.0
Gig1/0/13 auto   off        0.0     n/a                 n/a   30.0
Gig1/0/14 auto   off        0.0     n/a                 n/a   30.0
Gig1/0/15 auto   off        0.0     n/a                 n/a   30.0
Gig1/0/16 auto   off        0.0     n/a                 n/a   30.0
Gig1/0/17 auto   off        0.0     n/a                 n/a   30.0
Gig1/0/18 auto   off        0.0     n/a                 n/a   30.0
Gig1/0/19 auto   off        0.0     n/a                 n/a   30.0
Gig1/0/20 auto   off        0.0     n/a                 n/a   30.0
Gig1/0/21 auto   off        0.0     n/a                 n/a   30.0
Gig1/0/22 auto   off        0.0     n/a                 n/a   30.0
Gig1/0/23 auto   off        0.0     n/a                 n/a   30.0
Gig1/0/24 auto   off        0.0     n/a                 n/a   30.0
```

Figure 9.9 The result of executing the show power inline command

9.3 Adding PoE devices (Exercise 24)

This exercise is a continuation of the previous exercise. We will study the distribution of power supply on the various ports of the switch to which IP phones will be connected.

Step 1. Connect 5 type 7960 IP phones to the switch

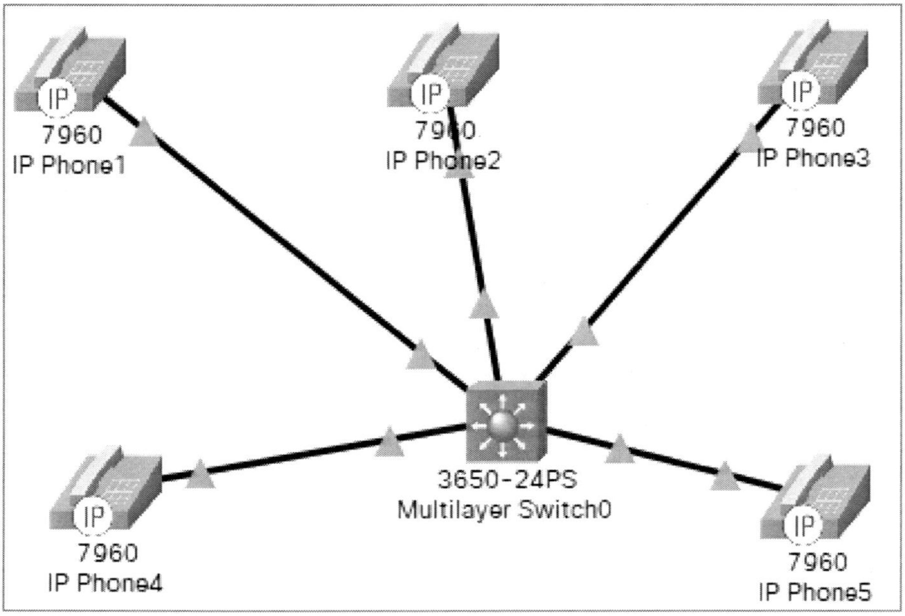

Figure 9.10 Network topology

Step 2. Using the appropriate IOS commands, check the distribution of power consumed on the Gig1/0/1 - Gig1/0/5 interfaces.

show power inline

```
Switch#
Switch#show power inline
Available:780.0(w)  Used:50.0(w)  Remaining:730.0(w)

Interface Admin  Oper       Power   Device               Class Max
                            (Watts)
--------- ------ ---------- ------- -------------------- ----- ----
Gig1/0/1  auto   on         10.0    IP Phone 7960        3     30.0
Gig1/0/2  auto   on         10.0    IP Phone 7960        3     30.0
Gig1/0/3  auto   on         10.0    IP Phone 7960        3     30.0
Gig1/0/4  auto   on         10.0    IP Phone 7960        3     30.0
Gig1/0/5  auto   on         10.0    IP Phone 7960        3     30.0
```

Figure 9.11 The result of executing the show power inline command

9.4 List of auxiliary files

- exercise23-adding-power-modules.pkt
- exercise24-adding-poe-devices.pkt

CHAPTER 10

CLOCK SYNCHRONIZATION

COMPUTER NETWORKS IN PACKET TRACER

FOR ADVANCED USERS

10 Clock Synchronization

10.1 NTP and PTP protocol

Part 1. Brief description of NTP protocol.

The Network Time Protocol (NTP) is used to synchronize the clocks of network devices.

Command	Description	Parameters
ntp master	Sets the router to the role of reference clock (i.e. time server)	*stratum* - integer from 1 to 15
ntp server	Notifies the client what the address of the time server is	*address* – IP address of the master, or time server
show ntp status	Displays NTP status (whether the clock is synchronized)	-

Table 10.1 The most important IOS commands for the NTP protocol

Part 2. Brief description of PTP protocol

The Precision Time Protocol (PTP) was implemented in PT 8.0.0 for the IE2000 switch.

Sources:
(Technology, 2017) [9]
(Cisco, Precision Time Protocol Software Configuration Guide for IE 2000U and Connected Grid Switches, 2022)[10]

The purpose of the PTP protocol is to enable Ethernet clock synchronization accuracy of less than 1 microsecond. It can be used to synchronize end devices.

Note: If the difference between the port time of a particular device and that of the MASTER device (see the parameter Offset From Master) exceeds the value of 500,000,000 ms (500 ms), the port status will change to UNCALIBRATED. This situation happens quite often in Packet Tracer because packets are sent at millisecond intervals.

[10] Cisco. Precision Time Protocol Software.

1 ms	$10^{-3}s = 0{,}001$ s
1 µs	$10^{-6}s = 0{,}000\ 001$ s
1 ns	$10^{-9}s = 0{,}000\ 000\ 001$ s

Table 10.2 SI sub-equivalents of 1 second

Command	Description	Parameters
`show ptp clock`	Displays clock information in PTP, e.g. priorities, time interval between current device and master.	-
`show ptp port`	Displays states and PTP clock information for individual ports.	*port (optional)* - port name and port number
`ptp mode`	Sets the mode of operation of the switch in the PTP protocol *	*boundary* – default border operation mode *e2etransparent* – transparent mode of operation, the device does not select the master, but packets *forward* – Passing packets are not processed (they are treated as multicast traffic)
`ptp priority1`	Sets the local priority of the so-called **Priority1**	Number - integer from 0 to 255
`ptp priority2`	Sets the local priority of the so-called **Priority2**	Number–integer from 0 to 255

Table 10.3 The most important IOS commands for the PTP protocol

*) PTP domain modes:

boundary – In this mode, the switch is configured to operate in boundary clock mode and participates in the selection of the best master clock in the domain. The selection is made from among all the clocks it can see, including itself.

If the switch does not detect a more accurate clock than itself, it becomes the master clock (Master). If a more accurate clock is detected, the switch synchronizes with that clock and becomes a slave clock.

forward – in this mode, the switch forwards incoming PTP packets as normal multicast traffic.

e2etransparent – In this mode, the switch is configured to operate in transparent **end-to-end** clock mode, that is, it does not synchronize its clock with the master clock. The switch does not participate in the selection of the master clock and uses the default PTP clock mode on all ports.

Source: (Cisco, Precision Time Protocol Software Configuration Guide for IE 2000U and Connected Grid Switches, 2022) [11]

10.2 Master-Slave synchronization between routers (Exercise 26)

Part 1. Topology.

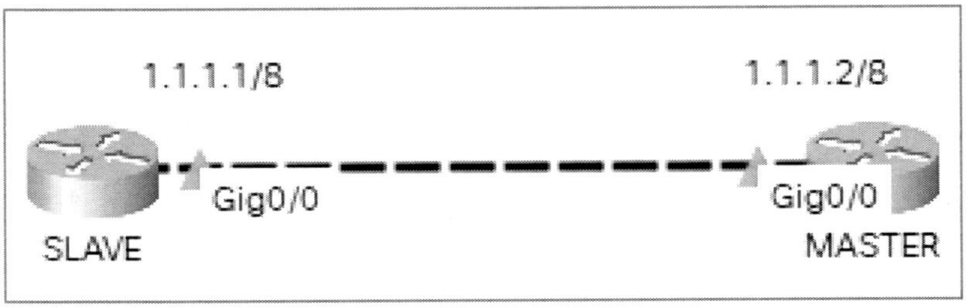

Figure 10.1 Master-Slave topology

Part 2. Plan of the exercise.

Step 1. Check the status of the clock on the MASTER router.

To do this, on the IOS command line, execute the commands:

```
enable
show  clock
```

```
MASTER#show clock
*9:19:9.544 UTC Mon Mar 1 1993
MASTER#
```

Figure 10.2 No drawing signature

Also:

```
show  ntp  status
```

[11] Cisco. Precision Time Protocol Software Configuration Guide, 2019.

```
MASTER#
MASTER#show ntp status
Clock is unsynchronized, stratum 16, no reference clock
nominal freq is 250.0000 Hz, actual freq is 249.0000 Hz, precision is 2**24
reference time is 00000000.00000000 (00:00:00.000 UTC Mon Jan 1 1990)
clock offset is 0.00 msec, root delay is 0.00  msec
root dispersion is 0.00 msec, peer dispersion is 0.00 msec.
loopfilter state is 'FSET' (Drift set from file), drift is - 0.000001193 s/s system poll
```

Figure 10.3 The result of the show ntp status command for the MASTER router

Step 2. Check the status of the clock on the SLAVE router.

To do this, on the IOS command line, execute the commands:

```
enable
show  clock
```

```
SLAVE#show clock
*9:24:23.593 UTC Mon Mar 1 1993
SLAVE#
```

Figure 10.4 The result of the show clock command for the SLAVE router

and

```
show  ntp  status
```

Step 3. On the MASTER router, activate the NTP service so that it acts as a time server.

```
SLAVE#
SLAVE#show ntp status
Clock is unsynchronized, stratum 16, no reference clock
nominal freq is 250.0000 Hz, actual freq is 249.0000 Hz, precision is 2**24
reference time is 00000000.00000000 (00:00:00.000 UTC Mon Jan 1 1990)
clock offset is 0.00 msec, root delay is 0.00  msec
root dispersion is 0.00 msec, peer dispersion is 0.00 msec.
loopfilter state is 'FSET' (Drift set from file), drift is - 0.000001193 s/s system poll
```

Figure 10.5 The result of the show ntp status command for the SLAVE router

Step 4. On the MASTER router, set the clock, for example, to the date of December 30, 2021 and the time 00:00:00.

```
enable
clock  set  00:00:00   30 December 2021
```

```
MASTER#
MASTER#clock  set  00:00:00   30 December 2021
MASTER#
MASTER#show clock
0:0:10.891 UTC Thu Dec 30 2021
```

Figure 10.6 Setting the clock for the MASTER router

Step 5. On the MASTER router, activate the NTP service so that it acts as a time server.

To do so, follow the commands:

enable

conf t

ntp master [*stratum*], stratum is integer number from 1 to 15.

Step 6. Wait a few minutes until the clock on the SLAVE router synchronizes with the clock on the MASTER router.

Step 7. Check NTP status on MASTER router.

```
MASTER#show ntp status
Clock is synchronized, stratum 1, reference is 127.127.1.1
nominal freq is 250.0000 Hz, actual freq is 249.9990 Hz, precision is 2**24
reference time is E54AA2F9.0000027E (0:4:9.638 UTC Thu Dec 30 2021)
clock offset is 0.00 msec, root delay is 0.00  msec
root dispersion is 0.00 msec, peer dispersion is 0.12 msec.
loopfilter state is 'CTRL' (Normal Controlled Loop), drift is - 0.000001193 s/s system
poll interval is 4, last update was 16 sec ago.
MASTER#
```

Figure 10.7 The result of the show ntp status command for the MASTER router

Step 8. Check NTP status and time on SLAVE router.

```
SLAVE#
SLAVE#show ntp status
Clock is synchronized, stratum 16, reference is 1.1.1.2
nominal freq is 250.0000 Hz, actual freq is 249.9990 Hz, precision is 2**24
reference time is 1B7DD41D.0000012E (14:13:49.302 UTC Sat Oct 29 2050)
clock offset is 0.00 msec, root delay is 0.00  msec
root dispersion is 10.23 msec, peer dispersion is 0.12 msec.
loopfilter state is 'CTRL' (Normal Controlled Loop), drift is - 0.000001193 s/s system
poll interval is 4, last update was 3 sec ago.
SLAVE#
SLAVE#show clock
0:7:15.744 UTC Thu Dec 30 2021
```

Figure 10.8 The result of the show ntp status command for the SLAVE router

10.3 Chain synchronization between routers (Exercise 26)

Part 1. Topology.

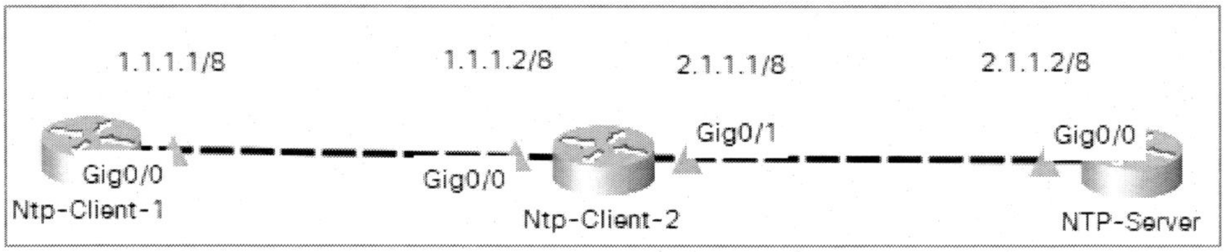

Figure 10.9 Client-Server chain topology

Part 2 Plan of the exercise.

Step 1. Set the clock on the NTP-Server router to, for example, the date November 15, 2022 and the time 12:00:00.

To do this, on the IOS command line, execute the commands:

```
enable
clock  set  12:00:00   15 November 2022
```

```
NTP-Server>
NTP-Server>enable
NTP-Server#clock  set  12:00:00   15 November 2022
NTP-Server#
```

Figure 10.10 Setting the clock for the NTP-Server router

Step 2. On the NTP-Server router, activate the NTP service so that it acts as a time server.

To do this, follow the commands:

```
enable
conf  t
ntp  master  3
```

```
NTP-Server#enable
NTP-Server#conf  t
Enter configuration commands, one per line.  End with CNTL/Z.
NTP-Server(config)#ntp  master  3
NTP-Server(config)#
```

Figure 10.11 Activating NTP for the NTP-Server router

Step 3. On the Ntp-Client-2 router, activate the NTP service so that it acts as a client.

To do this, follow the commands:

```
enable
conf  t
ntp  server  2.1.1.2
```

```
Ntp-Client-2>
Ntp-Client-2>enable
Ntp-Client-2#conf  t
Enter configuration commands, one per line.  End with CNTL/Z.
Ntp-Client-2(config)#ntp  server  2.1.1.2
Ntp-Client-2(config)#
```

Figure 10.12 Configuring NTP for the NTP-Client-2 router

Step 4. On the Ntp-Client-1 router, activate the NTP service so that it acts as a client.

To do this, follow the commands:

```
enable
conf  t
ntp  server  1.1.1.2
```

```
Ntp-Client-1>
Ntp-Client-1>enable
Ntp-Client-1#conf  t
Enter configuration commands, one per line.  End with CNTL/Z.
Ntp-Client-1(config)#ntp  server  1.1.1.2
Ntp-Client-1(config)#
```

Figure 10.13 Configuring NTP for the NTP-Client-1 router

Note: The next steps should be performed after waiting a time of at least 5 minutes. The further away the router is from the NTP-Server router, the longer the synchronization time will.

Step 5 Check the NTP status and time on the Ntp-Client-1 router.

```
Ntp-Client-1#show ntp status
Clock is synchronized, stratum 3, reference is 1.1.1.2
nominal freq is 250.0000 Hz, actual freq is 249.9990 Hz, precision is 2**24
reference time is E6F12C0F.00000255 (12:5:35.597 UTC Tue Nov 15 2022)
clock offset is 0.00 msec, root delay is 0.00  msec
root dispersion is 25.72 msec, peer dispersion is 0.12 msec.
loopfilter state is 'CTRL' (Normal Controlled Loop), drift is - 0.000001193 s/s system
poll interval is 4, last update was 1 sec ago.
Ntp-Client-1#
Ntp-Client-1#
Ntp-Client-1#show clock
12:5:59.843 UTC Tue Nov 15 2022
Ntp-Client-1#
```

Figure 10.14 Result of show ntp status, show clock commands for NTP-Client-1 router

Step 6. Check the NTP status and time on the Ntp-Client-2 router.

```
Ntp-Client-2#sh ntp status
Clock is synchronized, stratum 2, reference is 2.1.1.2
nominal freq is 250.0000 Hz, actual freq is 249.9990 Hz, precision is 2**24
reference time is E6F12C42.000001F6 (12:6:26.502 UTC Tue Nov 15 2022)
clock offset is 0.00 msec, root delay is 0.00  msec
root dispersion is 16.48 msec, peer dispersion is 0.24 msec.
loopfilter state is 'CTRL' (Normal Controlled Loop), drift is - 0.000001193 s/s system
poll interval is 5, last update was 7 sec ago.
Ntp-Client-2#show clock
12:6:39.68 UTC Tue Nov 15 2022
Ntp-Client-2#
```

Figure 10.15 Result of show ntp status, show clock commands for NTP-Client-2 router

10.4 Slave-Master-New Master Synchronization (Exercise 27)

Part 1. Topology and assumptions.

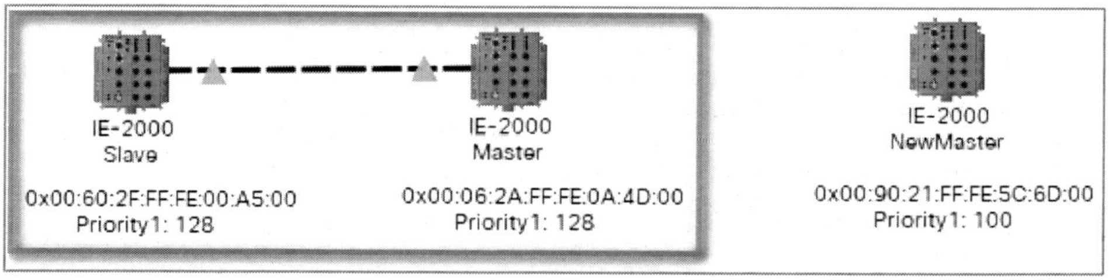

Figure 10.16 Slave-Master-NewMaster topology

The topology contains three IE-2000 devices (so-called Boundary Clock), with the following data, given in the table.

Host name	Clock Id	Priority1
Slave	0x00:60:2F:FF:FE:00:A5:00	128
Master	0x00:06:2A:FF:FE:0A:4D:00	128
NewMaster	0x00:90:21:FF:FE:5C:6D:00	100

Table 10.4 Main data of IE-2000 devices

Part 2. Plan of the exercise.

Step 1. Create topology according to the drawing.

Step 2. Display the configuration of the slave switch regarding time synchronization.

```
ptp mode boundary
ptp time-property persist 300
```

Figure 10.17 Checking the PTP configuration for a slave switch

Step 3. Display the master switch configuration for time synchronization.

```
ptp mode boundary
ptp time-property persist 300
```

Figure 10.18 Checking the PTP configuration for the master switch

Step 4. Check the status of the Fa1/1 port on the slave switch.

To do this, execute the command:

`show ptp port Fa1/1.`

```
Slave# show ptp port Fa1/1
 PTP PORT DATASET: FastEthernet1/1
  Port identity: clock identity: 0x00:60:2F:FF:FE:00:A5:00
  Port identity: port number: 1
  PTP version: 2
  Port state: SLAVE
  Delay request interval(log mean): 5
  Announce receipt time out: 3
  Announce interval(log mean): 1
  Sync interval(log mean): 0
  Delay Mechanism: End to End
  Peer delay request interval(log mean): 0
  Sync fault limit: 500000000
```

Figure 10.19 Checking the Fa1/1 port configuration for the slave switch

Step 5. Check the status of the Fa1/1 port on the master switch.

To do this, execute the command:

`show ptp port Fa1/1.`

```
Master#show  ptp  port  Fa1/1
 PTP PORT DATASET: FastEthernet1/1
  Port identity: clock identity: 0x00:06:2A:FF:FE:0A:4D:00
  Port identity: port number: 1
  PTP version: 2
  Port state: MASTER
  Delay request interval(log mean): 5
  Announce receipt time out: 3
  Announce interval(log mean): 1
  Sync interval(log mean): 0
  Delay Mechanism: End to End
  Peer delay request interval(log mean): 0
  Sync fault limit: 500000000
```

Figure 10.20 Checking Fa1/1 port configuration for master switch

Step 6. Connect the **Master** switch to the **NewMaster** switch.

Note 1: The NewMaster switch has a higher priority **Priority1.**

Note 2: Click the [Fast Forward Time] button several times.

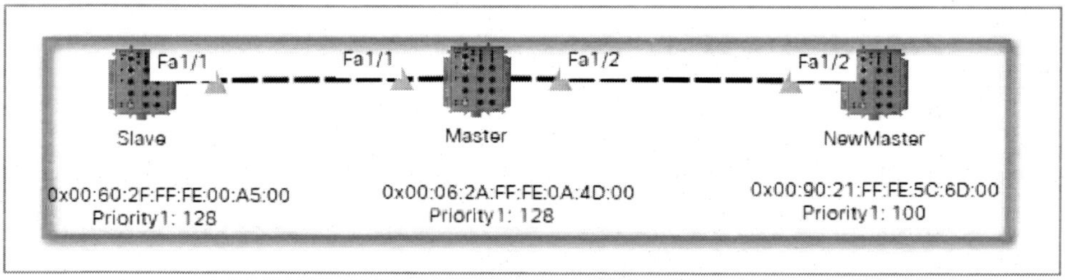

Figure 10.21 Synchronization in the Salave-Master-NewMaster topology

Step 7. Check the status of the PTP clock on the slave switch.

```
Slave#show ptp clock
 PTP CLOCK INFO
  PTP Device Type: Boundary clock
  PTP Device Profile: Default Profile
  Clock Identity: 0x00:60:2F:FF:FE:00:A5:00
  Clock Domain: 0
  Number of PTP ports: 10
  Priority1: 128
  Priority2: 128
  Clock Quality:
        Class: 248
        Accuracy: Unknown
        Offset (log variance): N/A
  Offset From Master(ns): 499872
  Mean Path Delay(ns): 500000
  Steps Removed: 2
  Local clock time: 03:26:05 UTC March 30 2011
```

Figure 10.22 PTP clock status on the slave switch

Step 8. Check the status of the PTP protocol on port Fa1/1 on the slave switch.

```
Slave#show ptp port Fa1/1
 PTP PORT DATASET: FastEthernet1/1
  Port identity: clock identity: 0x00:60:2F:FF:FE:00:A5:00
  Port identity: port number: 1
  PTP version: 2
  Port state: SLAVE
  Delay request interval(log mean): 5
  Announce receipt time out: 3
  Announce interval(log mean): 1
  Sync interval(log mean): 0
  Delay Mechanism: End to End
  Peer delay request interval(log mean): 0
  Sync fault limit: 500000000
```

Figure 10.23 protocol status on port Fa1/1 on the slave switch

Step 9. Check the status of the PTP timer on the master switch

```
Master#show ptp clock
 PTP CLOCK INFO
  PTP Device Type: Boundary clock
  PTP Device Profile: Default Profile
  Clock Identity: 0x00:06:2A:FF:FE:0A:4D:00
  Clock Domain: 0
  Number of PTP ports: 10
  Priority1: 128
  Priority2: 128
  Clock Quality:
        Class: 248
        Accuracy: Unknown
        Offset (log variance): N/A
  Offset From Master(ns): -1000000
  Mean Path Delay(ns): 64
  Steps Removed: 1
  Local clock time: 03:27:57 UTC March 30 2011
```

Figure 10.24 PTP clock status on master switch

Step 10 Check the status of the PTP protocol on port Fa1/1 on the master switch.

```
Master#show ptp port Fa1/1
 PTP PORT DATASET: FastEthernet1/1
  Port identity: clock identity: 0x00:06:2A:FF:FE:0A:4D:00
  Port identity: port number: 1
  PTP version: 2
  Port state: MASTER
  Delay request interval(log mean): 5
  Announce receipt time out: 3
  Announce interval(log mean): 1
  Sync interval(log mean): 0
  Delay Mechanism: End to End
  Peer delay request interval(log mean): 0
  Sync fault limit: 500000000
```

Figure 10.25 PTP protocol status on port Fa1/1 on the master switch

Step 11. Check the status of the PTP protocol on port Fa1/2 on the master switch.

```
Master#show ptp port Fa1/2
 PTP PORT DATASET: FastEthernet1/2
  Port identity: clock identity: 0x00:06:2A:FF:FE:0A:4D:00
  Port identity: port number: 2
  PTP version: 2
  Port state: SLAVE
  Delay request interval(log mean): 5
  Announce receipt time out: 3
  Announce interval(log mean): 1
  Sync interval(log mean): 0
  Delay Mechanism: End to End
  Peer delay request interval(log mean): 0
  Sync fault limit: 500000000
```

Figure 10.26 PTP protocol status on port Fa1/2 on the master switch

Step 12. Check the status of the PTP timer on the NewMaster switch.

```
NewMaster#show ptp clock
 PTP CLOCK INFO
  PTP Device Type: Boundary clock
  PTP Device Profile: Default Profile
  Clock Identity: 0x00:90:21:FF:FE:5C:6D:00
  Clock Domain: 0
  Number of PTP ports: 10
  Priority1: 100
  Priority2: 128
  Clock Quality:
        Class: 248
        Accuracy: Unknown
        Offset (log variance): N/A
  Offset From Master(ns): 0
  Mean Path Delay(ns): 0
  Steps Removed: 0
  Local clock time: 03:29:15 UTC March 30 2011
```

Figure 10.27 PTP clock status on the NewMaster switch

Step 13. Check the status of the PTP protocol on port Fa1/1 on the NewMaster switch.

```
NewMaster#
NewMaster#show ptp port Fa1/2
 PTP PORT DATASET: FastEthernet1/2
  Port identity: clock identity: 0x00:90:21:FF:FE:5C:6D:00
  Port identity: port number: 2
  PTP version: 2
  Port state: MASTER
  Delay request interval(log mean): 5
  Announce receipt time out: 3
  Announce interval(log mean): 1
  Sync interval(log mean): 0
  Delay Mechanism: End to End
  Peer delay request interval(log mean): 0
  Sync fault limit: 500000000
```

Figure 10.28 PTP protocol status on port Fa1/2 on the NewMaster switch

Step 14. Check the current time difference between Slave and NewMaster, using the command:

`show ptp clock`

```
Slave#show ptp clock
 PTP CLOCK INFO
  PTP Device Type: Boundary clock
  PTP Device Profile: Default Profile
  Clock Identity: 0x00:60:2F:FF:FE:00:A5:00
  Clock Domain: 0
  Number of PTP ports: 10
  Priority1: 128
  Priority2: 128
  Clock Quality:
        Class: 248
        Accuracy: Unknown
        Offset (log variance): N/A
  Offset From Master(ns): 500032
  Mean Path Delay(ns): [illegible]
  Steps Removed: 2
  Local clock time: 03:31:32 UTC March 30 2011
```

Figure 10.29 Time difference between Slave and NewMaster [ns].

Note: If the difference between the port time of a particular device and that of the MASTER device (see the parameter Offset From Master) exceeds 500,000,000 ns (500 ms), the port status will change to **UNCALIBRATED.** This situation happens quite often in Packet Tracer because packets are sent at millisecond intervals.

10.5 Synchronization in boundary, e2eforward, transparent modes (Exercise 28)

Part 1. Topology and assumptions.

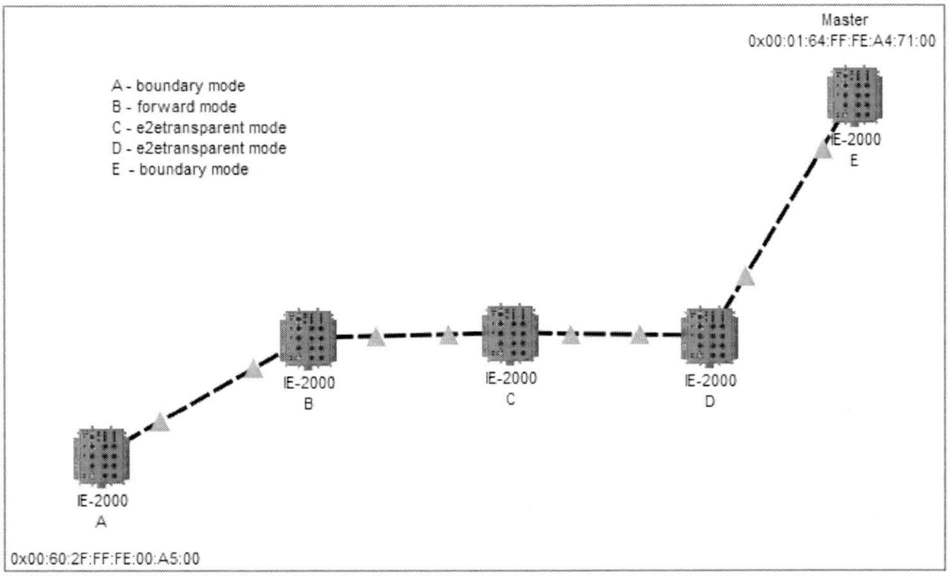

Figure 10.30 Topology with boundary+e2eforward+transparent clocks

Name of the device	Clock ID	Priority1	Mode of operation	The role of the device
A	0x00:60:2F:FF:FE:00:A5:00	128	boundary	SLAVE
B	-	-	forward	-
C	-	-	e2etransparent	-
D	-	-	e2etransparent	-
E	0x00:01:64:FF:FE:A4:71:00	128	boundary	MASTER

Table 10.5 Data for PTP

Part 2. Plan of the exercise.

Step 1. Create a topology according to the figure.

Step 2. Set the clock on switch E to, for example, the date 1.11.2022 and the time 00:00:00.

To do this, on the E switch command line, execute the commands:

```
enable
clock  set  00:00:00   1 November 2022
```

Step 3. Set the **boundary** mode on switch **A.**

To do this, on the command line of Switch A, execute the commands:

```
enable
conf  t
ptp mode boundary
```

Step 4. Set the **forward** mode on switch **B.**

To do this, on the command line of Switch B, execute the commands:

```
enable
conf  t
ptp mode forward
```

Step 5. Set the **e2etransparent** operation mode on switch **C**.

To do this, on the command line of Switch C, execute the commands:

```
enable
conf  t
ptp mode e2etransparent
```

Step 6. Set the **e2etransparent** operation mode on switch **D.**

To do this, on the command line of Switch D, execute the commands:

```
enable
conf  t
ptp mode e2etransparent
```

Step 7. Set the **boundary** mode on the **E** switch.

To do this, on the command line of Switch E, execute the commands:

```
enable
conf  t
ptp mode boundary
```

Step 8 Enter simulation mode to observe PTP movement. Turn on the [Play] button to start the simulation.

Figure 10.31 [Play] button in simulation mode

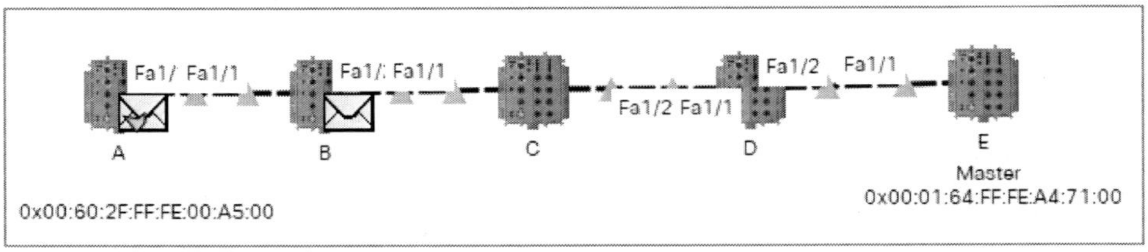

Figure 10.31 Observation of PTP packets in simulation mode

Watch for PTP packages.

Simulation Panel

Event List

Vis.	Time(sec)	Last Device	At Device	Type
	0.121	--	C	PTP
	0.122	C	B	PTP
	0.122	--	C	PTP
	0.123	C	B	PTP
	0.123	B	A	PTP
	0.124	B	A	PTP
	0.994	--	E	PTP
	0.994	--	E	PTP
	0.995	E	D	PTP
	0.995	--	E	PTP
	0.996	E	D	PTP
	0.996	D	C	PTP
	0.997	D	C	PTP
	0.997	C	B	PTP
	0.998	C	B	PTP
	0.998	B	A	PTP
	0.999	B	A	PTP
	1.121	--	C	PTP
	1.121	--	C	PTP
	1.121	--	C	PTP
	1.122	C	B	PTP
	1.122	--	C	PTP
	1.123	C	B	PTP
	1.123	B	A	PTP

Figure 10.32 Observation of PTP packets in [Simulation Panel].

Step 9. Wait about 3 to 4 minutes, for the clocks to synchronize.

Step 10. After waiting for some time, check the status of port Fa1/1 on switch A.

Execute the command

`show ptp port Fa1/1`

Check that the status of port Fa1/1 is **SLAVE**.

```
A#show ptp port Fa1/1
 PTP PORT DATASET: FastEthernet1/1
  Port identity: clock identity: 0x00:60:2F:FF:FE:00:A5:00
  Port identity: port number: 1
  [illegible]
  Port state: SLAVE
  Delay request interval(log mean): 5
  [illegible]
  Announce interval(log mean): 1
  Sync interval(log mean): 0
  Delay Mechanism: End to End
  Peer delay request interval(log mean): 0
  Sync fault limit: 500000000
```

Figure 10.33 The result of the command: show ptp port Fa1/1

Step 11. Check the clock values of the individual switches.

On each switch, execute the command

`show ptp clock`

PTP time on A should be synchronized with PTP time on E.

```
E#show ptp clock
 PTP CLOCK INFO
  PTP Device Type: Boundary clock
  PTP Device Profile: Default Profile
  Clock Identity: 0x00:01:64:FF:FE:A4:71:00
  Clock Domain: 0
  Number of PTP ports: 10
  Priority1: 128
  Priority2: 128
  Clock Quality:
        Class: 248
        Accuracy: Unknown
        Offset (log variance): N/A
  Offset From Master(ns): 0
  Mean Path Delay(ns): 0
  Steps Removed: 0
  Local clock time: 13:04:02 UTC November 24 2015
```

Figure 10.34 The result of the command: show ptp clock in E

```
D#show ptp clock
 PTP CLOCK INFO
  PTP Device Type: End to End transparent clock
  PTP Device Profile: Default Profile
  Clock Identity: 0x00:0D:BD:FF:FE:CE:C6:00
  Clock Domain: 0
  Number of PTP ports: 10
  Delay Mechanism: End to End
  Local clock time: 04:58:05 UTC March 30 2011
```

Figure 10.35 The result of the command: show ptp clock in D

```
C#show ptp clock
 PTP CLOCK INFO
  PTP Device Type: End to End transparent clock
  PTP Device Profile: Default Profile
  Clock Identity: 0x00:60:47:FF:FE:D9:DB:00
  Clock Domain: 0
  Number of PTP ports: 10
  Delay Mechanism: End to End
  Local clock time: 04:31:46 UTC March 30 2011
```

Figure 10.36 The result of the command: show ptp clock in C

```
B#show ptp clock
 No clock information is available in forwarding mode.
B#
B#
```

Figure 10.38 The result of the command: show ptp clock in B

```
A#show ptp clock
 PTP CLOCK INFO
  PTP Device Type: Boundary clock
  PTP Device Profile: Default Profile
  Clock Identity: 0x00:60:2F:FF:FE:00:A5:00
  Clock Domain: 0
  Number of PTP ports: 10
  Priority1: 128
  Priority2: 128
  Clock Quality:
        Class: 248
        Accuracy: Unknown
        Offset (log variance): N/A
  Offset From Master(ns): -32
  Mean Path Delay(ns): 4000096
  Steps Removed: 1
  Local clock time: 13:07:11 UTC November 24 2015
```

Figure 10.37 The result of the command: show ptp clock in A

The clock date on A is **November 24 2015** and the clock date on E is **November 24 2015**, so the both device A are E are synchronized.

10.6 List of auxiliary files

- exercise25-ntp-master-slave-synchronization.pkt
- exercise26-ntp-chain-synchronization.pkt
- exercise27-ptp-slave-master-new-master-synchronization.pkt
- exercise28-ptp-advanced-synchronization.pkt

CHAPTER 11

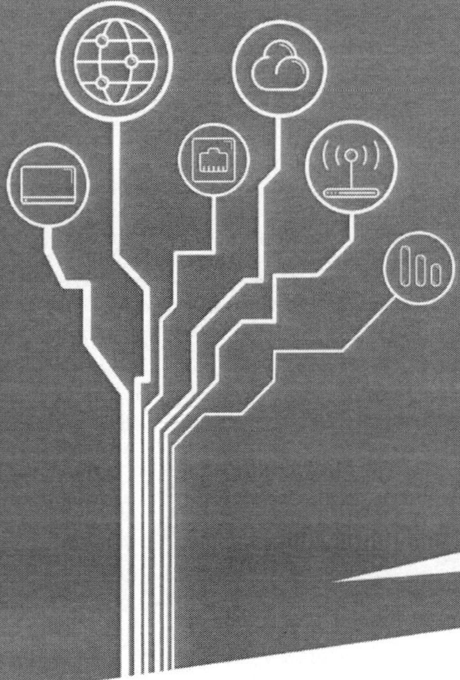

SERVER SERVICES

COMPUTER NETWORKS IN PACKET TRACER

FOR ADVANCED USERS

11 Server Services

11.1 Http SERVICE (Exercise 29)

Part 1. Introduction.

In Packet Tracer you can create your own web pages (simple and complex) using HTML, CSS, JS files. They can be hosted on PT-Server type servers using HTTP service.

Part 2. File preparation.

Prepare the following files:

- my_styles.css
- my_java_script.js
- index.html
- index2.html
- index3.html
- image2.html
- picture1-40x40.png
- picture2-154x167.png
- picture3-222x148.png
- picture4-350x196.png

Part 3. Plan of the exercise.

Step 1. In Notepad, create code containing the following CSS cascading styles

Save this code in a file **my_styles.css**

```
BODY, P, UL, TD, TH, DIR, .bodyText {
    font-family: Arial, Helvetica, Verdana, Geneva, Arial,
sans-serif;
    font-size : 10pt;
    color: Black;
    background-color: Yellow;
}
h1  {font-size: 14pt/14pt; font-weight: bold; color: Red;}
.head {font-size: 12pt; font-weight: bold; color: #990000;}
```

```
p.textbody {text-align: justify; line-height: 17pt;}
.font10pt {font-size: 10pt;}
.font12pt {font-size: 12pt;}
a:link {color: #996600; text-decoration: none;}
a:visited {color: #996600; text-decoration: none;}
a:hover {color: #CC0000; text-decoration: underline;}
a:active {color: #990000; text-decoration: none;}
#watermark_box {
position:relative;
display:block;
}
img.watermark {
position: absolute;
top: 1px;
left: 1px;
}
```

Step 2. In Notepad, create a code containing the following codes for Java Script.

Save this code in a file **my_java_script.js**

```
<!--
function my_function()
{
   alert('An internal script was run!');
}
// -->
```

Step 3 In Notepad, create a code containing the following codes for the main file.

Save this code in a file **index.html**

```
<html>

<head>
<link rel="stylesheet" href="my_styles.css">
<script>
function MyFunction()
{
   alert('An internal script was run !');
}
```

```
</script>
</head>
<body>
<h1> My website at Cisco Packet Tracer</h1>
<hr>
<p><center>MENU:</center></p>
<p><center><button type="button"
onclick="MyFunction()">Launch of internal Java
Script</button></center></p>
<p><center><a href="index2.html"> Launch of external Java
Script</a></center></p>
<p><center><a href="index3.html"> Displaying images
</a></center></p>
<p><center><a href="image2.html"> Testing images imported
from Packet Tracera</a></center></p>
<p><center><a href="index.html">RETURN</a></center></p>
</body>
</html>
```

Step 4. In Notepad, create code containing the following codes for the index2.html file

Save this code in a file **index2.html**

```
<html>
<head>
<link rel="stylesheet" href="my_styles.css">
</head>
<body>
<script language="javascript"
src="my_java_script.js"></script>
<center><font size='+2' color='blue'> Launch of external
script</font></center>
<hr>
<br><button type="button" onclick="my_function()">Launch of
external script</button>
<a href='index.html'>RETURN</a>
</body>
</html>
```

Step 5. In Notepad, create a code containing the following codes for the index3.html file.

Save this code in a file **index3.html**

```
<html>
<head>
<link rel="stylesheet" href="my_styles.css">
</head>
<body>
<center><font size='+2' color='blue'> Displaying images
</font></center>
<center><p>
<a href='index.html'>RETURN</a><br>
This is the image in resolution 154px x 167px<br>
<img src="/picture2-154x167.png"/><br>
This is the image in resolution 222px x 148px<br>
<img src="/picture3-222x148.png"/><br>
This is the image in resolution 350px x 196px<br>
<img src="/picture4-350x196.png"/>
</p></center>
</body>
</html>
```

Step 6. In Notepad, create a code containing the following codes for the image2.html file.

Save this code in a file **image2.html**

```
<html>
<head>
<link rel="stylesheet" href="my_styles.css">
</head>
<body>
<center><font size='+2' color='blue'> Imported images
</font></center>
<center><p>
<a href='index.html'>RETURN</a><br>
<img src="\picture1-40x40.png"/>
</p></center>
</body>
```

Step 7. Create a topology to test the site.

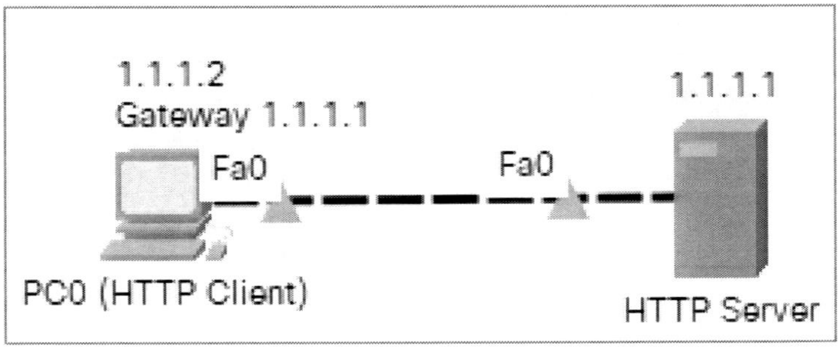

Figure 11.1 Network topology tested

Step 8. On the server in the HTTP service, delete all files.

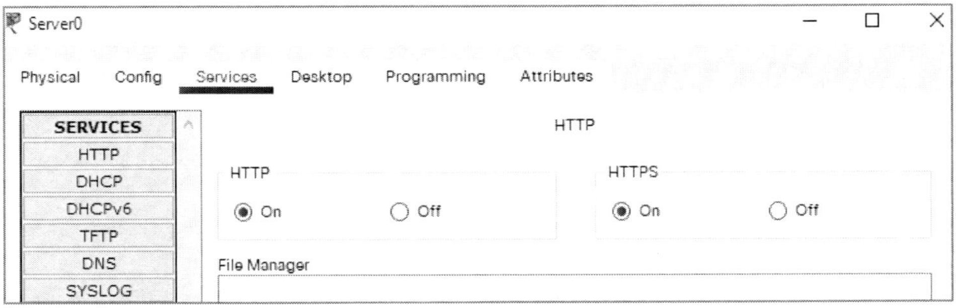

Figure 11.2 http service

Step 9. Open File Manager under [Services][HTTP].

Step 10. Import **index.html** file

Import a file named [**index.html**] into File Manager on the HTTP service.

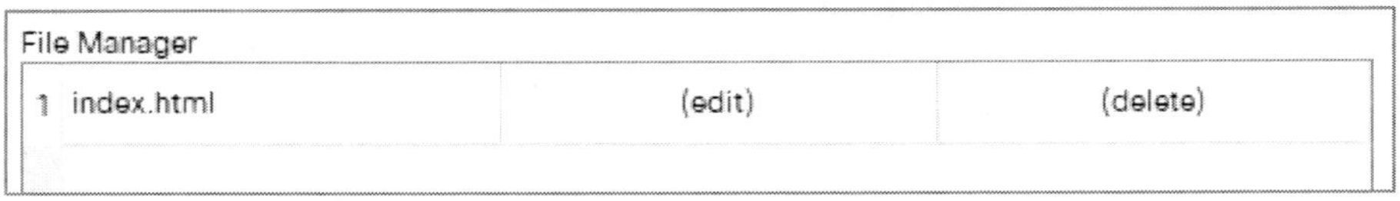

Figure 11.3 Importing an index.html file

Step 11. Import the **index2.html** file

Import a file named **[index2.html]** into the File Manager on the HTTP service

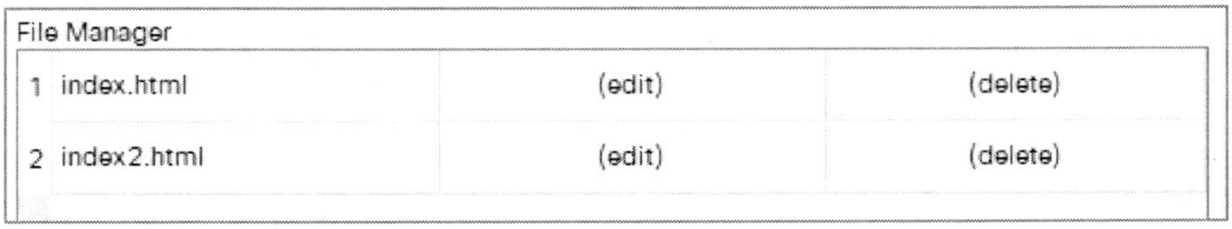

Figure 11.4 Importing the index2.html file

Step 12. Import the **index3.html** file

Import a file named [**index3.html**] into the File Manager on the HTTP service

File Manager

1	index.html	(edit)	(delete)
2	index2.html	(edit)	(delete)
3	index3.html	(edit)	(delete)

Figure 11.5 Importing the index3.html file

Step 13. Import **my_java_script.js**

Import a file named [**my_java_script.js**] into the File Manager in the HTTP service

File Manager

	File Name	Edit	Delete
1	image2.html	(edit)	(delete)
2	index.html	(edit)	(delete)
3	index2.html	(edit)	(delete)
4	index3.html	(edit)	(delete)
5	my_java_script.js	(edit)	(delete)

Figure 11.6 Importing my_java_script.js file

Step 14. Import **my_styles.css**

Import a file named [**my_style.css**] into the File Manager on the HTTP service

File Manager

	File Name	Edit	Delete
1	image2.html	(edit)	(delete)
2	index.html	(edit)	(delete)
3	index2.html	(edit)	(delete)
4	index3.html	(edit)	(delete)
5	my_java_script.js	(edit)	(delete)
6	my_styles.css	(edit)	(delete)

Figure 11.7 Importing my_styles.css file

Step 15. Import **image2.html**

Import a file named [**image2.html**] into File Manager on the HTTP service

File Manager

	File Name	Edit	Delete
1	image2.html	(edit)	(delete)
2	index.html	(edit)	(delete)
3	index2.html	(edit)	(delete)
4	index3.html	(edit)	(delete)
5	my_java_script.js	(edit)	(delete)
6	my_styles.css	(edit)	(delete)

Figure 11.8 Importing the image2.html file

Step 16. Import picture1-40x40.png

Import a file named [**picture1-40x40.png**] into the File Manager in the HTTP service .

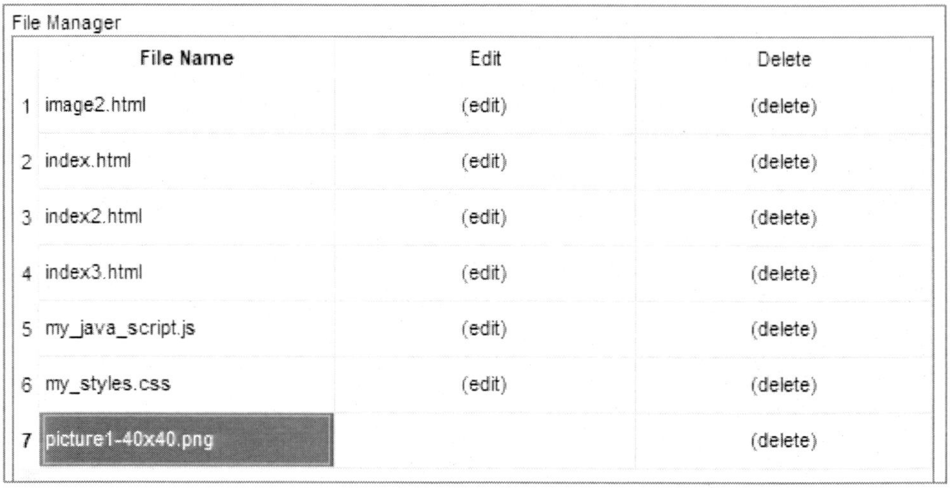

Figure 11.9 Import of picture1-40x40.png file

Step 17. Check the performance of **http://1.1.1.1**

In the server, open a page with the address **[http://1.1.1.1].**

Figure 11.10 Home page with menu

Step 18. Check the operation of the first menu item (Launch of internal JS script)

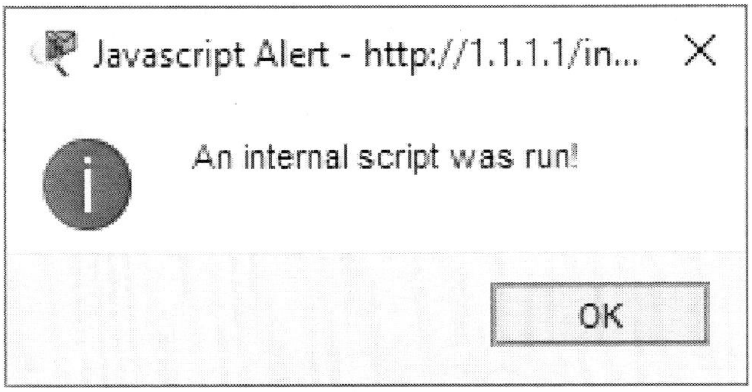

Figure 11.11 Running an internal script

Step 19. Check the operation of the second menu item (external JS script)

Figure 11.12 Running an external script

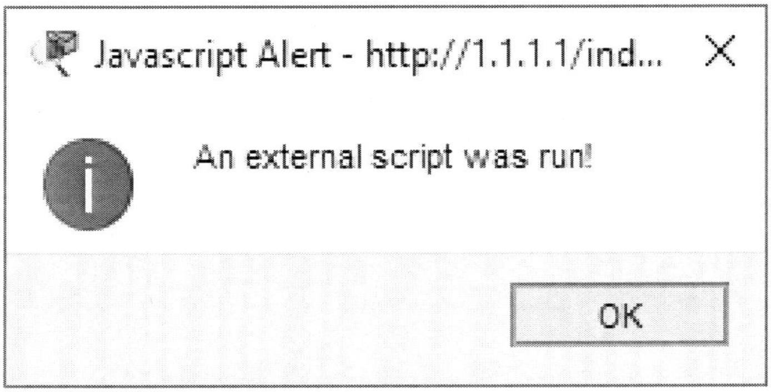

Figure 11.13 Running an external script

Step 20. Check the operation of the third menu item (Display images)

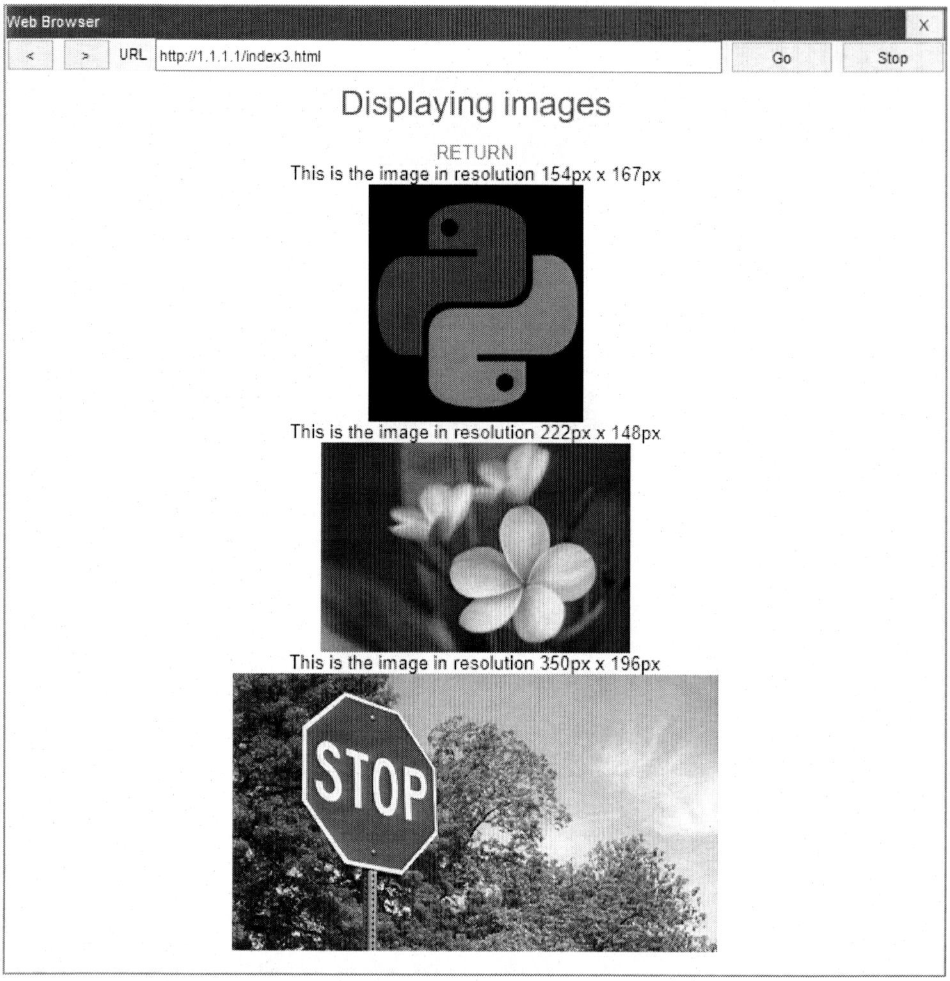

Figure 11.14 Displaying images

Step 21. Check the operation of the fourth menu item (Imported images)

Figure 11.15 Displaying imported images

11.2 FTP SERVICE (Exercise 30)

Part 1. Introduction.

In Packet Tracer, you can import (copy) files to the local disk C: on **PC-PT** using the **Text Editor** applet in the **[Desktop]** tab and then send them to the **Server-PT** using **FTP**.

Figure 11.16 Text Editor application

Part 2. Network topology.

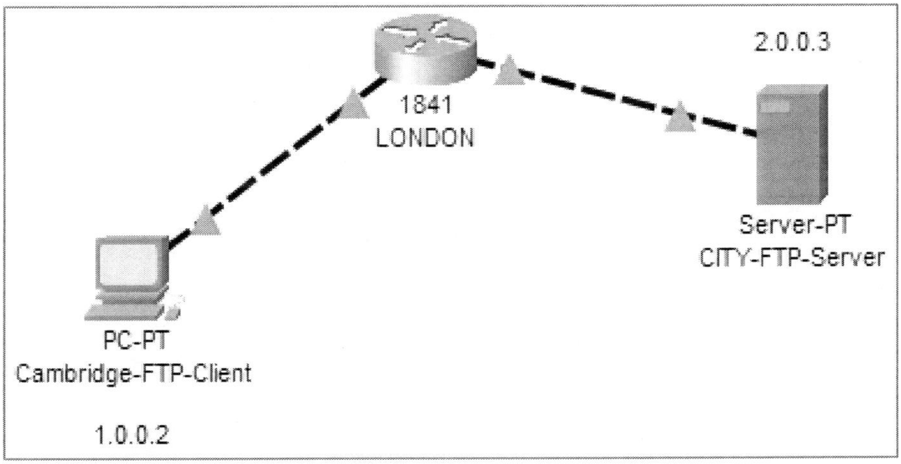

Figure 11.17 Network topology

Part 3. Plan of the exercise.

Step 1 On **CITY-FTP-Server,** using the **FTP** service, delete all files, for account **cisco**:

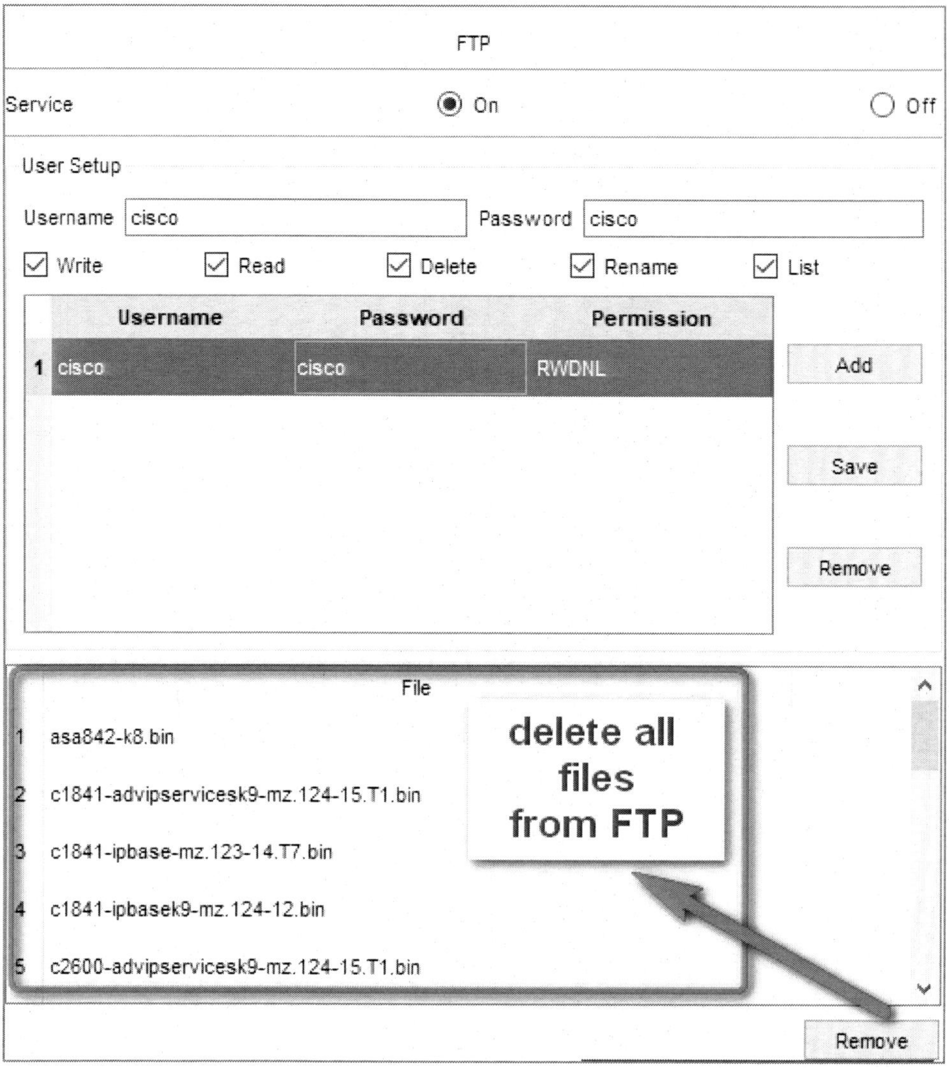

Figure 11.18 List of files in the FTP service

In FTP account should be no files.

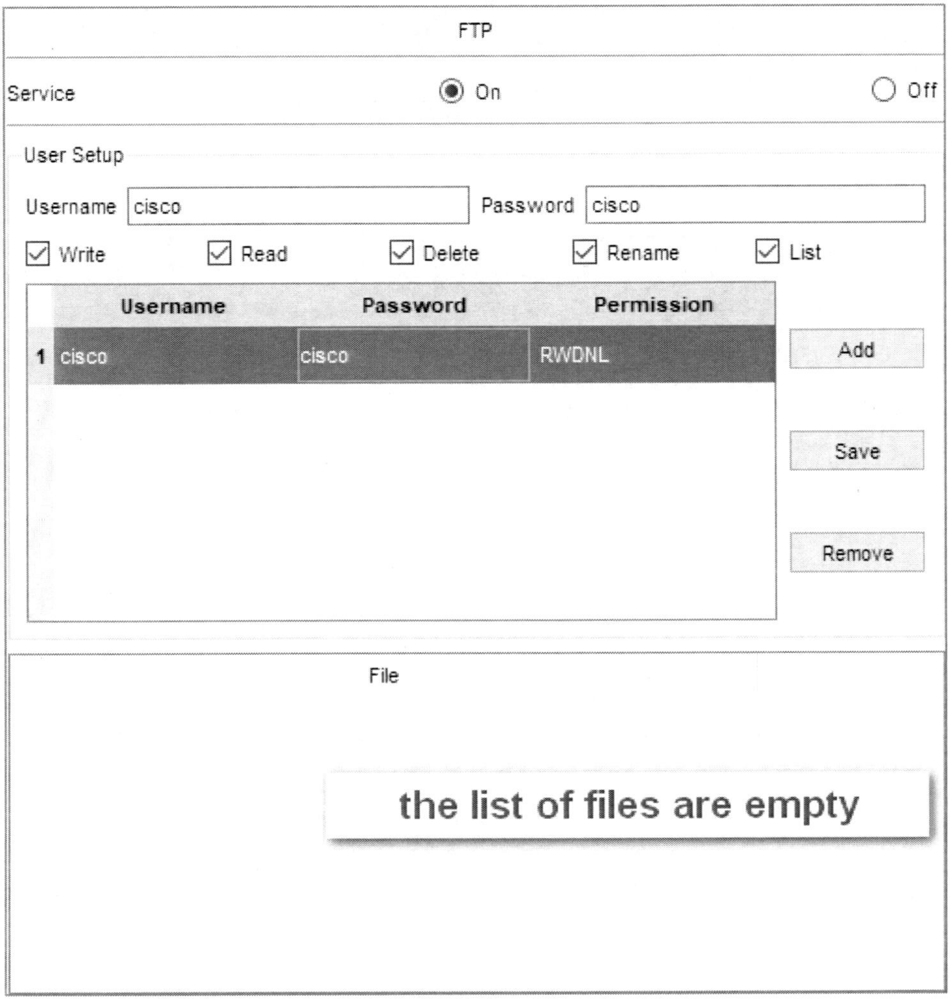

Figure 11.19 Empty list of files in the FTP service

Step 2. On the **Cambridge-FTP-Client,** using the **Text Editor,** place (import) the bellow named files:

- cambridge_description.txt,
- city_of_london.txt,
- cost_of_grocery_food.txt,
- cost_of_property.txt.

on local disk C: and additionally delete file **sampleFile.txt**.

```
C:\>dir

 Volume in drive C has no label.
 Volume Serial Number is 5E12-4AF3
 Directory of C:\

1/1/1970     1:0 PM                530        cambridge_description.txt
1/1/1970     1:0 PM                406        city_of_london.txt
1/1/1970     1:0 PM                857        cost_of_grocery_food.txt
1/1/1970     1:0 PM                1111       cost_of_property.txt
                2904 bytes              4 File(s)
```

Figure 11.20 List of files on C: disk in Cambridge-FTP-Client

Step 3. In **CITY-FTP-Server**, create a new account for FTP server:

- FTP server's address: 2.0.0.3
- Username: **George**
- Password: **george123**
- Permissions: **Write, Read, Delete, Rename, List**

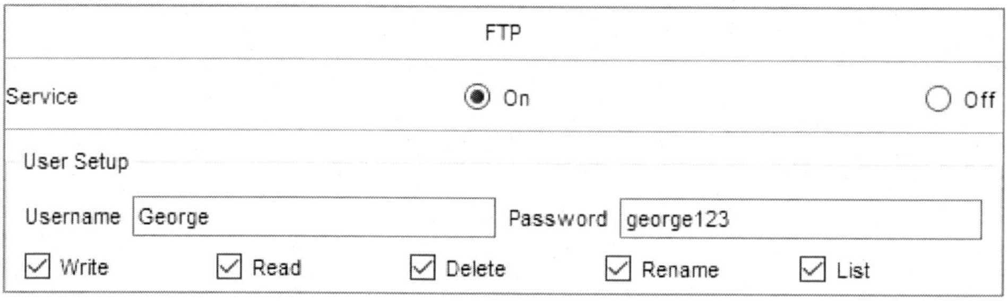

Figure 11.21 Creating a new account on the FTP server

	Username	Password	Permission
1	cisco	cisco	RWDNL
2	George	george123	RWDNL

Figure 11.22 New account on the FTP server

Step 4. In **Cambridge-FTP-Client**, log into George's account on the FTP server:

- FTP server's address: 2.0.0.3

- Username: George
- Password: george123

```
C:\>ftp 2.0.0.3
Trying to connect...2.0.0.3
Connected to 2.0.0.3
220- Welcome to PT Ftp server
Username:George
331- Username ok, need password
Password:
230- Logged in
(passive mode On)
ftp>
```

Figure 11.23 Logging into an FTP server

Step 5. Display the accessible commands, you can use on the FTP server

- Command: **?**

```
ftp>?
            ?
            cd
            delete
            dir
            get
            help
            passive
            put
            pwd
            quit
            rename
ftp>
```

Figure 11.24 List of commands on the FTP server

Step 6. List actual content on the FTP server:

- Command: **dir**

```
ftp>dir

Listing /ftp directory from 2.0.0.3:
ftp>
```

Figure 11.25 Actual content on the FTP server

Step 7. Using the **PUT** command, copy to the FTP server, the following files:

- cambridge_description.txt,
- city_of_london.txt,

- cost_of_grocery_food.txt,
- cost_of_property.txt.

```
ftp>put cambridge_description.txt

Writing file cambridge_description.txt to 2.0.0.3:
File transfer in progress...

[Transfer complete - 530 bytes]

530 bytes copied in 0.08 secs (6625 bytes/sec)
ftp>put city_of_london.txt

Writing file city_of_london.txt to 2.0.0.3:
File transfer in progress...

[Transfer complete - 406 bytes]

406 bytes copied in 0.085 secs (4776 bytes/sec)
ftp>put cost_of_grocery_food.txt

Writing file cost_of_grocery_food.txt to 2.0.0.3:
File transfer in progress...

[Transfer complete - 857 bytes]

857 bytes copied in 0.077 secs (11129 bytes/sec)
ftp>put cost_of_property.txt

Writing file cost_of_property.txt to 2.0.0.3:
File transfer in progress...

[Transfer complete - 1111 bytes]

1111 bytes copied in 0.076 secs (14618 bytes/sec)
ftp>
```

Figure 11.26 Copying files to an FTP server

Step 8. Using the DIR command, check the contents of the FTP server

```
ftp>dir

Listing /ftp directory from 2.0.0.3:
0   : cambridge_description.txt                                    530
1   : city_of_london.txt                                           406
2   : cost_of_grocery_food.txt                                     857
3   : cost_of_property.txt                                         1111
ftp>
```

Figure 11.27 Viewing a list of files on an FTP server

Step 9. End the FTP session by using the **quit** command.

```
ftp>quit

221- Service closing control connection.
C:\>
```

Figure 11.28 End of FTP session

Step 10. On **CITY-FTP-Server,** go to the **FTP** service, check if these files exist.

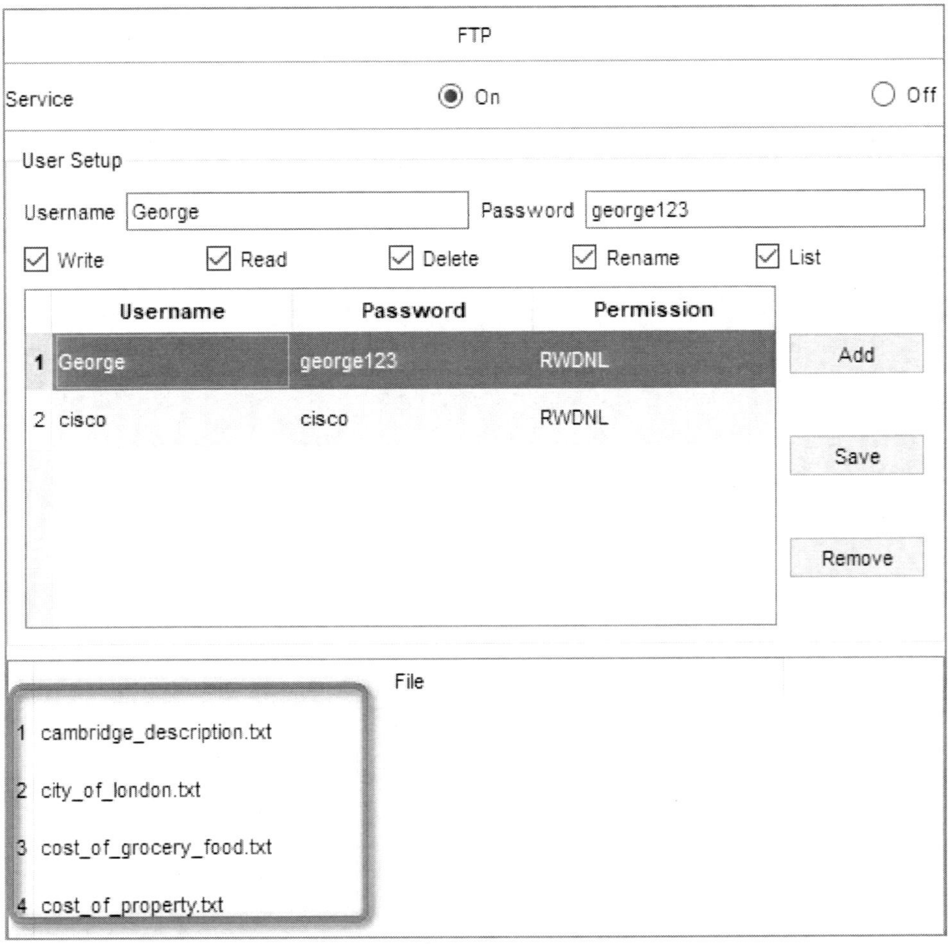

Figure 11.29 List of files in the FTP service

11.3 Email Service (Exercise 31)

Part 1. Introduction.

In Packet Tracer, you can create your own mail servers by configuring the mail domain and SMTP protocols in them, as well as accounts for users.

Part 2. Assumption.

IP addressing of devices is ready and working properly.

Part 3. Topology.

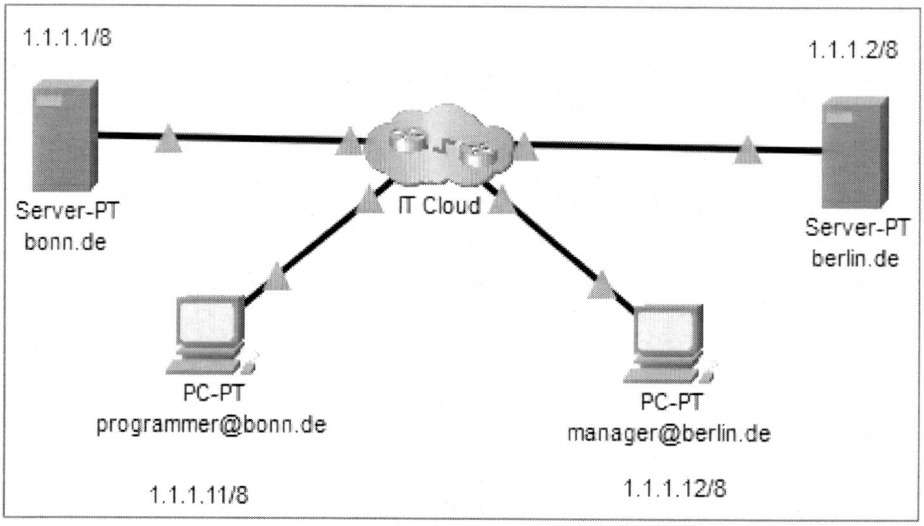

Figure 11.30 Topology of a network using EMAIL service.

Domain's name	Account's name	Account's address	Incoming mail server	Outgoing mail server	Login and password
bonn.de	programmer	programmer@bonn.de	bonn.de	bonn.de	programmer python123
berlin.de	manager	manager@berlin.de	berlin.de	berlin.de	manager reganam456

Table 11.1 EMAIL service configuration data

Part 4. Plan of the exercise.

Step 1. Configure the DNS service on the **bonn.de** server

Figure 11.31 Configuration of DNS service in bonn.de server

Step 2. Configure the DNS service on the **berlin.de** server

Figure 11.32 Configuration of DNS service in berlin.de server

Step 3. Configure the EMAIL service on the **bonn.de** server

Go to the **[Services]** tab and select the **[EMAIL]** service.

Enable the **[SMTP Service]** and **[POP3 Service]** options.

Transcribe the appropriate data from the table to the configuration fields.

To set the domain name, click the button [**Set**].

To add an email account, click the [+] button.

Figure 11.33 Adding a programmer mail account on the bonn.de server

Step 4. Configure the EMAIL service on the **berlin.de** server

Go to the [**Services**] tab and select the [**EMAIL**] service

Enable the **[SMTP Service]** and **[POP3 Service]** options.

Transcribe the appropriate data from the table to the configuration fields.

To set the domain name, click the button [**Set**].

To add an email account, click the [+] button.

Figure 11.34 Adding a manager email account on the berlin.de server

Step 5. Configure the programmer's computer (programmer@bonn.de), using the Email applet, which is located in the **[Desktop]** tab.

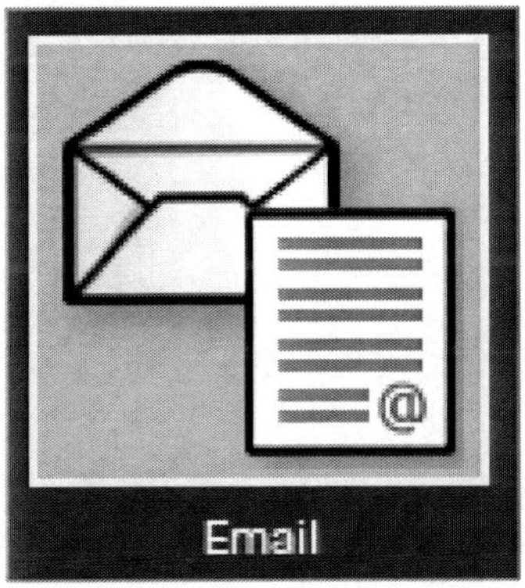

Figure 11.35 Email application (mail client)

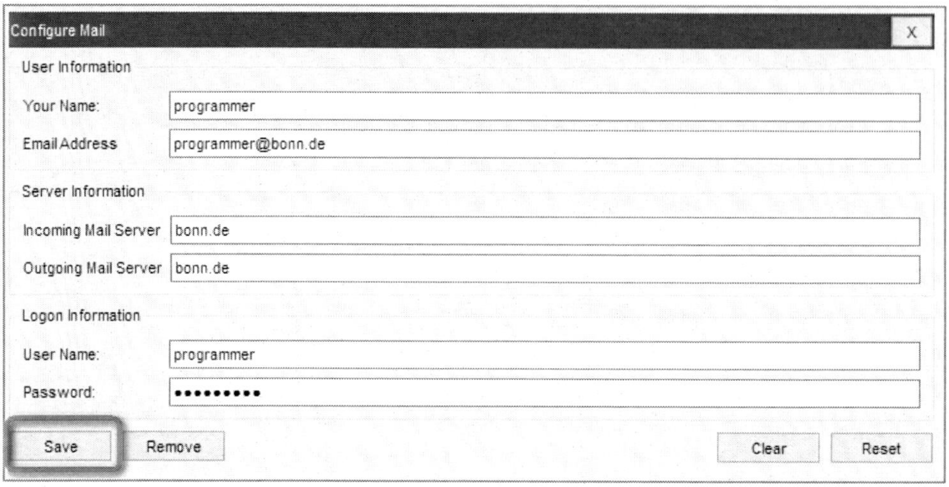

Figure 11.36 Setting up a programmer mail account in the mail client

Step 6. Repeat the same steps for the manager's computer (manager@berlin.de).

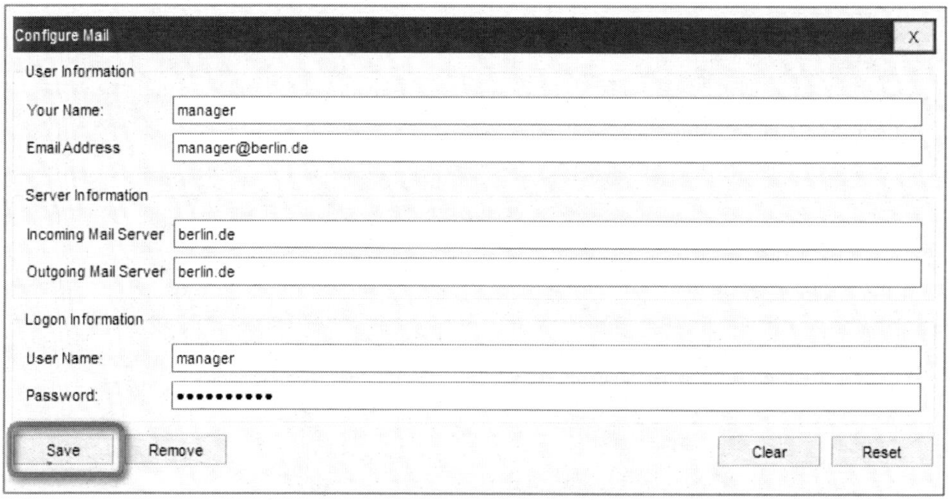

Figure 11.37 Configuration of manager mail account in mail client

Step 7. Test sending messages from the programmer to the manager.

To do this on the developer's computer, go to the [**Desktop**] tab, launch the [**Email]** applet, and then click the [**Compose**] button.

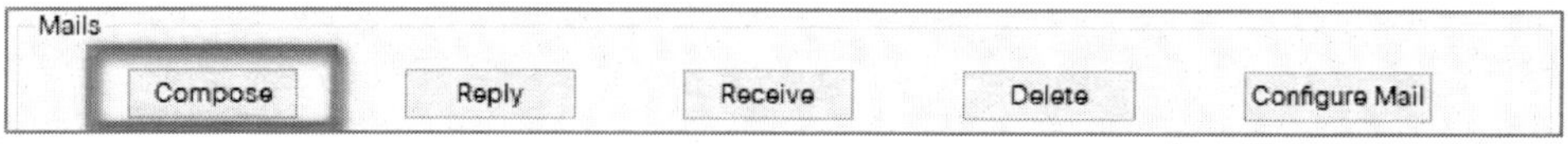

Figure 11.38 Creating messages in the mail client

In the [**To**:], [**Subject:**] fields, enter the appropriate data, put the message content and click the [**Send**] button.

Figure 11.39 Sending a message to a manager

At the bottom of the window you will get additional information about the sent message.

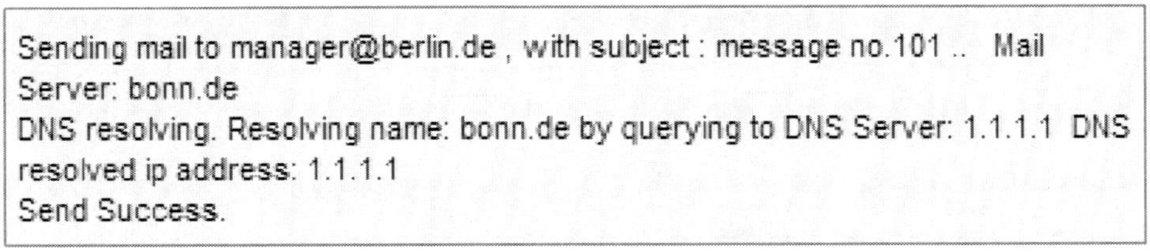

Figure 11.40 Information after sending a message to the manager

On the manager's computer, go to the [**Desktop**] tab, launch the [**Email**] applet, and then click the [**Receive**] button.

Figure 11.41 Receiving messages by a manager in the mail client

The message received is:

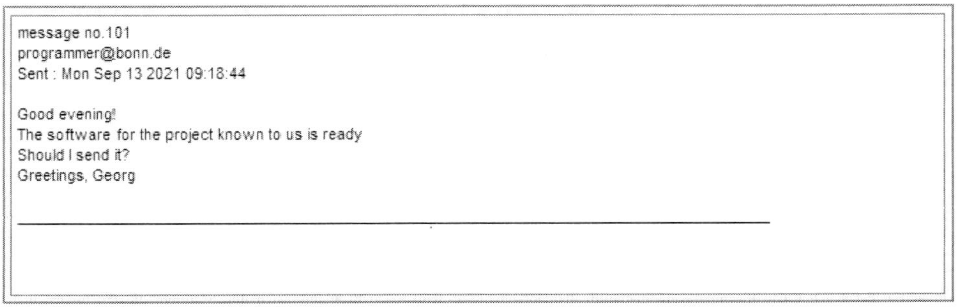

Figure 11.42 Received message in the mail client (manager)

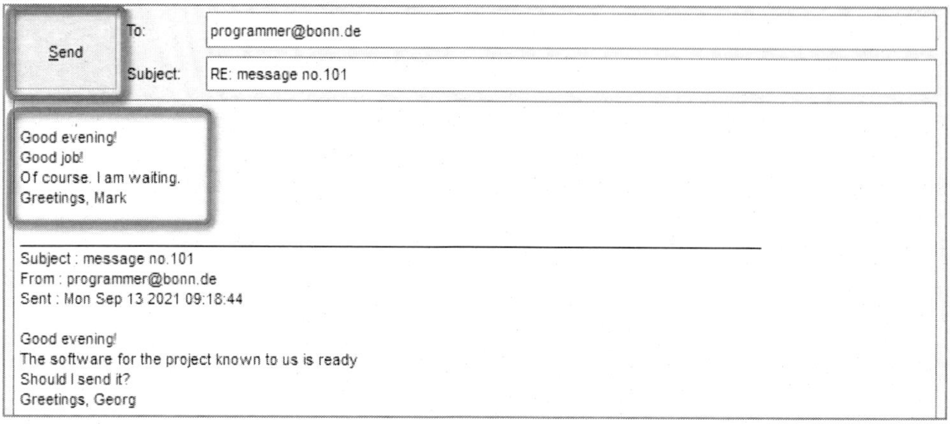

Figure 11.43 Sending message in the mail client (from manager to programmer)

11.4 List of auxiliary files

- cambridge_description.txt,
- city_of_london.txt,
- cost_of_grocery_food.txt,
- cost_of_property.txt.
- exercise29-http-service.pkt
- exercise30-ftp-service.pkt
- exercise31-email-service.pkt
- image2.html
- index.html
- index2.html
- index3.html
- my_java_script.js
- my_styles.css
- picture1-40x40.png
- picture2-154x167.png
- picture3-222x148.png
- picture4-350x196.png

CHAPTER 12

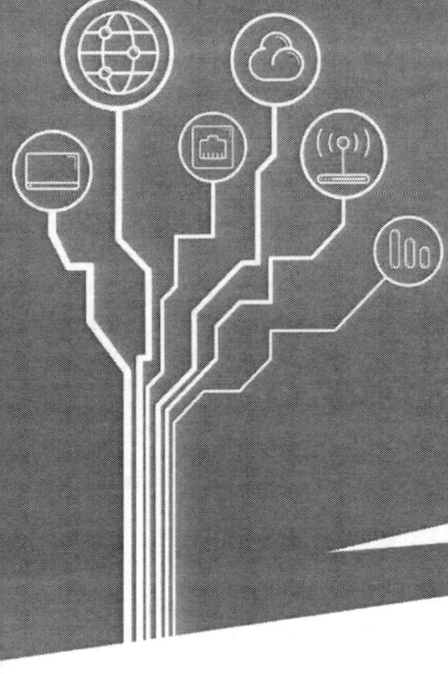

IPV6 PROTOCOL

COMPUTER NETWORKS IN PACKET TRACER

FOR ADVANCED USERS

12 IPV6 PROTOCOL

12.1 Introduction to IPV6

Part 1. Previous versions of the IP protocol at the network layer.

The Internet Protocol was created by the U.S. Department of Defense's Defense Advanced Research Projects Agency (DARPA) in the early 1970s. After creating the pioneering ARPANET project (the world's first wide area network), DARPA began multidirectional work on data transfer technologies.

In 1972, **Robert E. Kahn** was hired at the DARPA Information Processing Technology Office.

Figure 12.1 Robert Elliott Kahn

Born. 23.02.1938, Brooklyn, New York. Source: (Wikipedia, https://en.wikipedia.org/wiki/Bob_Kahn, 2022).

Robert Kahn worked on two projects: satellite transmission of Internet packets and radio transmission of Internet packets. At the time, he saw the possibilities that lay in communicating via these packets.

In 1973, **Vinton Cerf** who developed the original ARPANET network protocol (NCP), joined Kahn to work with him on an open communications architecture model and the development of a new protocol for ARPANET.

Figure 12.2 Vinton Cerf

Born. 23.06.1943, New Haven, Connecticut. Source: (Wikipedia, https://en.wikipedia.org/wiki/Vint_Cerf, 2022)

In 1973, **Kahn and Cerf** developed the basis for a new system that used only one common Internet protocol.

Vinton Cerf was also inspired by **Hubert Zimmerman** and **Louis Pouzin**, who created the French CYCLADES network, similar to the American one.

In doing so, it became possible to connect almost all networks, including those not based on **TCP/IP**.

A computer called a **network gateway** (later this name was changed to **router** to avoid confusion with other types of network gateways) is hooked up to each of the networks being connected and performs the translation (forwarding) of packets between them.

The DARPA agency has begun working with BBN Technologies, at Stanford University and London's College University, to develop other versions of the protocol for different devices. Four versions of the protocol were created: **TCP V1, TCP V2**, a split version of

TCP V3 and **IP V3** in the spring of 1978, and then the stable version **TCP/IP V4**, the standard that is still used on the Internet today.

IP versions 1 through 3 were experimental versions designed between 1973 and 1978. The following Internet Experiment Note (IEN) documents describe version 3 of the Internet Protocol, prior to the modern version of IPv4:

- IEN 2 (*Comments on Internet Protocol and TCP*), dated August 1977 describes the need to separate the TCP and Internet Protocol functionalities (which were previously combined.) It proposes the first version of the IP header, using 0 for the version field.
- IEN 26 (*A Proposed New Internet Header Format*), dated February 1978 describes a version of the IP header that uses a 1-bit version field.
- IEN 28 (*Draft Internetwork Protocol Description Version 2*), dated February 1978 describes IPv2.
- IEN 41 (*Internetwork Protocol Specification Version 4*), dated June 1978 describes the first protocol to be called IPv4. The IP header is different from the modern IPv4 header.
- IEN 44 (*Latest Header Formats*), dated June 1978 describes another version of IPv4, also with a header different from the modern IPv4 header.
- IEN 54 (*Internetwork Protocol Specification Version 4*), dated September 1978 is the first description of IPv4 using the header that would be standardized in RFC 760.

The dominant network protocol in the network layer used (ISO/OSI model) and in the Internet layer (TCP/IP model) is IPv4. The number 4 identifies the protocol version found in each IP datagram. IPv4 is described in RFC 791 (1981).

Part 2. What is IPV6?

IPV6 is a way (protocol) of addressing that enables the generation of many more network addresses compared to the number of addresses in IPV4 (the main purpose of this protocol), based on the use of a 128-bit address.

Protocol	**Number of address bits**	**Maximum number of addresses**
IPV4	32	2^32= **4 294 967 296**
IPV5 **(ST2)**	32	A protocol is not another version of the IP protocol, but this version has been designed for a set of **ST protocols** (*The Internet Stream Protocol – source : https://datatracker.ietf.org/doc/html/rfc1819*
IPV6	128	2^128= **3,4028236692093846346337460743177E+38**

Table 12.1 Comparing IPV4 and IPV6 protocols

The maximum number of IPV4 addresses is exactly 2^{32}**.That's about 4 billion**.

The maximum number of IPV6 addresses is exactly 2^{128}**. This is about 340 sextillion.**

n	Value 2^n
2	4
3	8
4	16
5	32
6	64
7	128
8	256
9	512
10	1 024
11	2 048
12	4 096
13	8 192
14	16 384
15	32 768
16	65 536
17	131 072
18	262 144
19	524 288
20	1 048 576
21	2 097 152
22	4 194 304
23	8 388 608
24	16 777 216
25	33 554 432
26	67 108 864
27	134 217 728
28	268 435 456
29	536 870 912
30	1 073 741 824
31	2 147 483 648
32	**4 294 967 296**

Table 12.2 Values of powers 2^N with exponents from 2 to 32

n	Value 2^n
100	1 267 650 600 228 230 000 000 000 000 000
101	2 535 301 200 456 460 000 000 000 000 000
102	5 070 602 400 912 920 000 000 000 000 000
103	10 141 204 801 825 800 000 000 000 000 000
104	20 282 409 603 651 700 000 000 000 000 000
105	40 564 819 207 303 300 000 000 000 000 000
106	81 129 638 414 606 700 000 000 000 000 000
107	162 259 276 829 213 000 000 000 000 000 000
108	324 518 553 658 427 000 000 000 000 000 000
109	649 037 107 316 853 000 000 000 000 000 000
110	1 298 074 214 633 710 000 000 000 000 000 000
111	2 596 148 429 267 410 000 000 000 000 000 000
112	5 192 296 858 534 830 000 000 000 000 000 000
113	10 384 593 717 069 700 000 000 000 000 000 000
114	20 769 187 434 139 300 000 000 000 000 000 000
115	41 538 374 868 278 600 000 000 000 000 000 000
116	83 076 749 736 557 200 000 000 000 000 000 000
117	166 153 499 473 114 000 000 000 000 000 000 000
118	332 306 998 946 229 000 000 000 000 000 000 000
119	664 613 997 892 458 000 000 000 000 000 000 000
120	1 329 227 995 784 920 000 000 000 000 000 000 000
121	2 658 455 991 569 830 000 000 000 000 000 000 000
122	5 316 911 983 139 660 000 000 000 000 000 000 000
123	10 633 823 966 279 300 000 000 000 000 000 000 000
124	21 267 647 932 558 700 000 000 000 000 000 000 000
125	42 535 295 865 117 300 000 000 000 000 000 000 000
126	85 070 591 730 234 600 000 000 000 000 000 000 000
127	170 141 183 460 469 000 000 000 000 000 000 000 000
128	340 282 366 920 938 000 000 000 000 000 000 000 000

Table 12.3 Values of powers 2^N with exponents from 100 to 128.

12.2 Tunneling in IPV6 protocol (Exercise 32)

Part 1. Topology.

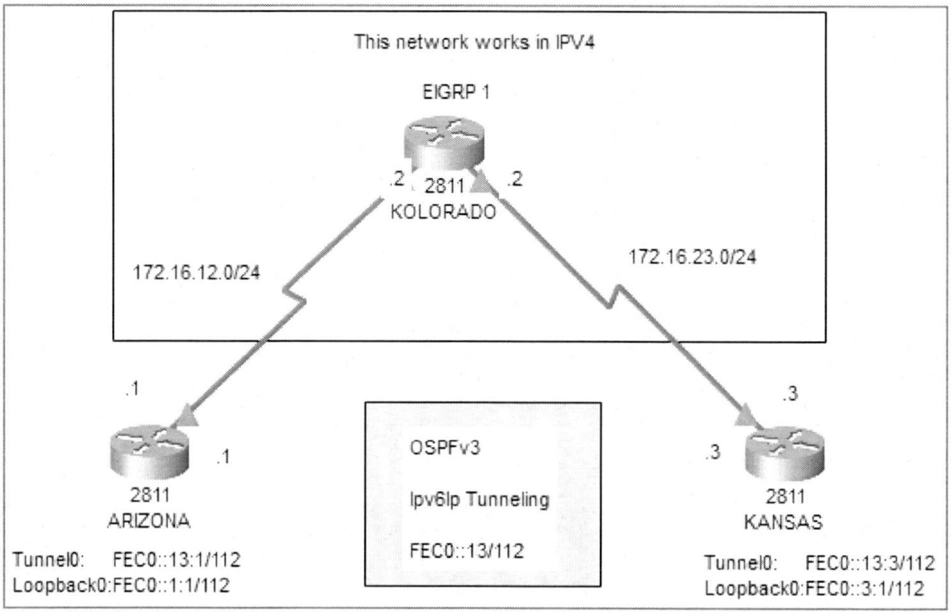

Figure 12.3 Network topology with tunneling

Name of device	Interface	AddressIPV4/Prefix	Address IPV6/Prefix
ARIZONA	Se1/0	172.16.12.1/24	-
ARIZONA	Loopback0	10.1.1.1/24	FEC0::1:1/112
ARIZONA	Tunnel0	-	FEC0::13:1/112
KOLORADO	Loopback0	10.1.2.1/24	-
KOLORADO	Se1/0	172.16.12.2/24	-
KOLORADO	Se1/1	172.16.23.2/24	-
KANSAS	Se1/1	172.16.23.3/24	FEC0::13:3/112
KANSAS	Loopback0	10.1.3.1/24	FEC0::13:3/112
KANSAS	Tunnel0	-	FEC0::3:1/112

Table 12.4 Addressing table for IPV6.

Part 2. Plan of the exercise.

Step 1. Make the network according to the topology drawing.

Step 2. Configure the KOLORADO router.

Assumptions: router works with IPV4 and EIGRP networks.

Configuration commands:

```
hostname KOLORADO

interface Loopback0
ip address 10.1.2.1 255.255.255.0

interface Serial1/0
ip address 172.16.12.2 255.255.255.0

interface Serial1/1
ip address 172.16.23.2 255.255.255.0

router eigrp 1
network 10.0.0.0
network 172.16.0.0
```

Step 3. Configure the ARIZONA router.

Assumptions: router works with IPV4 (EIGRP), IPV6 (OSPF) networks.

Configuration commands:

```
hostname ARIZONA
ipv6 unicast-routing

interface Loopback0
ip address 10.1.1.1 255.255.255.0
ipv6 address FEC0::1:1/112
ipv6 ospf 1 area 0

interface Tunnel0
ipv6 address FEC0::13:1/112
ipv6 ospf 1 area 0
tunnel source Serial1/0
tunnel destination 172.16.23.3
tunnel mode ipv6ip
interface Serial1/0
ip address 172.16.12.1 255.255.255.0
```

```
router eigrp 1
network 10.0.0.0
network 172.16.0.0

ipv6 router ospf 1
```

Step 4. Configure the KANSAS router.

Assumptions: router works with IPV4 (EIGRP), IPV6 (OSPF) networks.

Configuration commands:

```
hostname KANSAS
ipv6 unicast-routing

interface Loopback0
ip address 10.1.3.1 255.255.255.0
ipv6 address FEC0::3:1/112
ipv6 ospf 1 area 0

interface Tunnel0
ipv6 address FEC0::13:3/112
ipv6 ospf 1 area 0
tunnel source Serial1/1
tunnel destination 172.16.12.1
tunnel mode ipv6ip

interface Serial1/1
ip address 172.16.23.3 255.255.255.0

router eigrp 1
network 10.0.0.0
network 172.16.0.0

ipv6 router ospf 1
```

Step 5. Verify communication between ARIZONA and KANSAS routers.

Make a ping to Loopback0:FEC0::3:1/112.

```
ARIZONA#ping FEC0::3:1

Type escape sequence to abort.
Sending 5, 100-byte ICMP Echos to FEC0::3:1, timeout is 2 seconds:
!!!!!
Success rate is 100 percent (5/5), round-trip min/avg/max = 2/7/10 ms
```

Figure 12.4 The result of the ping command FEC0::3:1

```
ARIZONA#
ARIZONA#traceroute FEC0::3:1
Type escape sequence to abort.
Tracing the route to FEC0::3:1

  1    FEC0::13:3 8 msec     11 msec    13 msec
ARIZONA#
```

Figure 12.5 The result of the traceroute FEC0::3:1 command

12.3 Configuring DHCP for IPV6 on the server (Exercise 33)

Part 1. Topology.

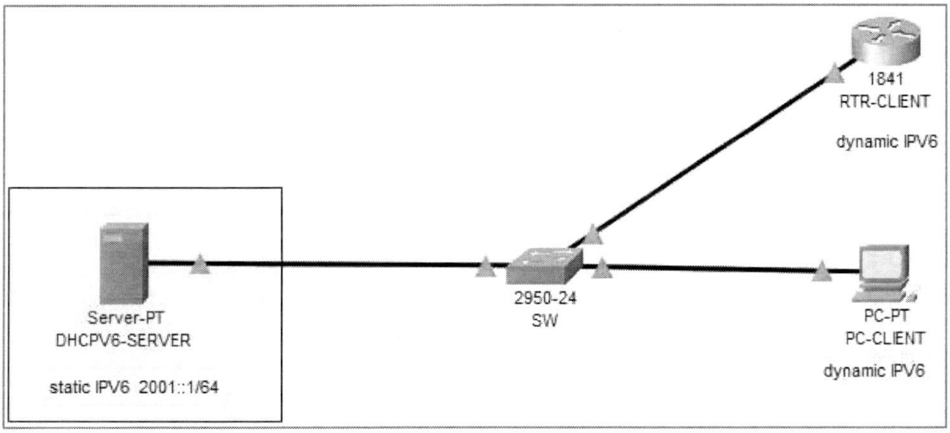

Figure 12.6 IPV6 network topology with DHCPV6-SERVER computer.

Part 2. Assumptions.

The DHCP pool for IPV6 addresses is to be located in the server. The parameters of the pool are listed in the table.

Name of the server	**DHCPV6-SERVER**
Server's address	**2001::1/64**
Interface	**Fa0**
DHCP pool's name	**dhcpPool**
DNS Server	**2001::1**
Domain Name	**itstart.pl**
Prefix Length	**64**
Valid Lifetime	**2592000**
Preferred Lifetime	**604800**

Table 12.5 DHCPv6 server configuration.

Part 3. Plan of the exercise.

Step 1. Make the network topology.

Step 2. Configure the DHCP server according to the given assumptions.

Step 3. On the **DHCPV6-SERVER** computer, select the tab [Services].

Step 4. Go to the section [DHCPv6].

Step 5. Enable the service [DHCPv6].

Step 6. Configure a pool named **dhcpPool**.

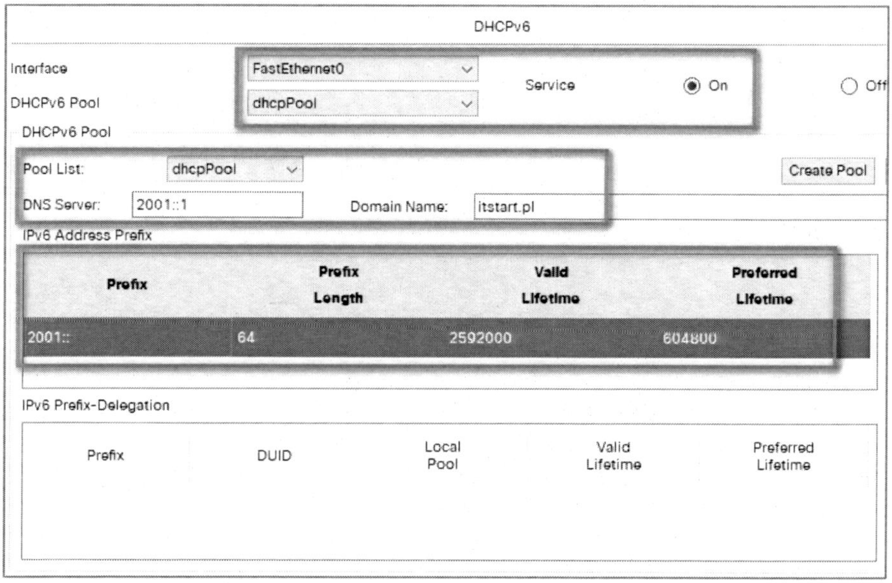

Figure 12.7 DHCPV6 server configuration.

Step 7. In RTR-CLIENT, configure the Fa0/0 interface.

Commands:

```
ip name-server 2001::1
interface FastEthernet0/0
ipv6 enable
ipv6 address dhcp
```

Step 4. In PC-CLIENT, configure the Fa0 interface for IPv6 as **'Automatic'.**

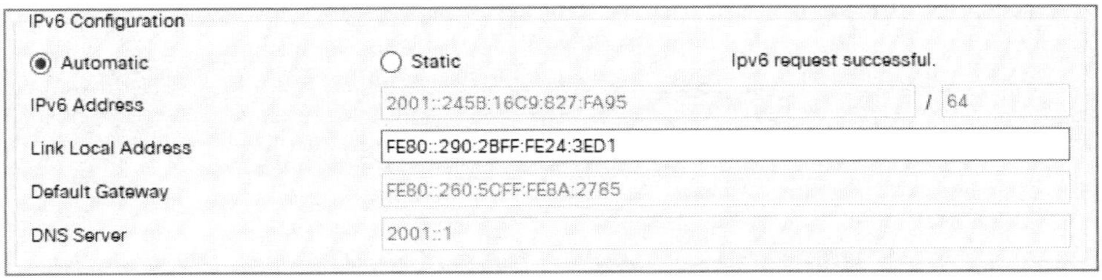

Figure 12.8 Fa0 configuration in PC-CLIENT.

Step 5. In PC-CLIENT check the automatic IPV6 addressing

```
C:\>ipv6config

FastEthernet0 Connection:(default port)

   Connection-specific DNS Suffix..: itstart.pl
   Link-local IPv6 Address.........: FE80::290:2BFF:FE24:3ED1
   IPv6 Address....................: 2001::245B:16C9:827:FA95
   Default Gateway.................: FE80::260:5CFF:FE8A:2785
   DHCPv6 IAID.....................: 1532855452
   DHCPv6 Client DUID..............: 00-01-00-01-2B-5A-B2-E9-00-90-2B-24-3E-D1
```

Figure 12.9 Fa0 redaction in PC-CLIENT.

Step 6. In RTR-CLIENT, check the IPV6 addressing assignment

Command:

```
show  ipv6  dhcp interface
```

```
RTR-CLIENT#show ipv6 dhcp interface
FastEthernet0/0 is in client mode
  State is OPEN
  Renew will be sent in 0d0h
  List of known servers:
    Reachable via address: FE80::260:5CFF:FE8A:2785
    DUID: 00-01-00-01-50-20-AC-AE-00-60-5C-8A-27-85
    Preference: 0
    Configuration parameters:
      IA PD: IA ID 1484959468, T1 0, T2 0
      Address: 2001::7BEF:6D5D:4129:4129/64
              preferred lifetime 604800, valid lifetime 2592000
              expires at October 31 2021 4:21:45 pm (2592000 seconds)
      DNS server: 2001::1
      Domain name: itstart.pl
      Information refresh time: 0
```

Figure 12.10 Fa0/0 configuration in RTR-CLIENT.

12.4 Configuring DHCP for IPV6 on a router (Exercise 34)

Part 1. Topology.

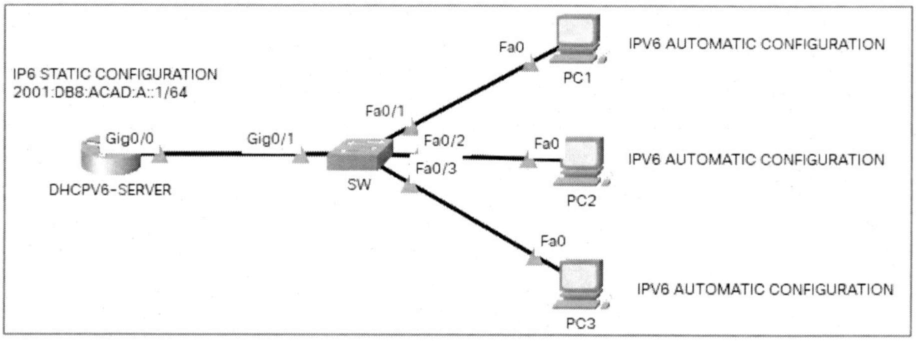

Figure 12.11 IPV6 network topology with DHCPV6-SERVER router.

Part 2. Assumptions.

The DHCP pool for IPV6 addresses is to be located in the router. The parameters of the pool are listed in the table.

Name of the server	**DHCPV6-SERVER**
Server's address	**2001:DB8:ACAD:A::1/64**
Interface	**Gi0/0**
DHCP pool name	**IPV6POOL**
DNS Server	**2001:DB8:ACAD:A::ABCD**
Domain Name	**itstart.pl**

Table 12.6 DHCPV6-SERVER router configuration.

Part 3. Plan of the exercise.

Step 1. Make the network topology.

Step 2. Configure the router according to the given assumptions.

Commands:

```
en
conf t
hostname DHCPV6-SERVER

ipv6 unicast-routing

interface GigabitEthernet0/0
ipv6 address FE80::1 link-local
ipv6 address 2001:DB8:ACAD:A::1/64
ipv6 dhcp server IPV6POOL
exit

ipv6 dhcp pool IPV6POOL
dns-server 2001:DB8:ACAD:A::ABCD
domain-name itstart.pl
end
```

Figure 12.12: On PC1 - PC3, configure the Fa0 interfaces for IPv6 as '**Automatic**'.

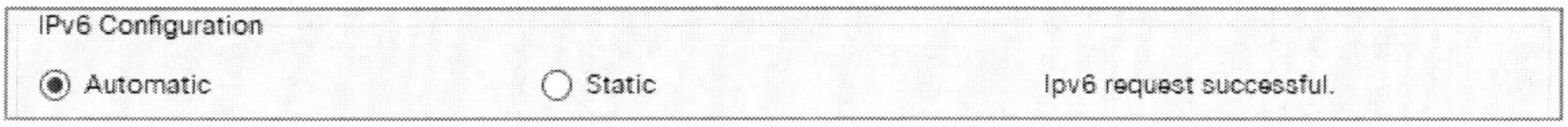

Figure 12.12 Automatic option for IPV6 configuration on PC1-PC3 compueters .

Step 4. In PC1, check the ping to DHCPV6-SERVER (2001:DB8:ACAD:A::1)

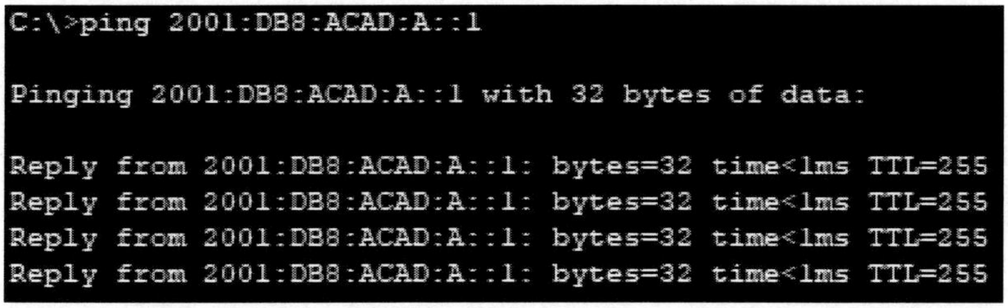

Figure 12.13 The result of the ping 2001:DB8:ACAD:A:1 command on PC1.

Step 5. On PC2, check the ping to DHCPV6-SERVER (2001:DB8:ACAD:A::1)

```
C:\>ping 2001:DB8:ACAD:A::1

Pinging 2001:DB8:ACAD:A::1 with 32 bytes of data:

Reply from 2001:DB8:ACAD:A::1: bytes=32 time<1ms TTL=255
Reply from 2001:DB8:ACAD:A::1: bytes=32 time<1ms TTL=255
Reply from 2001:DB8:ACAD:A::1: bytes=32 time<1ms TTL=255
Reply from 2001:DB8:ACAD:A::1: bytes=32 time<1ms TTL=255
```

Figure 12.14 The result of the ping 2001:DB8:ACAD:A:1 command in PC2.

Step 6. In PC3, check the ping to DHCPV6-SERVER (2001:DB8:ACAD:A::1)

```
C:\>ping 2001:DB8:ACAD:A::1

Pinging 2001:DB8:ACAD:A::1 with 32 bytes of data:

Reply from 2001:DB8:ACAD:A::1: bytes=32 time<1ms TTL=255
Reply from 2001:DB8:ACAD:A::1: bytes=32 time<1ms TTL=255
Reply from 2001:DB8:ACAD:A::1: bytes=32 time<1ms TTL=255
Reply from 2001:DB8:ACAD:A::1: bytes=32 time<1ms TTL=255
```

Figure 12.15 The result of the ping 2001:DB8:ACAD:A:1 command in PC3.

12.5 List of auxiliary files

- exercise32-ipv6-tunneling.pkt
- exercise33-configuring-dhcp-for-ipv6-on-server.pkt
- exercise34-configuring-dhcp-for-ipv6-on-router.pkt

CHAPTER 13

HOT STANDBY ROUTER PROTOCOL

COMPUTER NETWORKS IN PACKET TRACER

FOR ADVANCED USERS

13 Hot Standby Router Protocol

13.1 FHRP – Type Protocols

What are FHRP protocols (**First Hope Redundancy Protocols**)?

FHRP protocols are special techniques that provide redundant default gateways for end devices, without the necessary additional end-user configuration. Using FHRP, two or more routers can share the same virtual IP address and MAC address and can act as a single virtual router. Hosts on the network are configured with the shared IP address as the default gateway. An example is the Cisco **Hot Standby Router Protocol (HSRP).**

What is Cisco HSRP?

Cisco HSRP (Hot Standby Router Protocol) is a redundant protocol for establishing a fault-tolerant default gateway.

Version	Designed for protocol	Group address	UDP port	Range of virtual MAC addresses
1	IPV4	224.0.0.2	1985	00:00:0C:07:AC:XX
1	IPV4	224.0.0.102	1985	00:00:0C:9F:FX:XX
2	IPV6	FF02::66	2029	00:05:73:A0:0X:XX

Table 13.1 HSRP versions

13.2 HSRP Configuration (Exercise 35).

In this exercise, we will demonstrate the idea of HSRP on routers R-AUSTIN and R-BOSTON, which serve as default gateways for hosts PC-CALIFORNIA and PC-DALLAS.

Required equipment:

- PC-PT – 2 pts
- Switch 2950-24TT – 2 pts
- Router 1841 – 3 pts

Device	Model	Interface	IP/Mask	Default gate
PC-CALIFORNIA	PC-PT	Fa0	1.1.1.1/8	1.1.1.2
PC-DALLAS	PC-PT	Fa0	4.1.1.1/8	4.1.1.2
R-AUSTIN	1841	Fa0/0	1.1.1.2/8	-
R-AUSTIN	1841	Fa0/1	3.1.1.2/8	-
R-BOSTON	1841	Fa0/0	1.1.1.3/8	-
R-BOSTON	1841	Fa0/1	3.1.1.3/8	-
R-DALLAS	1841	Fa0/0	3.1.1.1/8	-
R-DALLAS	1841	Fa0/1	4.1.1.2	-

Table 13.2 Network addressing (Austin, California, Boston, Dallas)

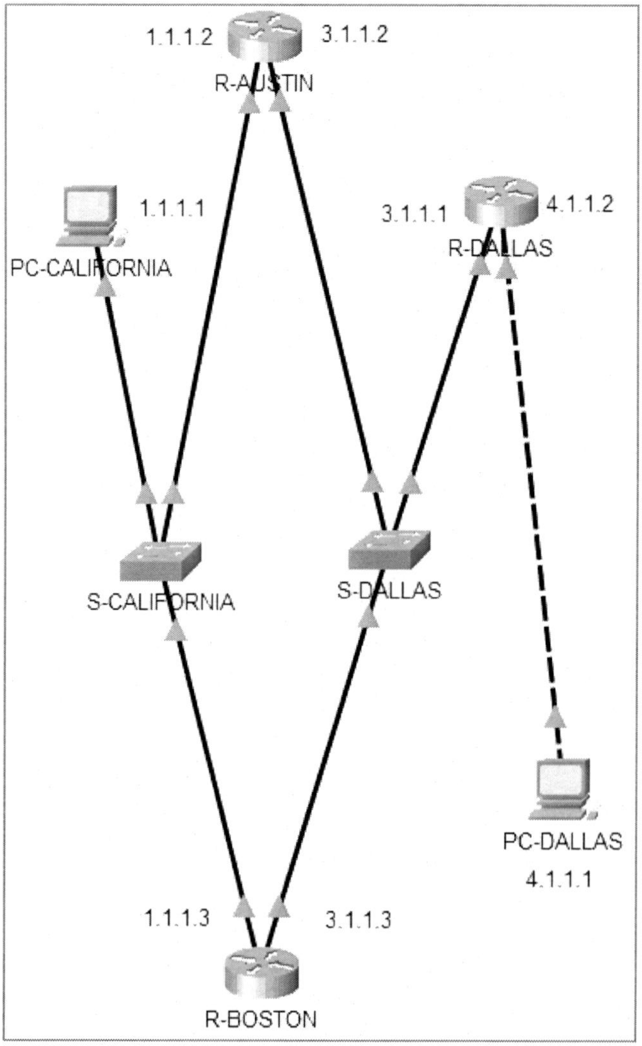

Figure 13.1 Network topology

Step 1. Make and configure the network according to the given assumptions.

Step 2. Configure RIPV1 dynamic routing correctly.

Step 3. Test the packet path from PC-CALIFORNIA to PC-DALLAS.

```
C:\>tracert 4.1.1.1

Tracing route to 4.1.1.1 over a maximum of 30 hops:

  1   0 ms      0 ms      0 ms      1.1.1.2
  2   0 ms      0 ms      0 ms      3.1.1.1
  3   1 ms      0 ms      0 ms      4.1.1.1
```

Figure 13.2 The path of the package goes through R-AUSTIN and R-DALLAS.

Step 4. Simulate Fa0/0 interface failure in R-AUSTIN

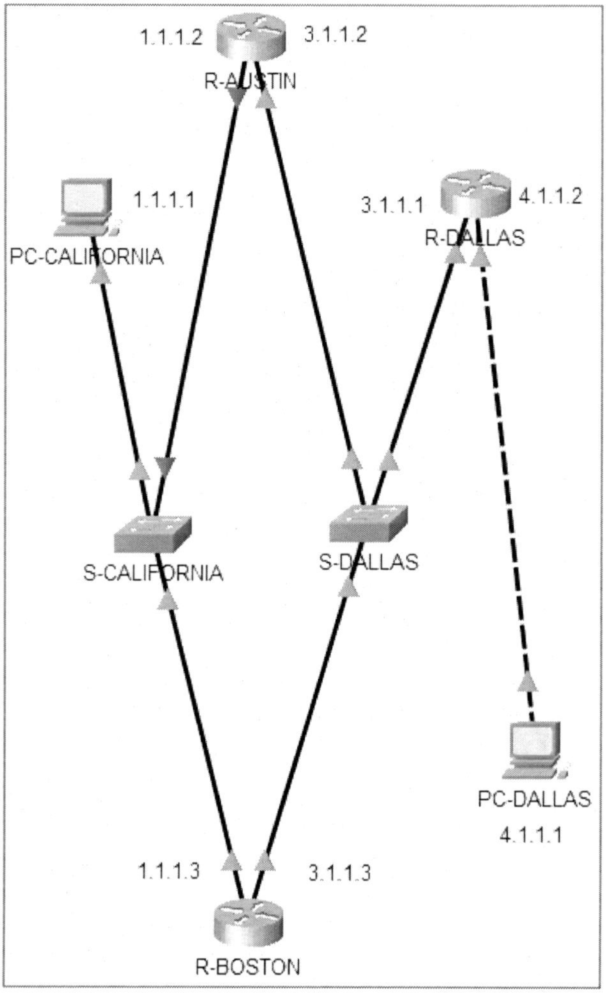

Figure 13.3 Network topology with Fa0/0 interface failure in R-AUSTIN

Step 5. Test the packet path from PC-CALIFORNIA to PC-DALLAS.

```
C:\>tracert 4.1.1.1

Tracing route to 4.1.1.1 over a maximum of 30 hops:

  1   *        *        *        Request timed out.
  2   *        *        *        Request timed out.
  3   *        *        *        Request timed out.
  4   *        *        *        Request timed out.
```

Figure 13.4 The result of the tracert command

NOTE: The default gateway in PC-CALIFORNIA is 1.1.1.2, but it has crashed, although a route through the R-BOSTON router is possible.

Step 6. Prepare the HSRP protocol configuration on R-AUSTIN.

In the R-AUSTIN router, run the commands:

```
en
conf  t
int fa0/0
standby  1  ip  1.1.1.7
standby  1  priority 110
standby  1  preempt
end
```

Step 7. Prepare the HSRP protocol configuration on R-BOSTON.

In the R-BOSTON router, run the commands:

```
en
conf  t
int fa0/0
standby  1  ip  1.1.1.7
standby  1  preempt
end
```

```
R-BOSTON#
%HSRP-6-STATECHANGE: FastEthernet0/0 Grp 1 state Speak -> Standby

%HSRP-6-STATECHANGE: FastEthernet0/0 Grp 1 state Standby -> Active
```

Figure 13.5 Messages after executing commands on the R-BOSTON router

Step 8. Modify the IP protocol configuration on PC- CALIFORNIA.

Set in PC- CALIFORNIA, Default gateway = 1.1.1.7

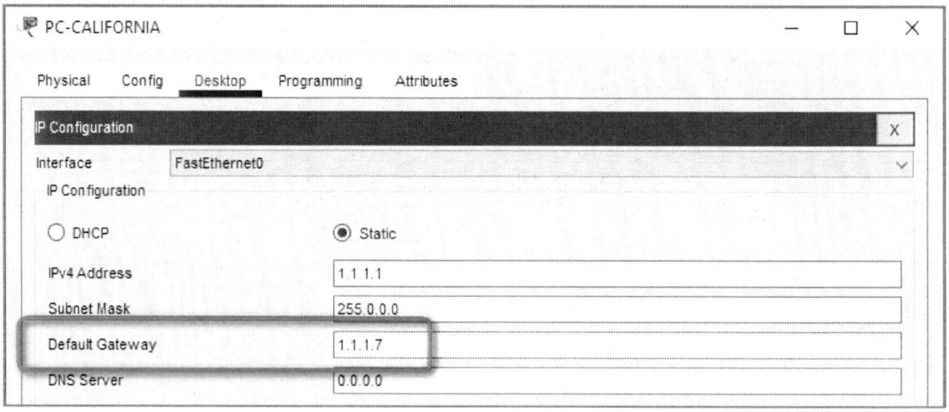

Figure 13.6 Changing the address of the default gateway in PC- CALIFORNIA

Step 9. Checking the packet route from PC-CALIFORNIA to PC-DALLAS before a failure.

```
C:\>tracert 4.1.1.1

Tracing route to 4.1.1.1 over a maximum of 30 hops:

  1   0 ms      0 ms      0 ms      1.1.1.2
  2   0 ms      0 ms      0 ms      3.1.1.1
  3   0 ms      0 ms      0 ms      4.1.1.1
```

Figure 13.7 The path of the package goes through R-AUSTIN and R-DALLAS.

Step 10. Checking the route of the packet from PC-CALIFORNIA to PC-DALLAS after simulating a failure at the Fa0/0 interface in R-AUSTIN.

```
C:\>tracert 4.1.1.1

Tracing route to 4.1.1.1 over a maximum of 30 hops:

  1   0 ms      0 ms      0 ms      1.1.1.3
  2   1 ms      1 ms      0 ms      3.1.1.1
  3   0 ms      0 ms      0 ms      4.1.1.1
```

Figure 13.8 The path of the package goes through R-BOSTON and R-DALLAS.

Observation: Address 1.1.1.7 is the so-called default virtual gateway.

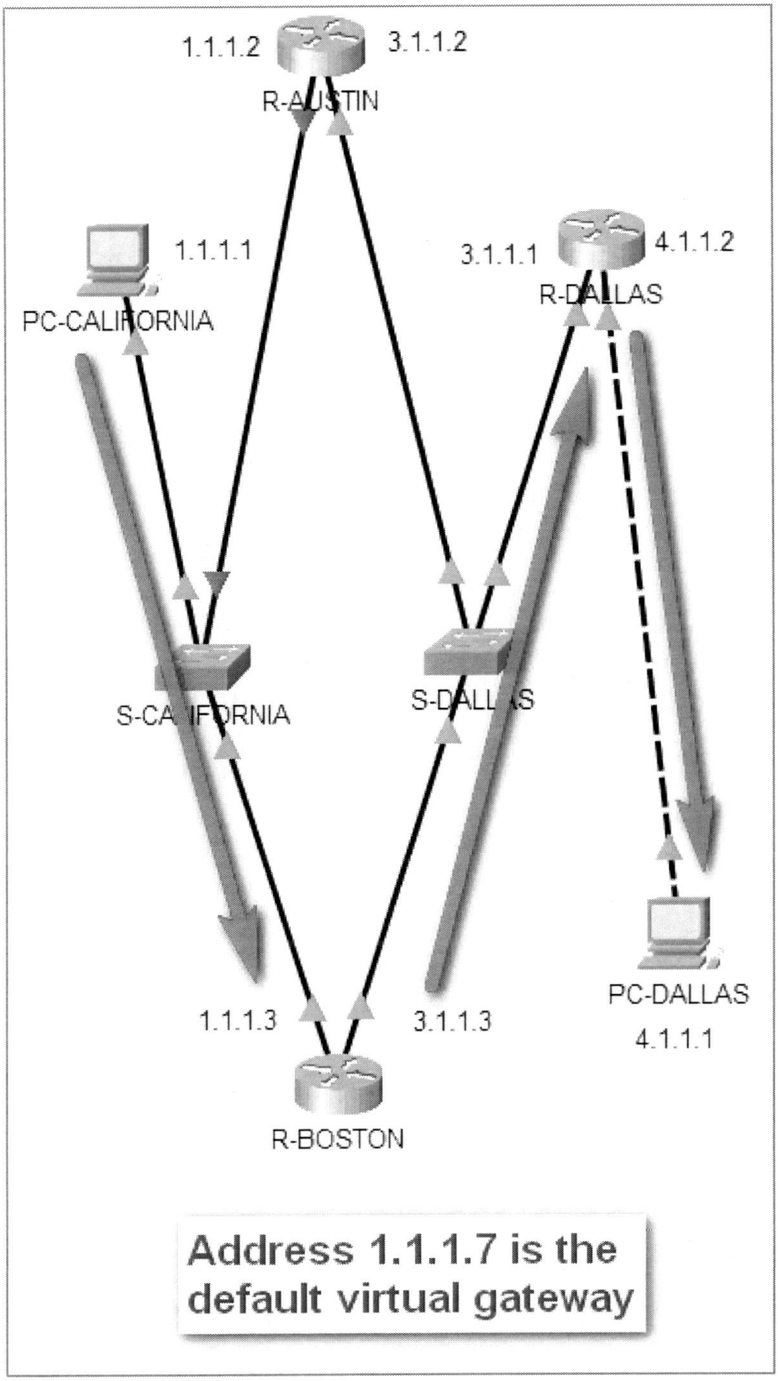

Figure 13.9 Route in case of R-AUSTIN failure

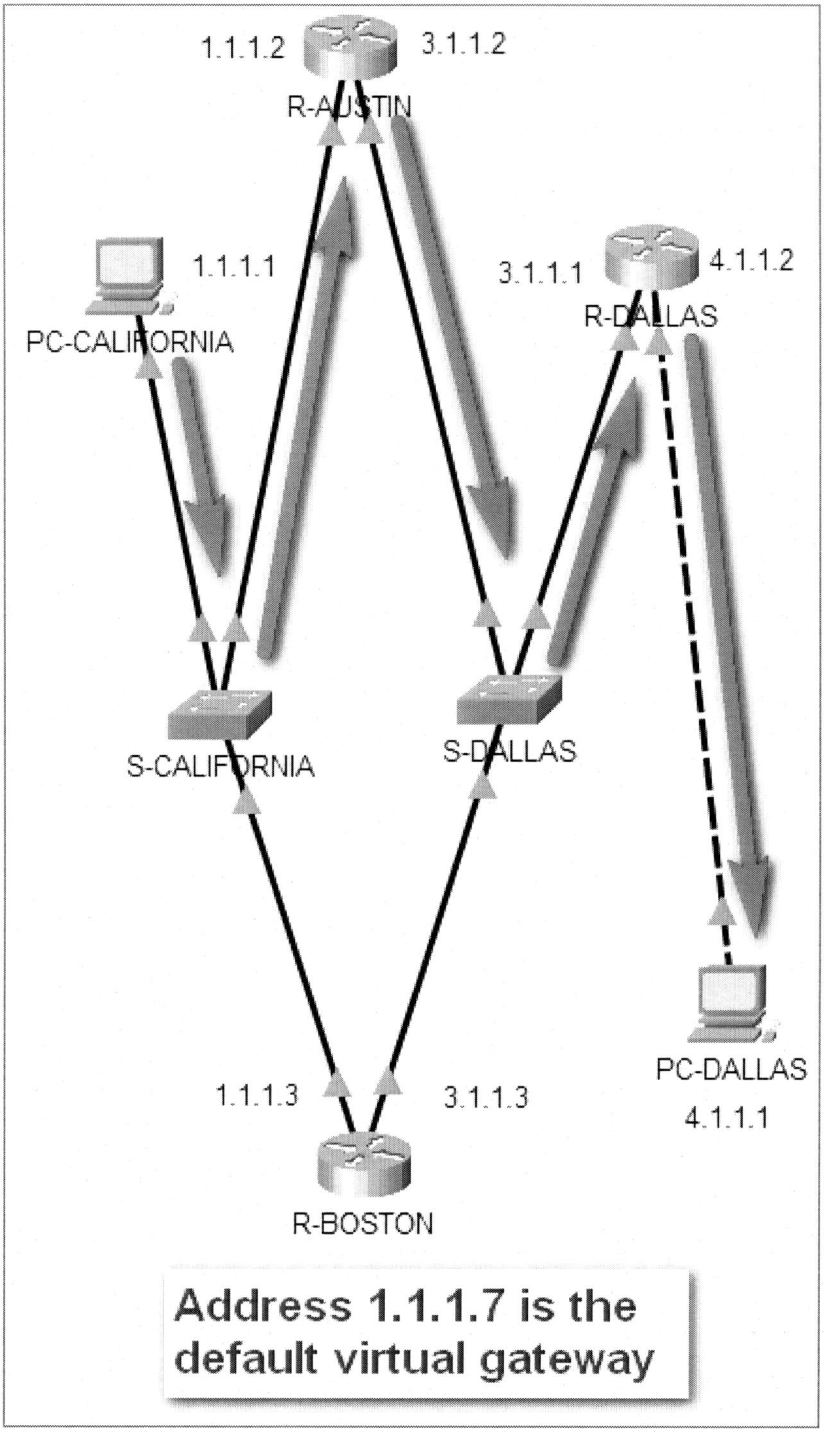

Figure 13.10 Route in case of failure R-BOSTON

13.3 HSRP Configuration (Exercise 36)

In the second example, we will demonstrate HSRP configuration on routers RTR1 and RTR3, which serve as default gateways for hosts on LAN-A and LAN-B. When configuring the HSRP protocol, a virtual gateway will be created that uses the same default gateway address for hosts on both LANs

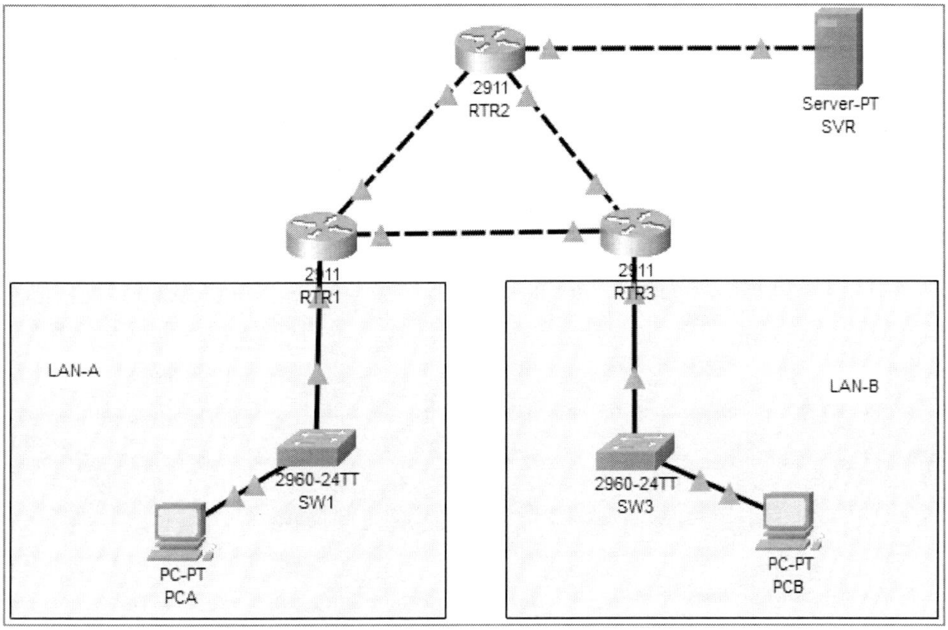

Figure 13.11 Network topology

If one gateway router becomes unavailable, the other router will take over using the same default gateway address that was used by the first router. Since the hosts on the LANs are configured with the virtual gateway's IP address as the default gateway, the hosts will regain connectivity to the remote networks once the remaining router is activated by HSRP.

Required equipment:

- Server-PT – 1 pts
- PC-PT – 2 pts
- Switch 2960-24TT – 2 pts
- Router 2911 –3 pts

Device	Model	Interface	IP/Mask	Default gateway
PCA	PC-PT	Fa0	192.168.1.101/24	192.168.1.1
PCB	PC-PT	Fa0	192.168.1.103/24	192.168.1.3
SVR	Server-PT	Fa0	10.100.100.2/30	10.100.100.1
SW1	2960-24TT	VLAN1	192.168.1.11/24	192.168.1.1
SW3	2960-24TT	VLAN1	192.168.1.13/24	192.168.1.3
RTR1	2911	Gi0/0	10.1.1.1/30	-
RTR1	2911	Gi0/1	192.168.1.1/24	-
RTR1	2911	Gi0/2	10.1.1.9/30	-
RTR2	2911	Gi0/0	10.1.1.2/30	-
RTR2	2911	Gi0/1	10.1.1.5/30	-
RTR2	2911	Gi0/2	10.100.100.1/30	-
RTR3	2911	Gi0/0	192.168.1.3/24	-
RTR3	2911	Gi0/1	10.1.1.6/30	-
RTR3	2911	Gi0/2	10.1.1.10/30	-

Table 13.3 Network addressing (RTR1, RTR2, RTR3, SW1, SW2)

Protocol	OSPF
Id	10
Area	0
Network	10.1.1.0/30
Network	192.168.1.0/24
Network	10.1.1.8/30
Protocol	static
Target network	0.0.0.0 0.0.0
Next hop address	10.1.1.2

Table 13.4 Routing configuration parameters for RTR1

Protocol	OSPF
Id	10
Area	0
Network	10.1.1.0/30
Network	10.1.1.4/30
Protocol	static
Target network	0.0.0.0 0.0.0
Next hop address	10.100.100.2

Table 13.5 Routing configuration parameters for RTR2

Step 1. In RTR2, make **default-information originate**

Protocol	OSPF
Id	10
Area	0
Network	10.1.1.4/30
Network	192.168.1.0/24
Network	10.1.1.8/30
Protocol	static
Target network	0.0.0.0 0.0.0
Next hop address	10.1.1.5

Table 13.6 Routing configuration parameters for RTR3

Step 2. Make and configure the network according to the given assumptions.

Step 3. Check the path of the package from PCA to SVR

```
C:\>tracert 10.100.100.2

Tracing route to 10.100.100.2 over a maximum of 30 hops:

  1   0 ms      0 ms      0 ms      192.168.1.1
  2   0 ms      0 ms      0 ms      10.1.1.2
  3   0 ms      0 ms      0 ms      10.100.100.2

Trace complete.
```

Figure 13.12 The path of the packet from PCA to SVR

Step 4. Check the path of the package from the PCB to the SVR

Step 5. Configure HSRP on the LAN interface G0/1 RTR1.

```
enable
conf  t
interface Gi0/1
standby version 2
```

Step 6. Configure the IP address of the virtual default gateway.

Comments:

This address must be configured on all hosts that require default gateway services. It replaces the physical address of the router interface that was previously configured on the hosts.

Multiple HSRP instances can be configured on a router. You must specify an HSRP group number to identify the virtual interface between routers in the HSRP group. This number must be consistent between the routers in the group. The group number for this configuration is 1.

```
standby 1 ip 192.168.1.254
```

Step 7. Designate an active router for the HSRP group.

Comments:

This is the router that will be used as the gateway device unless it fails or the path to it becomes inactive or unusable. Specify the router's interface priority. The default value is 100. A higher value will determine which router is the active router. If the priorities of the routers in the HSRP group are the same, the router with the highest configured IP address will become the active router.

```
standby 1 priority 150
```

Comments:

RTR1 will act as the active router, and traffic from the two LANs will use it as the default gateway.

Step 8. If it is desirable for the active router to resume this role when it becomes available again, configure it with the preempt option. The active router will take over the role of the gateway when it is operational again.

```
standby 1 preempt
```

Step 9. Configure RTR3 as a standby router (Configure RTR3 interface connected to LAN-B).

```
standby version 2
standby 1 ip 192.168.1.254
```

Step 10. Check the HSRP configuration in RTR1.

```
show standby
```

Step 11. Check the HSRP configuration in RTR3.

```
show standby
```

Step 12. Check the summary of HSRP statuses in RTR1.

show standby brief

Step 13. Check the summary of HSRP statuses in RTR3.

```
show standby brief
```

13.4 List of auxiliary files

- exercise35-hsrp.pkt
- exercise36-hsrp.pkt

CHAPTER 14

ADVANCED PHYSICAL TOPOLOGY

COMPUTER NETWORKS IN PACKET TRACER

FOR ADVANCED USERS

14 Advanced Physical Topology

14.1 Creating the Intercity physical topology (Exercise 37)

Part 1 Assumptions for the exercise.

The exercise demonstrates the creation and configuration of the following physical topology structure: **US-STATE → CITY → Building→ Main Closet → Rack**

Name	Type
˅ US-STATE	Intercity
˅ CITY	City
˅ Building	Building
˅ Main Closet	Wiring Closet
˅ Rack	Rack
Power Distribution Device0	Device
Router0	Device
Multilayer Switch0	Device
Wireless LAN Controller0	Device

Figure 14.1 Multi-level physical topology structure

Graphic files (background-images for topology levels) required for the exercise:

- us-state.png (level Intercity)
- city.png (level City)
- building.png (level Building)

A reminder of the meaning of the icons (buttons) in the toolbar in [Physical] mode.

Figure 14.2 Physical topology navigation panel

Figure 14.3 Button that causes the transition to the superior level in the physical topology.

Figure 14.4 Button that causes the creation of a new city in the physical topology.

Figure 14.5 Button that causes the creation of a new city in the physical topology.

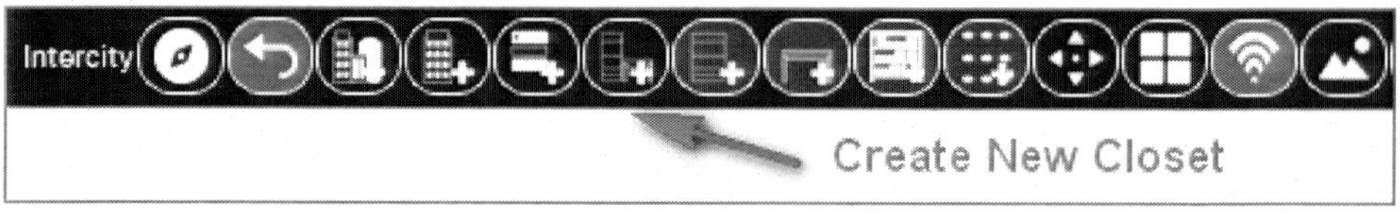

Figure 14.6 Button that causes the creation of a new patch cabinet in the physical topology.

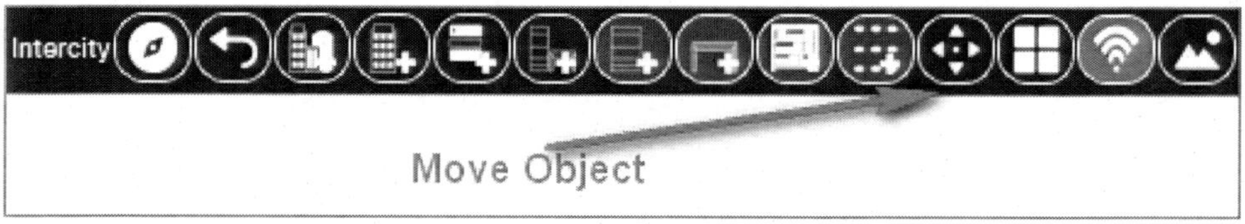

Figure 14.7 Button to move devices in the physical topology .

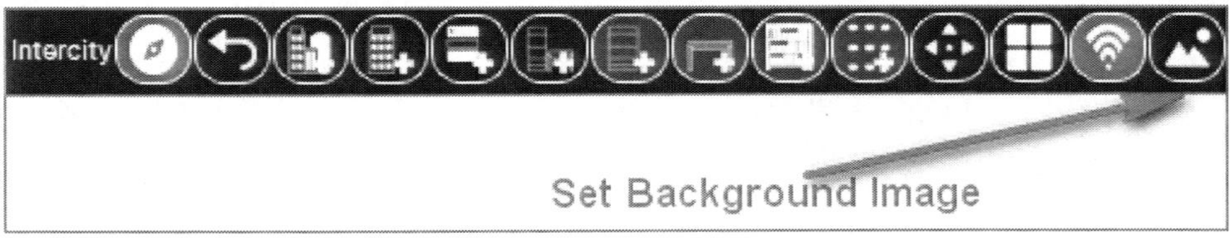

Figure 14.8 Button to change the background of devices in the physical topology.

Figure 14.9 Button that causes the creation of a new generic container in the physical topology.

Part 2. Plan of the exercise.

Step 1. Start the Packet Tracer program.

Step 2. Change the background at the **Intercity level [Set Background Image]** → **[us-state.png]** → **[Apply]**.

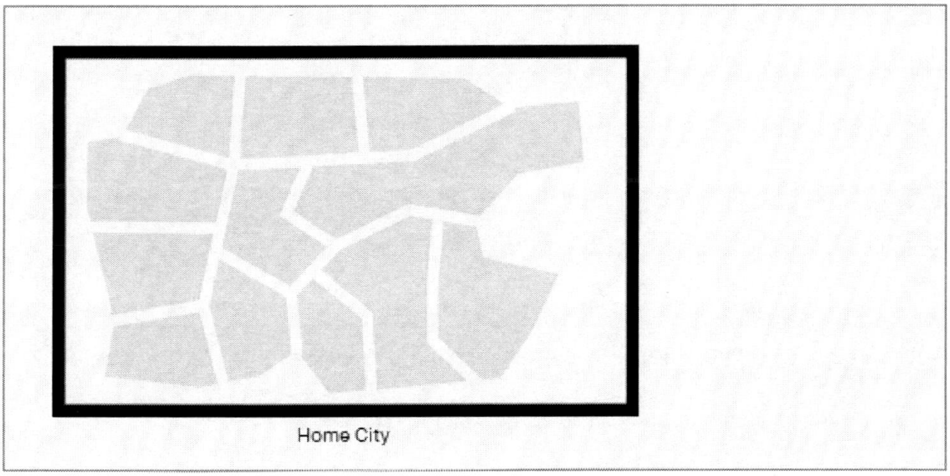

Figure 14.10 The appearance of the topology before the changes.

Figure 14.11 The appearance of the topology after changing the background.

Step 3. Rename [**Home City]** to **[CITY**] and go to the **[CITY]** level.

Step 4 Change the background at the **CITY** level [**Set Background Image**] → [**city.png**] → [**Apply**].

Step 5. Rename **[Corporate Office]** to **[Building]** and go to the **[Building]** level.

Figure 14.12 City-level background.

Step 6. Change the background at the Building level [**Set Background Image**] → [**building.png**] → [**Apply**].

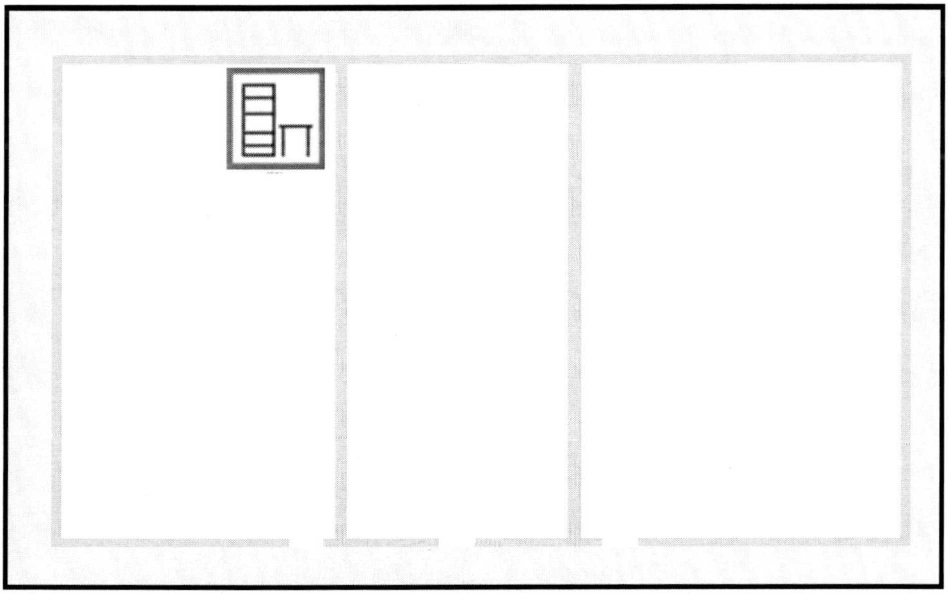

Figure 14.13 Background at the Building level

Step 7. Change the name of the **[Main Wiring Closet]** to **[Main Closet].**

Figure 14.14 Main Closet

Step 8. Go to the **[Main Patch Closet]** level.

Step 9 Insert the shelves in the **[Create New Rack]** cabinet into the **[Main Rack]** object.

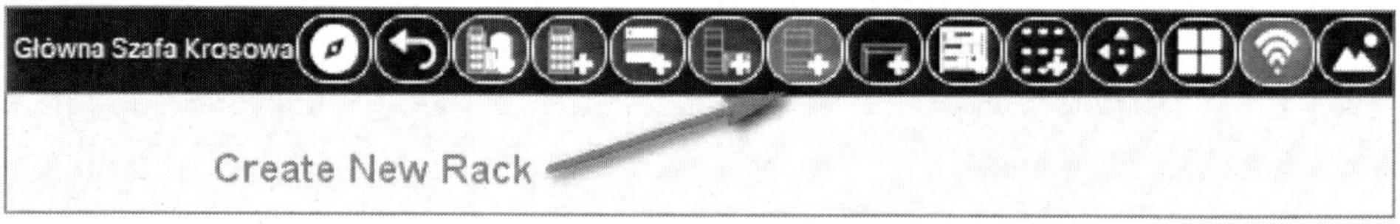

Figure 14.15 Inserting shelves into the Main Closet

Step 10 Insert several network devices at the **[Main Closet]** level.

For example:

- Router ISR4331
- Multilayer switch 3650-24PS
- WLC-2504

Figure 14.16 Inserting network devices into the Main Closet

Step 11. Check the hierarchical structure of the physical topology.

Use the **[Navigation panel]** button in the toolbar in [**Physical**] mode.

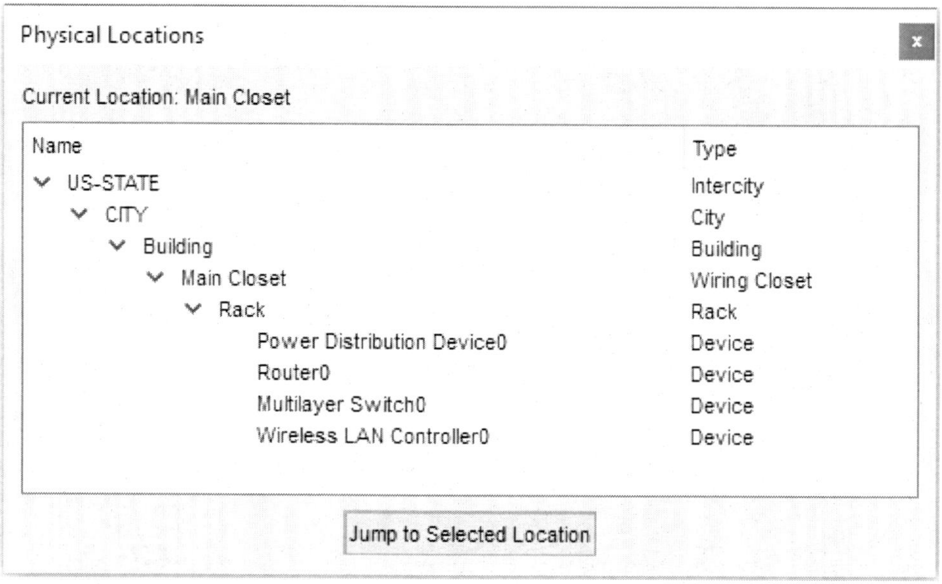

Figure 14.17 Physical topology navigation panel

14.2 Creating the one city physical topology (Exercise 38)

Part 1. Introduction to the exercise.

This exercise is an extension and supplement to the description contained in our Publisher's book titled **"MANAGING COMPUTER NETWORKS IN PACKET TRACER - BASIC KNOWLEDGE". - Chapter 10 - Physical Topology in the Cisco Packet Tracer".**

Part 2. Goal.

Placing devices in Packet Tracer physical storage.

Part 3. Plan of the exercise.

Step 1. Start the Packet Tracer program.

Step 2. Go to the [Home City] level and remove all objects that can be removed.

NOTE: Main Wiring Closet CANNOT BE REMOVED - so rename it to **'SAN JOSE CLOSET'**.

Figure 14.18 Renaming the Main Wiring Closet object

You have obtained the following initial physical topology structure.

Step 3. Go to the [Intercity] level and start creating the **Three Cities** infrastructure.

Graphic files (background-images for topology levels) required for the exercise:

- california2.png
- san-jose.png
- downtown-san-jose.png

Step 4. Go to the [Intercity] level and configure the [**california2.png**] background.

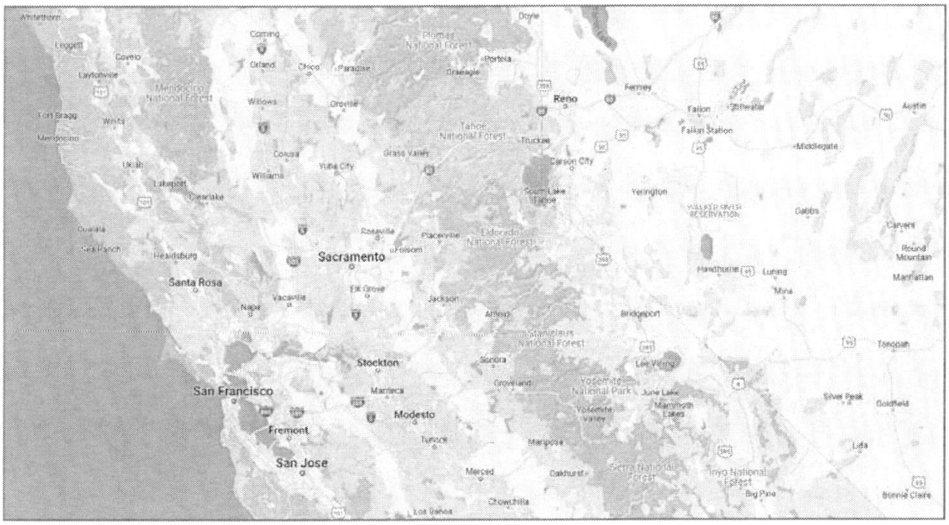

Figure 14.19 Intercity level

Step 5. Go to the **[Intercity]** level and insert a new city **[SAN JOSE].**

Figure 14.20 Intercity level and new city

Step 6. Go to the **[SAN JOSE]** level and configure the **[san-jose.png]** background.

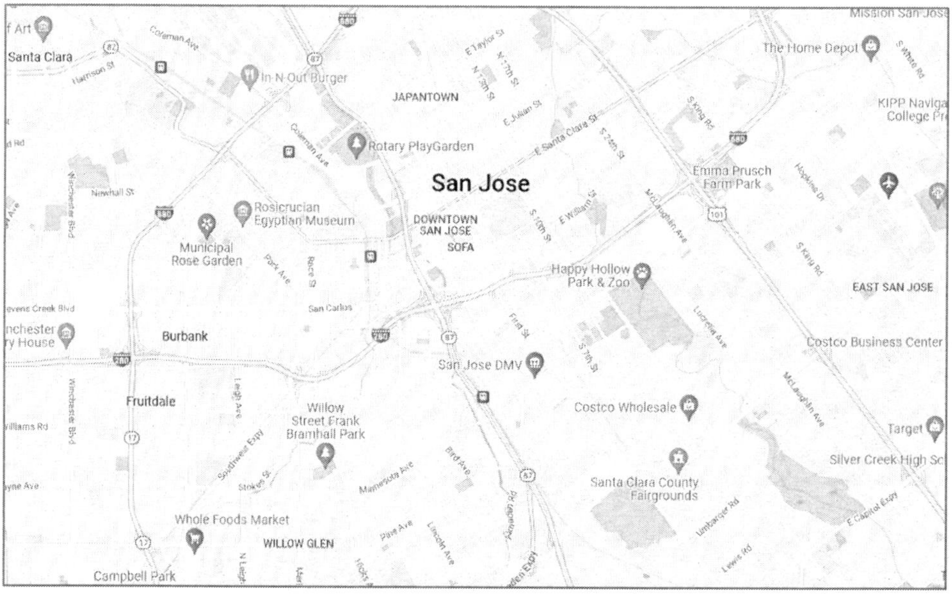

Figure 14.21 SAN JOSE level

Step 7. On the **[SAN JOSE]** level, insert a new building and rename it **[Downtown San Jose].**

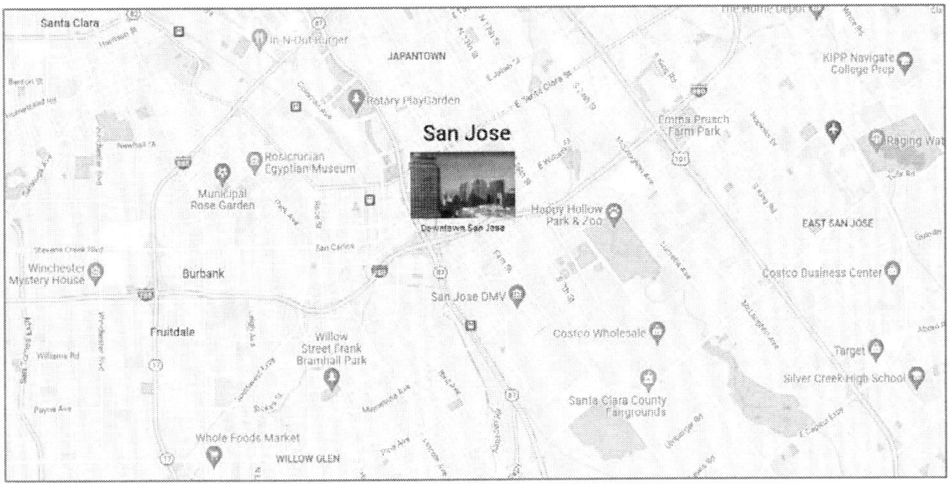

Figure 14.22 SAN JOSE level and Downtown San Jose

Step 8. Go to the **[Downtown San Jose]** level and configure the **[downtown-san-jose.png]** background.

Step 9. Go to the **[Intercity]** level and move the **[SAN JOSE CLOSET]** object to the **Downtown San Jose** level

Figure 14.23 Downtown San Jose level

Step 10. Go to level [**SAN JOSE CLOSET**].

In the **SAN JOSE CLOSET** rename Rack into [**SAN JOSE-RACK**].

Step 11. Insert new shelves into the level [**SAN JOSE-CLOSET**].

Figure 14.24 Button [Create New Inventory Shelf]

Step 12. Rename the shelves to **[SAN JOSE-STORE].**

Figure 14.25 Renaming shelves

Step 13. Insert various devices into the new shelves in the **[SAN JOSE-STORE]** warehouse, for example:

- ISR4331
- ISR4321
- 2911
- 2960

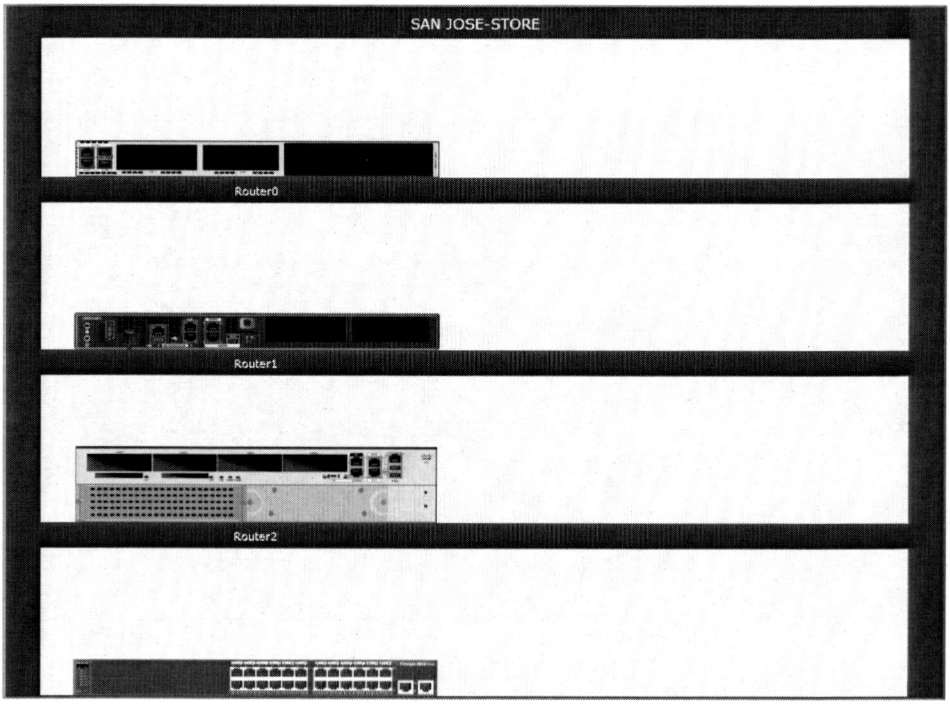

Figure 14.26 New devices in SAN JOSE-MAGAZINE

- Laptop-PT

- PC-PT

Figure 14.27 New devices in SAN JOSE-STORE (cont.).

Step 14. Verify that the new devices are in the logical topology

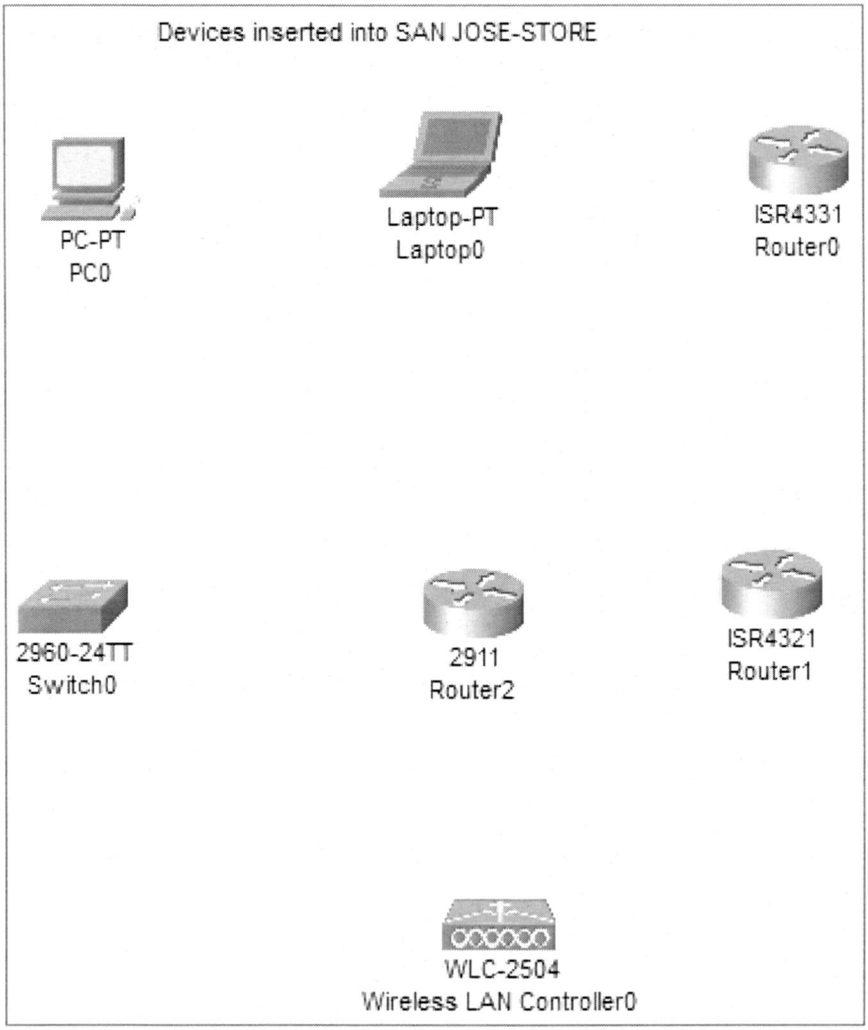

Figure 14.28 View of new devices in SAN JOSE-STORE in logical topology

14.3 Physical topology of the local network (Exercise 39)

Part 1. Goal.

Create a local area network (physical and logical) in Packet Tracer

Part 2 Physical network topology.

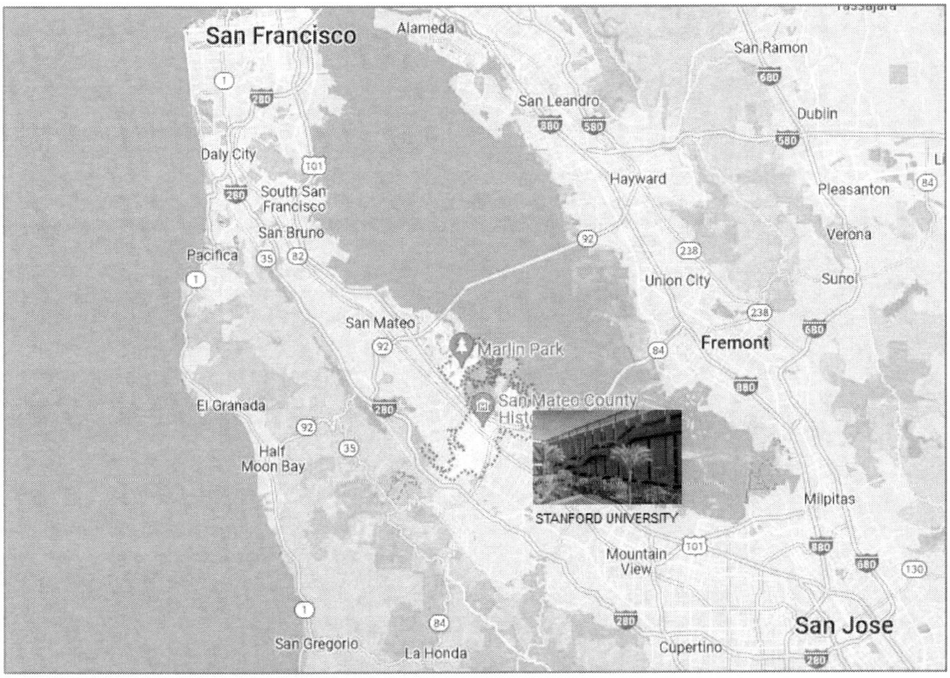

Figure 14.29 Physical topology→ Intercity level

Figure 14.30 Physical topology→ STANFORD UNIVERSITY level

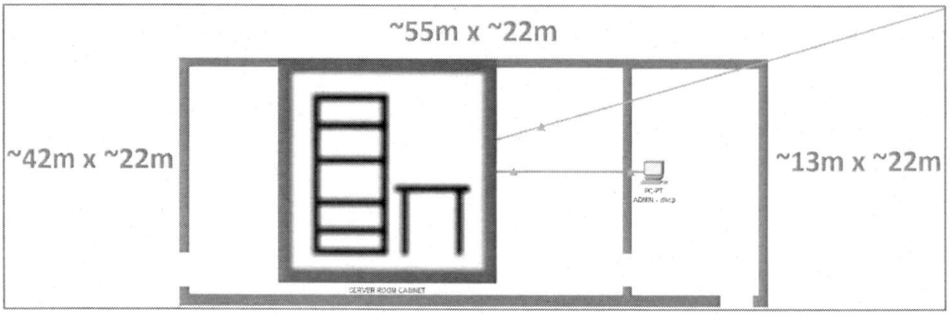

Figure 14.31 Physical topology→ STANFORD-SERVER ROOM level

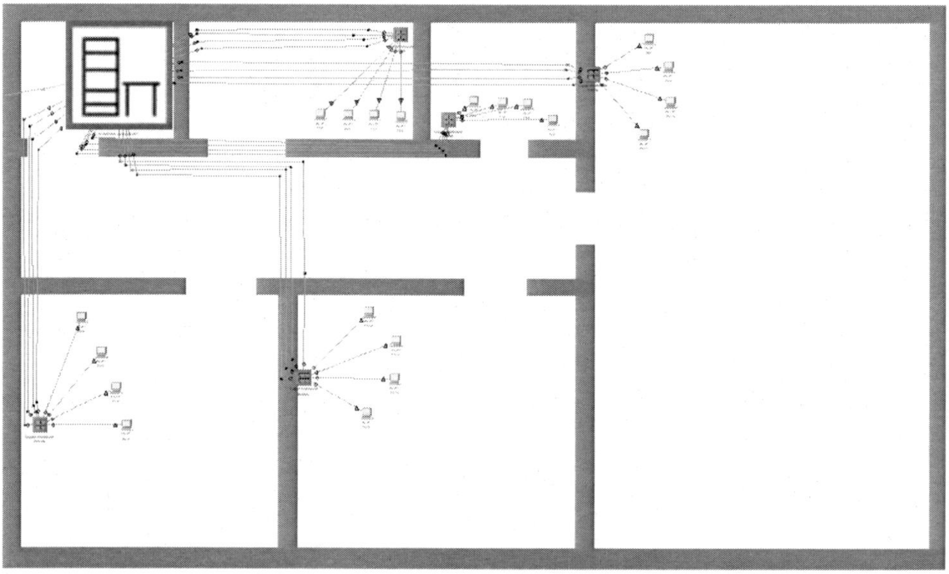

Figure 14.32 Physical topology→ STANFORD-LAN level

Files required for physical topology:

- california1.png
- stanford-university.png
- stanford-server-room.jpg
- stanford-lan.png

Part 3. Plan of the exercise

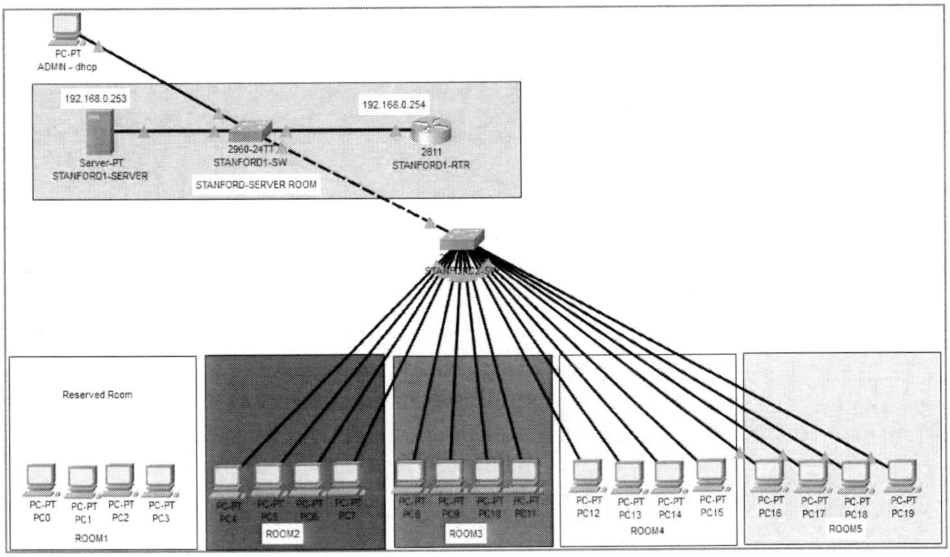

Figure 14.33 Logical topology

Part 4. Creating a physical topology.

Step 1. At the Intercity level, insert an image from the file california1.png.

Step 2. At the Intercity level, insert STANFORD UNIVERSITY.

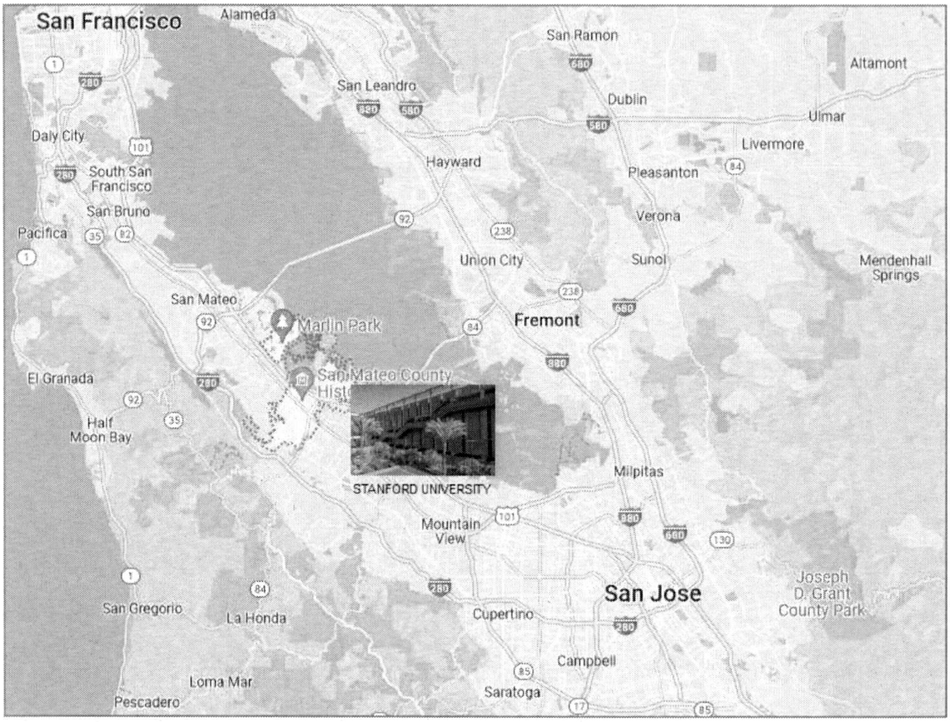

Figure 14.34 Physical topology - Intercity level

Step 3. At the STANFORD UNIVERSITY level, insert buildings:

- STANFORD-SERVER ROOM,
- STANFORD-LAN.

Step 4. Insert an image from the file stanford-university.png at the STANFORD UNIVERSITY level.

Figure 14.35 Physical topology – STANFORD UNIVERSITY level

Step 5. Insert an image from the file stanford-server-room.png at the STANFORD-SERVER ROOM level.

Step 6. Insert objects at the STANFORD-SERVER ROOM level:

- SERVER ROOM CABINET,
- ADMIN-dhcp.

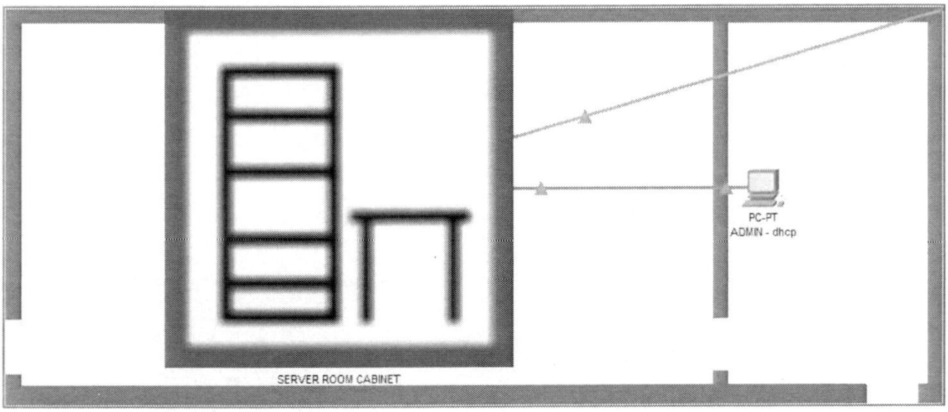

Figure 14.36 Physical topology – STANFORD-SERVER ROOM

Step 7. At the STANFORD-LAN level, insert an image from the stanford-lan.jpg file.

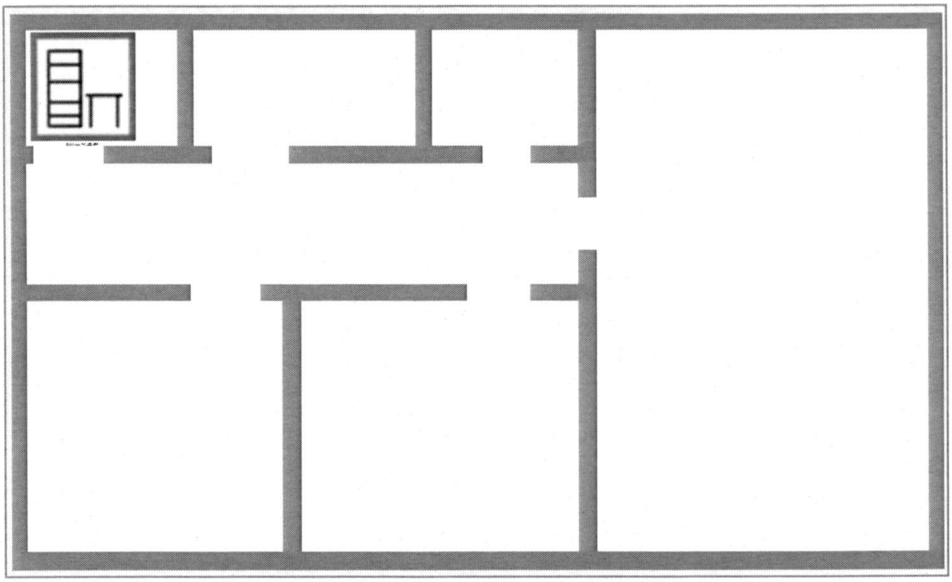

Figure 14.37 Physical topology - STANFORD-LAN

Part 5. Installing equipment in SERVER ROOM CABINET.

Step 1. At the **SERVER ROOM CABINET** level

At the **SERVER ROOM CABINET** physical level, insert a new rack into it. Change the name of the crawlspace cabinet to **STANFORD1**.

Step 2. Install the following devices and network hardware in the **STANFORD1** rack:

- Cooper Patch Panel – 1 pts
- Router 2811 – 1 pts
- Switch 2960 – 1 pts
- Server PT – 1 pts

Note: Maintain 1U spacing between devices.

Step 3. Change the descriptions and names of the devices in the **STANFORD1** rack according to the table below.

Type of device	Description of the device	Device's Host name	Number of ports

Cooper Patch Panel	STANFORD1-A	Not applicable	24 x RJ-45
Router 2811	STANFORD1-RTR	STANFORD2-RTR	2 x FastEthernet
Switch 2960	STANFORD1-SW	STANFORD2-SW	24 x FastEthernet 2 x GigaEthernet
Server-PT	STANFORD1-SERVER	Not applicable	1 x RJ-45

Table 14.1 Names of devices in the STANFORD1 rack

Step 4. Use the Cooper Straight-Through cable to connect the server's Fa0 port to the 2950 switch's Gi0/2 port.

Step 5. Use the Cooper Straight-Through cable to connect the router's Fa0/1 port to the 2950 switch's Gi0/1 port.

Figure 14.38 Physical topology - Cable types

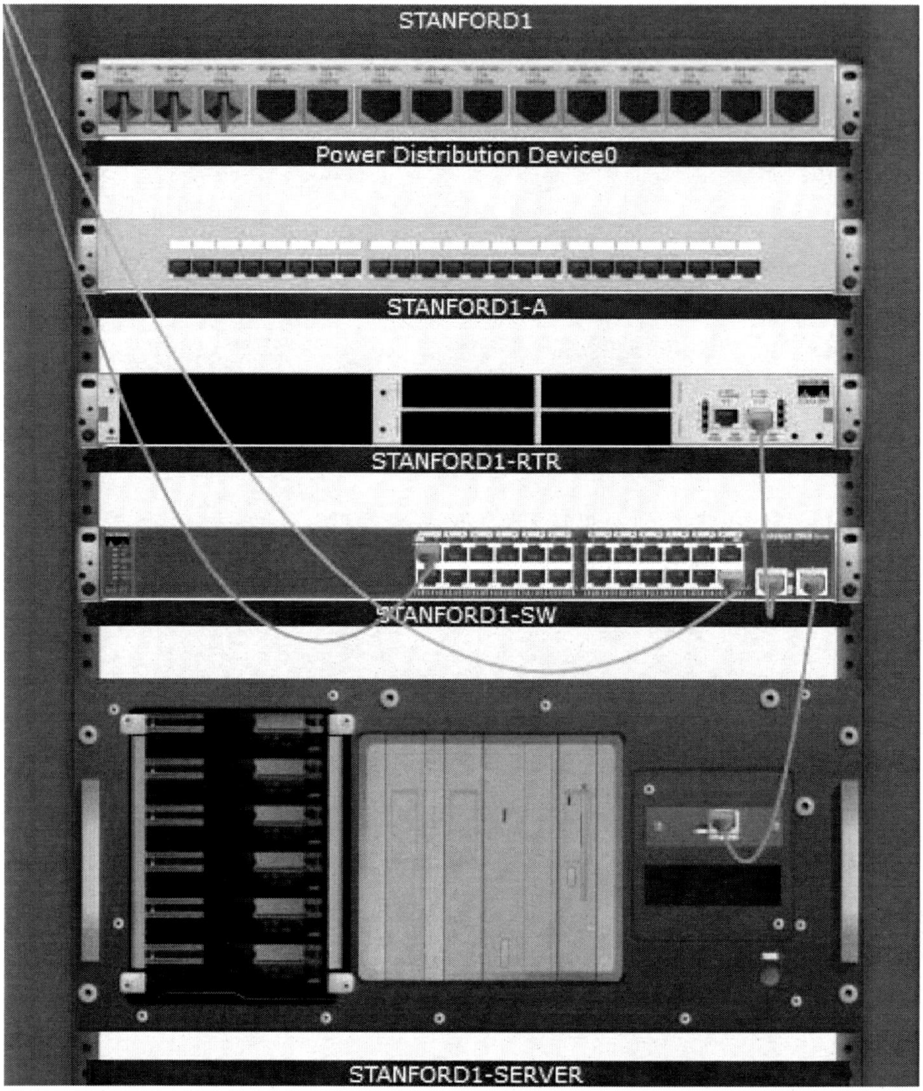

Figure 14.39 Physical topology - Interconnections between devices

Part 6. Installing equipment in STANFORD-LAN CABINET.

Step 1. At the physical level of STANFORD-LAN CABINET, insert a new rack. Rename it to **STANFORD2**.

Step 2. Install the following devices and network hardware in the STANFORD2 rack:

- Cooper Patch Panel – 1 pts
- Switch 2960 – 1 pts

Maintain 1U spacing between devices.

Step 3. Change the descriptions and names of the devices in the STANFORD2 rack according to the table below.

Type of the device	Description of the device	Host name of the device	Number of ports
Cooper Patch Panel	STANFORD2-A	Not applicable	24 x RJ-45
Switch 2960	STANFORD2-SW	STANFORD2-SW	24 x FastEthernet, 2 x GigaEthernet

Table 14.2 Names of devices in the STANFORD2 cabinet

Part 7. Implementation of cabling in STANFORD-LAN.

Step 1. Go to the STANFORD-LAN physical level.

Step 2. In the rooms in STANFORD-LAN, mount Cooper Wall Mount outlets - 5 pts on the walls. (Each outlet has 4 RJ-45 ports).

Figure 14.40 Physical topology - Outlet selection

The outlets should be arranged according to the diagram below.

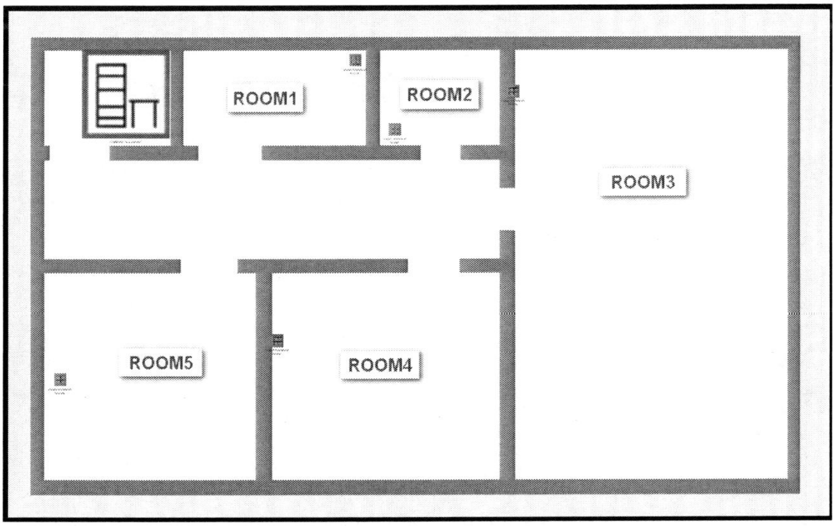

Figure 14.41 Physical topology - Example of outlet layout in rooms

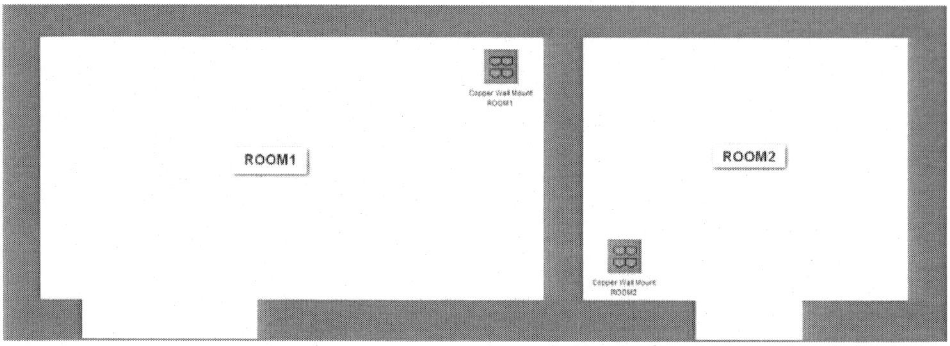

Figure 14.42 Physical topology - Example of outlet layout (zoom – cont.)

Figure 14.43 Physical topology - Example of outlet layout (zoom - cont.)

Step 3. Change the symbology (the names of the sockets, numbered in ascending order, clockwise and starting with the prefix ROOM).

Step 4. Make the wiring connecting the outlets to the patch panel according to the table below.

Note 1: Cabling should be run perpendicularly, along walls, or floors, ceilings, and the length of the cable must not exceed 90 meters.

Note 2: If the total length of the cable will exceed 90 m, move the room outlet to a location that will allow the cable length to be reduced to less than or equal to 90 m.

Patch Panel port designation	Patch Panel Punch Down Number	Socket designation	Punch Down Number in the outlet
Jack1	PunchDown1	ROOM1	PunchDown1
Jack2	PunchDown2	ROOM1	PunchDown2
Jack3	PunchDown3	ROOM1	PunchDown3
Jack4	PunchDown4	ROOM1	PunchDown4

Jack5	PunchDown5	ROOM2	PunchDown1
Jack6	PunchDown6	ROOM2	PunchDown2
Jack7	PunchDown7	ROOM2	PunchDown3
Jack8	PunchDown8	ROOM2	PunchDown4
Jack9	PunchDown9	ROOM3	PunchDown1
Jack10	PunchDown10	ROOM3	PunchDown2
Jack11	PunchDown11	ROOM3	PunchDown3
Jack12	PunchDown12	ROOM3	PunchDown4
Jack13	PunchDown13	ROOM4	PunchDown1
Jack14	PunchDown14	ROOM4	PunchDown2
Jack15	PunchDown15	ROOM4	PunchDown3
Jack16	PunchDown16	ROOM4	PunchDown4
Jack17	PunchDown17	ROOM5	PunchDown1
Jack18	PunchDown18	ROOM5	PunchDown2
Jack19	PunchDown19	ROOM5	PunchDown3
Jack20	PunchDown20	ROOM5	PunchDown4

Table 14.3 Patch Panel STANFORN2-A Ports – Sockets

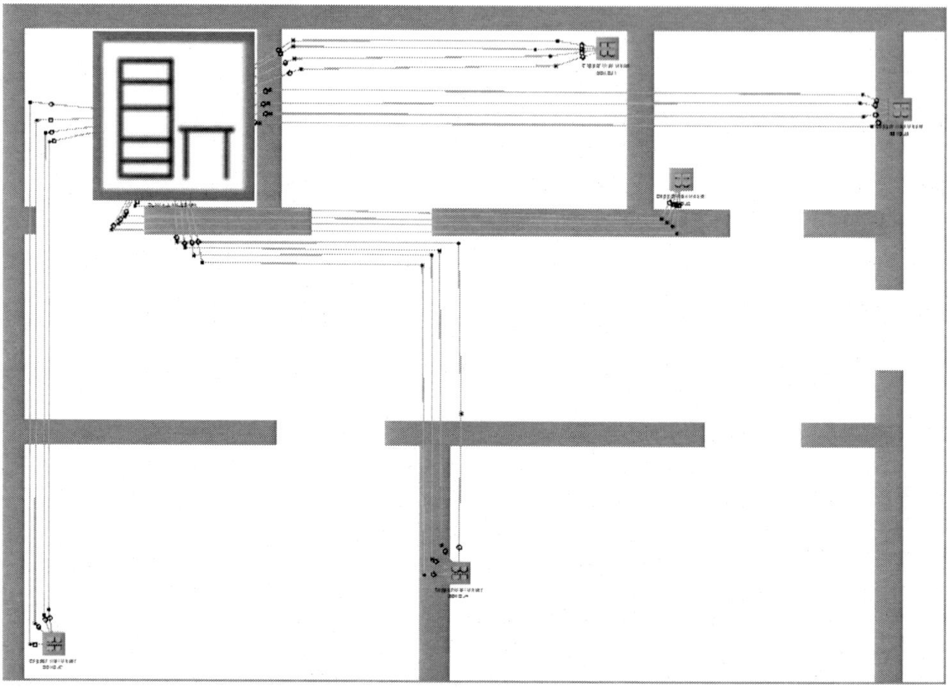

Figure 14.44 Physical topology - Example of cabling layout in rooms

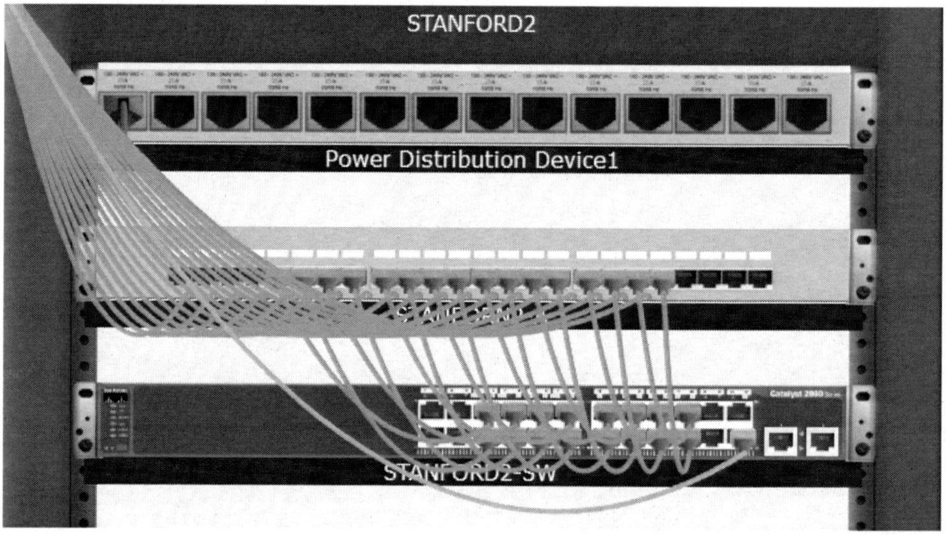

Figure 14.45 Physical topology - Appearance of connections in the STANFORD2 rack

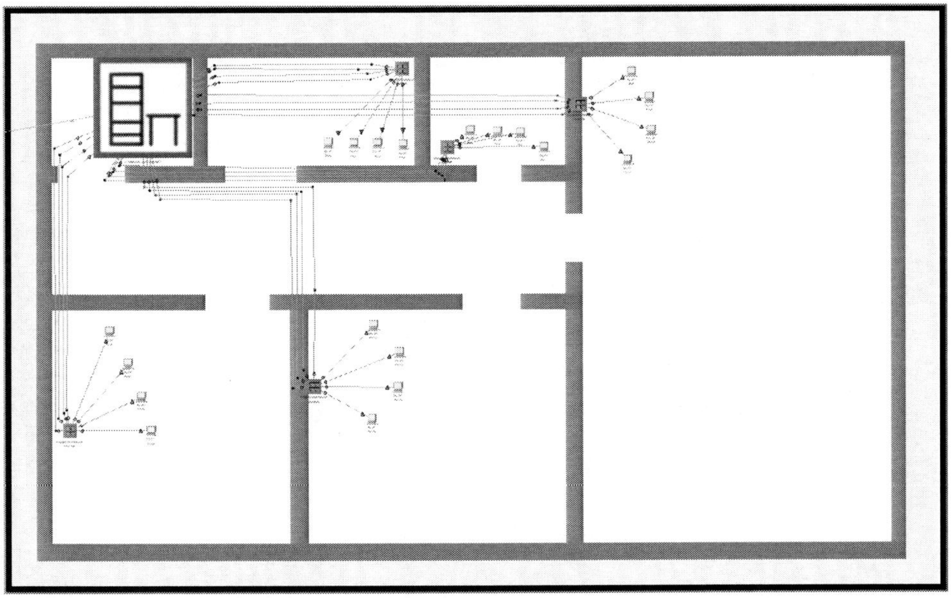

Figure 14.46 Physical topology - Example of cabling layout in rooms and connecting computers to outlets in STANFORD-LAN (green color - UTP cable, straight)

Part 8. Provision of cabling for computers.

Step 1. Insert from one to a maximum of four computers into each room, depending on space and needs.

Step 2. Label the computers according to the table and connect them to the corresponding ports on the outlets.

Computer designation	Socket designation	Port number on the outlet
PC0	ROOM1	Jack1
PC1	ROOM1	Jack2
PC2	ROOM1	Jack3
PC3	ROOM1	Jack4
PC4	ROOM2	Jack1
PC5	ROOM2	Jack2
PC6	ROOM2	Jack3
PC7	ROOM2	Jack4
PC8	ROOM3	Jack1
PC9	ROOM3	Jack2

PC10	ROOM3	Jack3
PC11	ROOM3	Jack4
PC12	ROOM4	Jack1
PC13	ROOM4	Jack2
PC14	ROOM4	Jack3
PC15	ROOM4	Jack4
PC16	ROOM5	Jack1
PC17	ROOM5	Jack2
PC18	ROOM5	Jack3
PC19	ROOM5	Jack4

Table 14.4 Patch Panel STANFORD2-A Sockets

Part 9. Crossover of outlets in the STANFORD-LAN CABINET.

Step 1. Go to the STANFORD-LAN server room.

Step 2. In the STANFORD-LAN cabinet, go to the STANFORD-LAN CABINET object.

Step 3. Perform port (slot) crossover on the STANFORD2-A patch panel (***ROOMS 2 THROUGH 5 ONLY***).

Using Cooper Straight-Through cables, connect the **Jack5 – Jack20** ports on the STANFORD2-A patch panel to the ports in Fa0/5 - Fa0/20 on the 2950 switch, according to the table.

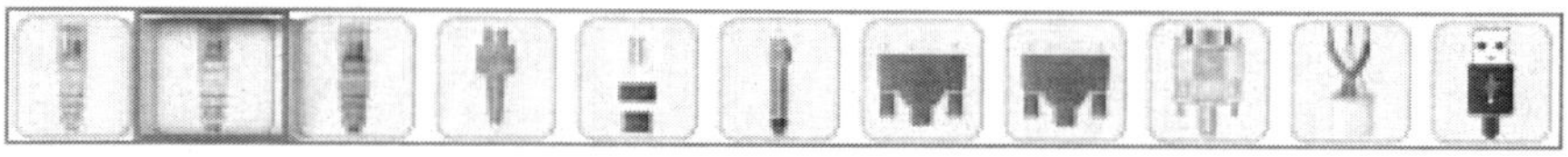

Figure 14.47 Physical topology - Types of cables

Note: This is a daunting task, as fitting the cable plug into the socket meets the already existing wiring - so choose the ports carefully and gently.

Patch panel socket	**Target device**	**Port number of the destination device**	**Room No.**
Source Port	**Destination Device**	**Destination port**	
Jack1	Reserved	Fa0/1	**1**
Jack2	Reserved	Fa0/2	**1**
Jack3	Reserved	Fa0/3	**1**
Jack4	Reserved	Fa0/4	**1**

Jack5	STANFORD 2-SW	Fa0/5	2
Jack6	STANFORD 2-SW	Fa0/6	2
Jack7	STANFORD 2-SW	Fa0/7	2
Jack8	STANFORD 2-SW	Fa0/8	2
Jack9	STANFORD 2-SW	Fa0/9	3
Jack10	STANFORD 2-SW	Fa0/10	3
Jack11	STANFORD 2-SW	Fa0/11	3
Jack12	STANFORD 2-SW	Fa0/12	3
Jack13	STANFORD 2-SW	**Fa0/13**	**4**
Jack14	STANFORD 2-SW	**Fa0/14**	**4**
Jack15	STANFORD 2-SW	**Fa0/15**	**4**
Jack16	STANFORD 2-SW	**Fa0/16**	**4**
Jack17	STANFORD 2-SW	**Fa0/17**	**5**
Jack18	STANFORD 2-SW	**Fa0/18**	**5**
Jack19	STANFORD 2-SW	**Fa0/19**	**5**
Jack20	STANFORD 2-SW	**Fa0/20**	**5**
Jack21	Reserved	Fa0/21	-
Jack22	Reserved	Fa0/22	-
Jack23	Reserved	Fa0/23	-
Jack24	Reserved	Fa0/24	-

Table 14.5 Patch Panel STANFORD2-A

Step 4. After the physical topology is done, arrange the logical topology of the STANFORD-LAN network.

The resulting logical topology of the PC0 - PC3 connection is omitted, because the cabling in the ROOM1 are reserved for the future.

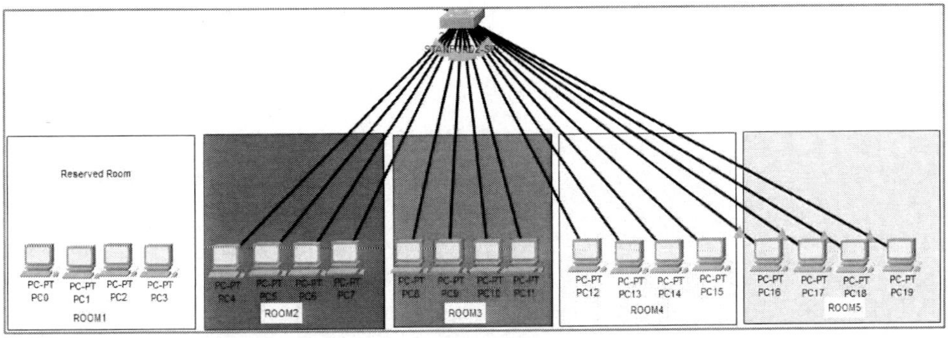

Figure 14.48 Intermediate state of logical topology

Part 10. STANFORD-SERVER ROOM connection with STANFORD-LAN.

Step 1. Connect the **STANFORD2-SW** switch, installed in STANFORD-LAN), to the **STANFORD1-SW** switch, installed in STANFORD-SERVER ROOM.

Device	Port	Device	Port
STANFORD1-SW	Fa0/24	STANFORD 2-SW	Fa0/24

Table 14.6 STANFORD1-SW - STANFORD-SW connection

Step 2. Check the physical topology.

Figure 14.49 Resulting physical topology

Choose the location of the devices so that the cable between the switches is not more than 90 meters long.

Step 3. Check the logical topology.

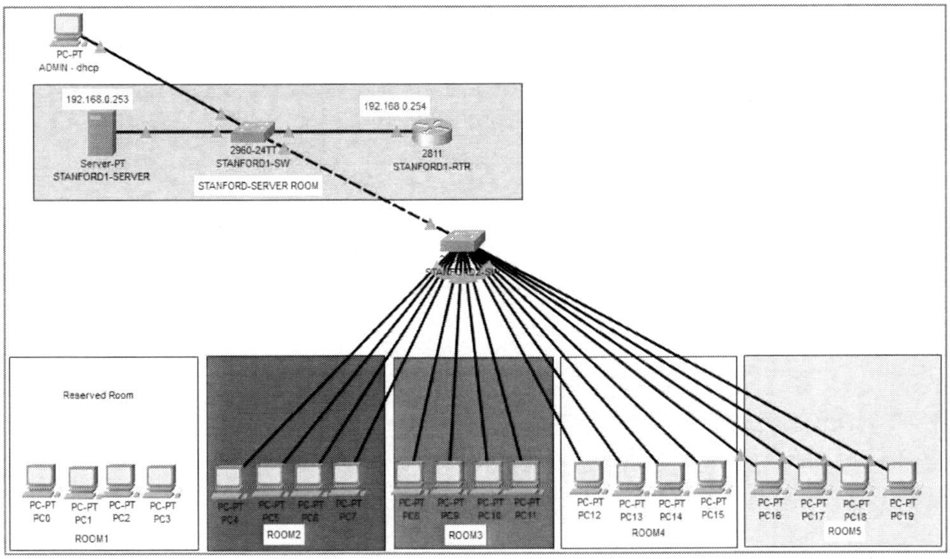

Figure 14.50 Resulting logical topology with server room

Part 11. Assumptions for IPV4 addressing.

- Automatic addressing (in STANFORD-SERVER ROOM, where is a DHCP server, assigning IP network addresses, default gateway, DNS address).
- The DHCP server automatically determines the /24 subnet mask (255.255.255.0).
- The DHCP server automatically determines the default gateway of the subnet (192.168.0.254).
- The DHCP server automatically determines the DNS address (192.168.0.253).
- The host with the address 192.168.0.253 is the DNS server.
- Addresses from 192.168.0.1 to 192.168.0.252 are available to computers - DHCP clients.

Part 12. Configuring the DHCP server on the router in STANFORD1-RTR.

Step 1. Configure the interfaces in STANFORD1-RTR

IOS commands:

```
enable
conf   t
hostname   STANFORD1-RTR
interface   Fa0/1
ip address   192.168.0.254     255.255.255.0
no shutdown
```

Step 2. Configure DHCP in STANFORD1-RTR

IOS commands:

```
enable
conf  t
ip dhcp excluded-address 192.168.0.253 192.168.0.254
dns-server  192.168.0.253
exit

enable
conf  t
ip dhcp pool  STANFORD
default-router 192.168.0.254
network  192.168.0.0  255.255.255.0
dns-server  192.168.0.253
exit
```

Part 13 Configuring the HTTP server in STANFORD1-SERVER.

Step 1. Create a website in STANFORD1-SERVER

Use **[Services]→[HTTP]** →index.html

Step 2. Contents of index.html file

```
<html>
<center><font size='+2' color='blue'>Cisco Packet Tracer
8.2</font></center>
<hr>Serwer HTTP is still just as available since the
immemorial days of Packet Tracer
<p> Web site information:
<br> Topic: local network equipment management
<br>Author: IT
<br> Date the exercise was created: 2022.10.31
<br> Place of origin of the exercise: Redwood
</html>
```

URL name	Address
www.stanford.redwood.california.org	192.168.0.253

Table 14.7 DNS server configuration in STANFORD1-SERVER

Step 1. Insert a Type A record into the DNS service.

Use **[Services]→[DNS] →** Service: On

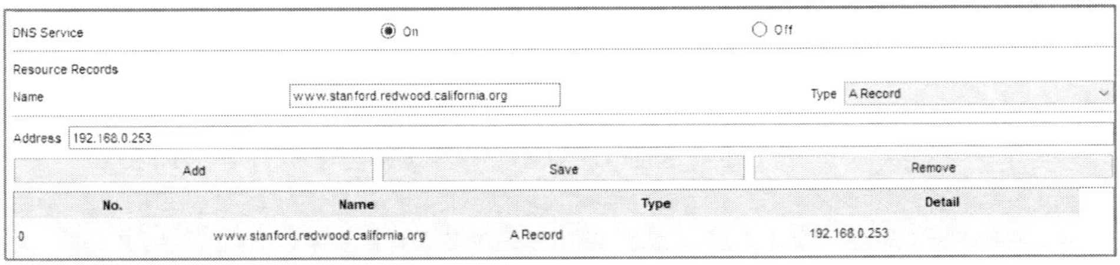

Figure 14.51 Configuration of DNS service in STANFORD1-SERVER

Part 14. Configuring clients in STANFORD-LAN.

Step 1. Set up DHCP service on all clients (computers)

Use **[Desktop] → [IP Configuration] → [FastEthernet0] → [DHCP] →** Enabling DHCP on client computers

Step 2. For example for PC4

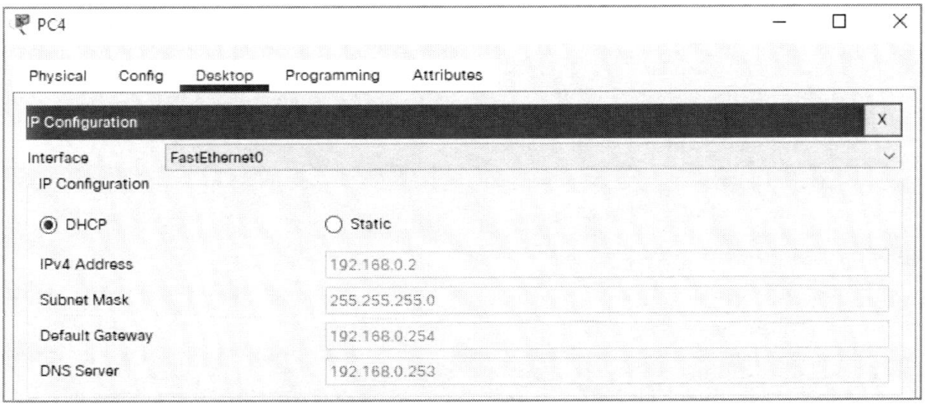

Figure 14.52 Configuration of dynamic addressing in PC4

Step 3. For example for PC19

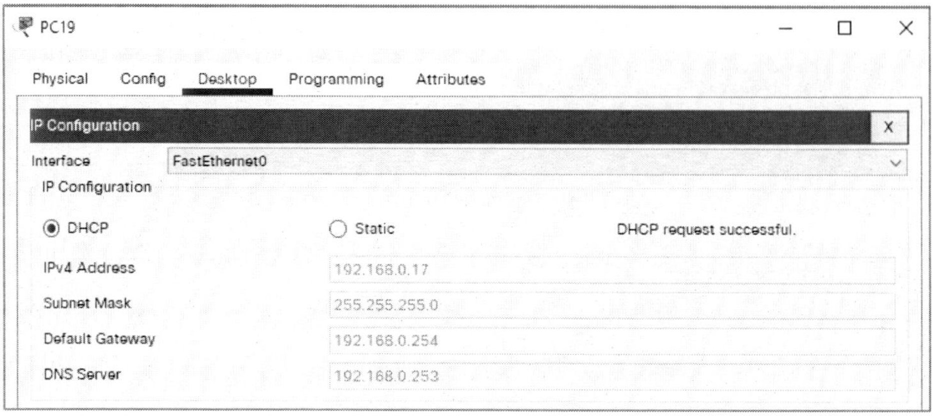

Figure 14.53 Configuration of dynamic addressing in PC19

Step 4. Verify server access **www.stanford.redwood.california.org** from PC19

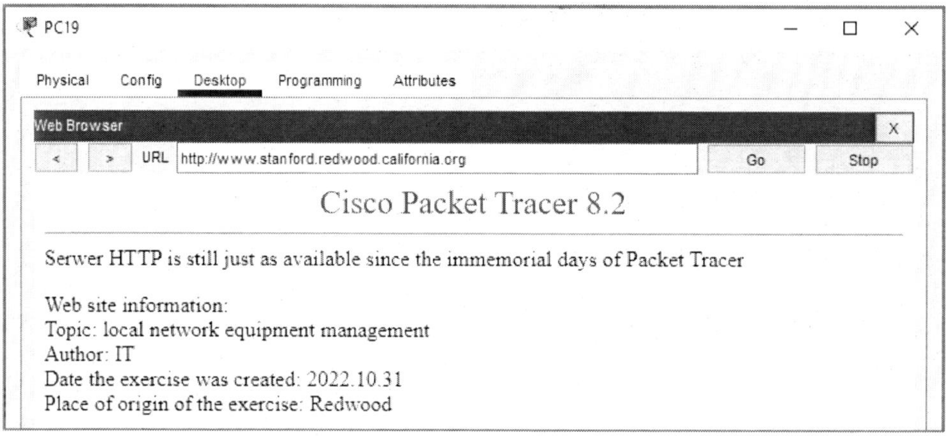

Figure 14.54 Site www.stanford.redwood.california.org

14.4 Physical topology for WAN (Exercise 40)

Part 1. Assumptions for network topology.

Files required for physical topology:

- california2.png
- sacramento-building.png
- san-francisco-building.png
- server-rooms.png

The physical topology of the 3 cities, for this exercise, consists of three cities:

- Sacramento
- San Francisco
- San Jose

Figure 14.55 Physical topology of WAN

There is a building with a server room in Sacramento.

There is a building with a server room in San Francisco.

There is a building with a server room in San Jose.

Part 2. Creating a physical topology.

Step 1. Start Cisco Packet Tracer 8 and enter the physical topology design mode.

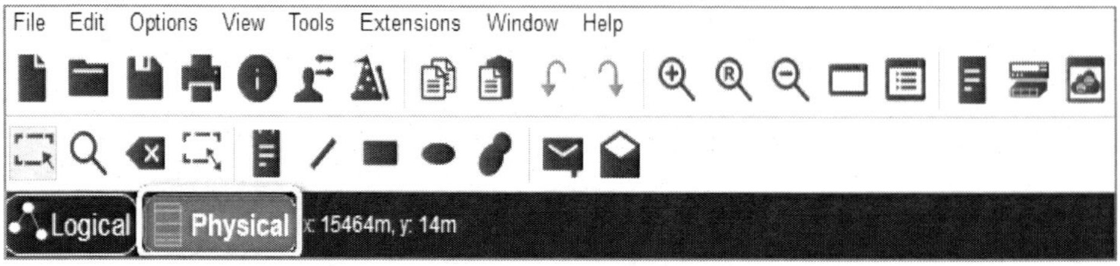

Figure 14.56 [Physical] mode.

Step 2. At the Intercity level, insert an image from the california2.png file.

Figure 14.57 [Intercity] level.

Use the [**Set Background Image**] button.

Figure 14.58 [Set Background Image] button.

Click the button **[Browse]**

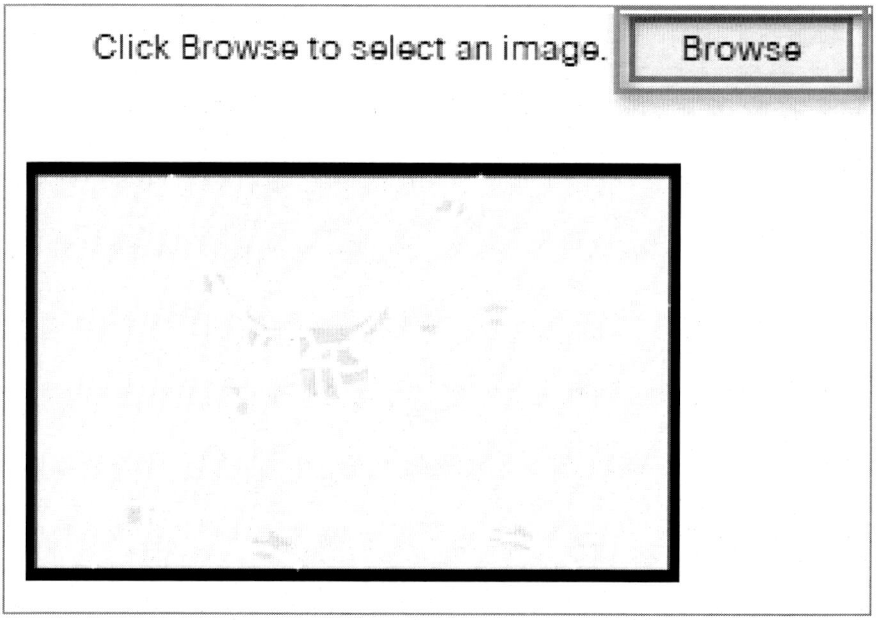

Figure 14.59 [Browse] button.

Select the file **california2.png**.

Figure 14.60 Selecting a background

Click the button **[Apply]**

Figure 14.61 [Apply] button.

Step 3. Move the Home City object and rename it to **Sacramento Building**.

Step 4. Move to the Sacramento Building level.

Step 5. At the Sacramento Building level, insert an image from the file **sacramento-building.png**.

Use the [**Set Background Image**] button.

Figure 14.62 Background view for Sacramento Buiding

Step 6. Rename the Corporate Office object to **Sacramento-Server Room**.

Figure 14.63 Changing the name of the Corporate Office to for Sacramento-Server Room

Step 7. Go to the Sacramento-Server Room level.

Step 8. Rename the Main Wiring Closet object to Sacrament-Cabinet.

Step 9. At the Sacramento-Server Room level, insert the image from the server-rooms.png file.

The server room consists of three rooms.

Use the **[Set Background Image]** button.

Move the Sacrament-Cabinet object to the middle room.

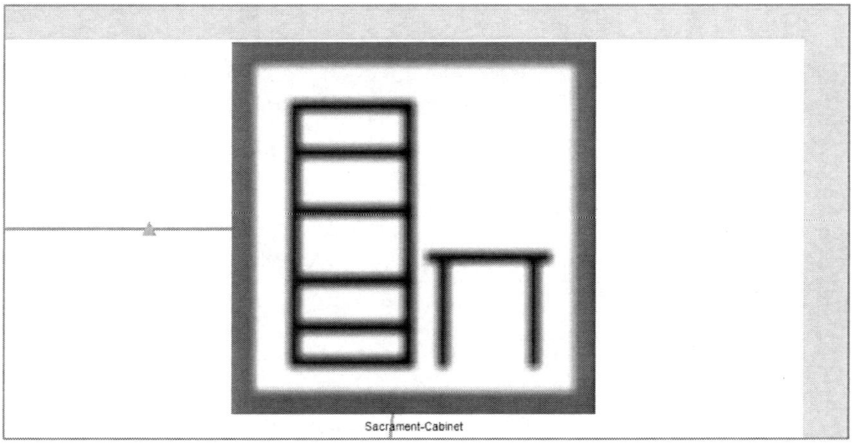

Figure 14.64 Sacrament Cabinet

Step 10. Return to Intercity level.

Figure 14.65 Intercity level view

Step 11. Insert a new object and rename it San Francisco Building**.**

Use the button **[Create New City]**

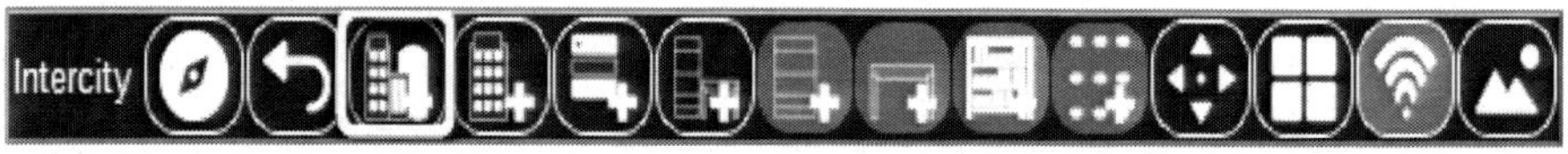

Figure 14.66 [Create New City] button

Figure 14.67 View of the San Francisco Building object

Step 12. At the San Francisco Building level, insert an image from the san-francisco-building.png file.

Use the button **[Set Background Image]**

Figure 14.68 Background of Sun Francisco Building object

Step 13. Insert a new Office Building object at the San Francisco Building level.

Use the button **[Create New Building]**

Step 14. Rename the Office Building object to San Francisco-Server Room

Figure 14.69 Changing the name of the Office Building to San Francisco-Server Room

Step 15. Go to San Francisco-Server level

Step 16. Insert an image from the server-rooms.png file at the San Francisco-Server Room level.

Use the button **[Set Background Image]**

Figure 14.70 The background of the San Francisco-Server Room facility

The server room consists of three rooms.

Step 17. Insert a new object (closet) at the San Francisco-Server Room level.

Use the button **[Create New Closet]**

Change the name of the closet to San Francisco-Closet. Move the San Francisco-Closet object to the middle room.

Figure 14.71 San Franciso-Closet object

Step 18. Return to Intercity level

Figure 14.72 Intercity topology

Step 19. Insert a new object and rename it San Jose Building.

Use the **[Create New City]** button.

Figure 14.73 [Create New City] button.

Step 20. At the San Jose Building level, insert an image from the file **san-jose-building.png**.

Use the **[Set Background Image]** button.

Step 21. At the San Jose Building level, insert a new Office Building object.

Use the [**Create New Building]** button.

Step 22. Change the name of the Office Building object to San Jose Building.

Figure 14.74 San Jose-Server at the San Jose Building level

Step 23. Go to the San Jose-Server Room level

Step 24. Insert an image from the **server-rooms.png** file at the San Jose-Server Room level.

Use the **[Set Background Image]** button.

Figure 14.75 San Jose-Server level

The server room consists of three rooms.

Step 25. Insert a new object (cabinet) on the San Jose-Server Room level.

Use the **[Create New Closet]** button.

Change the name of the closet to **San Jose-Rack**.

Move the **San Jose-Rack** object to the middle room.

Figure 14.76 San Jose-Rack on the level of San Jose-Server

Step 26. Return to Intercity level.

Figure 14.77 Intercity level

Step 27. Check physical topology structure and device locations

Use the **[Navigation Panel]** button.

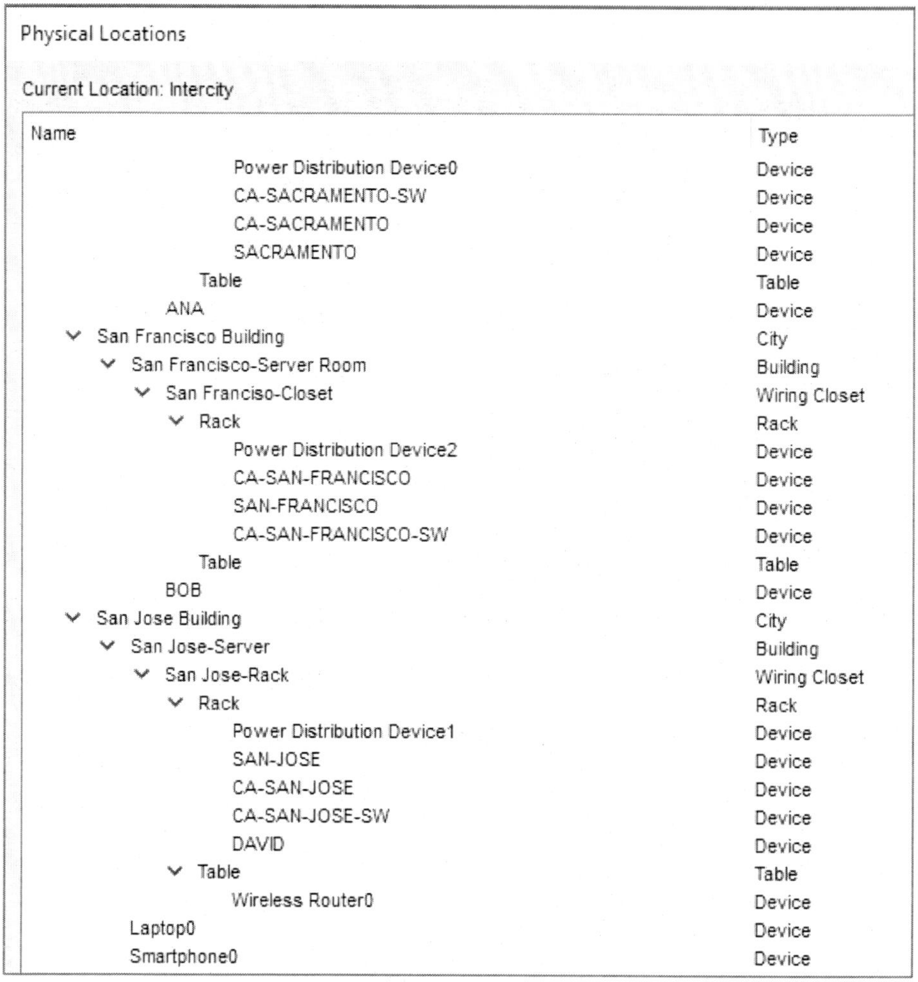

Figure 14.78 Physical topology structure

Part 3. Preparation of intermediary devices.

Type of device	**Device model (module)**	**Number of devices**
L3-Multilayer Switch	3650-24PS (**GLC-LH-SMD**)	4 for one switch
L3-Multilayer Switch	3650-24PS (**AC-POWER-SUPPLY**)	2 for one switch
Router	2811 (**NM-1FE-FX**)	3 for one router
L2-Switch	2960-24TT	3

Table 14.8 Devices required for physical topology and modules

	Equipment	Quantity	Names
Sacramento-Cabinet	3650-24PS	1	SACRAMENTO
	2811	1	CA-SACRAMENTO
	2960-24TT	1	CA-SACRAMENTO-SW
San Francisco-Cabinet	3650-24PS	1	SAN-FRANCISCO
	2811	1	CA-SAN-FRANCISCO
	2960-24TT	1	CA-SAN-FRANCISCO-SW
San Jose-Cabinet	3650-24PS	1	SAN-JOSE
	2811	1	CA- SAN-JOSE
	2960-24TT	1	CA- SAN-JOSE-SW

Table 14.9 Location of equipment

Part 4 Configuring hardware (intermediary devices).

Step 1. Use the topology created previously.

Step 2. Prepare a reference 3650 multilayer switch as specified.

Insert Multilayer Switch0 into logical topology.

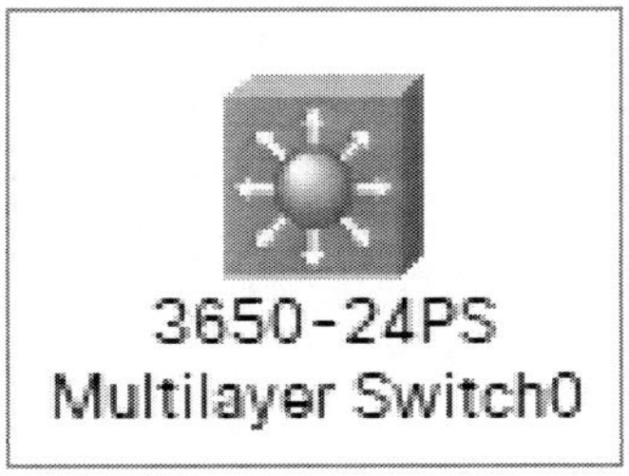

Figure 14.79 Multilayer switch 3650

Step 3. Insert the two **AC-POWER-SUPPLY** modules into their respective slots.

Step 4. Insert the four **GLC-LH-SMD** fiber optic modules (transceivers) into the corresponding slots.

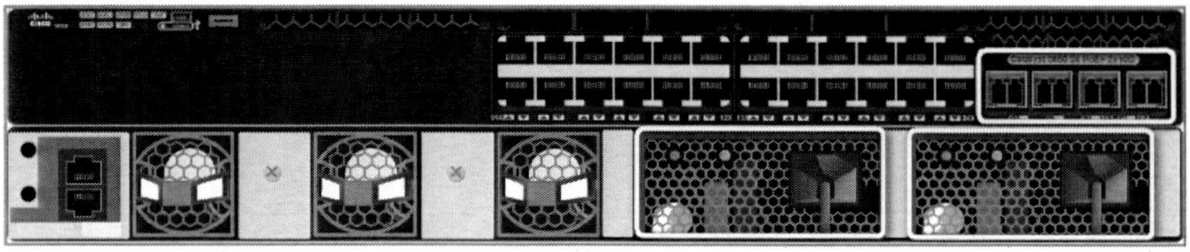

Figure 14.80 Multilayer 3650 switch with GLC-LH-SMD modules

Step 5. Prepare a model 2811 router as specified.

Figure 14.81 Router 2811

Step 6. Insert one **NM-1FE-FX** fiber optic module (tranceiver) into the appropriate slot.

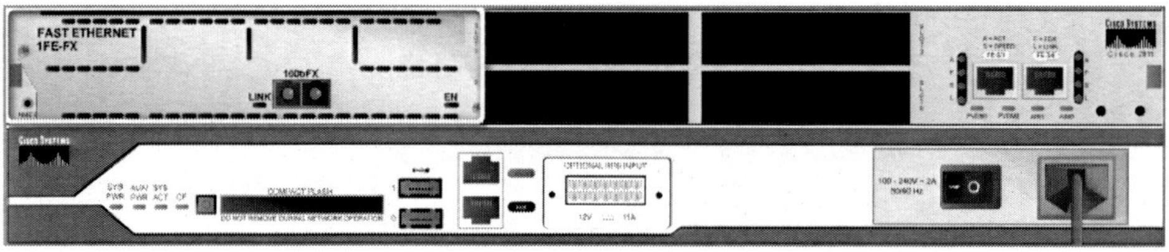

Figure 14.82 Router 2811 with NM-1FE-FX module

Step 7. Prepare a model 2960 single layer switch as specified.

Figure 14.83 Single layer switch 2960

Step 8. Select three model devices and copy them twice.

Use: Edit → Copy, Edit→ Paste

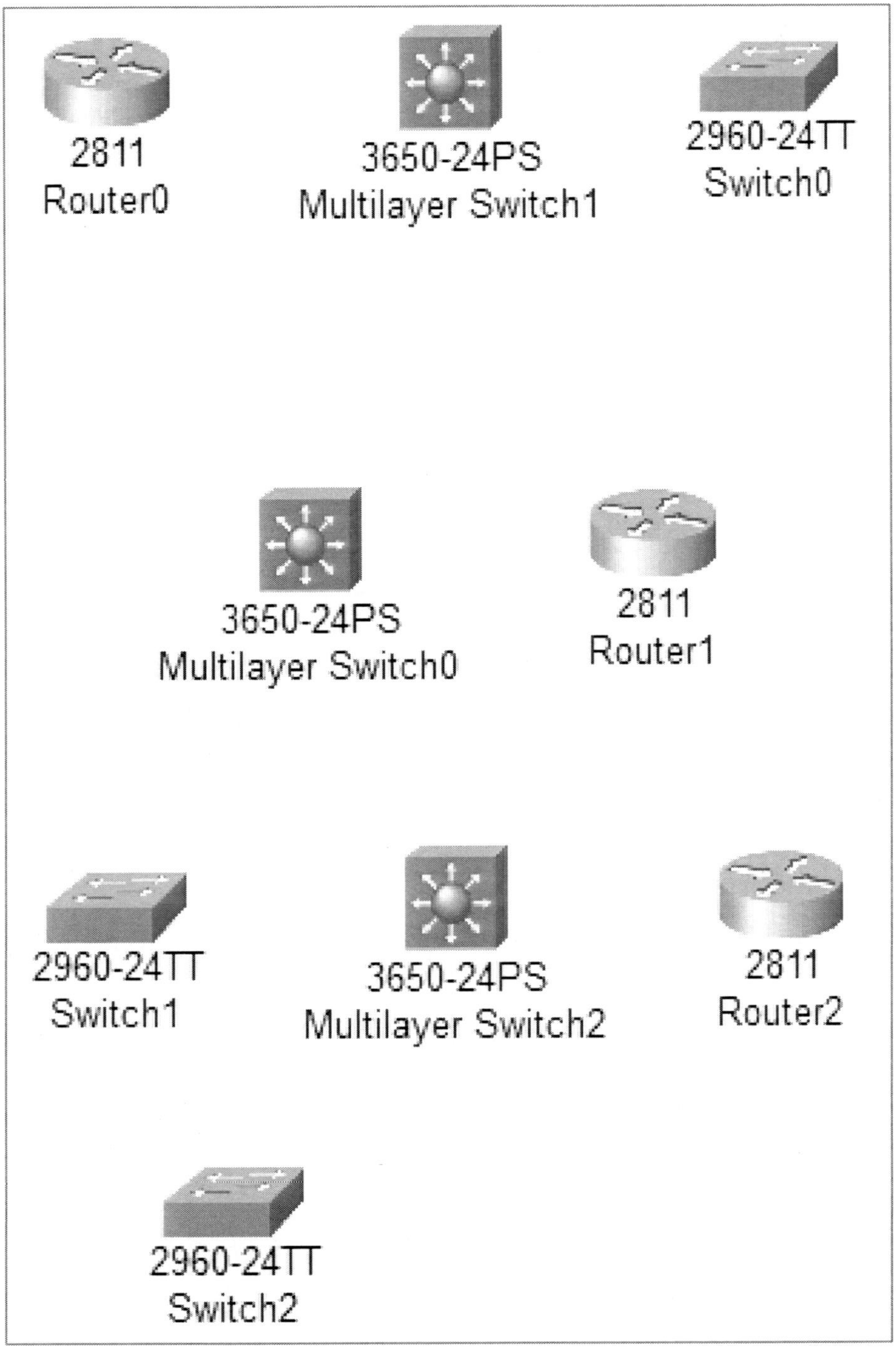

Figure 14.84 Intermediary devices in a logical topology

Step 9. Change the names (display names, host names) adequately according to the assumptions.

Type of device	Names (Display Name, Host Name)	Location
3650-24PS	SACRAMENTO	Sacramento-Cabinet
2811	CA-SACRAMENTO	Sacramento-Cabinet
2960-24TT	CA-SACRAMENTO-SW	Sacramento-Cabinet
3650-24PS	SAN-FRANCISCO	San Francisco-Closet
2811	CA-SAN-FRANCISCO	San Francisco-Closet
2960-24TT	GSP-SW	San Francisco-Closet
3650-24PS	SAN JOSE	San Jose Rack
2811	CA-SAN-JOSE	San Jose Rack
2960-24TT	CA-SAN-JOSE-SW	San Jose Rack

Table 14.10 Device names

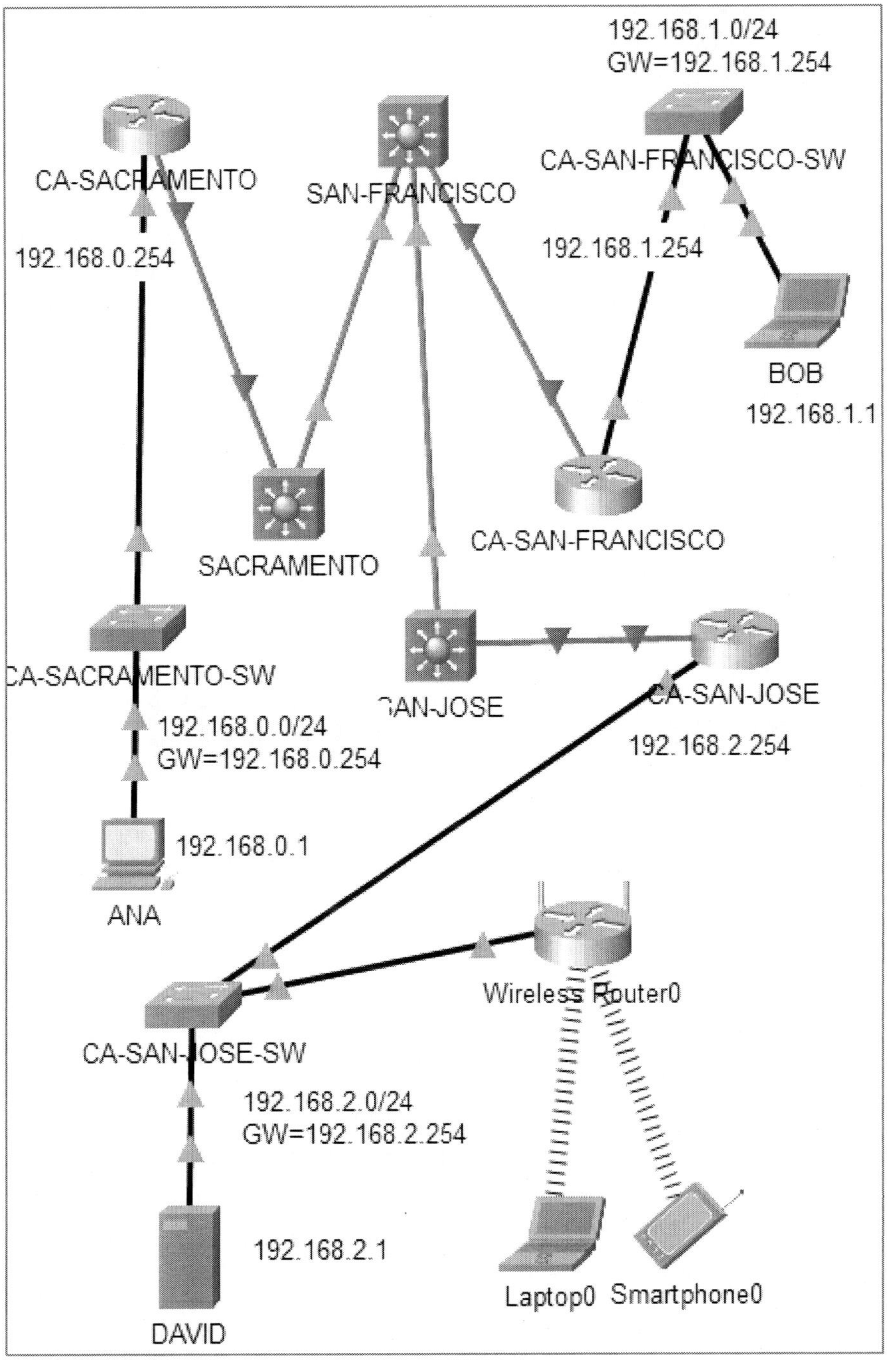

Figure 14.85 Intermediary devices after renaming

Step 10. Move the devices to their proper location. Change the locations of the devices according to the physical topology.

Step 11. Move on to the physical topology.

Step 12. Use the [Move Object] button to move the devices to their correct locations.

Step 13. Arrange the devices in the cabinets according to the following rule.

The principle of installation of devices: (from top to bottom)

- Switch 3650-24PS
- Router 2811
- Switch 2960-24TT

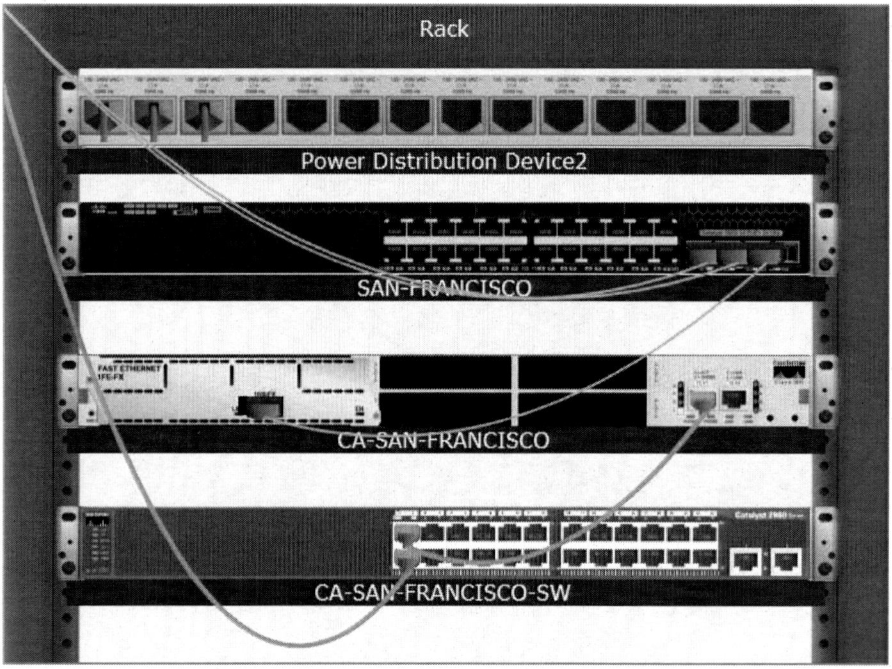

Figure 14.86 San Francisco-Closet

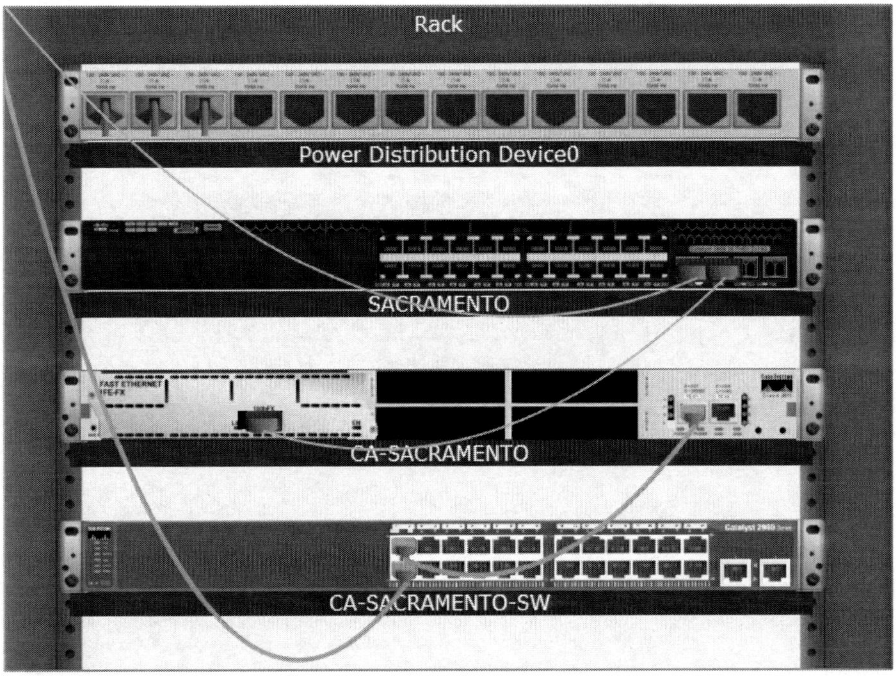

Figure 14.87 Sacramento-Cabinet

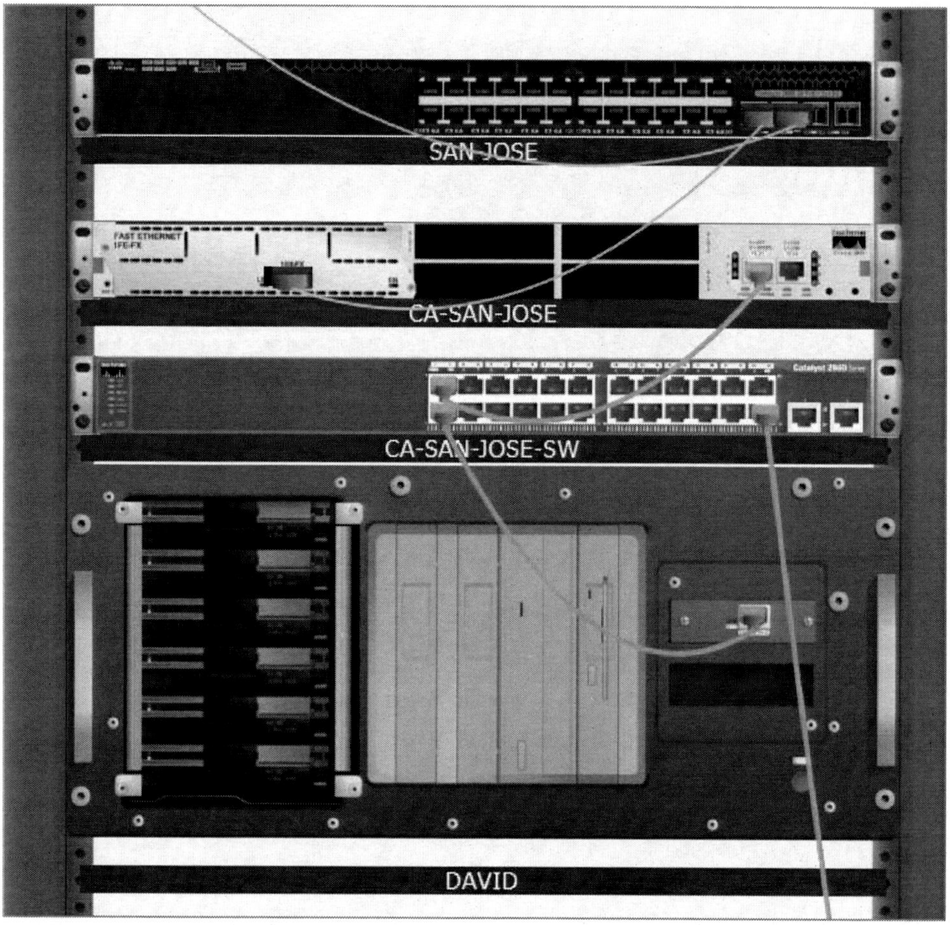

Figure 14.88 Jan-Jose-Cabinet

Step 14. Return to the Intercity level.

Step 15. Check the physical topology structure and device locations.

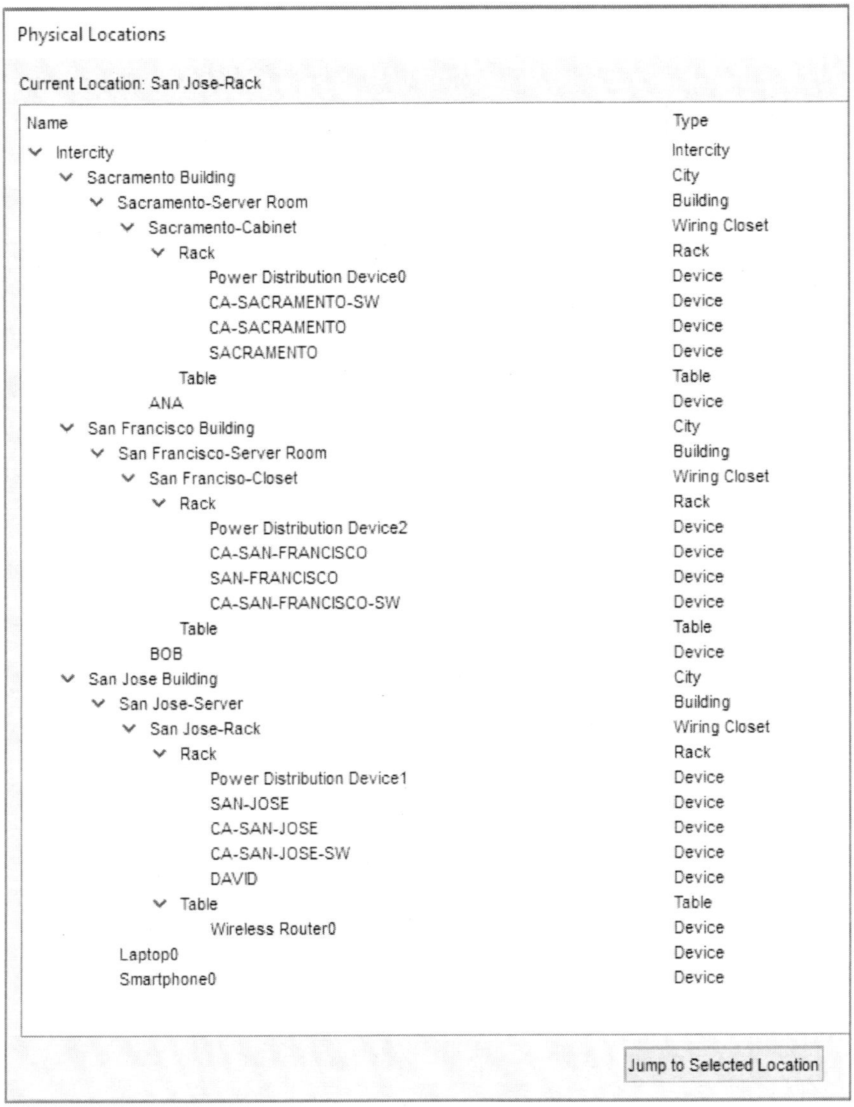

Figure 14.89 Physical topology structure .

Part 5. New wiring symbology.

Step 1. Familiarize yourself with the wiring symbology in the logical topology.

In logical topology mode (Logical), the wiring types are located in the lower left corner of the Packet Tracer program window and look the same as in previous versions of the program.

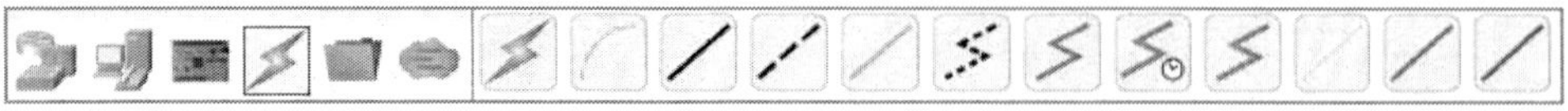

Figure 14.90 Types of cabling in a logical topology

Step 2. Familiarize yourself with the wiring symbology in the physical topology .

In physical topology mode (Physical), the types of cabling look different than in logical topology mode. In the latest version of Packet Tracer, the cable symbols have been changed to the following plug symbols - see the Plug Types table.

Figure 14.91 Types of plug-ins in the physical topology

Symbol	Description of plug / cable /.
	Console cable plug (Console-Roll Over) blue color
	Straight twisted-pair cable connector (Straight-Through) – green color
	Twisted pair twisted pair cable connector (Cross-Over) – orange color
	Fiber optic plug (Fiber)
	Telephone plug (Phone)
	BNC coaxial plug (Coaxial)
	Serial plug (Serial DCE)
	Serial plug (Serial DTE)
	IoT plug (Internet of Things)
	USB plug

Table 14.11 Types of plug-ins in the physical topology

14.5 List of auxiliary files

- building.png
- california1.png
- california2.png
- sacramento.png
- sacramento-area-business-park.png
- sacramento-building.png
- san-francisco-building.png
- san-jose-building.png
- server-rooms.png
- exercise37-physical-topology.pkt
- exercise38-physical-topology.pkt
- exercise39-physical-topology.pkt
- exercise40-physical-topology.pkt

CHAPTER 15

COMMAND PROMPT COMMANDS

15 Command Prompt Commands

15.1 Tabular summary of commands

Command	Description	Options
ipv6config	Configuring IPV6 addressing for the interface	IPV6 address, prefix, default gateway, DNS server address
ping	Testing communication between hosts (for IPV4 and IPV6)	-n number of ICMP packets, -v TOS, -t, destination host address
ipconfig	Configuring IPV4 addressing for the interface	IPV4 address, subnet mask, default gateway
nslookup	Checks existing DNS servers on the network	host domain name
netsh interface ipv6 show neighbors	Displaying the physical address of the nearest router	-

Table 15.1 Command table in Command Prompt

15.2 Ipv6config and ping

Syntax:

```
ipv6config { /? | /renew | /release | <IPv6
address>/<prefix> [<default gateway> [<DNS server>]] }
```

renew – reload network card configuration for IPV6
release – delete network card configuration for IPV6
IPv6 address – address in IPV6 format
prefix – prefix for IPV6 address
default gateway – address of default gateway
DNS server – address of DNS server

```
ping [-n count | -v TOS | -t ] target
```

count – number of packages ICMP
TOS – type of service (numeric value from 1 to 255) sent in the packet
t – Looping ICMP packets
target – address (IPV4 or IPV6) of the target host

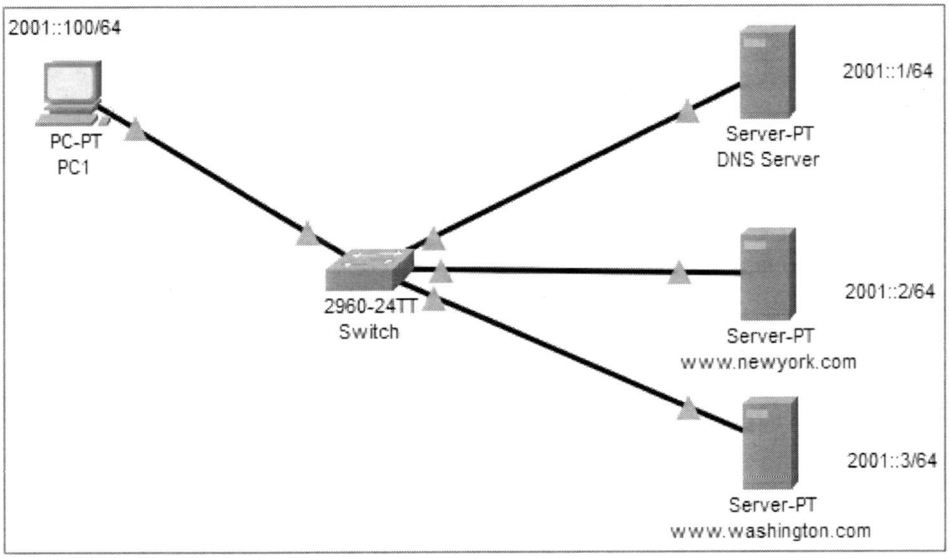

Figure 15.1 IPV6 logical topology for testing commands.

Step 1. Make the topology according to the figure.

Step 2. Go to the [Desktop] tab on PC1.

Step 3. Run the [Command Prompt] applet.

Step 4. Execute the ipv6config command (with sample parameters).

```
ipv6config   2001::100/64  2001::1  2001::1
```

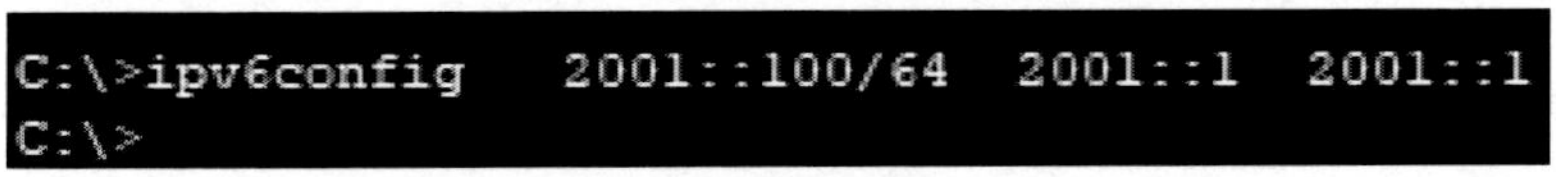

Figure 15.2 ipv6config command

Step 5. Check the addressing of PC1.

```
ipv6config   /all
```

```
C:\>
C:\>ipv6config   /all

FastEthernet0 Connection:(default port)

   Connection-specific DNS Suffix..:
   Physical Address................: 0009.7CE7.3671
   Link-local IPv6 Address.........: FE80::209:7CFF:FEE7:3671
   IPv6 Address....................: 2001::100
   Default Gateway.................: ::
   DNS Servers.....................: 2001::1
   DHCPv6 IAID.....................: 816894081
   DHCPv6 Client DUID..............: 00-01-00-01-9A-71-7A-85-00-09-7C-E7-36-71
```

Figure 15.3 ipv6config /all command

Step 6. Check the communication from PC1 to the DNS Servers, www.newyork.com, www.washington.com .

Note: For IPV6 addressing, this is the only way to execute the ping command. In visual mode [using the envelope], you can only ping between IPV4 addresses.

```
ping 2001::1
ping 2001::2
ping 2001::3
```

Note: In Packet Tracer, DNS service for IPV6 is not implemented.

```
C:\>ping 2001::1

Pinging 2001::1 with 32 bytes of data:

Reply from 2001::1: bytes=32 time<1ms TTL=128
Reply from 2001::1: bytes=32 time=2ms TTL=128
Reply from 2001::1: bytes=32 time<1ms TTL=128
Reply from 2001::1: bytes=32 time<1ms TTL=128

Ping statistics for 2001::1:
    Packets: Sent = 4, Received = 4, Lost = 0 (0% loss),
Approximate round trip times in milli-seconds:
    Minimum = 0ms, Maximum = 2ms, Average = 0ms

C:\>ping 2001::2

Pinging 2001::2 with 32 bytes of data:

Reply from 2001::2: bytes=32 time<1ms TTL=128
Reply from 2001::2: bytes=32 time<1ms TTL=128
Reply from 2001::2: bytes=32 time<1ms TTL=128
Reply from 2001::2: bytes=32 time<1ms TTL=128

Ping statistics for 2001::2:
    Packets: Sent = 4, Received = 4, Lost = 0 (0% loss),
Approximate round trip times in milli-seconds:
    Minimum = 0ms, Maximum = 0ms, Average = 0ms

C:\>ping 2001::3

Pinging 2001::3 with 32 bytes of data:

Reply from 2001::3: bytes=32 time<1ms TTL=128
Reply from 2001::3: bytes=32 time<1ms TTL=128
Reply from 2001::3: bytes=32 time=2ms TTL=128
Reply from 2001::3: bytes=32 time<1ms TTL=128

Ping statistics for 2001::3:
    Packets: Sent = 4, Received = 4, Lost = 0 (0% loss),
Approximate round trip times in milli-seconds:
    Minimum = 0ms, Maximum = 2ms, Average = 0ms
```

Figure 15.4 Results of ping commands

15.3 Ipconfig and nslookup

Syntax:

```
ipconfig { /? | /renew | /release | <IP> <subnet mask>
[<default gateway>] }
```

renew - renew IPV4 addressing
release - remove IPV4 addressing
IP - address in IPV4 format

default gateway - address of the default Gateway

```
nslookup host
nslookup  domain_name
```

host - searches for the DNS server address
domain_name - searches for the DNS server address and the address of the desired domain name in the DNS system

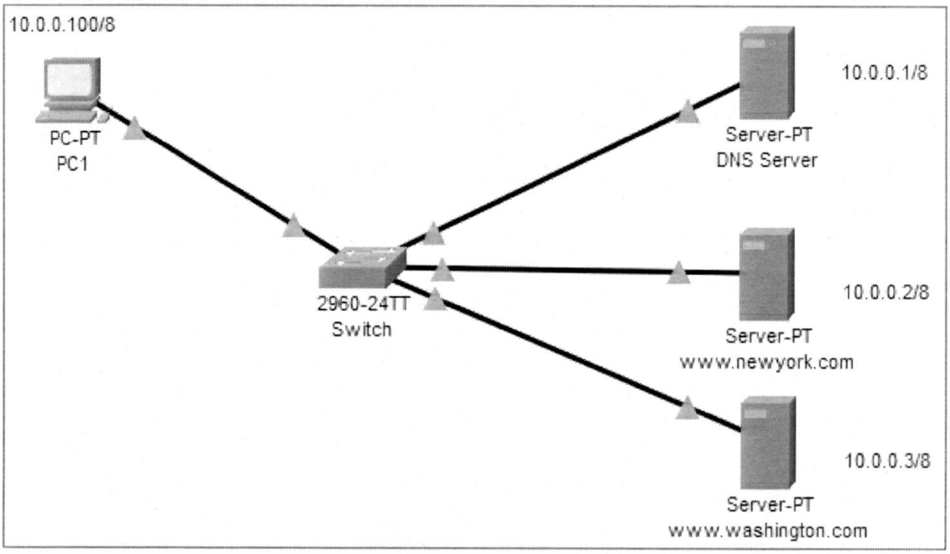

Figure 15.5 IPV4 topology for testing commands.

Step 2. Configure two type A records on the DNS server.

No.	Name	Type	Detail
0	www.newyork.com	A Record	10.0.0.2
1	www.washington.com	A Record	10.0.0.3

Figure 15.6 Type A records in a DNS server

Step 3. Go to the [Desktop] tab on PC1.

Step 4. Run the [Command Prompt] applet.

Step 5. Run the ipconfig command (with sample parameters).

```
ipconfig  10.0.0.100  255.0.0.0  10.0.0.1
```

```
C:\>ipconfig   10.0.0.100  255.0.0.0  10.0.0.1
C:\>
```

Figure 15.7 ipconfig command

Step 6. Set the DNS server address on PC1.

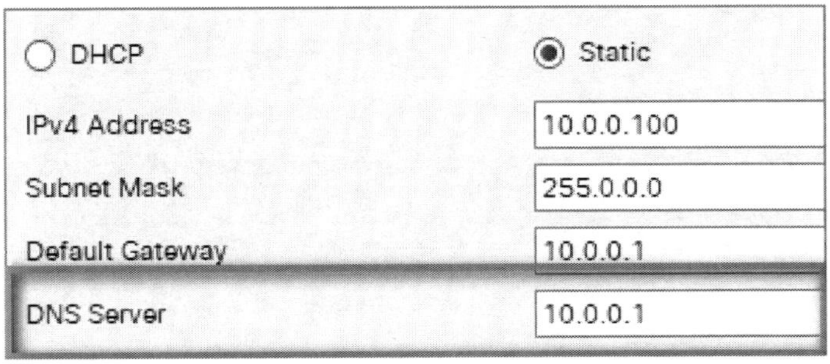

Figure 15.8 Setting the DNS address

Step 7. Check the addressing of PC1.

```
ipconfig  /all
```

```
C:\>
C:\>ipconfig  /all

FastEthernet0 Connection:(default port)

   Connection-specific DNS Suffix..: 
   Physical Address................: 0009.7CE7.3671
   Link-local IPv6 Address.........: FE80::209:7CFF:FEE7:3671
   IPv6 Address....................: ::
   IPv4 Address....................: 10.0.0.100
   Subnet Mask.....................: 255.0.0.0
   Default Gateway.................: ::
                                     10.0.0.1
   DHCP Servers....................: 0.0.0.0
   DHCPv6 IAID.....................: 816894081
   DHCPv6 Client DUID..............: 00-01-00-01-9A-71-7A-85-00-09-7C-E7-36-71
   DNS Servers.....................: ::
                                     10.0.0.1
```

Figure 15.8 The result of the ipconfig /all command

Step 8. Check the DNS server addressing on PC1.

```
nslookup  www.newyork.com
nslookup  www.washington.com
```

```
Cisco Packet Tracer PC Command Line 1.0
C:\>nslookup www.newyork.com

Server: [10.0.0.1]
Address:  10.0.0.1

Non-authoritative answer:
Name:   www.newyork.com
Address:   10.0.0.2

C:\>nslookup www.washington.com

Server: [10.0.0.1]
Address:  10.0.0.1

Non-authoritative answer:
Name:   www.washington.com
Address:   10.0.0.3
```

Figure 15.9 nslookup command

15.4 Netsh interface ipv6 show neighbors

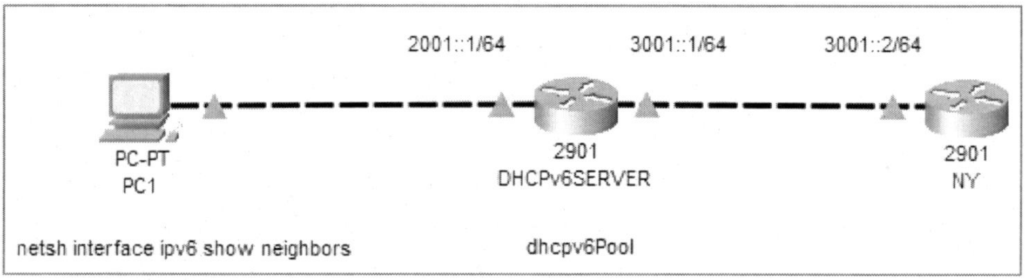

Figure 15.10 IPV6 network topology for netsh

Step 1. Make an IPV6 topology according to the figure.

Step 2. On the **DHCPv6SERVER** router, perform the configuration of a pool named **dhcpv6Pool.**

Commands:

```
ipv6  dhcp  pool  dhcpv6Pool
address prefix 2001::/64  lifetime  172800 86400
dns-server 2001::1
domain-name ny.com
```

Step 3. On the **DHCPv6SERVER** router, perform the configuration of the **Gig0/0** interface.

```
interface GigabitEthernet0/0
ipv6 address 2001::1/64
ipv6 nd managed-config-flag
ipv6 dhcp server dhcpv6Pool
```

Step 4. On the **DHCPv6SERVER** router, perform the configuration of the **Gig0/1** interface

```
interface GigabitEthernet0/1
ipv6 address 3001::1/64
```

Step 5. Note the MAC address of the **Gig0/0** interface in DHCPv6SERVER **.**

`00E0.A3EB.A501`

Step 6. Enable DHCP for IPV6 on the PC1 interface.

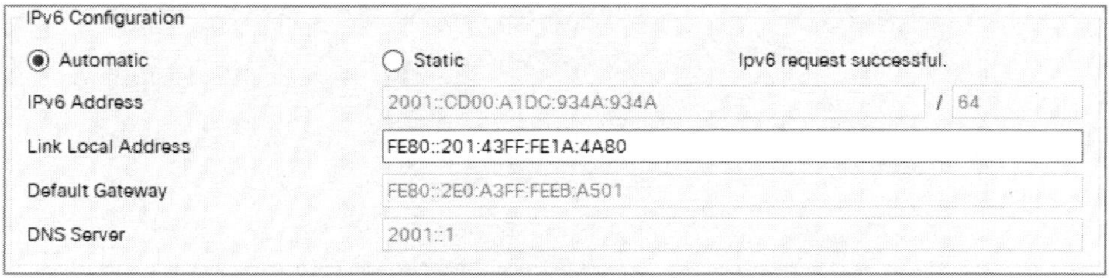

Figure 15.11 Example of IPV6 address confiirmation

Step 7. On PC1, execute the command: **`netsh interface ipv6 show neighbors`**.

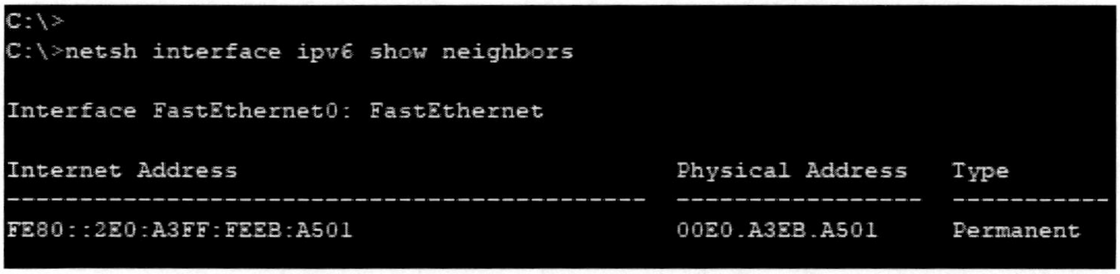

Figure 15.12 The netsh interface ipv6 show neighbors command

The second column should contain the physical address of the nearest router, consistent with the address obtained in step 5. The interface with this physical address is connected to the FastEthernet0 interface of the computer.

15.5 Directory Commands

Command: `mkdir`

Create a directory on the C drive:

Examples:

```
mkdir  DOWNLOAD
mkdir  DOCS
```

Command: `dir`

Display a list of directories and files on the C drive:

Examples:

```
dir
```

```
C:\>dir

 Volume in drive C has no label.
 Volume Serial Number is 5E12-4AF3
 Directory of C:\

3/1/1993     0:5 PM     <DIR>                 DOCS
3/1/1993     0:3 PM     <DIR>                 DOWNLOAD
1/1/1970     1:0 PM              26           sampleFile.txt
                26 bytes                3 File(s)
```

Figure 15.13 The result of the dir command

Command: `cd`

Change the current directory.

Examples:

```
cd DOCS
```

```
C:\>cd DOCS
C:\DOCS>
```

Figure 15.14 The result of the cd command

```
cd ..
```

```
C:\DOCS>
C:\DOCS>cd ..
C:>
```

Figure 15.15 The result of the cd command ..

```
cd  /
```

```
C:\DOCS>
C:\DOCS>cd /
C:>
```

Figure 15.16 The result of the cd / command.

Command: `delete`

File deletion.

Examples:

```
delete sampleFile.txt
```

```
C:>delete sampleFile.txt
C:>dir

 Volume in drive C has no label.
 Volume Serial Number is 5E12-4AF3
 Directory of C:

3/1/1993     0:5 PM     <DIR>                DOCS
3/1/1993     0:3 PM     <DIR>                DOWNLOAD
                 0 bytes              2 File(s)
```

Figure 15.17 delete command

Command: `rmdir`

File deletion.

Examples:

```
rmdir DOWNLOAD
```

```
C:>DIR

 Volume in drive C has no label.
 Volume Serial Number is 5E12-4AF3
 Directory of C:

3/1/1993     0:5 PM     <DIR>                DOCS
3/1/1993     0:3 PM     <DIR>                DOWNLOAD
                 0 bytes              2 File(s)
C:>rmdir DOWNLOAD
C:>dir

 Volume in drive C has no label.
 Volume Serial Number is 5E12-4AF3
 Directory of C:

3/1/1993     0:5 PM     <DIR>                DOCS
                 0 bytes              1 File(s)
```

Figure 15.18 rmdir command

Command: `exit`

Exit the command interpreter (close the **Command Prompt** applet).

15.6 List of auxiliary files

- commands-config-ipv4.pkt
- commands-config-ipv6.pkt
- commands-directories.pkt
- commands-netsh-interface-ipv6-show-neighbors.pkt

CHAPTER 16

INDEX OF TABLES

COMPUTER NETWORKS IN PACKET TRACER

FOR ADVANCED USERS

16 Index of Tables

CHAPTER 17

INVENTORY OF EXERCISES AND LIST OF SUPPORT FILES

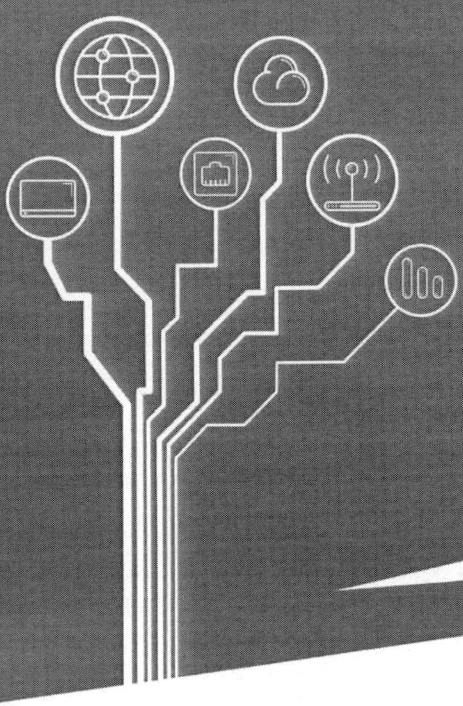

COMPUTER NETWORKS IN PACKET TRACER

FOR ADVANCED USERS

17 Inventory of Exercises and List of Support Files

Chapter	List of auxiliary files
Using Multiuser Mode	dns-config.txt ftp-config.txt index.html style.css exercise1-internal-network-topology-in-the-server-room.pkt exercise2-external-networks-topology.pkt exercise3-server-room-pc1.pkt exercise3-external-networks-pc2.pkt
Packet Tracer in Linux	exercise4-ubuntu.pkt exercise5-windows.pkt exercise6-windows.pkt exercise6-ubuntu.pkt
Device Pairing Technology and Tethering	exercise7-bluetooth-pairing.pkt exercise8-tethering-in-smartphone.pkt
Mobile GSM Telephony	exercise9-two-mobile-gsm-networks.pkt exercise10-three-mobile-gsm-networks.pkt
Network Controller	exercise11-network-controller.pkt exercise12-network-controller.pkt exercise13-network-controller.pkt exercise14-network-controller.pkt exercise15-network-controller.pkt exercise16-network-controller.pkt
Wireless Network Controllers	biology.html biology.jpg biology.png biotechnology.html biotechnology.jpg biotechnology.png building.png campus.png exercise17-wlc-pt.pkt exercise18-wlc-pt.pkt exercise19-wlc-2504.pkt exercise20-wlc-2504.pkt www.institute.com-index.html
Integrated Industrial Routers	exercise21-isr819hg-4g-iox-basic-configuration.pkt exercise22-isr819hg-4g-iox-running-virtual-machine.pkt
Hot Swapping Devices	exercise23-adding-power-modules.pkt exercise24-adding-poe-devices.pkt
Clock Synchronization	exercise25-ntp-master-slave-synchronization.pkt exercise26-ntp-chain-synchronization.pkt exercise27-ptp-slave-master-new-master-synchronization.pkt exercise28-ptp-advanced-synchronization.pkt
Server Services	cambridge_description.txt, city_of_london.txt,

	cost_of_grocery_food.txt, cost_of_property.txt. exercise29-http-service.pkt exercise30-ftp-service.pkt exercise31-email-service.pkt image2.html index.html index2.html index3.html my_java_script.js my_styles.css picture1-40x40.png picture2-154x167.png picture3-222x148.png picture4-350x196.png
IPV6 Protocol	exercise32-ipv6-tunneling.pkt exercise33-configuring-dhcp-for-ipv6-on-server.pkt exercise34-configuring-dhcp-for-ipv6-on-router.pkt
Hot Standby router Protocol	exercise35-hsrp.pkt exercise36-hsrp.pkt
Advanced Physical Topology	exercise37-physical-topology.pkt exercise38-physical-topology.pkt exercise39-physical-topology.pkt exercise40-physical-topology.pkt building.png california1.png california2.png city.png downtown-san-jose.png sacramento.png sacramento-area-business-park.png sacramento-building.png sacramento-iron-point-business-park.png san-francisco-building.png san-jose.png san-jose-building.png server-rooms.png stanford-lan.jpg stanford-server-room.png stanford-university.png us-state.png
Command Prompt Commands	commands-config-ipv4.pkt commands-config-ipv6.pkt commands-directories.pkt commands-netsh-interface-ipv6-show-neighbors.pkt

Table 17.1 List of supported files in exercises described in the book.

CHAPTER 18

BIBLIOGRAPHY

18 Bibliography

Academy, C. N. (2022, 11 1). Cisco Packet Tracer 8.2.0 FAQ.

Academy, C. N. (2022, 11 1). Online help for the program Cisco Packet Tracer.

Calhoun, P., Montemurro, M. i Stanley, D. (2022, 11 5). Control And Provisioning of Wireless Access Points (CAPWAP). *Control And Provisioning of Wireless Access Points (CAPWAP).*

Cisco. (2022, 11 5). End User License Agreement. *End User License Agreement.*

Cisco. (2022, 11 5). Precision Time Protocol Software Configuration Guide for IE 2000U and Connected Grid Switches.

Cisco. (2022, 11 5). Precision Time Protocol Software Configuration Guide for IE 2000U and Connected Grid Switches. *Precision Time Protocol Software Configuration Guide for IE 2000U and Connected Grid Switches*(Precision Time Protocol Software Configuration Guide).

Cisco.live. (2019). Technical Documentation Ciscolive.com. Las Vegas. Retrieved from https://www.ciscolive.com/c/dam/r/ciscolive/us/docs/2017/pdf/BRKRST-2293.pdf

Cisco800. (2022, 11 5). Cisco 800 Series Integrated Services Routers Software Configuration Guide. Cisco.

IOx-Application-Hosting. (2022, 11 5). IOx Application Hosting. Cisco.

Technology, R. U. (2017, 5 2). Precision Time Protocol. University of Technology in Rzeszow.

Wikipedia. (2022, 11 1). *https://en.wikipedia.org/wiki/Bob_Kahn.*

Wikipedia. (2022, 11 1). *https://en.wikipedia.org/wiki/Vint_Cerf.*

www.cisco.com. (2022, 11 5). VLANs on Wireless LAN Controllers Configuration Example. *VLANs on Wireless LAN Controllers Configuration Example.* Cisco.